THE
DWIGHT HARRINGTON TERRY
FOUNDATION

This volume is published with the assistance of the Foundation established at Yale University by the late Dwight H. Terry of Bridgeport, Connecticut, through his gift of $100,000 as an endowment fund for the delivery of lectures on "Religion in the Light of Science and Philosophy," and for the "publication and dissemination of said lectures and other utterances or literature originating outside the Foundation, which are in line with the objects therein specified . . ."

THE

PROBLEM OF KNOWLEDGE

Philosophy, Science, and History since Hegel

by

ERNST CASSIRER

TRANSLATED BY WILLIAM H. WOGLOM, M.D.,
AND CHARLES W. HENDEL

WITH A PREFACE BY CHARLES W. HENDEL
Professor of Moral Philosophy and Metaphysics,
Yale University

27228

NEW HAVEN

YALE UNIVERSITY PRESS

LONDON, GEOFFREY CUMBERLEGE, OXFORD UNIVERSITY PRESS

1950

To

the Rector and Faculty of Gothenburg University
with cordial thanks for the Gothenburg years

PREFACE

WHEN ERNST CASSIRER left Sweden in May, 1941, to come to Yale University as Visiting Professor of Philosophy he left behind in Sweden an important work in manuscript form, fulfillment of a lifetime project, the fourth and final volume of the series on the "Problem of Knowledge in Philosophy and Science in Modern Times." It would have been hardly wise for him to bring this newly completed manuscript with him on the voyage to America—the ship on which he traveled was the last one permitted by the German Government to come from Sweden to the United States, and it was stopped and searched. Cassirer's intention was to have typewritten copies made and dispatched later; but with the entry of the United States into the war that, too, was postponed. It was only after his death that the copy of the manuscript was obtained by Mrs. Cassirer on a visit to Sweden in 1946.

The work here presented is a translation of that book, whose exact title in the original German was *Das Erkenntnisproblem in der Philosophie und Wissenschaft der neueren Zeit. Vierter Band: Von Hegel's Tode bis zur Gegenwart. 1832–1932.* The translation is the first English version of any of that series and it is being published prior to a German edition.

Professional students of philosophy are familiar with the three preceding volumes of the *Erkenntnisproblem* and can readily appreciate the significance of the present volume which brings the study of the problem of knowledge down into contemporary science and philosophy. It is now possible for others besides the special scholars in the subject to become acquainted with the work of Cassirer through *The Philosophy of Ernst Cassirer*, Volume VI in "The Library of Living Philosophers," published in 1949 under the enterprising editorship of Professor Paul Arthur Schilpp (Evanston, Illinois). Many will also have read Cassirer's last two books composed in English, the *Essay on Man* (1944) and the *Myth of the State* (1946), both published by the Yale University Press, and the essays, *Rousseau, Kant, Goethe*, translated by James Gutmann, P. O. Kristeller, and J. H. Randall, Jr. (Princeton University Press, 1945). A few notes on the writing of the present work and on its place in Cassirer's philosophy may be of interest to this ever-widening circle of readers.

It is appropriate, in what follows, to quote some passages from the

excellent short biography in the memorial volume of 1949 just mentioned. It is called "Ernst Cassirer: His Life and His Work," and was
written by Dimitry Gawronsky, a devoted and intimate friend of Cassirer's for many years, who possessed the kind of insight often given to
one who has enjoyed such a profound and enduring personal relationship.

The manuscript of Cassirer's book bears this dedication: "To the
Rector and Faculty of Gothenburg University with cordial thanks for
the Gothenburg years." The "Gothenburg years" were a memorable
part of the "long Odyssey" of his academic life, as Cassirer described it
later in his farewell address to the faculty and students of philosophy at
Yale. (P. 56.) [1] Of that Swedish sojourn Gawronsky has written:

. . . in September, 1935, Cassirer went to Goeteborg.

He stayed in Sweden for almost six years; and those years . . . were very
fruitful years for him. In 1937 he published his book on *Determinismus und
Indeterminismus in der modernen Physik.* Cassirer himself regarded this book
as one of his most important achievements. His capacity to penetrate into all
the details of the most intricate problems of modern physics . . . is truly
amazing. Cassirer had been prompted to embark upon this difficult task by a
prolonged and somewhat confused discussion which had arisen among several
leading physicists and which had touched upon the fundamental problems of
epistemology, especially upon the principle of causality. . . .

No sooner had Cassirer finished his epistemological interpretation of the
quantum theory than he began working on the fourth volume of the *Erkenntnisproblem.* In this volume . . . Cassirer is giving us an integral analysis of
the development of epistemological and logical problems for the period of
the last hundred years—from the middle of the nineteenth century to prac-
tically our own day. This volume also contains a critical analysis of all important movements in the realm of contemporary philosophy. (Pp. 29–30.)

The fourth volume of the *Erkenntnisproblem* was, in a sense, a sequel
to the *Determinismus* but it was above all the completion of a long program whose execution covered the whole period from 1902 to 1940. As
Gawronsky remarked in "Cassirer's Contribution to the Epistemology
of Physics" (another chapter in the aforementioned volume): "To this
problem—the contribution of exact science to epistemology—Cassirer
devoted constant and assiduous study throughout his entire life." (Pp.
218–219.)

Upon receiving his Doctorate from Marburg University, Cassirer . . . at
once began working on a new problem, which grew out of his research on
Leibniz [*Leibniz' System in seinen wissenschaftlichen Grundlagen*]—he decided to give a comprehensive picture of the development of epistemology in

1. The page references in this Preface are all to *The Philosophy of Ernst Cassirer.*

the philosophy and science of modern times. . . . His work developed rapidly, and as early as 1904 the two volumes of his *Erkenntnisproblem* . . . were finished. . . . In 1906 the first volume . . . was published, followed by the second one in 1908 [1907].[2] The outstanding qualities of this work were rapidly recognized by students of philosophy all over the world; it appeared in several editions and slowly became one of the standard works on the history of human thought. Cassirer's original intention had been to give a broad picture of modern European thought as it led to, and culminated in, the philosophy of Kant. This he did in the first two volumes. . . . Years later [1920] he added one more volume, in which he set forth the development of epistemology in post-Kantian philosophy. . . . (Pp. 12–14.)

Then another twenty years and the writing of the fourth volume was begun.

The manuscript of this volume has the following notation in parenthesis at the end: "Von 9. Juli bis 26. November 1940." According to Mrs. Cassirer this note records the fact that "unbelievable as it may seem the whole book was composed between July 9th and November 26th 1940." She recalled that "it was the time when Belgium, France, and Holland were overrun, Norway and Denmark were occupied, and we never knew whether Hitler would appear the next day in Sweden." Of course, she added, her husband "had worked all his life on the problem and had thought out long beforehand what he wanted to say." It is evident, too, when we consider the original subtitle, "from the death of Hegel to the present," with the dates given—1832 to 1932—that the book must have been planned at the time of the centenary of Hegel's death. Its final completion in the darkest hour of Europe is remarkable testimony to the philosophical poise and the great power of concentration which were so characteristic of the author.

Gawronsky offers the following estimate of the whole of Cassirer's achievement in all the four volumes of the *Erkenntnisproblem.*

The more one studies this work of Cassirer, the more one admires the intellectual scope of the man who was able to write it. Immense was the number of books Cassirer had to study and familiarize himself with in the interest of this work. And yet, this is the least spectacular part of it. Really amazing is Cassirer's ability to penetrate scores of individual systems of thought, reconstruct them in all their peculiarities, accentuate all that is original and fruitful in them, and reveal all their weaknesses and inconsistencies. Cassirer had an incredibly fine mind for the slightest nuances of thought, for the minutest differences and similarities, for all that was fundamental or of secondary importance; with steady grasp he picked up the development through all its stages and ramifications; and, in showing how the *same* concept acquired a

2. Gawronsky erroneously gives the date 1908.

different meaning, according to the diverse philosophical systems in which it was applied as a constructive element, Cassirer laid the first foundation for the ideas which he later developed as his theory of "symbolic forms." Scores of Italian and German, French and English philosophers, almost or completely fallen into oblivion, came back in Cassirer's book to new life and historical importance . . . He was the first to introduce into the history of philosophy such names as Kepler, Galileo, Huygens, Newton, and Euler, by giving a detailed analysis of their philosophical conceptions, scientific methods and achievements, and by proving their fundamental importance for the theory of knowledge. . . . Yet Cassirer's greatest achievement in this work consisted in the creation of a broad general background by connecting the evolution of knowledge with the totality of spiritual culture: mythos and religion, psychology and metaphysics, ethics and aesthetics . . . (Pp. 14–15.)

The fourth volume, with which we are here concerned, is distinguished by a special method of dealing with the subject matter. The author tells of this himself in his Introduction, where he briefly reviews the modern period and then describes the particular features of the last hundred years and how differently the problem of knowledge must be treated in reference to this changed situation. "The relation of philosophy to the various sciences has altered fundamentally in this period of unceasing progress in specialization." Formerly philosophy "*directed* scientific knowledge toward new goals and opened new paths." Now "it allows itself to be led by the sciences and forced in a prescribed direction by each of them in turn." Moreover, the sciences themselves have become more sharply differentiated from each other and each one goes its own way and develops its own concepts and methodology. To understand the *problem* of knowledge in this period, then, calls for much more than was attempted in the three previous volumes of the series, more than a study of "the manifold and delicate interweavings" of philosophical systems with the various particular sciences. To quote Cassirer's words at the close of his Introduction: it "requires a persistent patient steeping of oneself in the work of the separate sciences, which must not only be investigated in respect to principles but explained concretely, that is, in the way they conceive and handle their primary and fundamental problems. I do not conceal from myself for a moment the enormous difficulty involved in this conception of the task, and during the course of the work I have become increasingly conscious of it."

The nineteenth century and the earlier twentieth witnessed the development of the biological sciences and history, both of which came to rank in importance with the mathematical and physical sciences that for so long had represented the ideal of knowledge both in method and achievement. These new disciplines, too, had their own forms of achieve-

ment. In recognition of this fact the book is divided into three parts:
the first on "Exact Science," the second on "The Ideal of Knowledge
and Its Transformations in Biology," and the third on the "Fundamental Forms and Tendencies of Historical Knowledge." The work ends
without any Conclusion to bring together the results or the problems of
the three parts, but in a sense the last paragraph of the author's Introduction supplies a conclusion. However, there is little doubt that had
Cassirer lived to be able to see his work through the press himself, he
would have added some further words expressing the sense of his whole
study and giving his own later judgment concerning its subject matter.

It has been observed by various critics, and by the contributors to
the volume on Cassirer, how fundamental mathematics and physics are
to his philosophy, and especially to his historical study of the problem of
knowledge. We have seen above how he naturally passed from an examination of the problems of contemporary physics, in the *Determinismus*,
to the writing of this fourth volume, whose first part consists of an
elaborate scrutiny of the epistemological problems arising *within* contemporary mathematics and physics. Gawronsky has stressed this point
several times, and quotes directly from Cassirer, " 'only in exact science
—in its progress which, despite all vacillation, is continuous—does the
harmonious concept of knowledge obtain its true *accomplishment* and
verification . . . ' " (P. 218.) Felix Kaufmann in his chapter, "Cassirer's Theory of Scientific Knowledge," speaks of the *Determinismus* as
"a work which offers perhaps the most accomplished elaboration of his
theory of science" (p. 194), and it was with this perfection of his own
theory behind him that Cassirer undertook his study of the contemporary problem of knowledge. Another contributor, Fritz Kaufmann, says
that the *Geschichte des Erkenntnisproblems* (as he designates it) "is
not only an inestimable source of authentic historical knowledge, but
interprets modern science and philosophy on the basis of a principle
which is truly congenial with them . . ." (P. 829.) Harold R. Smart,
in his contribution, "Cassirer's Theory of Mathematical Concepts,"
writes of Cassirer's "profound and critical study of the history of mathematics in its relations both with philosophy and with the other sciences . . . " (p. 241), and this is precisely what is undertaken for both
mathematics and physical science in the first part of the present volume.

The second part, on "The Ideal of Knowledge and Its Transformations in Biology," will be somewhat new matter even for scholars who
have known the work of Cassirer in his other books. Here is a fresh study
of theoretical developments in the science of biology. It is not so evident
from Cassirer's earlier writings what interest or position he would take
in the discussions of biological science during the past hundred years.

It is significant that none of the twenty-seven authors of the recent volume in "The Library of Living Philosophers" has made Cassirer's views of biology the subject of his essay. The themes are mathematics, physical science, language, art, literature, criticism, culture, ethics, myth, social science, anthropology, history, humanism, neo-Kantianism, and phenomenology. Gawronsky, who had access to the manuscript of the present volume and who knew Cassirer's mind well, makes this pregnant observation, however, about his work in the study of Kant. "Perhaps the most important of these contributions is Cassirer's analysis of the fundamental ideas of Kant's *Kritik der Urteilskraft* and his explanation of why Kant based his theory of judgment upon two seemingly so different roots as the philosophy of art, on the one hand, and biology, on the other." (Pp. 22–23.) This indicates an approach to the study of biological knowledge by way of Kant's *Critique of Judgment*. It must also be remembered that Cassirer's first preoccupation was with Leibniz who continued to influence him all his life, and that he was even more profoundly and constantly at home with the thought of Goethe. We can see here the ways in which Cassirer would have developed an interest in the knowledge of the phenomena of life. But this second part of his book is not simply using biological thought to illustrate a philosophical position taken beforehand; its argument evolves out of the actual discussions of the method and the goal of knowledge *within* biology.

The third part, treating of the "Fundamental Forms and Tendencies of Historical Knowledge," is, as we might expect, full of original and new material. Here is a theme the author could treat *con amore*, for his own genius lay in his historical understanding and insight. On the occasion of Cassirer's sixtieth birthday an international group of admirers of his work chose to honor him with a volume entitled *Philosophy and History* (edited by Raymond Klibansky, Oxford, the Clarendon Press, 1936), which stresses, of course, the inspiration and the significance of the conjunction of history with philosophy in his work. The historian Hajo Holborn, in his memorial address in 1945, spoke of Cassirer's "capacity to project himself into the psychological and mental environment of a past age or of an individual thinker of the past . . . " (p. 44), and of his gift at the same time of putting himself into the position of the person to whom he was speaking so that the forms of past civilization would be "made a part of the consciousness of the modern individual and of present-day civilization." (P. 43.) John Herman Randall, Jr., writing on "Cassirer's Theory of History as Illustrated in His Treatment of Renaissance Thought," gives an excellent rendering of a passage from *Zur Logik der Kulturwissenschaften* which begins as follows: " 'The task of history does not consist merely in making us *acquainted with* past existence and life, but in showing us how to *interpret its meaning,*' " and ends with the idea that no facts or monuments ever " 'become history for us until in these monuments we see symbols, through which we can not only recognize definite forms of life, but by virtue of which we can restore them for ourselves.' " (Pp. 701–702.) In this third part of the volume are to be seen the sources of those ideals of history and historical interpretation which are exemplified with supreme art and imagination by Cassirer.

In the concluding sentences of his Introduction Cassirer wrote: "The era of the great constructive programs, in which philosophy might hope to systematize and organize all knowledge, is past and gone. But the demand for synthesis and synopsis, for survey and comprehensive view, continues as before . . . " The work here presented offers just such a synoptic view and one who reads it will, under the guidance of this fine mind, gain an insight into the rich and complex thought of the nineteenth and twentieth centuries. Precisely because it includes so much—mathematics, physical science, biological science, and history—and is so full of reference to the whole cultural milieu, it is liable to criticism from those who may expect more of it than it pretends to offer. We are given such a vista that we look to see everything there, and of course we do not find it. For it is not meant to be a complete history even of the individual sciences. For example, Cassirer works through the vitalistic controversy in biology but he does not go so far as we should expect of one writing at the present moment. And in the study of the problem of knowledge in history, he closes with Fustel de Coulanges. But much has happened in the study of history since then. There has developed the whole new concept of economic history, and historians have arisen with quite other ideas than those here singled out for treatment. On this score various critics have already asked pertinent questions the answers to which they had hoped to hear from Cassirer himself. Holborn noted that Cassirer had "avoided the discussion of the social and political forces" in history. (P. 43.) Randall and Fritz Kaufmann have both commented on the fact that "economic determinism" is hardly even mentioned. (Pp. 704 and 838.) It might be said, in reply, that Cassirer had already dealt with "determinism" in history and that the particular brand of it labeled "economic" was sufficiently taken care of in his general discussion of causal knowledge. The subject of the book is not *all* of the theorizing in the sciences of mathematics, physics, biology, and history but only that which has to do with the "method" in each of the disciplines and the conception of the knowledge sought for or believed to be attainable in each one of them. Purely scientific or historical theories that do not carry with them any new or distinctive conception of the nature of knowledge and the getting of knowledge are not strictly relevant to the subject of the book. But such observations can be only a partial answer to the criticisms. The author himself would never have been content with such a reply. He wrote this book in one long draught of inspiration during the anxious months in 1940 when Western Europe was threatened with complete military conquest. When Cassirer inscribed the subtitle, "from the death of Hegel to the present," that was "the present." Had he been able to recover the manuscript himself during the years remaining to him he would certainly have revised and added to it, for he always wanted to address himself to the contemporary mind and situation. When he came to America he wrote for readers in this country and referred to the trends of thought here so that what he had to say would be relevant and up to date. Many of the scholars who have written about his work in the light principally of what was published years ago in Germany have had to take special account of this recent development in Cassirer's thought, and time and time again they have had to qualify what they were saying about his whole philosophy by referring to the new aspects of it in the *Essay on Man* and the *Myth of the State*. So we have every reason to believe that this fourth volume of the *Problem of Knowledge* would have been really brought down to "the present" if the author had been spared to resume work on his long-cherished theme.

In regard to the translation itself a word of explanation is in order. Only one who is native to the German language and scholarship in science and philosophy would be competent to do justice to the author and render his meaning exactly and in all its nuances. On the other hand the American and English reader must be addressed in his own turns of thought, and the metaphors and allusions should be the ones that are natural and meaningful to him. It would take another Cassirer adequately to translate Cassirer. There is a special difficulty about this particular book because it deals with the intricacies of science as well as philosophy and involves the employment of the technical language of several scientific disciplines. The primary translator, Dr. William H. Woglom, has demonstrated a most unusual gift of rendering German into a literary English form without foreign idiom and turns of expression that so often betray the fact of translation. In order to bring Dr. Woglom's version into conformity with philosophical usage and with what I know of Cassirer's thought from my close personal association with him I have made the final revisions of the translation. We are both much indebted to the generous services of two of my colleagues at Yale University for the proper technical and scientific terms. Professor Oystein Ore kindly read Chapters I–IV on mathematics, comparing them with the German text, and Professor Henry Margenau did the same for

Chapter V on physics. If there are still errors of terminology and meaning, the fault is unwittingly my own. In spite of all the care that has gone into the making of this translation, the collaborators know that it will have errors and faults, but they hope that the reader will find it enlightening and interesting so that he will not be too much aware of the fact that he is meeting with the mind of Ernst Cassirer at second hand.

It had been our hope, before his death intervened, to have Cassirer invited to Yale University again in order to give the Terry Lectures. He had so much that would have been welcome to that particular audience. It is appropriate, therefore, that this book should be brought out partly through a grant from the Terry Lectureship Fund.

Mrs. Cassirer has been a constant encouragement and help to both translators. Mr. Eugene Davidson, editor of the Yale University Press, has taken a great personal interest in the work. We are indebted to Mr. Ronald Grider for his conscientious work in looking up quotations and checking references, and to Miss Mabel R. Weld who has taken great pains to obtain accuracy and consistency in our copy. My wife has served as the "general reader" in the interest of clarity.

CHARLES W. HENDEL

Yale University
August 1, 1949

CONTENTS

Part III

FUNDAMENTAL FORMS AND TENDENCIES OF HISTORICAL
KNOWLEDGE

INTRODUCTION

THE PROBLEM of the nature and origin of human knowledge is not a late product of philosophical speculation. It is rather one of those fundamental problems of humanity to which we cannot assign any definite historic beginning, since the earliest traces of it are found in the primitive strata of mystical and religious thinking. Even in myth and religion all that is distinctive of man is associated with the miracle of knowledge. This miracle reveals the nature of man and his likeness to God, *yet* in it man also realizes, in the deepest and most painful way, the very limitations of his own nature. Knowledge assures him of his divine origin, yet through it he at once sees himself cut off and banished, as it were, from the original ground of all things. He is condemned to a long laborious way of search and research, from which there is no final escape. In the very consciousness that there *is* a knowledge and a truth is the awareness at the same time that the possession of absolute truth is denied to man. To this religious pessimism the Greeks were the first to take a definitely opposite view. It was a decisive affirmation that knowledge is certainly possible to man. There was no longer that sense of a "fall" of man and of an estrangement from the ultimate ground of things, but on the contrary a conviction that knowledge is the one power which can sustain and unite man forever with the ultimate being. That way to union with reality is what Greek philosophy aims to show. The more deeply reason is absorbed in its own being, and the more conscious it becomes of its own true worth, the further it penetrates into the Being of things. For there is no sharp line that separates truth from reality, thought from Being. This fundamental meaning of Greek philosophy is realized fully in Plato. With him the problem of being and the problem of knowledge, "ontology" and "logic," are bound together in indissoluble unity. We can succeed in defining what True Being is only when we have first attained clarity on the nature of knowing and have a certain answer to the question: What is knowledge?

In the early dawn of the Renaissance modern philosophy returned to that Platonic position. Here philosophical speculation and the first rudiments of exact science meet. To Galileo the "new science" of dynamics, which he founded, meant first of all the decisive confirmation of what Plato had sought and demanded in his theory of ideas.

It showed that the whole of Being is pervaded through and through with mathematical law and thanks to that is really accessible to human knowledge. The first definite proof of that harmony of truth and reality upon which, in the end, all possibility of knowledge rests was afforded not by mathematics but by natural science.

What was for Galileo and Kepler, as well as for Descartes and Leibniz, the certain and secure foundation of all knowledge became actually the problem, however, for Kant, who had passed through the school of Hume's skepticism. Metaphysics is denied the power to solve the basic problem of knowledge: how a priori synthetic judgments are possible. All previous attempts in this direction belonged to the realm of pure fancy. The solution must be sought by new means, and not until they are successful can the answer be given whether and within what limits metaphysics is really possible. Thus the order of the problem is reversed. What had formerly been accepted as the real basis for truth is now recognized as questionable and attacked with critical arguments. In this reversal Kant saw the essence of his philosophical achievement and with it he believed he could effect that "complete revolution" in metaphysics which he compared with the revolution achieved by Copernicus in the domain of astronomy.

But those who followed systems of thought immediately after Kant, and believed themselves with their systems directly in line with him, actually did not follow in his footsteps. They did not see in his "transcendental" formulation of the problem a sure means for determining the limits of pure reason but actually took it to be an instrument for freeing reason from all the restrictions formerly laid upon it. The critical idealism of Kant was transformed into an absolute idealism which proposed to achieve what Plato had promised but had been unable to accomplish because of the dualistic nature of his cosmology. Logic and dialectics were now no longer to be regarded as a mere organon for a knowledge of reality, but were thought to contain this knowledge in all its fullness and totality and to allow of its being made explicit. Herewith the realm of philosophic thought appeared to be fixed for the first time, and its goal attained, the identity of reality and reason. This was where Hegel believed his *Science of Logic* stood. His reproach to Kant as well as to all earlier logic was this: that they were not able to rise above the "formal" point of view, and accordingly were left hanging, suspended in pure abstraction and speculation. According to Hegel this is not the way to escape from the circle of subjectivism. The "dead bones" of logic must be revivified with the spirit so as to have new content and meaning. This is precisely what the dialectic method promises, and what it alone can achieve.

Pure science presupposes . . . deliverance from the antithesis of consciousness and reality. It comprises thought in so far as this is one with fact, or the fact itself in so far as it is pure thought . . . Pure science itself is so little formal—it is so little devoid of the material for an actual and true knowledge—that its content is the only absolute truth; or, if one still prefers to employ the word matter, it is the truly existing matter, but matter not in the form of an external something, since it is pure thought and accordingly absolute form itself. Hence logic is to be taken as being the system of pure reason rather than the realm of pure thought. This realm is truth, truth as it is unveiled and self-existent. Therefore it may be said that the content of logic is the representation of God, as He is in His eternal essence and before the creation of nature and any mortal mind.[1]

But Hegel's system does not stay in the empty spaces of metaphysics. Its intention is to open the way to a very definite and concrete undertaking of scientific knowledge. Its aim is not only to win for history its rightful place at the side of science; it sees in history the realization and true expression of all the knowledge that the mind possesses from its own nature and resources. Here is the new positive demand represented by Hegel, and, by virtue of it, he imparted the most powerful and lasting impulse to the logic of the "Geisteswissenschaften." [2] In the domain of science, however, Hegel's system not only failed to disclose any similar result, but also led him and his disciples and successors to everlasting blundering and pretensions that necessarily deprived speculative philosophy of any credit among empirical investigators. It was on this point that the first scornful attacks were made.

Helmholtz was one of the first to raise the cry: "Back to Kant!" The sterility of metaphysical systems and their eventual collapse were in no way convincing proof to him, as they were to so many other scientific investigators in the second half of the nineteenth century, that philosophy as such was exhausted. He had been deeply impressed not only by Kant but even by Fichte, whose system he had early assimilated, and he declared that the latter's theory of the I

1. G. W. F. Hegel, Einleitung, *Wissenschaft der Logik,* "Werke" (2. Aufl. Berlin, Duncker & Humblot, 1841), III, 33.

2. "Geisteswissenschaften" is almost untranslatable. The French "moral sciences" is an approximation. It is the knowledge relating to man, society, history, the arts, religion, etc., as contrasted with the knowledge of the physical and natural sciences. (C. W. H.)

and the not-I was not opposed to science in any important respect. In fact such an explanation of sense perception was in the most perfect accord with later empirical conclusions regarding the physiology of the sense organs.[3] Here a new and unique bond was forged between empirical science and philosophy, for now the leading role fell no longer to mathematics and mathematical physics, as it had in the seventeenth and eighteenth centuries, but to physiology and psychology. Furthermore, the movement back to Kant first received its distinctive character through this interpretation by Helmholtz. While he was unable to follow Kant in the handling of the problem of the origin of geometrical axioms and in his view of arithmetic and the concept of numbers, he nonetheless regarded Kant's theory of given a priori forms of intuition as "a very clear and happy statement of the case" because, as a psychologist and physiologist interested in sensation, he explained the philosophical view in accordance with his own theory of the law of specific nerve energies. For Johannes Müller's discovery of this law had appeared to Helmholtz "as in a certain sense the empirical realization of Kant's theoretical explanation of the nature of the human understanding." [4] Thus Helmholtz gave the *"theory of knowledge"* a new content and relevance, without being conscious of making any serious change in the meaning of Kant's basic concept of the "transcendental."

From the early 1860's this view of knowledge, newly sprung from the soil of the physiology of sensation and colored by it, permeated general philosophical discussion more and more widely and finally won an unquestioned predominance. As a consequence, the earlier orientation of this fundamental problem of philosophy underwent a radical change. A characteristic example will show how deep and far reaching it was. The work of Eduard Zeller *On the Significance and Problem of the Theory of Knowledge* (1862) is historically of importance because here the expression "theory of knowledge" first seems to have been coined. But still more important is the position thereafter assigned to it in the body of the basic philosophical sciences. In place of the metaphysical orgy inspired by post-Kantian philosophy, a complete sobriety appears. Logic has abandoned every pretension of reaching to the heart of absolute being and no longer purports to be the "representation of God" in His eternal essence. But neither is it to remain content with developing formal laws of thought and deduction. What logic seeks to clarify is the problem of

---

3. H. Helmholtz, "Über das Sehen des Menschen," *Vorträge und Reden* (1855) (4. Aufl. Braunschweig, Friedrich Vieweg & Sohn, 1896), I, 89.

4. Helmholtz, *Handbuch der physiologischen Optik* (2. Aufl. Hamburg und Leipzig, Leopold Voss, 1896), § 17, S. 249.

the knowledge of reality; and this cannot be solved in any other way than by analyzing and tracing to their original conditions the ideas of the human mind which form the basic material for all empirical knowledge. Only so is it possible to answer the question what "truth" may be ascribed to these ideas, that is to say, how much they owe to subject or to object.

Yet with all this Zeller thinks he is merely taking up again the problem posed by Kant in his *Critique of Pure Reason.* He is as little conscious of its distortion toward a "psychologism" as Helmholtz was when he explained Kant's fundamental precepts in the light of sensory physiology. "The way we have to proceed to obtain exact concepts," says Zeller, "can be decided by reference only to the conditions under which the formation of our concepts takes place according to the nature of the mind; it is just these conditions that the theory of knowledge ought to investigate and to determine, accordingly, whether and with what presuppositions the human mind is capable of a knowledge of truth." The theory of knowledge and not mere logic is thus declared to be the formal basis for all philosophy; from it must come the ultimate decision as to the proper method for philosophy and for science in general. In this way, according to Zeller, the magic circle of speculative thinking and the Hegelian system can actually be broken through. "The present status of this science in Germany," as he says,

proves that it has reached one of those turning points that lead in favorable cases to a rebuilding on new foundations, and in unfavorable cases to dissolution and death. Instead of the splendid and concordant systems that ruled German philosophy in rapid succession for half a century, there is presented at the moment the spectacle of unmistakable bewilderment and uncertainty by which even the worthiest endeavors of philosophy are smothered and its keenest inquiries paralyzed in respect to their effect upon the whole; and the relationship of philosophy to the special sciences has so altered that philosophy in general has actually more to learn from them now than it has had for some decades, while on the other hand it has more and more confirmed in them the prejudice against any need of philosophy for their purposes, and even made them feel that they should not be troubled by it in their work. No proof is required to show that this is not a healthy condition. In general where there is a continuous development the need appears from time to time of a return to the starting point, of recalling the original problems and again attempting a solution in the original spirit, though perhaps by other means. For German philosophy such a moment now appears to have arrived. The beginning of the period of evolution reached by modern philosophy is Kant, and the scientific achievement with which he broke the new way in his theory of knowledge. Everyone who wishes to improve the bases of our philosophy will have to go back to this inquiry first of all and must investigate the questions which Kant presented to us in the spirit of his own *Critique*, in order to avoid the errors Kant made—and to do so from the riches of scientific experience of our century.[5]

In setting forth this general program Zeller indicated the direction that German philosophy was to follow for decades, a phase that in the end almost seemed to gain sole mastery.

Developments in France and in England took a different course. In both countries Hegel's system exerted a strong influence, evident even in thinkers who, like Taine or Renan, started from quite other, or actually opposite, fundamental assumptions. But scientific thought there never fell under the spell of the Hegelian method, not in the same sense and to the same degree, as in Germany. It continued as before to follow in the classical paths of French and English philosophy: of Descartes or Bacon. How strongly and how persistently the Cartesian spirit especially continued its sway is shown by the example of that thinker who, above all others, has determined the development of French philosophy for the past hundred years. Comte's *Course of Positive Philosophy* plays almost the same role in French thought of the nineteenth century that Kant's *Critique of Pure Reason* has played in Germany. It became the focus and intellectual rallying point of all efforts toward a renaissance of logic and epistemology. It was a fundamental tenet with Comte that logic should not attempt to pursue any speculative and metaphysical aims and that it must take form and build itself solely as a methodology of empirical science. Nevertheless, the way in which he represented and prosecuted this his fundamental thesis differed sharply and characteristically from the conception of the "empirical" logic that John Stuart Mill sought to establish with his *System of Logic, Ratiocinative and Inductive.* Close as the relationship and community of interest may seem between Comte and Mill at first glance, the two men are sharply separated in their basic interpretation of the meaning and task of science itself. Comte's idea of experience is defined and oriented very differently from that of Mill.

In the final analysis experience for Mill remains simply an aggre-

5. E. Zeller, "Über Bedeutung und Aufgabe der Erkenntnistheorie," *Vorträge und Abhandlungen,* Zweite Sammlung (Leipzig, Fues Verlag [R. Reisland], 1887), S. 489–490.

gate. It is a sum of individual observations held together by the loose tie of association and constantly extended by the act of "inductive inference," which is taken as a fact but remains a strange riddle in so far as the ground of its validity is concerned. Mill thus established that form of "positivism" that admits only particulars and facts as foundations of the knowledge of truth and reality. All the so-called "universals" must be reduced to the individual particulars and resolved into the simple data of sensory perception.

For Comte, on the contrary, the relation between universal and particular in scientific knowledge is determined in a wholly different way. The task of science, as he sees it, does not consist in the establishment of facts but in gaining laws and these are never to be attained simply by the assembling of particulars; laws are the expression of relations that can be discovered and confirmed only by a specific activity, the function of relational thinking. Because of this point of departure Comte's logic acquires a pronounced constructive aspect. His positivistic method proposes to do more than establish fixed, unchangeable features in all *events*. There is the higher and still more difficult order of things—that which constitutes the real object of *philosophic* knowledge—that of our concepts themselves. The order in which we take up the basic problems of scientific knowledge and the way in which we relate some of them with others is by no means a matter of indifference. On the contrary, all the certitude and precision of which knowledge is capable depend upon the right method of relationship and systematic coherence. If one single link should be dropped or inserted at the wrong place, the fundamental goal of all positive knowledge will be missed. The basic law of positivism is that every proposition must be strictly traced back to a simple statement of a fact if it is to have any real and intelligible meaning.[6] Yet the facts as such are in no sense of the same sort or of the same value but form a series according to the degree of their inherent generality. There are "general facts," as well as particular facts, and there is a rigorous and unambiguous passage from one to the other. Thus for Comte knowledge does not mean at all what it means to Mill—a conclusion "from particulars to particulars." It has a definite logical *structure* and is tied down to a determinate order, a "hierarchic" series, the principle of which philosophical thought can generally ascertain. In working out this problem Comte shows himself much more closely allied to the spirit of the Hegelian logic

6. This "criterion of meaning," which has been made the keystone of modern "logical positivism" by Schlick and Carnap, had already been formulated by A. Comte. See, for example, his *Discours sur l'esprit positif,* ed. C. LeVerrier (Paris, Garnier), première partie, p. 31.

than to the inductive logic of Mill; not in content, to be sure, but in basic tendency.

What is common to Comte and Mill is basically only the negative tendency: the rejection of all "theological" and metaphysical thinking. In everything that is really positive Comte goes a way of his own that is entirely different. Whenever he proclaims observation to be the supreme principle of knowledge, it still remains true for him, on the other hand, that thought not only has a part in observation but that it has its own unalterable rhythm to which it is bound. This rhythm is no longer determined, as in Hegel, by the "self-activity" of the pure concept, through the three stages of the dialectical method. It emerges, rather, from the phenomena themselves, which are so arranged in series that they advance from the simple to the complex. When we pass from inorganic to organic nature and, having arrived there, ascend from the world of plants and animals to that of man, we encounter a constantly increasing complexity in phenomena. But thought proves quite equal to its task; indeed the very complexity itself comes to be a peculiar and unfailing source of strength for thought. Each new object becomes a stimulus and a challenge to the development of a new instrument of human knowledge which is proper to the object. In this way, according to Comte, the human mind has advanced from astronomy to physics, from physics to chemistry, and from chemistry to biology, to reach at last its proper and highest goal in the doctrine concerning the order of the human world, in "social physics." In all this the question is never the mere amassing of empirical material from every field; it requires much more, that all phases of knowledge and all the various methods at its command should be grasped in their natural order so that a unified organism of knowledge may be built up. Once this has occurred and the theoretical pattern of knowledge has been established, then the practical application will follow. Even this latter will never come about by mere groping attempts or by a mere reshuffling of details. Philosophical synthesis must precede social organization and social synthesis, and Comte was convinced that in his "positive philosophy" he had fused both problems into one and solved them in principle.[7]

But Comte was perhaps the last thinker to grasp the problem of philosophy and the general theory of knowledge in its universal extent. For him there is never any antithesis between the "positive" spirit and the systematic spirit, between the "factual" and the "ra-

---

7. See especially the first and second lectures in his *Cours de philosophie positive,* as well as the *Discours sur l'esprit positif,* in the Introduction to Comte's *Traité philosophique d'astronomie populaire* (1884).

tional." Each one conditions and requires the other; for all that is factual gains its value for knowledge primarily through becoming a phase and an element in a rational order. In virtue of this basic conviction Comte wages a continuous struggle on two different fronts. True scientific positivism is, as he constantly emphasizes, opposed to the mistaken tendency to unify knowledge no less than to the other mistaken tendency toward many details. He attacks the "mystic" mind, content with vague, general, and specious solutions, as well as the "empirical" mind that sticks by particulars as particulars.[8]

For this reason Comte saw real danger in the increasing fragmentation of knowledge. He meant to oppose this tendency toward "specialization," not only in theory but in practice as well, and the thoroughgoing reform of education that is the very heart and essence of positivism is directed above all to this end. It is precisely here that Comte sees the necessary spiritual and social function of philosophy for which nothing else can be substituted and from which it never can be dispossessed. The special task of philosophy must always be to oppose the intellectual division of labor, no matter how useful and even indispensable it may be to the progress of science. Philosophy can never deny its own universal character, and if it yields to the spirit of mere facts, if it ceases to be systematic and "encyclopedic," it will really have renounced itself.

In this respect Comte adhered steadfastly to the classical, rationalistic ideal. With Descartes he interpreted philosophy as the unity of human knowledge, as that *sapientia humana*, at which all separate forms of knowledge are ultimately aiming and to which they attach themselves as members rendering lasting service.

In the final analysis one should think only of one single science: the science of man, or, more exactly expressed, social science, of which our own existence constitutes at once the principle and the purpose and in which the rational study of the external world naturally comes to merge, for this double reason that the science of nature is a necessary constituent of and a basic preamble to social science.

Not until this last purely human goal of all science has been recognized will science be capable, in Comte's opinion, of a rigorous systematization. We cannot succeed in this as long as we stay within the realm of purely physical phenomena. The material world is infinite in time and space, so that all knowledge of it must have a merely provisional and inconclusive character. Here research can never hope to attain the goal, for after all it remains rudimentary and prepara-

---

8. Comte, *Discours*, première partie. See especially, *Cours*, cinquante-sixième leçon.

tory. The situation does not change until we assign to research another task and select another focal point for it. The true center of knowledge lies not in the world but in mankind; not in the universe but in humanity. Even astronomy, complete as it is, reaches its true perfection only when it is viewed in this light. It would be wholly inadequate were one to relate it to the universe instead of to mankind, for all our actual research is of necessity restricted to our own world, which represents a vanishingly small part of a universe of which the complete exploration is virtually denied us.[9] Astronomy and physics, chemistry and biology relate in the end to a knowledge of man, and aim to prepare the way for it, for mankind or humanity is the one truly universal concept into which all our knowledge must ultimately flow.[10]

On the basis of this conviction, which is not only logical but ethical as well, Comte protested unceasingly against the fateful dismemberment of knowledge, favored by a false system of education and academic routine of which the evil consequences were becoming more and more noticeable. Yet Comte was witnessing only the beginning of a process that dominated all scientific research in the second half of the nineteenth century and more than any other thing stamped its character upon it.

Even the development of the problem of knowledge could not escape this tendency toward specialized isolation. Reviewing the history of this problem from its first traces in Greek philosophy to its inclusion in the great metaphysical systems in the first half of the nineteenth century, and contrasting it with the philosophical investigation of the past hundred years, one might think for a moment that the problem was actually discovered during this latter period. All that the earlier epochs produced appears to have been the merest preliminary, forshadowing the modern development but not to be compared with it in either content or scope. Never before in the history of philosophy has the problem of knowledge stood so in the limelight; never before have such manifold and searching investigations, reaching out to include the very last details, been devoted to it. Yet it is highly questionable whether this vast extension of the problem has gone hand in hand with an equal profundity. For philosophy is gradually losing the leadership in this domain that it had held and treasured for centuries. The individual sciences will no longer delegate their authority but mean to see and judge for themselves. Certainly this drive toward self-examination and autonomy has produced

9. *Discours,* première partie, § 4.
10. *Ibid.,* troisième partie, § 20.

most important and valuable results; but at the same time it has led to an inclusion under the term "theory of knowledge" of enterprises that have little more in common than the name. The controversy over psychologism, waged for a time with such vehemence, is one of the best known and most significant signs of how little the various trends of investigation could come together on the task proposed and the very conception of the problem. No longer did the various special sciences receive the problem from the hands of philosophy; on the contrary, each one sought to formulate the problem independently, and in accordance with its own peculiar interests and tasks. When one examines the various theories of knowledge that have been in competition with each other during recent decades, one can discover for each of them its peculiar origin in some particular discipline or other. Just as we find a psychologism, so we find a logical formalism, mathematicism, physicalism, biologism, and historicism. Even within certain fundamental lines of philosophical thought that are closely related to one another and seem actually to spring from the same source, the different ways of formulating the problem of knowledge are to be noticed and felt at every step.

Thus, to recall but one single characteristic example, in the development of neo-Kantianism the theory of Cohen and Natorp is sharply opposed to that of Windelband and Rickert: a dissimilarity that flows of necessity from their general orientation, determined in the one case by mathematical physics, in the other by history. Each of these formulations of the question, connected with a different discipline, contains important and fertile problems. But everyone pretends to speak not only for his own department of knowledge but for the whole of science, which he believes himself to represent and to embody in an exemplary fashion. Thus arise ever new discords and constantly sharper conflicts, and there is no tribunal that can compose these quarrels and assign to each party its respective rights.

The relation of philosophy to the various sciences has altered fundamentally in this period of unceasing progress in specialization. In this respect a sharp line separates the present from the past. In antiquity and in the Middle Ages, throughout the Renaissance, and in the great philosophical systems of the seventeenth and eighteenth centuries there is no doubt that philosophy had an independent and distinctive role to play in erecting the structure of scientific knowledge. It was not content with recording the contents of knowledge already acquired or with further working over it systematically. Philosophy then *directed* scientific knowledge toward new goals and opened new paths.

This relationship had appeared with notable precision and clarity in Greek philosophy. There is no denying that Plato shaped his conception of knowledge on the pattern of mathematics, and his theory of ideas not only owes separate fundamental insights to mathematics but is determined throughout its whole structure by this science. On the other hand, his theory far transcends whatever Greek mathematics could present in the way of stable results, and Plato seems to have given to the mathematics of his time much more than he took from it. He set before it a pure "idea" of mathematics, a model and an archetype, and demanded of inquiry that it should shape its course according to this pattern traced out by philosophic thought and progressively approach it. We can follow in detail how his immediate disciples understood this demand and how they complied with it. They carry out Plato's philosophical postulates to the letter. They create the science of stereometry, which Plato declares in his *Republic* to be a necessary intermediate between geometry and astronomy. They propound the first scientific theory of irrational ratios, which serves to do away with the logical objection to "incommensurable" quantities. And, finally, they develop, in direct continuity with a problem set by Plato, a theory of the movement of the heavenly bodies that became not only in content but in method a model for all scientific astronomy.

What Plato had done for mathematics, Aristotle did for biology. Not only did he conceive of it as a self-contained whole; he was the first to provide a conceptual language for its separate parts. In an admirable essay Hermann Usener has described this brilliant taxonomic work, which was carried out under the influence of Plato's Academy and for centuries thereafter determined the form of scientific investigation. "The creation not of Greek science alone but generally of classical antiquity," he writes, "is the work of two, or at the very most three generations: those of Plato, Aristotle, and the latter's immediate disciples. No single page in history records a similar phenomenon." [11] What had come to pass can be understood only by recalling that here there was no question of constructing a whole out of its separate parts, but that the idea of science, as conceived by Plato and maintained and developed by Aristotle, was that of a true "organic" whole: a whole that, in accordance with the Aristotelian definition of organic, preceded its parts.

Modern philosophy could not achieve its own most important results until it had rediscovered this ancient ideal independently and

11. H. Usener, "Organisation der wissenschaftlichen Arbeit" (1884), *Vorträge und Aufsätze* (Leipzig und Berlin, B. G. Teubner, 1907), S. 73–74.

on its own initiative, and imbued it with new life. Of course during the Middle Ages this ideal was never extinguished. Thomas Aquinas is also the great disciple of Aristotle, in that the all-encompassing spirit of the Greek thinker's philosophy continued to live and work in him. His *Summae* attempt not only to synthesize the knowledge of his time but are inspired by one uniform, predominant design. Yet however great he admits the claims of philosophic and scientific reason to be, Saint Thomas can never declare this the true and ulti-mate principle of knowledge. All knowledge is conditional, and it is null and void in so far as it does not depend upon an authoritative source of another kind and origin. The phrase "without faith there is no knowledge," is valid for Aquinas as it is throughout the Middle Ages. Thus for him, as for Bonaventura, the "reduction of all knowl-edge to theology," becomes the fundamental and leading principle of inquiry, though he defines in a different way the relation of reason to revelation, of philosophy to theology.

The Renaissance proved itself in very truth a new birth, in that it not only revived the various philosophical theories of antiquity but also recovered the spirit by which they had been created. The first centuries of the Renaissance were content in general to tie up with some doctrine or other. But so long as they sought to establish anew the Platonic, the Aristotelian, the Stoic, the Epicurean, and the Skeptic systems, all these remained mere heirlooms of which it was impossible to take complete possession. Descartes, precisely because of his unhistorical temper, was the first to succeed in the historic act of liberation. For he never merely took over conclusions but re-embodied in himself the original power of philosophical thinking. He filled all science with this power and he thereby discovered a new universal form of science, and the Cartesian method and the Carte-sian system are but the discovery of science and establishment of this new form: The thought of the *mathesis universalis* as it opened up before the mind of Descartes in his first great discovery, analytical geometry, is the common bond uniting every part of the Cartesian philosophy with every other part into one indissoluble whole. Even mathematics, so Descartes declared in his *Rules for the Direction of the Mind,* cannot fulfill its true philosophical mission as long as it is satisfied with only solutions of partial problems, and is nothing more than a theory of figures or numbers. So considered, it remains but an ingenious and sterile intellectual game. It will be really under-stood in principle and its philosophical import recognized only when it succeeds in advancing from a special to a universal science—a science of all that can be reduced to order and measure and thus is accurately known. From this point onward there follows a transformation and reorganization not only of geometry but also of optics and all other departments of physics and astronomy, anatomy and physiology, general biology, and medicine. Much of what Descartes sought to construct in this way has proven to be untenable, and the edifice of his natural philosophy has had to be pulled down bit by bit. But the spirit of his method and its universalistic purpose have remained embedded in mathematics and in modern natural science, where they have held good as a permanent and effective force.

The same spirit also dominates the philosophy of Leibniz and inspires all its special doctrines. The plan of a universal encyclopedia is the grand leading motive of all his scientific and philosophical inquiry. It attended him all life long, and there is no single work that does not relate to it in some way or another; everything focuses on this one central point. Hence there is no waste or dispersion in the immeasurable fullness of Leibniz' creativity. He found constantly verified, in this abundance of matter, the fundamental principle that he expressed as follows: "the sciences concentrate as they expand." It was not only a briefer compass that he wished to attain but complete intellectual penetration and the most intense concentration. He was convinced, too, that all this could only be achieved by philosophical thought. Thus the idea of the universal encyclopedia was for him an indispensable element in his project of *philosophia perennis.* "Never," he declared, "has any century been riper for this great task than our own, which seems destined to reap the harvest of all those that have gone before." [12]

Kant had not the same immediately productive role as Descartes and Leibniz in the development of mathematics and natural philosophy. He did not grapple directly with these sciences but confronted them as a philosophical observer, a critic and analyst. His transcendental method has to assume the "fact of the sciences" as given, and seeks only to understand the possibility of this fact, its logical conditions and principles. But even so, Kant does not stand merely in a position of dependence on the factual stuff of knowledge, the material offered by the various sciences. Kant's basic conviction and presupposition consist rather of this, that there is a universal and essential *form* of knowledge, and that philosophy is called upon and qualified to discover this form and establish it with certainty. The critique of reason achieves this by reflective thought upon the function of knowl-

---

12. For Leibniz' outline of *scientia generalis* and for the universal encyclopedia see the description by L. Couturat, *La Logique de Leibniz* (Paris, Félix Alcan, 1901), chaps. v–vi.

edge instead of upon its content. It discovers this function in judgment, and to understand judgment in its universal structure and in its specification in different lines becomes one of the main problems of the critique. Here it is that Kant found the strictly unifying, systematic, and organizing principle of knowledge. He can show the special structure of metaphysical and mathematical thinking and of the general and special sciences and of physics and biology, all by reference to the distinction between analytical and synthetic judgments, between empirical and a priori propositions, and between causal and teleological judgments. For him, too, the theory of knowledge in all its ramifications remains a closely organized whole within which every part is assigned its own definite place.

Such a universalistic way of thinking no longer obtains in the second half of the nineteenth century. Thinkers like Spencer still attempt to draft a synthetic philosophy, but it is precisely in them that one perceives very clearly how they fall into a one-sided dependence upon special scientific facts and theories, for example, the theory of evolution. The mood for an a priori metaphysic is gone, and with it, too, that for any thoroughgoing systematic thinking. Comte, as we have already seen, was still strongly obsessed by this desire for unification and saw in it the true characteristic mark of the philosophic spirit. Despite his emphasis on the factual and on the "positive" foundations of knowledge, he was convinced that all knowledge must relate itself in the end to a single objective—that set for him by his idea of humanity. Knowledge was no longer anchored to mere mathematics and natural science but to ethics and sociology, and only here in its final destination was it to achieve and securely retain its real unity. As long as one is confined to the realm of purely objective contemplation, as long as one starts from external nature instead of from man, just so long will all knowledge retain, in a certain sense, an irreducible complexity. Classical rationalists succumbed to self-deception when they believed they had conquered this multiplicity and become its intellectual master by transforming all knowledge into mathematics. The pan-mathematics of Descartes is no solution of the problem, for it does violence to the phenomena. We must realize that in the progress from astronomy to physics, from physics to chemistry, and from chemistry to biology, new and unusual modifications arise from time to time that can neither be traced back to earlier ones nor derived from the general content of mathematics, from number and measure. It is impossible to reduce all scientific concepts to the single type of mathematics; and just as little possible to explain all phenomena by a single law. It is enough if the inevitable diversity of objects known and methods of knowing is such that these can be arranged in a definite series; that they follow from one another in accordance with a uniform principle. This sort of homogeneity and not abstract identity is the true ideal.[13] But this homogeneity can be attained in full measure only if the point of orientation is transferred from the object to the subject; if the problem of knowledge is viewed not from the standpoint of the universe but from that of man himself. Then everything at once falls into perfect unity. The sciences constitute a single, concordant, and hierarchically organized system, because each has its own definite function to fulfill in the construction of man's intellectual cosmos and thus acquires its specific meaning. Comte hoped in this way to improve radically the prevailing scientific spirit by rescuing it from its "blind and distracting passion for specialization" and giving it by degrees the true philosophic character so essential to its mission.[14]

But the task became more and more difficult to accomplish. The progress of science not only multiplied incessantly the number of problems and interests; it compelled also a constantly increasing specialization in research. The conformity of knowledge to its objects seemed more surely achieved the more patiently each individual science pursued its special subject into all the details of its structure and the more exclusively each was guided by its own subject alone. Therewith the sciences were more and more sharply differentiated but at the same time they became more and more strangers to each other. Nothing more seemed to remain for the logic of research than to confirm this situation, and either tacitly or expressly approve it. But with this the problem of knowledge had lost the stable foundation that it had preserved despite all the incessant struggle during the centuries past.

The very possibility of a unified formulation of this problem has become doubtful, to say nothing of its solution. Is there really any such thing as "knowledge" after all, or do we not fall into a spurious and inadmissible abstraction in advancing such a concept? Is it not the right and the duty of each science to go its own way, unconcerned with all the others, and to develop its own concepts and methodology? But in such a case philosophy and science present a difficult problem for the historian of the theory of knowledge, since there is no longer a uniform theme upon which he can lay hold and by which he can orient himself.

In an earlier inquiry, attempted in the preceding three volumes of

13. See *Cours de philosophie positive*, première leçon. *Discours*, première partie, § 4.
14. *Discours*, troisième partie, § 17.

this work (published in German), it was necessary always to survey the field of the various philosophic systems in order to present the inner development of the problem of knowledge. We had to follow out the manifold and delicate interweavings of these systems with the various concrete sciences. Yet philosophical speculation still retained its primacy throughout, as the perfect and wholly adequate *expression* of the total motif of knowledge. This orientation fails us when we turn to the philosophy of the past hundred years, for in this period philosophy no longer can or will make the same claim which it always insisted upon in earlier times. Instead of assuming the role of leader and representing a determinate ideal of truth in the pride of its own strength and on its own responsibility, it allows itself to be led by the sciences and forced in a prescribed direction by each of them in turn. There are now as many single forms of theory of knowledge as there are different scientific disciplines and interests. Were we content to follow only the most important of these during the second half of the nineteenth and at the opening of the twentieth century we should have a comprehensive and highly variegated picture, to be sure, but it would be incomplete and inadequate by reason of this very complexity. We should have a glimpse of the conflict among the schools, but it could teach us nothing about the real, inner, moving forces of the problem of knowledge itself; these must be sought elsewhere. They lie, often deeply hidden, within the sciences, and during the period with which we are now concerned not only has each one of these undergone the most profound changes in content but revolutionary movements have actually taken place within them that have shaken the foundations upon which the sciences had formerly built.

This appears most clearly among the exact sciences. In geometry, the system of Euclid, which had enjoyed uncontested supremacy for centuries, is ousted from its eminence; the discovery of non-Euclidean geometry introduces entirely new questions for mathematical thought and forces it to a new interpretation of its own logical structure. In the natural sciences, the conception of the world entertained by classical physics becomes more and more open to doubt; the mechanistic view of the universe is staggered by the quantum theory and the special and general theories of relativity.

But changes no less deep and searching come about in other domains. It is during this period that biology seems first to have attained scientific maturity. It not only acquired an incalculable store of new and independent insights that far surpassed the whole achievement of previous centuries, but seemed to have found in the Darwinian theory the first theoretically adequate answer that promised to solve conclusively the riddle of life. Even here, however, doubt and conflict soon set in and hardly any biologists remain today who would see a conclusive doctrine in Darwinism, the end rather than the beginning. As for the science of history, its problem first became clear during this period, when the real "historical concept of the world" began to take shape for the first time. This too, was only possible through constant controversies regarding the method of history that became progressively acrimonious.

All this must restrain the historian of the theory of knowledge for the moment unless he is willing to remain with the peripheral movements instead of tracing them back to their intellectual center. Accordingly we choose for the present treatise a method different from that of the preceding inquiry. We shall not follow out the findings attained in the theory of knowledge by reference to the philosophical classics of the period under discussion, but shall try to penetrate the motives that led to their discovery. Only thus is it possible to overcome the separatist tendencies that seem at first glance the distinguishing mark and, to a certain extent, the stigma of the theory of knowledge during the past century. The fact cannot be denied or remedied, to be sure, but it can be understood at its source and in its relative historical as well as its logical necessity. When the situation is looked at in this way the problem of knowledge is clearly seen to have taken a new turn and acquired a much more complex structure than in the earlier centuries; but at least it ceases to be a chameleon, assuming all the various colors in turn.

From the richness as well as the divergence and conflict of individual tendencies and efforts a unified and comprehensive tendency begins to disclose itself. But of course all this requires a persistent, patient steeping of oneself in the work of the separate sciences, which must not only be investigated in respect to principles but explained concretely, that is, in the way they conceive and handle their primary and fundamental problems. I do not conceal from myself for a moment the enormous difficulty involved in this conception of the task, and during the course of the work I have become increasingly conscious of it. If, nevertheless, I venture to embark on this labor it is with the conviction that only by so doing is there any possibility of approaching the goal that all *philosophic* historical writing must set for itself. For it dare not and indeed is not content to describe certain trains of thought in their origins and temporal order, but intends to explain their general purport and results and show not only what they have been and how they have historically come to be but also their significance as systems. The era of the great constructive programs, in which philosophy might hope to systematize and organize all knowledge, is past and gone. But the demand for synthesis and synopsis, for survey and comprehensive view, continues as before, and only by this sort of systematic review can a true historical understanding of the individual developments of knowledge be obtained.

PART I

EXACT SCIENCE

I

The Problem of Space and the Development of Non-Euclidean Geometry

IN ALL the history of mathematics there are few events of such immediate and decisive importance for the shaping and development of the problem of knowledge as the discovery of the various forms of non-Euclidean geometry. Gauss, the pioneer, who seems to have been in possession of all its fundamental concepts as early as the beginning of the nineteenth century, hardly dared mention them at first. He guarded his secret carefully because he had no hope that the new problem would be understood and because, as he said in a letter, he feared the "hue and cry of the blockheads." At the beginning of the period now under discussion, the third decade of the nineteenth century, appeared the works of Lobachevski and of John Bolyai the younger; but although these could not fail to direct the attention of mathematicians to the question, its full significance in respect to general logic was appreciated only after Riemann had formulated it precisely and more or less conclusively in his dissertation *On the Hypotheses Underlying Geometry* (1854 but not published until 1868). Even the very title of this work suggests the revolution in thinking that had come about in mathematics, for Riemann speaks of "hypotheses," where his predecessors had spoken of "axioms." Where absolute and self-evident propositions had been envisioned he sees "hypothetical" truths that are dependent upon the validity of certain assumptions, and no longer expects a decision on this validity from logic or mathematics but from physics. He explains that the problem of the "intrinsic principle of the dimensions of space" can be solved only if one starts from an interpretation that has already been verified by experience and for which Newton laid the foundation and then, impelled by facts that it will not explain, gradually adapts it to them. Investigation should serve only to insure that research in the future shall not be thwarted by restricted concepts and that progress in recognizing new connections shall not be hindered by traditional prejudices.[1] The whole character of mathematics appeared radically changed by this view, and axioms that had been regarded for centuries as the supreme example of eternal truth now seemed to belong to an entirely different kind of knowledge. In the words of Leibniz, the "eternal verities" had apparently become merely "truths of fact."

It was obvious that no simple mathematical question had been raised here; the whole problem of the truth of mathematics, even of the meaning of truth itself, was placed in an entirely new light. The fate not only of mathematics but of logic as well now seemed to depend upon the direction in which the solution was sought and where it would be found. In antiquity there had been an indissoluble partnership between geometrical and philosophical ideas of truth; they developed with and within one another, and the Platonic concept of the theory of ideas was possible only because Plato had continually in mind the static shapes discovered by Greek mathematics. On the other hand, Greek geometry did not achieve completion as a real system until it adopted Plato's manner of thinking. Its ideal of science was wholly determined by this, and Euclid's "Elements" are the end and the crown of its endeavor. They were correlated throughout with the work of Plato's Academy and were meant to complete the undertaking begun by its great mathematicians, especially by Eudemos and Theaetetus. The concepts and propositions that Euclid placed at the apex of his system were a prototype and pattern for what Plato called the process of synopsis in idea. What is grasped in such synopsis is not the peculiar, the fortuitous or unstable; it possesses universally necessary and eternal truth. Even modern philosophy holds steadfastly to this basic concept. In his theory of mathematical intuition Descartes relied wholly upon the ancient scientific ideal. He distrusted the validity and fertility of syllogistic thinking; but the immediate certainty that characterizes geometrical intuition was never seriously questioned even in his methodical doubt. What this intuition gives us cannot be proved, in the sense of a logical deduction, but there is no need of proof: it is self-evident. It shines by its own and not by reflected light, and herein lies the final and only possible criterion of truth, behind which one cannot go. Truth consists in the indubitable concepts of the "pure and attentive mind," concepts which come out of the light of reason alone.[2]

1. B. Riemann, *Über die Hypothesen, welche der Geometrie zu Grunde liegen* (1854), Neuausgabe von Hermann Weyl, 1919 (3. Aufl. Berlin, Julius Springer, 1923).

2. For Descartes' theory of intuition see especially *Regulae ad directionem ingenii,* "Oeuvres" (Paris, Léopold Cerf, 1908), X, Regula III, 368 ff.

But Leibniz is essentially more skeptical about the value of geometrical intuition as the sole and sufficient criterion of truth, declaring the Cartesian standard of "clear and distinct ideas" inadequate as long as there is no measure of the clarity and distinctness of an idea. Merely appealing to a psychological feeling of evidence can never suffice, for mathematics can furnish us with enough examples of how seriously such a feeling can deceive us and lead us astray.[3] That two lines which continually approach one another, and whose distance apart can become less than any given amount however small, must finally intersect seems at first glance an assertion that is immediately certain; nevertheless the relation of the hyperbola to its asymtotes shows that it is false. Hence Leibniz will not allow the axioms of Euclidean geometry to stand as absolutely undemonstrable propositions. For him they are merely preliminary stages, which must be traced back by increasingly finer analysis to antecedent propositions. The demand for a proof of these axioms runs through all his philosophical and mathematical writings, and constitutes an essential part of his *Characteristica generalis*. Indeed, even for such propositions as that the whole is greater than its parts Leibniz offered an explicit proof.[4] Thus the belief in the immediate certainty and persuasiveness of geometrical "evidence" was profoundly shaken within the confines of classical rationalism itself, not to be reinstated even by Kant's theory of the a priori forms of pure intuition—if this theory be interpreted in its true sense, "transcendentally," instead of psychologically. Yet Kant describes the familiar and fundamental tenet of rationalism when he sets down pure mathematics as a discipline "that carries with it apodictic certainty; that is to say, absolute necessity, not based upon experience, and consequently a pure product of reason." [5] Even the radical skepticism of Hume had not ventured to assail this position. In the first statement of his theory, in the *Treatise of Human Nature*, Hume extended his doubting even to mathematical knowledge and declared it invalid as measured by his standard of truth, sensory perception. Later, however, he expressly retracted this judgment, conceding to mathematics its certainty in view of the argument that it refers not to *matters of fact* but solely to *relations of ideas*. Between ideas there are rigorously necessary and

3. G. W. Leibniz, "Meditationes de cognitione, veritate et ideis," *Die philosophischen Schriften von Gottfried Wilhelm Leibniz*, ed. C. J. Gerhardt (Berlin, Weidmannsche Buchhandlung, 1880), IV, 422 ff.; *Hauptschriften zur Grundlegung der Philosophie*, ed. Cassirer, Erster Bd. (2. Aufl. Leipzig, Felix Meiner, 1924), II, 22 f.

4. Leibniz, "Brief an Johann Bernoulli vom 23. August 1696," *Mathematische Schriften*, ed. C. J. Gerhart, Erste Abteil. (Halle, H. W. Schmidt, 1855), III, 321 f.

5. Immanuel Kant, *Prolegomena*, § 6.

unalterable relations, just because they depend upon nothing that exists in the universe but owe their being purely to the activity of thought.[6]

Rationalists and empiricists still seemed fully in agreement about all this until the beginning of the nineteenth century—for even Locke's theory of mathematical intuition agrees line for line with that of Descartes.[7] Then suddenly they were shaken in their belief as the first systems of non-Euclidean geometry appeared. If geometry owes its certainty to pure reason, how strange that this reason can arrive at entirely different and wholly incongruous systems, while claiming equal truth for each! Does this not call in question the infallibility of reason itself? Does not reason in its very essence become contrary and ambiguous? To recognize a plurality of geometries seemed to mean renouncing the unity of reason, which is its intrinsic and distinguishing feature. Still less than in earlier times could mathematical thinking in the nineteenth century hope to evade the problem thus posed by recourse to an infallible and absolutely evident "intuition." For through the recent advances in mathematics intuition had not only been steadily driven back but a real "crisis in intuition" had come about. In the development of mathematical thought there are many and famous examples which nourish and permanently support the suspicion that intuition is not valid as proof. Nothing seems intuitively more certain, for example, than that a curved line must have a definite direction at every point: a definite tangent. But Weierstrass was able to show that there are functions which are continuous throughout and yet cannot be differentiated, and which therefore correspond to curves for which the given condition is suspended. Similarly Peano later demonstrated the existence of a "curve" that filled a whole square and was thus, in the sense of intuitive interpretation, a highly paradoxical creation; while Möbius proved that there are polyhedra whose volume cannot be calculated in any way.[8] Nothing of all this suggested that the epistemological significance of geometrical intuition should simply be disclaimed, for such prominent geometricians as Felix Klein argued strongly in its favor. But it did

6. David Hume, *An Inquiry Concerning Human Understanding*, § 4, Part I.

7. For further details see Ernst Cassirer, *Das Erkenntnisproblem* (3. Aufl. Berlin, Bruno Cassirer, 1922), II, 255 ff.

8. For further details see Felix Klein, *Elementarmathematik vom höheren Standpunkte aus*, "Die Grundlehren der mathematischen Wissenschaften," XIV–XVI (3. Aufl. Berlin, Julius Springer, 1925), II, 17 ff.

On the "crisis in intuition" in modern mathematics see an article by Hans Hahn, "Krise der Abschauung," *Krise und Neuaufbau in den exakten Wissenschaften* (Leipzig und Wien, Franz Deuticke, 1933), S. 41 ff.

lead to the demand that the customary naïve reliance on intuition cease and give way to another and more critical attitude. If, as the example from Weierstrass shows, even the idea of a curve was not more or less self-evident; if one could say that from a purely mathematical standpoint "nothing would seem more obscure and indefinite than this idea," [9] it is obvious how much the conception of what is "clear and distinct" had altered since the time of Descartes. Thus the non-Euclidean geometries not only declined to yield ground to the Euclidean on the score of the logical rigor of their deductions but they were not to be worsted by the appeal to intuition. This became especially clear with the discovery that they could be translated into certain theorems of Euclidean geometry and immeasurably clarified thereby. Of the several geometries, hyperbolic, elliptic, and parabolic, the first was established by Beltrami, and developed by Helmholtz,[10] from the relations obtaining on a so-called pseudospherical surface, while elliptic geometry was demonstrable from the relations on the surface of a sphere, and in general by the geometry of surfaces with constant positive curvature. In his essay *On So-called Non-Euclidean Geometry*, published in 1871, Felix Klein showed that the entire system thereof can be derived from Euclidean geometry,[11] a fact that makes illusory every preference for one over the other on the score of absolute worth and proves that they share the same fate in respect to "truth," since any contradiction in one is inevitably attended by similar contradictions in the others. His proof was completed and made still more rigorous by Hilbert, who showed in his *Foundations of Geometry* that the theorems of the various systems are reflected not only in one another but in the purely analytical theory of real numbers, so that every contradiction in them must also appear in this theory.

In the field of mathematics itself the new conception made its way quite rapidly and, it would appear, without any violent internal dissension. By constrast, however, the misgivings encountered in the realm of philosophy were all the stronger. Notable thinkers not only entertained serious doubts as to the admissibility of non-Euclidean geometry, but even declared it an absurdity which philosophy must resist with all the means at its command. These different attitudes can

9. F. Klein, *Gesammelte mathematische Abhandlungen* (Berlin, Julius Springer, 1921), I, 38 f.

10. H. Helmholtz, "Über die Tatsachen, welche der Geometrie zu Grunde liegen" (1868), and "Über den Ursprung und die Bedeutung der geometrischen Axiome" (1870), *Vorträge und Reden*, II, 3 ff.

11. Klein, "Über die sogenannte Nicht-Euklidische Geometrie," *Gesammelte mathematische Abhandlungen*, I, 244 ff.

be explained by the distinctive character and the traditional assumptions, respectively, of mathematical and philosophical thought.

Mathematics is, and always will be, a science of pure relations, and in its modern form it is precisely this feature that has become more and more pronounced. When figures of any sort are mentioned and their nature is investigated the inquiry is never into their actual existence but into their relations to one another, in which alone mathematics is interested. Indeed in so far as mathematical thought is concerned their existence does not matter. The single elements receive their roles, and hence their significance, only as they fit together into a connected system; thus they are defined through one another, not independently of one another. Hilbert has expressed and clarified this feature of mathematical thinking with the greatest precision in his theory of "implicit definition." It is clear that for this theory any given geometry can be from the first nothing but a certain system of order and relations, whose character is determined by principles governing the relationships, and not by the intrinsic nature of the figures entering into it. The same system can acquire as many and as highly varied elements as one wishes without in any respect losing its identity. Hence the points, straight lines, and planes of Euclidean geometry can be replaced in an endless number of ways by other and entirely different objects without the least change in the content and truth of the corresponding theorems.[12] For neither system depends upon something that is assumed to be a definite content of geometrical knowledge; their foundations are erected upon the laws of combination and determined by them.

But philosophy found it difficult to achieve this sort of abstraction —long so natural and familiar to mathematics—for it was feared that the firm ground of "truth" would be lost. In his *Critique of Pure Reason* [13] Kant declared that philosophy would have to renounce the proud name of an ontology that presumed to furnish in a systematized doctrine synthetic a priori judgments on all existence. This claim would have to give way to the more modest one of a simple analysis of pure understanding. But the post-Kantian systems brushed this warning aside. They started from ontology and metaphysics, and every critique of knowledge that came within their purview was instinctively transformed into an ontological inquiry. This

12. For examples see H. Weber—J. Wellstein, "Euklidische Geometrie im parabolischen Kugelgebüsche," *Enzyklopädie der Elementar-Mathematik* (3. Aufl. Leipzig und Berlin, B. G. Teubner, 1915), II, 33.

13. I. Kant, *Kritik der reinen Vernunft* (3. verbesserte Aufl. Riga, J. F. Hartknoch, 1790), S. 303.

transformation and confusion touched the problem of space more closely because even the greatest philosophical mathematicians had given it their attention. Descartes, for example, connected it as intimately as possible with the problem of number by his discovery of analytical geometry, thereby giving the problem of space an entirely new orientation. But in the development of his metaphysics space appears to be not so much a certain pattern of order beside that of number as some sort of absolute thing in the form of extended substance. Leibniz objected to this metaphysical hypostatizing, this assumption that space is real, by emphasizing its ideal character. This character should in no way cast doubt on the objectivity of space and turn it into a "mere idea" in the subjective, psychological sense, but rather define this objectivity in its proper and only justifiable meaning, thus establishing the inevitable validity of geometrical truths. But in the seventeenth and eighteenth centuries Newton was awarded the palm over Leibniz on this score. Space continued to be defined as absolute and its reality constituted, for both physicists and philosophers, the essential subject of investigation.

It is easy to understand how paradoxical non-Euclidean geometry must have been to such a way of thinking. Nothing shocked those philosophers who were first to discuss the possibilities of the new geometry more than the sharp division between their own ontological formulation of the problem and that made from the standpoint of a logical critique of knowledge. If there were different systems of geometrical axioms, there must be different kinds of space, which in turn involved different worlds. But if this were admitted the essential claim of philosophy to be a rigorously uniform and comprehensive knowledge of truth seemed forever lost. Hence it was believed that in taking sides against mathematical speculation in this matter one was fighting for the fundamental rights and the essential business of philosophy, an attitude particularly evident in Lotze. The very fact that he incorporated his discussion on "metageometry" in his *Metaphysik*, instead of in his *Logik*, is characteristic and he was already making the inquiry take a definite line. He saw in metageometrical speculation "a unique, vast, and consistent error," and declared it not only the right but the imperative duty of philosophy to oppose this error with the utmost vigor. "I am entirely unable to convince myself that many of my colleagues who approve the new theories can so easily understand what is to me wholly unintelligible. I am afraid that with the timidity of their calling, they do not do such hard thinking about this borderland of mathematics and philosophy as they do in the name of philosophy about much of the speculation of the present day." [14] Upon closer examination it appears, however, that Lotze himself did not escape the "delusive play with ambiguities" with which he reproached metageometry,[15] for he viewed the problem of space not in the immanent sense of mathematics but objectively, asking whether a definite, absolute thing to which he gave the name space has certain properties or not. It seemed to him the most utter nonsense to ascribe to this thing simultaneously, as the various geometries appear to do, qualities that are incompatible with one another.

Wundt is more cautious in his criticism, though he too refuses to admit that the newer speculation has any epistemological value. His objection is that although the balancing of possibilities may be an attractive intellectual pastime, it can furnish no evidence of any value in respect to truth. "This question is on a par with that raised more than once in the older ontology: whether or not the real world is the best among all possible worlds. No one since Kant has hesitated to reply that the real world is the only one that exists, and that nothing at all can be said about the nature of worlds that do not exist." [16] Since our ideas must be based upon reality if they are to have any objective value, there is no sense in trying to conjure up new worlds and new kinds of space by mere differences in mathematical concepts. "The opinion that holds it possible to imagine a space of varying shape . . . is to be compared not with the opinion that we could imagine men who carry their heads in their hands instead of on their shoulders, but rather with this further one that we are in a position to summon such men of fiction actually into being." [17]

The "profound misunderstanding between philosophy and mathematics" that Lotze deplored could hardly be removed by this sort of criticism, which was conspicuously wide of the mark and unsuited to the real importance of the problem. But by the time Lotze and Wundt had stated their objections mathematics itself had already done all it could to clarify the misunderstandings. In 1872 the so-called "Erlanger Program" of Felix Klein appeared. Under the title *Comparative Reflections on the More Modern Geometrical Investigations* and offering for the first time a comprehensive survey of the various possible geometries from a rigorously uniform and systematized standpoint, it was a highly significant advance not only in a

14. H. Lotze, "Deductionen des Raumes," *Metaphysik,* Zweites Buch (Leipzig, S. Hirzel, 1879), S. 234.

15. *Ibid.,* S. 245.

16. W. Wundt, "Der mathematische Raumbegriff," *Logik* (2. Aufl. Stuttgart, Ferdinand Enke, 1893), I, 496.

17. *Ibid.,* S. 498.

mathematical sense but also as a critique of knowledge. Now at last the problem could be assigned its own rightful place. Klein restricted himself to its formal and analytical clarification, expressly avoiding all ontological opinions on the reality of space. The early discoverers of non-Euclidean geometry had not been careful to keep within these bounds, believing in their delight over the revelation that they had finally found the clue to the secret of space, which they thought Euclidean geometry had failed to disclose. Abandoning the axiom of parallels, Bolyai entered the discussion with the statement that through the new geometry "the theory of real, absolute space" had been founded for the first time.[18] In opposing this assertion from the standpoint of pure mathematics Klein shows that this science has to do solely with relations, which must on no account be confused with existence. He confines the discussion strictly to the field of mathematics, forbidding all excursions into the ontological and the metaphysical. In his *Lectures on the Development of Mathematics in the Nineteenth Century* he described in detail how many unfortunate mistakes had been caused by the transfer of certain thoroughly justifiable and fertile mathematical investigations to a wholly different sphere, with consequent destruction of their original sense. Thus an objective significance had been attributed by philosophers and mystics of all sorts to the purely internal mathematical proposition that the measure of curvature in Euclidean and non-Euclidean space is constant, as though this proposition conferred on space some sort of intuitively comprehensible property.[19] All this Klein avoided in his "Erlanger Program" by giving priority to questions of the content and task of geometry. But since Euclidean geometry had expanded to a pan-geometry the problem required a new solution in respect to logic and a critique of knowledge. Searching for an answer, Klein introduced the theory of groups, which furnished the first really adequate and collective orientation of the problems set by the new geometry; for this theory is one of the most important phases of mathematical thinking, though it was not revealed in all its fertility until the nineteenth century. In his *Philosophy of Mathematics* Hermann Weyl says emphatically that the group is perhaps the most characteristic mathematical concept of that period.[20] And indeed

18. See Klein, "Über die sogenannte Nicht-Euklidische Geometrie," *Gesammelte mathematische Abhandlungen*, I, 312.

19. Klein, *Vorlesungen über die Entwicklung der Mathematik im 19. Jahrhundert*, "Die Grundlehren der mathematischen Wissenschaften," XXIV–XXV (1926), I, 152 f.

20. H. Weyl, "Philosophie der Mathematik und Naturwissenschaft," Zweite Abteil., *Natur, Geist, Gott*, "Handbuch der Philosophie" (München und Berlin, R. Oldenbourg, 1927), S. 23.

this concept, while limited at first to certain important applications in special fields, became of increasingly general significance and finally proved to be a dominant point of view whence the whole panorama of mathematical problems can be surveyed. This may be because the theory of groups penetrates most deeply into the essentially mathematical view, not dealing with numbers or quantities as separate mathematical objects, but inquiring into the legitimacy of *operations*. Leibniz had already recognized that the focal point of mathematics lies here, and his attempts to construct a comprehensive system and a universal mathematics were aimed in this direction. In the eighteenth century the theory of groups had proved fruitful in algebra at the hands of Lagrange and Cauchy, the latter of whom was the first to raise the theory of substitutions to the rank of a finished discipline.[21] But even with Galois, the real pioneer in this field, the significance of the group theory far outstrips the uses that he makes of it for the theory of algebraic equations. The advance from the theory of numbers to the far more comprehensive theory of operations is plainly apparent in his work.[22]

Later the theory of groups was introduced into geometrical research by Lie and Klein; here too it showed immediately its inherent organizing power and the dark cloud that until then had lain over geometrical speculation was illumined by one single flash. The group is defined as a set of well-defined operations $A, B, C \ldots$ such that any two operations A, B combined yield an operation that is a member of the unit; as a complementary condition it is required that besides A the reciprocal element A^{-1} be present in the group. Klein thought it a real advantage of the theory that it eliminated all "appeal to fantasy."[23] The concept of groups is manifestly characteristic of "a wholly intellectual mathematics that has been purged of all intuition; of a theory of pure forms with which are associated not quantities or their symbols, numbers, but intellectual concepts, products of thought, to which actual objects or their relations *may*, but *need not*, correspond."

The plan of such a mathematics had already been advanced in 1867 by Hermann Hankel in his *Theory of Complex Number Systems*, who had expressly declared it a "requisite for the establishment of a

---

21. See L. Brunschvicg, "Les Racines de la vérité algébrique," *Les Etapes de la philosophie mathématique* (2e éd. Paris, F. Alcan, 1922), p. 550 ff.

22. For further details see E. Picard, *Les Sciences mathématiques en France depuis un demi-siècle* (Paris, Gauthier-Villars et Cie., 1917), p. 1 ff.

23. Klein, *Vorlesungen über die Entwicklung der Mathematik im 19. Jahrhundert,* "Die Grundlehren der mathematischen Wissenschaften," XXIV (1926), I, 335.

general arithmetic," [24] but now it turns out that this concept is no less fruitful and necessary for the systematization of geometry. The specific difference that separates the various geometries from one another can now be expressed with the greatest clarity and significance. The answer to the problem is not only most gratifying from a logical standpoint; it is surprisingly simple as well. Every geometry in its general concept and aim is a theory of invariants with respect to a certain group, and the special nature of each depends upon the choice of this group. Not every observation of a special object, and not every proof bearing on it, has the characteristics of a *geometrical* proposition. There are such proofs, relating to the position of an object in space or to some particular shape such as a triangle with sides of specified length. Propositions such as that a point has the coordinates 2, 5, 3 are of a spatial nature but are not geometrical definitions, for a proposition like this relates only to a system of coordinates that is fixed once for all; it belongs rather to a science that has to individualize each point and conceive its attributes separately: to topography or, if you will, to geography. Only properties that are characterized by an invariance with respect to certain transformations can be called "geometrical." This is first worked out by Klein for that "principal" group which is determining for Euclidean geometry. It is an inquiry into all those properties of a spatial figure that remain invariant throughout all the motions of space and its similarity transformations, and through the process of reflection as well as throughout all transformations compounded of these. Such properties are independent of the position occupied in space by the figure under investigation as well as of its absolute size and the order in which its parts are arranged. But nothing compels us to stop with the "principal group," determining for Euclidean geometry. Adequate as it is from a practical standpoint for all life's purposes and for our mastery of the physical world, others can be ranged alongside it that are theoretically justifiable to the same degree. As a generalization for all geometry, then, there arises this following comprehensive statement: "*Given a manifold, and in it a transformation group; one should investigate the figures belonging to the manifold with a view to finding the properties that are not changed by the transformations of the group.*" [25]

24. H. Hankel, *Vorlesungen über die Complexen Zahlen* (Leipzig, Leopold Voss, 1867), Teil I, S. 9 f.

25. Klein, "Vergleichende Betrachtungen über neuere geometrische Forschungen," *Gesammelte mathematische Abhandlungen* (1929), I, 463; "Systematik und Grundlegung der Geometrie," *Elementarmathematik,* II, 140 ff.

From this fundamental conception of the matter Klein develops the various kinds of geometry. He studies the ordinary metric geometry, affine geometry, projective geometry (as a theory of invariance of the projective transformations), the geometry of reciprocal radii, and analysis situs. The question which of them is the most "true" seems now to have lost its significance. All are equally rigorous and therefore equally justifiable in theory, for they differ only in respect to the system of transformations upon which they are based and the one upon which they establish the totality of the invariant properties. Here our thinking obviously is not committed at the outset to a single fixed system but can choose one and modify it freely. For there is no question yet of any result or of ascertaining something prescribed and imposed by the nature of the subject. It is only a simple question that is asked and it springs in a certain sense from the inner being of that thought itself. Reflection on and puzzling over what geometry is according to its own concept and problem must finally lead to further extension of the brand of science that was first developed for historic reasons. With this methodical interpretation it is clear that there can no longer be any more conflict between the various systems than there is between philosophy and mathematics. For whatever answer philosophy in its role as the knowledge of reality, as the doctrine of "being as being," may give to the problem of the nature of reality, the answer will not be dictated by mathematics, which now appears wholly as a science of pure form. Yet on the other hand philosophy cannot and dare not attack or reject what mathematics has to teach about pure form or about the logical structure of space but must build on it as on a sure foundation.

Even more significant in respect to the general theory of knowledge is another point of view to which Klein is led in the course of his investigation. That one geometry can have no advantage over another so far as its "truth" is concerned has already been shown. But what of universality? Must we declare all systems equivalent in this respect, too, or can some distinction be drawn? Can a sort of hierarchy be imagined, with the particular at the bottom and the general at the top? Klein did, in fact, establish such an ascending series, in which Euclidean geometry was assigned its definite place, and in so doing he substituted for the earlier obscure and unanswerable question, which of the various geometries is the most justifiable, one to which an exact reply can be given. There seem to be no degrees of precision among the various geometries; all are equally true and equally necessary. A difference in rank becomes recognizable, however, when we compare the various transformation groups upon which they are founded, for these groups are not simply juxtaposed but arranged in a series. So, for example, projective geometry is placed above ordinary metric geometry because the group of projective transformations contains as a part of itself the "principal" group upon which Euclidean geometry rests. Affine and projective geometry acknowledge as geometrical properties only those that are not changed by parallel or central projection, and thus to a certain extent widen the horizon of Euclidean geometry by adding parallel or central projection to figures that are similar in the ordinary sense.

When this point of view is logically developed it becomes clear that the differences assumed to exist among the various geometrical figures are not to be regarded as absolute, given, and fixed once for all by their nature; on the contrary, they shift about within the separate geometries, for the manner and principle of putting them together decides what are to be regarded as "the same" or "not the same." In Euclidean geometry similar triangles, which are distinguishable only through their absolute position in space and the length of their sides, are not different figures but one single figure; from a conceptual point of view their differences are explained as inconsequential or fortuitous. It is obvious that this is an immense step forward in thinking compared with the view of ordinary perception, which recognizes only a this and now, i.e., only individualized and spatially determined figures. This method of "equivalence" or of definition by abstraction is one of the operations fundamental to mathematical thought in general.[26] But such abstraction can go far beyond any use made of it in Euclidean geometry. What seems there an impassable barrier as a distinction between essential beings can be regarded from another point of view as something relative, and so explained from the standpoint of geometrical abstraction as of no importance.

In passing from one geometry to another the peculiar change in meaning is constantly seen. For example, in affine geometry there is no longer a question of length and angle. The concept of the major axes of a conic section is done away with and likewise the distinction between a circle and an ellipse. On the other hand, the distinction between finite and the *infinite extension* of space and all that relates thereto is maintained. And so the division of conic sections into ellipses, hyperbolas, and parabolas remains in force. In the transition to projective geometry, however, even the eminent position of infinity comes to an end and eventually only one kind of conic section remains. This peculiar process of breaking down distinctions goes even farther when we go on to analysis situs, which treats of the

26. H. Weyl, "Philosophie der Mathematik," *Natur* . . . , S. 8 ff.

totality of the properties that remain intact with respect to all continuous one-to-one transformations. Here the distinction between a cone, a cube, and a pyramid simply disappears; they are no longer different but only one structure, because any one can be changed into the other by a continuous transformation.

No matter how paradoxical and elusive such abstractions may seem from a naïve standpoint it must not be forgotten that the paradox, if such it be, does not first appear with the transition from Euclidean to the higher geometries. The real "hiatus" is not between the old and the new but between the point of view of ordinary sense perception and the world of geometrical ideas. In proportion as geometrical concepts gain in elegance and precision, the "world of space" is transformed for us, and other and deeper strata come to light. "The gradual separation of affine and projective geometry from metric," says Klein, "may be compared with the procedure of the chemist, who isolates increasingly valuable constituents from a compound by using constantly stronger analytical reagents; our reagents are first affine and then projective transformations." [27] The analogy lies in this, that in progressing from metric to affine and projective geometry we lay bare, as it were, deeper and deeper layers of spatial forms because we reach those basic spatial elements that prove invariant not only with respect to the relatively limited transformations of the "principal group," but to those going on and on without end.

With this interpretation as a basis it is possible to meet one of the principal objections leveled by philosophical criticism against modern geometrical theories. Their chief offense, it seems, is the violation of a fundamental postulate contained a priori in the idea of space itself. Space must be a *unity*, whereas the recognition of non-Euclidean geometry would turn it into a heterogeneous plurality. As long as one clings to a substantialistic view of space the criticism is wholly justifiable and irrefutable, for space then appears as something self-subsistent, something that geometry should acknowledge in such a way as to render a complete and faithful *representation*. But when different geometries offer different pictures, when one insists, for instance, that the curvature of space equals zero, others that it is positive or negative, then the unity and definiteness of the original is gone beyond repair, and in trying to define it we fall immediately into antinomies.

Yet it is easily seen that these contradictions should not be charged against geometrical abstraction but are derived from a false posing

27. Klein, *Elementarmathematik,* II, 142.

of the problem which has been injected from without. Geometry is a pure science of relations which has to do not with the ascertaining of objects and their characteristics, substances and their properties, but with orders of ideas alone. The question, too, about the unity of space can therefore be posed only in this sense, that it concerns not the substantial but the formal or "ideal" unity. This should have been all the more readily understood by the philosophy of the nineteenth century, for the foundations had been laid long before. Even in the philosophical systems of the seventeenth and eighteenth centuries we find a new theory of space, which breaks with the substantialistic interpretation and subjects it to critical analysis. It was Leibniz and not Kant who was the first to explain that space is pure "form": an order of coexistence, as time is an order of succession. Thus the view of modern mathematics was really anticipated by philosophy. "Space is indeed something," wrote Leibniz to Conti in expounding his opposition to the Newtonian theory, "but just as time is; each is a general order of things. Space is the order of coexistences, and time is the order of successive existences. They are veritable things but they are ideal ones like numbers." [28]

A glance at Klein's presentation of geometry shows that here the purely ideal, the systematic, unity of space appears to be in no way abandoned but on the contrary is more firmly established than ever; for the general form of space, the form of "possible coexistence," is assumed and employed by all geometries as an undeviating and fundamental concept. In this respect they closely resemble one another, but they differentiate this space form by approaching it with different questions and considering it under the aspect of different transformation groups. Yet even here the unity and continuity of thought are preserved throughout, for the various geometries do not exist side by side promiscuously and without relationship; they develop one from the other in accordance with a rigorously determined principle. Hence we are enabled to survey the entire series of possible geometries at a glance, from the ordinary metric geometry up to analysis situs and the theory of sets, and to see them as a connected whole. *Now* it is clear that the idea of several geometries not only does not exclude the idea of one single geometry but inevitably demands it, and that the unity of space is therefore neither suspended nor endangered. To attain this viewpoint, of course, modern geometrical

28. Leibniz, "D'une lettre de Leibniz à Conti," *Opera omnis* . . . , éd. L. Dutens (Geneva, Fratres de Tournes, 1768), III, 446. For a more extensive discussion of Leibniz' theory of space see E. Cassirer, *Leibniz' System in seinen wissenschaftlichen Grundlagen* (Marburg, 1902), S. 245 ff.

concept formation had to pass beyond the confines of spatial intuition. It in no way ignored intuition; quite the contrary, it was everywhere associated with it. "To pursue a geometrical train of thought by pure logic," says Klein, "without seeing constantly before my eyes the figure to which it refers is impossible, at any rate for me." Yet he says, too, that intuition as such is not enough, because it is "essentially inexact." Its inaccuracy must be done away with by constant revision and "idealization," for only thus can we arrive at absolutely precise and really universal statements. Geometrical axioms are the requirements by virtue of which "precise assertions are put into the vague intuitions." [29] But here, of course, another question intrudes that is of basic significance for the theory of mathematical knowledge. By what right do we undertake this "idealizing?" Is it not safer, and less biased scientifically, to accept the given as given and stop there? Is it permissible to modify arbitrarily the inexactness that is proper to all empirical intuition and introduce extraneous statements? In order to provide an answer we must widen the scope of our investigation, for now the question of the origin of geometric thought takes its place beside that of the content of the geometrical axioms and the logical relationship of the various systems to one another. Since the former question has constantly engaged mathematical and philosophical thought and strongly affected the development of epistemology during the second half of the nineteenth century, we now turn to the discussion of it.

29. Klein, "Zur Nicht-Euklidischen Geometrie," *Mathematische Annalen*, XXXVII (1890); *Gesammelte mathematische Abhandlungen* (1921), I, 381, 386.

II

Experience and Thought in the Construction of Geometry

RATIONALISM as a whole has remained firmly convinced that mathematics is the paragon of a priori knowledge, and empiricism itself has hardly ventured to touch this conviction (see p. 23). Kant declared mathematics to be a shining example of the progress we can make in knowledge independently of experience.[1] But the value and cogency of his illustration appeared to be seriously undermined by the discovery of non-Euclidean geometry. Here Gauss immediately drew the most radical consequences for the theory of knowledge. Arithmetic and analysis, based as they are on the idea of pure number, remained for him the purely rational knowledge. He dismissed geometry, however, from their company and placed it on the side of the empirical sciences. Thus he was led to attempt a solution of the problem, "which geometry is true," which is the one existing in reality, by measurements on empirical bodies. "We must humbly confess," he wrote in a letter to Bessel, "that whereas number is a product of the mind space has a reality outside the mind whose laws we cannot prescribe a priori." [2]

Once this conclusion had been drawn a serious flaw was revealed in the edifice that until then had stood so firm. Since the time of the Pythagoreans there had been an intimate association, not to say an indissoluble correlation, between the theory of numbers and the theory of extension: between arithmetic and geometry. They had received their scientific foundations at the same time and from the same philosophical spirit, and their connection was still further strengthened when Descartes discovered analytical geometry. If this tie were broken, if the origin of number were sought in the mind and the origin of space "outside" it, then the former unity of mathematics would be gone and it would comprise entirely different classes of objects and go back to different sources of knowledge.

Yet the fact of the plurality of geometries seemed to permit no other explanation. If no difference could be shown among them in respect to the rigor of their deductions, if from a logical standpoint all had arisen on the same plane, the exceptional and preferred posi-

---

1. I. Kant, Einleitung, *Kritik der reinen Vernunft* (2. Aufl.), S. 8.
2. C. F. Gauss, "Werke" (Leipzig, B. G. Teubner, 1900), VIII, 201.

tion of Euclidean geometry, which no one wished to dispute, could be understood only by the fact that one resorted to another court of appeal.

Ordinary empiricism, as represented in Mill's logic, for example, found no difficulty in solving the problem, referring the origin of mathematical concepts to experience, which it regarded as merely the sum of single sensory percepts. But mathematics, more rigid in its demands, was not satisfied with this solution. If geometrical thinking were to be included in the realm of empirical thinking, the endeavor must first be made to strip the latter of pure sensation and establish it on other and firmer ground. Among mathematicians the most energetic and logical advance in this direction was made by Moritz Pasch, in his *Lectures on Modern Geometry*.[3] Here for the first time proof seems to have been brought that geometrical empiricism need not result in any relaxation of geometrical rigor but can rather lead even to an increase in rigor. He declared in his Preface that in the preceding efforts to establish geometry on a new basis that could satisfy the increasingly severe demands of the time the empirical origin of geometry had not proven its value decisively.

If geometry is to be regarded as a science born of direct and exact observation of nature, a science that seeks by purely inductive means to win from immediately observed simple phenomena the laws of complicated phenomena, then one is indeed compelled to reject many a traditional idea; but if we do so, the material to be worked up will be brought back to its proper domain and the ground for a whole series of controversies will be eliminated. No matter how many sorts of speculation may still be associated with geometry, its fruitful application in the natural sciences and in practical life rests upon the fact that its concepts originally corresponded to empirical objects. As long as one limits himself from first to last to this empirical core, geometry retains the character of a natural science, distinguished from the other parts of science by the fact that it needs to derive very few of its concepts and laws immediately from experience.

Pasch relied on no philosophical authority in support of this contention, yet it is clear that he was following in the main the path of positivism and wanted to see its program accomplished in geometry.

Comte had maintained that geometry, like mathematics in general, is a science not of concepts but of facts, since all real knowledge as such is concerned with facts and must limit itself to ascertaining

---

3. M. Pasch, *Vorlesungen über neuere Geometrie,* "Die Grundlehren der mathematischen Wissenschaften," XXIII (2. Aufl. 1926), S. v.

them. But the long-standing primacy of mathematics was not in the least impugned and its value to knowledge was no less highly prized than in the systems of classical rationalism. For Comte drew a sharp distinction between what he called particular facts and general facts. Mathematics occupied itself exclusively with *faits généraux* and remained in that realm. That the very idea of a *fait général* contains a difficult problem, that it at least requires a theoretical foundation and vindication—all this seems hardly to have been recognized by Comte. No serious doubts about the possibility of deductive inference appear to have disturbed him. But he thought induction the real basis of certainty, and ranked it higher than deduction.[4] He believed, therefore, that mathematics owes its precision not to the rigor of its proofs, but to the fact that it deals with the simplest phenomena. As size and number are inherent in all natural phenomena they, first of all, must force themselves upon the mind and they, above all other characteristics, can be elevated to the rank of positive knowledge.[5]

Still the thesis that there is no difference in principle between empirical and geometrical knowledge remains with Comte, as in other systems of empiricism, essentially a bare postulate, and in a certain sense it is set up and defended only as epistemological dogma. Pasch, on the contrary, made the concrete attempt to show in detail what an empirical geometry must be like and how it can be built up from the first with scientific rigor. In so doing he naturally had to discard the Euclidean definitions of a point, a straight line, and a plane. Considered from his point of view they are empty, since they do not go back to any observable facts. They could be obtained from such facts by idealization, by certain limit processes, but the necessity of and the right to such a procedure are precisely what is in doubt here. The most important question, then, is what can be substituted for these elements, with which all geometrical thinking must begin. Any definition must be renounced, for no explanation can replace the means whereby alone it is possible to understand these simple figures, which cannot be derived from others, namely, the reference to appropriate natural objects. We recognize as such only material things and processes, to which we must therefore cling as the necessary foundation for all geometrical abstraction, though we allow ourselves certain simplifications in their description. A point is not something which has no parts, a line is not length without breadth; but rather a point

4. See in particular A. Comte's *Système de politique positive* (Paris, L. Matthius, 1851), I, 517 ff.

5. For the place of mathematics in Comte's system see especially his *Cours de philosophie positive,* deuxième et troisième leçons.

is a material body whose division does not lie within the limits of observation. Accordingly even the use of the various axioms is subject from the first to definite restrictions. If, for example, the proposition be advanced that a straight line, and only one, can always be drawn between two points, the points to be thus connected must not be assumed to lie too close together. So, too, one cannot use as often as one pleases, for one and the same figure, the axiom that if A and B are any two points, then a point C can be so chosen that B will lie on the line AC. Of course a perfectly clearcut limit cannot be set in these matters. "But one must beware of concluding, in the absence of a clearly prescribed restriction, that there is no such restriction." Even the application of the basic axioms and geometrical principles is not unlimited, for as they have been acquired by experience from objects that were relatively nearby, their unrestricted employment beyond this circumscribed field is not justified without more ado." [6] Pasch showed that a geometry such as he demanded would be possible and he showed, also, what form it should take.

But the fact of pure mathematics which Kant invoked in his *Critique of Pure Reason* and on which his conclusions there were based was not therewith set aside. It survives, at least as a historical fact, and as such demands explanation. Why has geometry from its first scientific beginnings taken this way of idealizing and held to it so consistently and, if the expression be allowed, so one-sidedly and obstinately? If it be a natural science, if its purpose be to assemble observations on material objects and systematize them in a prescribed way, its course must seem an odd detour if not a serious error. A natural science that was guided at first by observation, but almost immediately turned its back thereon to introduce elements that were not susceptible to observation and from which it drew purely logical deductions, would sin against the first commandment of intellectual procedure and the scientific view of things. If geometry be an experiential science, the precision of which it boasts would certainly have to lie in the accuracy of the empirical sources of its concepts. Thus it would have to justify itself by constant increase and refinement of its means of observation and by what grows out of this, the more and more exact tests of its fundamental principles and basic facts.

Yet this road was obviously as little followed in the system of Pasch as in any earlier geometrical system. He turned rather to the procedure that reached its logical completion in Hilbert's *Foundations of Geometry* and the method of implicit definition there employed. So

6. M. Pasch, "Von der geraden Linie," *Vorlesungen über neuere Geometrie*, § 1, S. 6, 16, 17, etc.

one could well apply Kant's expression to Pasch's system, that in it geometrical knowledge begins indeed with experience but does not for that reason arise from experience. Here, too, the essential thing is that working over of thought by which certain basic concepts ordinarily derived simply from intuition are first given a strictly logical meaning, e.g., the concept of "between." Hence Pasch's work had a historical effect that hardly tallied with its systematic purpose, for it actually paved the way for logicism and formalism rather than for geometrical empiricism.

An attempt at a thoroughgoing foundation for empiricism was made by Helmholtz. What distinguishes the achievements of Helmholtz in this field is that he placed the problem in a large context and grasped it in its truly universal extent. He was interested in it not only as a mathematician but also because from all sides of his scientific activities he was directed to it. He had investigated the problem of space not only as a geometrician and philosopher but as a physiologist and psychologist as well, and the problem was in a way the focal point of all his research. In his superb development of physiological optics he wanted to help empiricism triumph over "innatism," by showing that space is not an "innate idea" but has its origin in empirical consciousness which can be proved beyond any doubt, and that it grows out of simple sense perception by way of association and "unconscious inference." One can fully understand the peculiar features of his theory of space by reference to the fact that Helmholtz was at once mathematician, physicist, and physiologist. He did not deny the a priori character of space in the Kantian sense, but he wanted to conceive it in such a way that it would not only agree with his fundamental notions of the physiology of the senses but would actually complete and support them.

Space in its most universal form, as "the possibility of coexistence" is an underived basic concept that does not come out of experience but rather lies at the base thereof. But this form must be regarded as absolutely universal, and it is so only if thought of as empty and free of content so that it can receive every content that could possibly enter it. Such a restriction lies in the set of axioms basic to every particular geometry. Here first the role of experience begins. Space is transcendental, underived and original, but the construction given it by the Euclidean system, in particular the validity of the axiom of parallels, cannot be derived from it as a pure form of intuition, as the historical existence of non-Euclidean geometry shows, and so the particular feature of the system must have another origin. The axioms of geometry are not necessary consequences of such a given a priori, transcendental form but must be regarded as expressing fundamental experiences of such a general sort that their empirical character is apt to be forgotten.

The process of measurement did not begin with geometry but has gone on in the everyday experience of space.

When we measure we simply perform with the best and most reliable means known to us what otherwise we are accustomed to do by observation in judging of distance by the eye or by touch or by pacing off. In the latter case our own bodies and their organs that we carry about with us in space are the tools of measurement; now the hands, now the legs, are our dividers; or the eye, turning in all directions, is the theodolite with which we measure arcs or plane angles.

In all these measurements, however, those made with our own bodily organs as well as those made with artificial instruments, an assumption is in force the validity of which is not established a priori but can only be derived from experience: we have to assume the existence of "rigid bodies" that are freely movable in space without change of form. The non-Euclidean geometries have the merit of teaching us that this assumption, though probable in the highest degree, is not logically necessary; that it goes at any rate beyond the realm of pure spatial intuition and contains a definite assumption as to the physical behavior of objects, that is to say, an empirical proposition.[7]

Helmholtz' exposition was based in particular on the concept of groups, though he had not grasped this idea so definitely nor applied it so explicitly as did Lie and Klein afterward. It was shown that in a three-dimensional space of constant curvature displacements are possible that depend upon six parameters; thus there is a sextuply infinite variety of movements. But now the point of difficulty in the problem, from an epistemological standpoint, was shifted. In order to obtain a trustworthy insight respecting the meaning and origin of the various systems of axioms it is no longer enough to analyze the idea of space; it is essential to keep in mind the group concept itself. And in that regard we are in a most favorable position, for the logical character of group theory is hardly in doubt, being immediately obvious from its applications and its evolution. Since its early development by Cauchy, Lagrange, and Galois the range of these applications has broadened continuously and extended to the most various fields of mathematics. The group concept is not restricted either to mathematics or geometry or to number or dimension. In it we rise

7. H. Helmholtz, "Über den Ursprung und die Bedeutung der geometrischen Axiome," *Vorträge und Reden*, II, 22 ff.

above any consideration of special elements of mathematical thought to a theory of *operations*. We are no longer concerned with the special content but rather with the very procedure of mathematics itself, for we have entered the realm of pure, "intellectual mathematics."

Poincaré appears to have been the first thinker to draw the consequences of this for the problem of geometry, and the result was a categorical denial of geometrical empiricism. For if the theory of the group is what must be introduced into the definition of geometry, and if each geometry can be designated as a theory of invariants in respect to a certain group, then a pure a priori element has entered into the conceptual definitions. This solved for him the problem of the dignity of geometry from the point of view of a criticism of knowledge. "The object of geometry," he explained,

is the study of a definite group, but the general idea of the group pre-exists, at least potentially, in our mind, having forced itself in not as a form of sensibility but as a form of our understanding. All we have to do is to choose among all possible groups the one that will constitute a standard for us, as it were, to which natural phenomena are referred. Experience guides us in this choice but does not dictate it; nor does it permit us to know which geometry is truer but only which is more "useful." [8]

Here the word *useful* or *convenient* requires, first of all, a detailed explanation, for one must guard against the danger that this will result in a general renunciation of all objective character and so leave the choice of a particular geometry to subjective preference. Klein rightly protested against any such view. "In respect to the modern doctrine of axioms," he observed,

we often fall right back into the line of philosophy that has long been known as *nominalism*, where interest is entirely lost in things themselves and in their properties, and the only discussion is about what we shall call them and according to what logical scheme we shall operate with these terms. . . . I myself do not share this view at all, holding it to be the death of all science: *The axioms of geometry are, as I believe, not arbitrary but rational propositions that in general are occasioned by the perception of space and are regulated as to their individual content by their suitability.*[9]

But even Poincaré himself had not understood his thesis in the way criticized here, though later many advocates of extreme nominalism

8. H. Poincaré, *La Science et l'hypothèse* (Paris, E. Flammarion, 1902), p. 90 ff.
9. F. Klein, *Elementarmathematik*, II, 202.

and conventionalism invoked his name. Poincaré would have been able to subscribe to these words of Klein without demur. He thought it unreasonable to appeal to experience to decide which geometry is "truer," if true be interpreted to mean reality that can be empirically established and of which something can be proved or disproved by direct observation; for in this respect all geometries are equally remote from reality, since they deal with figures that are removed from all possibility of experiment. One can never experiment with ideal straight lines and circles; every answer received by experiment always has to do with the nature and behavior of material objects. But it may very well be that certain basic experiments made on these objects may lead to the development of a geometry that is conformable with them and represents them in the simplest manner. For example, we derive from experience the presupposition that it is possible for an object to move freely in all directions without any change in shape, and accordingly we eliminate from the possible geometries a definite group for which this assumption does not hold good. And the limitation can go even farther. Geometrical thinking is hereby more exactly determined through experience but it is not founded upon it. Experience is not the means of proving geometrical truths, though it can well serve as "occasional" cause, in furnishing a motive for and an invitation to the development of certain aspects of these truths and the choice of one above the others. This made the position clear in essentials as against the systems of geometrical empiricism.

The form of empiricism that professes to derive axioms from experience and regards them as simple copies of given, observable facts does not make sense, as Poincaré declared. Axioms are always free adventures of mathematical thought containing statements that transcend all observation. What can be ascertained is their fruitfulness for the order of physical constituents; but even that can never so succeed in this fashion that we get hold of any one single axiom for experimental verification; we can only compare the whole geometrical system with the entire order of experience.

If this be the procedure of empirical verification of geometrical propositions, then verification plainly has another and much more complicated meaning here than is supposed in a strict geometrical empiricism. The advantage of simplicity will always remain with the Euclidean system, according to Poincaré. It is simpler not only because of fixed mental habits that we have developed, or because we may have immediate intuition of Euclidean space, but rather in the same way as a polynomial of the first degree is simpler than one of the second. A mathematical analyst who knew nothing of their geometrical significance would be able to recognize that the formulas of spherical geometry are more complicated than those of plane geometry. Poincaré was likewise convinced that the whole of our physical experience will never furnish us with a compelling motive to prefer one variation over others among the geometrical assumptions; in this case, too, it would always be simpler and more to the point to set up special hypotheses about physical data (such as the propagation of light in a straight line) rather than touch the foundations of the Euclidean system. Hence this system has just as little to fear from future experience as it has little chance of being proved or established immediately through present experience.[10]

The subsequent development of physics did not confirm this prediction, for it showed there may be cases that neither induce nor oblige the physicist to shrink back in alarm from the use of a non-Euclidean geometry. But from a purely epistemological standpoint Poincaré's theory is broad enough even to reckon with this fact. The theory allows in general that for the application of geometry we have to look to experience as a principle of selection, even though it does not become thereby a *ground* on which one can justify the use of the particular geometry in preference to any other. If this view be accepted it is unnecessary, in order to solve the riddle of the applicability of mathematics, to go back to some sort of pre-established harmony between reason and reality as in rationalism or to see in mathematical concepts simple copies of reality or extracts and abstractions thereof, as in empiricism. The autonomous nature of mathematical thought may now be recognized in full measure, and we may see convincing proof of this autonomy precisely in the possibility of setting up a plurality of entirely independent systems of axioms. On the other hand, mathematical thinking is no longer enthroned in solitary grandeur above the world of the senses, as in the idealism of antiquity. However little it is derived from the sense world it still displays a constant readiness for sense material, and here the modern concept of axioms differs characteristically from the ancient. They are no longer assertions about contents that have absolute certainty, whether it be conceived as purely intuitive or rational. They are rather proposals of thought that make it ready for action—thought devices which must be so broadly and inclusively conceived as to be open to every concrete application that one wishes to make of them in knowledge. If one accepts this sense of "axioms," which was first made fully clear in the modern logic of mathematics, then the conflict about the truth of the different systems of axioms of geometry will

10. See Poincaré, *op. cit.*, chaps. iii–v.

become futile, for these systems do not pretend to answer an ontological question. They lay no claim to represent a certain object called "space," whether transcendent or phenomenal, since the representations would necessarily conflict. Axioms are not pictures but patterns, in the sense that they do not describe any given thing but are designs or plans for future completion. According to modern views a system of axioms is not to be thought of as establishing anything factual, but solely as a "logical blank form of the possible sciences." [11] To make such forms as diverse and as exact as possible is always a justifiable and necessary task of knowledge, and the development of science has shown again and again that even empirical knowledge itself makes much greater progress and becomes more resourceful just in proportion as it gives scope for thought instead of trying from the first to limit and restrict it to the empirically given and known.

11. See H. Weyl, "Philosophie der Mathematik," *Natur* . . . , S. 21.

III

Order and Measurement in Geometry

HERODOTUS is authority for the statement that Egypt is the homeland of geometry, and that the Greeks owed their first knowledge of it to the Egyptians. But in consequence of the transplantation it underwent an immediate, characteristic, and decisive change in significance, for what had been mere practical rules, accumulated over the course of centuries, was now made the subject of theoretical inquiry, a development that ancient historians regarded as the chief accomplishment of Greek mathematics. In his commentary on Euclid, Proclus preserved a statement of Eudemos, according to which Pythagoras was the first to raise mathematics to the dignity of a liberal education by returning to its general principles and treating its problems as purely intellectual, with no restriction to particular matters. This was the real stroke by which an empirical art of mensuration was made all at once the very center of the true, philosophical sort of knowledge.

"From the moment when the Greek philosophers begin to draw attention to themselves through their accomplishments in method," said Hermann Hankel in his *History of Mathematics,*

the view of mathematics was radically altered. Whereas in ancient civilizations it was only a routine trade, a collection of rules handed down by tradition, isolated, uncomprehended, obviously empirical and adapted only to the crudest sort of practice, the Greek genius recognized instantly that it concealed something infinitely more valuable, something worthy of more than passing thought, something that could be reduced to general laws—in short, a scientific content.[1]

The Greeks were able to unearth this hidden wealth because the idea of measure lay at the heart of their view of the world and of all their thinking. Restricted to no particular sphere and not exhausted by any special application, this idea represented the very essence of thinking and of being. To discover the "limits and the proportions of things" was the task of all knowledge.[2] But the concept extended far beyond this purely intellectual achievement, since it was the core not

1. H. Hankel, *Zur Geschichte der Mathematik in Altertum und Mittelalter* (Leipzig, B. G. Teubner, 1874), S. 88 f.
2. See Plato, *Philebus,* ed. Apelt (Leipzig, Felix Meiner, 1912), S. 18 ff.

only of all cosmic but also of the human order, and lay at the center
of ethics as well as of logic. For the earlier Greek thinkers the two
phases of the concept of measure were still undistinguished from each
other. Heraclitus saw in the concept of measure the bond that united
world events and human existence; chaos would overtake both were
they not bound according to fixed measure. This grand universal
view can be traced in all that the Greeks had to say about the significance and value of geometry, and it guided and controlled single
phases of investigation as well.[3] Through it geometry became a
paradigm of knowledge, in the Platonic sense; the eternal example
and model through which the nature and task of learning become
clear.

The idea of measure retained its primacy in mathematical and
philosophical thinking for centuries. Only with the Renaissance does
a change in the orientation of mathematics become noticeable; one
that takes away not one iota of the significance of the concept, though
it was no longer regarded as the sole object and focal point of methodical knowledge. There can be no doubt that the definition of modern
mathematics as the science of measurable quantities is too narrow.
Projective geometry and the theory of operations, analysis situs and
group theory, have revealed provinces that elude this definition and
yet are models of true, rigorous mathematical thinking. If we seek a
comprehensive explanation today of all objects of mathematical
thought we must go back to the general idea of order-form or rela-
tion-form. "The object of pure mathematics," we might say, "is
constituted by the relations that can be conceptually established between any elements of thought whatsoever, when considered as contained in a well-ordered multiplicity; the law of the order of this multiplicity must underlie our choice of object." [4]

The first thinker to hold this modern idea of mathematics, at least
as a postulate, and to draw decisive philosophical consequences therefrom, was Leibniz. Neither algebra nor geometry was for him the
really basic mathematical science but the theory of combinations.
This is concerned not with number or size but with the pure form of
the connection and it studies the laws of such form. "Thus," wrote
Leibniz, "there results a hitherto unknown or neglected subordination
of algebra to the science of combinations; that is to say, a subordina-

3. See G. Milhaud, *Les Philosophes-géomètres de la Grèce* (2e éd. Paris, J. Vrin,
1934).

4. E. Papperitz, "Über das System der rein mathematischen Wissenschaften," *Jahres-
ber. d. Deutsch. Math. Verein,* I (1890–91) (Berlin, George Reimer, 1892), 36. For analogous definitions by B. Peirce, B. Kempe, and I. G. Grassman see A. Voss, *Über das
Wesen der Mathematik* (3. Aufl. Leipzig, 1922), S. 26.

tion of the science that deals with quantitative relations to one that treats quite generally all the relations—expressions that have to do with order, similarity, in short, a subordination of the science of quantity to the science of quality." [5]

This idea of the "universal mathematic" goes far beyond even what Descartes had taught. To Leibniz it meant a complete reorganization of geometry which would take a direction opposite to that of Descartes' analytical geometry. Leibniz laid the foundations for it in his outlines of analysis situs and geometrical characteristic. But the trend of these projects became wholly clear only later, when geometrical thought had undergone development on its own account. Hermann Grassmann was the first to continue the investigations of Leibniz.[6] But the power of the new thought was shown above all in the constantly increasing self-sufficiency of pure projective thinking with respect to metric thinking in the development of modern geometry. The beginnings of it were already evident in the seventeenth century, with Desargues and Pascal, but the process attained full maturity and a consciousness of its methodological independence only with Poncelet, who first set up a program for a geometry that was based no longer on ideas of size and measure but on the concept and the study of pure relationship of position. His *Traité des propriétés projectives des figures* (1822) was significant not only from a mathematical but from a general epistemological standpoint as well, because he adopted Leibniz' principle of continuity and sought to give it validity in a new way, by introducing into geometry the idea of the imaginary.[7]

In general when we follow up the history of projective geometry it is really remarkable to see how much of it is taken up with purely methodological considerations.[8] Here we feel ourselves to be on new ground that needs to be explained in principle. This was already expressed in the title of Steiner's most important work, called *Systematic Development of the Dependence of Geometrical Figures upon One Another*. Its basic idea is that if a rigorously scientific foundation for geometry is to be laid it is not enough merely to place

5. G. W. Leibniz, "Mathesis universalis," *Mathematische Schriften,* ed. Gerhardt (1863).

6. H. Grassmann, *Geometrische Analyse, geknüpft an die von Leibniz erfundene Characteristik* (Leipzig, Weldmannsche Buchhandlung, 1847).

7. For details see Cassirer, *Leibniz' System,* S. 225 ff.

8. For the history of projective geometry see Klein's *Vorlesungen über die Entwicklung der Mathematik im 19. Jahrhundert,* I, 118 ff.; and particularly M. Dehn's *Die Grundlegung der Geometrie in historischer Entwicklung,* "Die Grundlehren der mathematischen Wissenschaften," XXIII, 209 ff.

the various figures side by side and examine each one separately; rather, a procedure must be specified by which, starting from a certain point, the different figures can be progressively generated. The whole system must be built up by the successive production of higher grades of figures from basic ones; in the plane—the straight line, the pencils of lines, and the plane itself; in space—the straight line, the plane pencils of lines and planes as well as bundles of lines and planes and space itself. Steiner thought this systematizing was the essential part of his work, for he wrote in his Preface: "The present book has sought to discover the organism through which various forms of phenomena in the world of space are connected one with another. . . . Order comes into chaos."

Nevertheless, the new program was first carried through rigorously by Staudt in his *Geometry of Position*.[9] For Poncelet and Steiner had still defined the truly fundamental concept of projective geometry, that is, the principle of "cross ratios," only metrically, as a relationship of lengths or distances in the ordinary sense. But Staudt wanted a new definition, independent of metric geometry, by means of which he could abandon the expression "cross ratio" and introduce instead the concept "throw." After the coordinates had thus been brought in projectively it became possible to construct a strictly projective geometry that contained the ordinary metric geometry and all other known geometries as special cases within itself and clarified their relations with one another. "Metrical geometry," declared Cayley, "is thus a part of descriptive geometry and descriptive geometry is *all* geometry." [10]

Here at last, then, the goal seemed to have been reached that Lobachevski also had had in mind when he called his work *Pangéométrie*. Projective geometry turned out to be the truly universal language, to which the ordinary metric geometry of measurement bore the relationship of a single idiom. The universal significance of projective geometry was expressed above all in the fact that it ignored the bounds within which Euclidean geometry was confined. A way had now been opened for the founding of a geometry without the postulate of parallels for, as Klein showed,[11] it was possible to construct projective geometry without this postulate.[12] From a

9. K. G. C. Staudt, *Geometrie der Lage* (Nürnberg, Bauer & Raspe, 1847); *Beiträge zur Geometrie der Lage* (Korn'schen Buchhandlung, 1857–60).

10. For details see Klein, *Vorlesungen über die Entwicklung der Mathematik im 19. Jahrhundert*, I, 132 ff., 147 ff.

11. Klein, "Über die sogennante Nicht-Euklidische Geometrie" (1871), *Gesammelte mathematische Abhandlungen*, 1, 303 ff.

12. For details see Dehn, "Das Parallelenpostulat," *Die Grundlegung der Geometrie in historischer Entwicklung* (2. Aufl. 1926), S. 193 ff., 209 ff.

purely epistemological standpoint the point of difficulty of the problem was thereby shifted. For while prior to that Euclidean geometry
had always been regarded as the normal instance, as it were, and it
was thought that an understanding of the non-Euclidean could be
achieved only by referring to it as the norm, now the view was reversed.

Klein himself did not conceive his interpretation of non-Euclidean
geometry to mean that he would simply find a model for it in the relationships of Euclidean metrical space but rather that he would
classify it under a comprehensive scheme of projective geometry. The
metric of parabolic geometry corresponding to Euclid's system here
shows itself to be less simple than the general "projective metric."
According to the projective concept of parallelism it is elliptic geometry, in which all planes and all straight lines in the same plane intersect, that becomes the conceptual basis of parabolic and hyperbolic
geometry.[13]

Thus came the primacy of the concept of order over that of
measurement which Leibniz had proposed. This was now carried
through for the whole realm of geometry. Here, too, one should start
out from relations of position, such as those of incidence, "Place a
point on a straight line," or, "pass through a point," and so on,
developing the fundamental axioms therefrom. The introduction of
measurement was only a second step, that now appeared for the first
time in its organic connection. It is characteristic of the thought of
modern geometry, as of modern physics, that in both cases the process
of measuring is recognized more and more clearly to be a *problem*, a
logical and epistemological one. What had been constantly practiced
before in the two sciences was seen from a different angle as soon as
one tried to make wholly clear the assumptions underlying mensuration. In geometry the discovery of the non-Euclidean systems first
demanded such a view and opened the way to it. In so doing, furthermore, the discourse, far from raising a question about the a priori
character of geometry, actually brought it into greater prominence.
The concept of space as such, when taken in its most general sense as
"order of coexistence," appeared to be an underivable basic concept.
The problem of the significance and role of experience arose only
when one dealt with the specification of this general space concept by
introducing a measurement. And here a new point of view appeared
which is derived from the consideration of motion.

The question how far the idea of motion is an "empirical" or "pure"
concept was variously answered in the course of the history of both

<hr>

13. H. Weber—J. Wellstein, "Elemente der Geometrie," *Enzyklopädie der Elementar-Mathematik,* I–III, II, 98, 196 ff.

philosophy and mathematics. The Greek mathematicians in general avoided bringing it in, fearing that they would incur the difficulties and antinomies shown in Zeno's dialectic; while Euclid, the Platonist, could not have the idea of movement, at any rate as an explicit factor, enter into the foundations of a science which Plato had called the "knowledge of the everlasting." The implicit connection that really obtained, however, lay deeply hidden and it became really clear only with the early epistemological studies of Helmholtz on the origin and significance of geometrical axioms. For here it was clear that a certain assumption was involved in Euclid's idea of congruence and all his proofs of it: the proof assumed that two figures that were to coincide must be moved toward one another, and that neither would change its shape and size during this motion. Modern geometry has taken the reverse way, which is logically more satisfactory and correct. It has placed certain propositions about motion at the forefront and from there showed how the structure of plane geometry is completed and under what conditions it agrees with the Euclidean system.[14]

Thus there remained but one epistemological difficulty to be overcome, though not a slight one, to be sure, for it struck deeply at the interpretation of the concept of science which classical tradition and philosophical idealism had created. "Motion of a body in space," said Kant, "does not appertain to a pure science, and consequently not to geometry, because the fact that something is capable of motion cannot be known a priori but only by experience." [15] In this sense it was also explained that the *Transcendental Aesthetic* could not comprise more than two elements, space and time, because all other concepts belonging to sensibility, even that of movement, which unites both space and time, presuppose something empirical.[16] If the distinction between the a priori and the empirical be understood in this sense, then it must be admitted that with assumptions about motion something empirical would have entered into geometry. In the transition to metric, indeed, such presuppositions are indispensable, and yet the rigidly scientific character of the various metric geometries is not to be questioned. It rests on the fact that we have to do not with categorical propositions about "the real in space" but with hypothetically deductive systems. In themselves the axioms say nothing about the empirical existence of things or events; they are merely "logical blank forms for possible sciences" (see above, p. 46).

Thus we return once more to the relation between experience and

14. Klein gives an abstract of these investigations in his *Elementarmathematik*, II, 174 ff.
15. I. Kant, *Kritik der reinen Vernunft* (2. Aufl.), S. 155.
16. *Ibid.*, S. 58.

thinking that Poincaré established in discussing the systematization of geometry. No geometry is absolutely derived from experience or given by it, but it can be so chosen that it will be best suited to certain problems set by experience and will solve them in the simplest way. The theory of relativity has shown that even physics in its own internal progress may be led to problems that require reference to a geometry other than the Euclidean. This merely proves anew what was already obvious in the whole conceptual development of projective geometry—that metric contains a variable element with respect to the constants of spatial form in general. Hence we choose just those determinate ideas and definitions of ordering that will enable us to construct the system of experience in the least complicated way.[17] In this respect the relationship between geometry and physics has certainly altered, for purely geometrical and physical presuppositions now so interlock that they cannot be treated as separate pieces which at best could be fitted in with each other in some way. They are moments of a unitary structure from the first, and only when we use them constantly in conjunction with each other do we have the means of "spelling out appearances in order to construe them as an experience." For that purpose the separation of the two types of assumption is possible and necessary in theory, but in practice they can exercise their functions only together and in relation to one another. In this way the geometrical and the physical are not only connected in the modern concept of the "metric field" but are finally interwoven, as it were. This shows that the physical laws no more than the geometrical laws admit of any separate proofs in experiment and that the "truth" of the whole theoretical construction alone can be demonstrated.[18]

A wholly new intellectual orientation is therewith achieved as regards the ideas of ancient geometry and classical physics, by which, as has been said, a "miraculous fusion of geometry and physics, of the laws of Pythagoras and Newton," has been attained.[19] But no logical break has occurred. Quite the contrary; if we look at the matter historically as well as systematically, we can bring the new ideal of knowledge into perfect continuity with the old.

17. For a discussion of definitions of ordering see H. Reichenbach, *Philosophie der Raum-Zeit Lehre* (Berlin und Leipzig, Walter de Gruyter & Co., 1928), S. 23 f.

18. See Weyl, "Philosophie der Mathematik," *Natur* . . . , S. 96; and Schlick, *Space and Time in Contemporary Physics* (Oxford, Clarendon Press, 1920), pp. 22 ff.

19. Max Born, *Die Relativitätstheorie Einsteins und ihre physikalischen Grundlagen* (Berlin, 1920), S. 227.

IV

The Concept of Number and Its Logical Foundation

THE DISCOVERY of non-Euclidean geometry endowed mathematics in the first half of the nineteenth century with a fresh and extraordinarily fruitful domain, but the new content thus disclosed could not be incorporated immediately with the well-organized classical form of the science. For a time it seemed as though its homogeneity had been lost forever—as though what had been regarded as a firmly united whole had been built of different parts that now appeared wholly disparate both in character and as types of knowledge. Gauss, declaring number "a product of our mind," was prepared to rank geometry with empirical knowledge and at the same time emphasized all the more strongly the strictly rational character of analysis.[1]

That this status of the problem should have been hardly satisfactory to philosophical thought can be readily understood. Philosophy in its own striving for unity had to make a continual effort to repair the rift in the edifice of mathematics. The concept of space and the concept of number, geometry and arithmetic, must be systematically deducible from one and the same principle, for otherwise that union by virtue of which they had not only developed side by side historically but also had interpenetrated and enriched one another would hardly be understandable. But once the conviction of the absolute character of the space concept, and consequently of the a priori nature of geometry, had been shaken, only one way seemed available for their reuniting if, indeed, it were to be possible at all. Would it not be simpler to renounce, now and forever, all belief in the "eternal and necessary" truths of mathematics and establish the whole science on a purely empirical basis? Ever since the days of Berkeley and Hume empiricist logic had consistently tried to do this, but all its attempts had bounded off of the ironclad theory of mathematical method. Now, finally, the time seemed to have come to drive rationalism from this its last and safest refuge.

The first to enter upon the task energetically and consistently was John Stuart Mill, though certainly he was far less well equipped for it than other thinkers who were closely allied to him in their fundamental epistemological views. For in contrast to Comte, whose every

1. See above, p. 37.

paragraph reveals a rigorous analytical mind and sound mathematical training, Mill was hardly in touch with real mathematical thought. The picture he gives of mathematical thinking was derived solely from his logical ideals and in the most curious way it often bypasses what mathematics actually is. Nowhere is this shown more clearly perhaps than in Mill's attempt to lay a foundation for arithmetical truths in inductive logic. He was determined that even such truths must fundamentally be nothing other than general experiential propositions, which originated from empirical generalizations and had always to be referred to definite physical facts. Accordingly all arithmetical expressions are about relationships in the material world that surrounds us, and thus they are accidental and variable in the same sense as all such relationships are. Hence growing up in a different environment would provide man not only with a different physics and geometry but also with a different arithmetic. It is not only possible, therefore, but even probable that in another world, say Sirius, other laws of number than ours may obtain—that 2×2 may equal not 4 but 5. We should not hesitate to agree, too, if it were a general law of nature that whenever two pairs of objects are placed side by side, or thought of together, a new object is created. Our concept of the relations of numbers depends then, like all other concepts, upon the nature of the sensory impressions received from the external world. "The reverse of the most familiar principles of arithmetic and geometry might have been made conceivable even to our present mental faculties, if those faculties had coexisted with a totally different constitution of external nature." [2]

The technically false reasoning that underlies this derivation of mathematical truths is easily seen through and it has often been emphasized in philosophical criticism.[3] Even sharper was the refutation by the mathematicians themselves, for they saw here in question all that they had labored over in ever increasing measure since the beginning of the nineteenth century, which was, in a certain sense, the very focus of their scientific work.

Gauss called mathematics the queen of the sciences, and arithmetic as in the ancient saying, the queen of mathematics.[4] Jacobi expressed himself still more sharply and pregnantly, calling the theory of num-

2. J. S. Mill, *An Examination of Sir W. Hamilton's Philosophy* (6th ed. London, Longmans, Green, 1869), p. 89.

3. One of the clearest and most convincing refutations of Mill's empirical arithmetic, from the philosophical side, is that of G. Heymans, *Die Gesetze und Elemente des wissenschaftlichen Denkens* (Leiden und Leipzig, 1890), I, 135 ff.

4. See Sartorius v. Walterschausen, *Gauss zum Gedächtnis* (Leipzig, S. Hirzel, 1856), S. 79.

bers the only purely mathematical discipline, since it had never stooped to any sort of practical use or been soiled, as it were, by the dust of the world. He said in a letter to Legendre that the "dignity of the human spirit," not utility, must be the only goal of science, and that in this respect a question of the theory of numbers was of equal significance with one that concerned the whole universe. To reduce arithmetical truths to merely factual truths therefore was intolerable, and virtually to impugn that dignity of the human spirit.[5]

In Jacobi's correspondence with Alexander von Humboldt on Leverrier's discovery of Neptune, he gave characteristic expression to his idea of the nature and value of the pure theory of numbers by reference to one of Schiller's well-known poems:

> *Zu Archimedes kam ein wissbegieriger Schüler,*
> *Weihe mich, sprach er zu ihm, ein in die göttliche Kunst,*
> *Die so herrliche Dienste der Sternenkunde geleistet,*
> *Hinter dem Uranus noch einen Planeten entdeckt.*
> *Göttlich nennst du die Kunst, sie ist's, versetzte der Weise.*
> *Aber sie war es, bevor noch sie den Kosmos erforscht.*
> *Was Du im Kosmos erblickst, ist nur der Göttlichen Abglanz:*
> *In der Olympier Schar thronet die ewige Zahl.*

> To Archimedes there came a scholar avid of learning.
> "Teach me," said he to the Master, "teach me the art divine
> That to astronomy rendered such truly magnificent service,
> Finding another planet beyond the orbit of Uranus."
> "Divine thou callest the art, it is," then answered the Master;
> "But it was so or ever it started to scan the heavens.
> All thou beholdest there is the gods' reflected splendor:
> With the Olympian band is enthroned eternal number."

The first prominent mathematician to restore this dignity by a strictly logical deduction of the theory of numbers was Frege, and his *Elements of Arithmetic* grew out of this endeavor. The pitiless acidity with which it exposed the psychological bias in Mill's theory of mathematics paved the way for Husserl's criticism in his *Logische Untersuchungen* (1900). According to Frege if the cooperation between philosophy and mathematics had led so far to no real result despite numerous attempts on the part of both it was because philosophy was still entangled in a prejudice of psychologism which it must lay aside if it was ever to recognize the true nature of mathe-

5. C. G. J. Jacobi, *Gesammelte Werke* (Berlin, G. Reimar, 1881), I, 453 ff. Letter to Legendre of July 2, 1830. The remarks of Gauss and of Jacobi are cited by L. Kronecker, "Über den Zahlbegriff," *Philosophische Aufsätze zu Ed. Zellers 50 jährigen Doktorjubiläum* (Leipzig, Fues [R. Reisland], 1887), S. 264.

matics.[6] An interpretation like that of Mill, which regarded number not as a definite concept but only as an idea "in the mind," consequently reducing it to the rank of the merely subjective, could never lead to any real development of the theory of numbers; it must always remain "an arithmetic of cookies or pebbles." The essential insight that Frege's book means to vindicate against such an interpretation was that the actual truth value of the science of numbers as well as its strictly objective character can be established only when we sharply distinguish it from anything having to do with "things." Statements about number and statements about objects are quite distinct in meaning, and whoever confuses the one with the other has not laid a foundation for arithmetic but rather has misunderstood and falsified its substance.

Ever since critical thinking was awakened in the mathematics of the nineteenth century and, largely through the influence of Weierstrass, became more exacting, the demand for a strictly logical derivation of the theory of numbers was constantly to the fore. It constitutes, so to speak, the moral issue of mathematics, upon which all endeavor must concentrate. A slipping over into psychologism was hardly possible here, even though noted mathematicians, with Helmholtz at their head, did try to find an explanation for the nature and essence of numbers not so much in logic as in psychology. In his essay "Numbers and Measurements from the Epistemological Standpoint," [7] Helmholtz started from the psychology of the act of counting to find by analysis a foundation for the development of arithmetic and its whole system of axioms. He believed that in so doing he had bridged the gap between mathematics and experience and thus indirectly found support and justification for the empiricism that he advocated in geometry. But he was far removed from an empiricism like Mill's. Arithmetical axioms for him were neither descriptions nor generalizations of physical facts, but arose from the pure form of the intuition of time which underlay the act of counting and was the condition of its possibility. In the realm of pure mathematics others, generally speaking, did not follow him. Here the Gauss-Jacobi interpretation was in the ascendancy, which held that arithmetic could more surely maintain its position as the queen of mathematics the more intrinsically self-contained it could be, developing its basic concepts with complete logical strictness and

---

6. G. Frege, *Die Grundlagen der Arithmetik* (Breslau, W. Koebner, 1884), S. v ff., § § 5–11, S. 5 ff.

7. H. Helmholtz, "Zählen und Messen," *Philosophische Aufsätze zu Ed. Zellers 50 jährigen Doktorjubiläum*, S. 17 ff.

without any reference to the world of intuition. The evolution that logic was undergoing furthered this tendency and seemed for the first time to promise that it would actually be carried through to fulfillment; for in the work of the founders of symbolic logic, that of Schröder and Boole and of Frege and Russell, the mathematicizing of logic had gone so far that a complete treatment of mathematics in terms of formal logic might well be expected to follow. In future it would be impossible to draw a real and sharp dividing line between the two except when one turned back to the historical differences in the development of logical and mathematical thinking.

Logic and mathematics, as Russell has declared, differ from one another as the boy from the man: logic is the youth of mathematics, mathematics the manhood of logic.[8] That characterizes a universal and pervasive trend in the mathematical thinking of the nineteenth century. To be sure, there were hard battles precisely about this decisive point. They began with the attacks of Poincaré on the claims of logic and the fundamental concepts of the theory of sets, and they seemed ultimately to lead to an absolute crisis in respect to the foundations of mathematics and to a sharp conflict between the "formalists" and the "intuitionists." [9] Yet although they were not at one about the foundations, the end in general was clear to all, for it had become more and more apparent that the whole fate of mathematics depended upon the solution of this problem. The arithmetizing of mathematics had made continuous progress since the first half of the nineteenth century. It began with a work by Cauchy, *Cours d'analyse* (1821), in which the doubt respecting the infinitely small that had troubled all theorizing about mathematical knowledge during the eighteenth century was for the first time dispelled. That the concept of limit formed the true basis for the "metaphysic of the infinitesimal calculus" had previously been declared by d'Alembert, but it was Cauchy who first succeeded in discovering the way that led to a basis of analysis free from logical objection and mastered the ambiguity of the concept of the infinitely small.[10]

He gave the first presentation of this subject based strictly on the concept of limit. What was here attained in respect to a special problem came to be recognized, toward the end of the century, as

8. B. Russell, *Introduction to Mathematical Philosophy* (New York, The Macmillan Company, 1919), p. 194.

9. For the historical development of the opposition between "formalists" and "intuitionists" see Hermann Weyl, "Über die neue Grundlagenkrise der Mathematik," *Mathematik Zeitschrift,* X (Berlin, Julius Springer, 1921), 39; also Richard Baldus, *Formalismus und Intuitionismus in der Mathematik* (Karlsruhe, G. Braun, 1924).

10. A. L. Cauchy, "Leçons sur le calcul infinitésimal," *Cours d'analyse* (1821).

a universal methodological postulate for mathematical thinking in general.

Felix Klein treated it as typical of modern mathematics, in that he recognized clearly and carried through completely this demand for the arithmetizing of mathematics. As he put it, "in the case of Euclid," and in the mathematical thinking of antiquity as a whole, "geometry, thanks to its axioms, was the rigorous foundation of general arithmetic, which included even irrational numbers. Arithmetic remained in this bondage to geometry until the nineteenth century. Since then, however, a complete transformation has occurred and arithmetic has achieved today sovereign authority as the really fundamental discipline." [11]

When one tries to survey the various attempts at a rigorous foundation for the theory of numbers and to classify them from a unified point of view, the first superficial impression is of two main trends according as one takes his point of departure from the cardinal number or from the ordinal. There was some dispute among mathematicians as to which concept deserved precedence. The cardinal number theory seemed to recommend itself because it could be more surely and clearly dissociated from all consideration of the psychological origin of number. It did not start with the act of counting or derive the individual numbers from such operations, but tried to gain the pure concept of number by reference to a purely objective content that is indispensable for all conceptual thinking. For such a basic content the cardinal number theory offered the existence of determinate classes and the relations between them. The class is herewith presented as prior to number and it forms those "logical constants" from which the entire content of the theory of numbers should be derived. It was Georg Cantor, above all, who centered attention upon this view in his *Elements of a General Theory of Sets* (1883). He saw in the theory the only road to a truly universal interpretation, above all because he came forward with a new claim as to the theory of numbers and created his own theory to prepare the ground for his conception of "transfinites." What he objected to in the ordinal theory was that it is confined from first to last to the domain of "finite numbers," whereas his own theory not only kept the way open for access to the nonfinite but concerned itself with "an expansion or continuation of the entire series of

11. See also *Elementarmathematik,* II, 225. On Cauchy see Klein, *Vorlesungen über die Entwicklung der Mathematik,* I, 84. In the philosophy of the nineteenth century Bolzano was a pioneer in this particular realm. Even prior to Cauchy he had grasped quite precisely the concept of continuity.

real numbers beyond the infinite." Not only the hope but the firm conviction was expressed that this expansion must in time be regarded as entirely simple, appropriate, and natural, and he contrasted the previous interpretation of the mathematically infinite, according to which a quantity increases beyond all bounds or decreases to any desired extent, with his own conception of what he called "the truly infinite." In the former case it was a variable infinite, whereas in the latter it was a thoroughly determinate infinite.[12]

It is obvious that metaphysical considerations played a role in this revival of the actual infinite even though Cantor strictly distinguished several kinds of infinite: the absolute infinite, as it is most completely realized in wholly independent, extramundane being, that is to say, in God; the infinite, as it is represented in the dependent, created world; and infinity, as it can be conceived in the abstract as mathematical quantity, number, or type of order. Efforts to view the problem of number from any other angle Cantor not only held to be futile but considered the expression of a skeptical attitude. It was on that account that he objected to the ordinal theory as Helmholtz and Kronecker tried to establish it.

The academic, positivistic skepticism that had risen to ascendancy in Germany as a reaction against the exaggerated Kant-Fichte-Hegel-Schelling idealism had now finally penetrated even arithmetic, where it seemed to be drawing its last possible conclusion and with the most extreme, and perhaps the most fatal, consequences to itself. In the true philosophical theory of number, according to Cantor, one should not begin with the ordinals, for these are rather the last and least essential things.[13]

It must seem strange indeed at first sight that a problem concerning pure mathematics, and wholly confined to it, should excite so much vehemence and such argumentation. From a purely mathematical standpoint it seems to make little difference whether one starts out from the cardinals or the ordinals in thinking of number, for it is clear that every deduction of the number concept must take both into account. Number is cardinal and ordinal in one; it is the expression of the "how many," as well as the determination of the position of a member in an ordered series. As the two factors are inseparable and really strictly correlative, philosophical criticism was right in insisting that it was fruitless to argue over which of these two

---

12. G. Cantor, *Grundlagen einer allgemeinen Mannigfaltigkeitslehre* (Leipzig, B. G. Teubner, 1883), § 1.

13. Cantor, *Zur Lehre vom Transfiniten* (Halle a. S., 1908), Teil I, S. 11 ff., Eng. trans. by P. E. B. Jordain (Chicago, Open Court Publishing Co., 1915), pp. 85 ff.

functions of number is primary and which is dependent upon the other and merely follows by implication.[14] The way to begin could at any rate be supported by certain formal and didactic considerations, but from a practical point of view that was of no compelling significance, since there was a necessity, in the case of either theory, of advancing from the starting point and going over to the other aspect. The ordinal theory had to do justice to the idea of plurality, of actual number, just as the cardinal theory had to show how numbers that were defined independently of one another could be arranged in a fixed series. As a matter of fact, both theories had the authority of distinguished mathematicians behind them; on one side were arrayed Dedekind and Peano, alongside of Helmholtz and Kronecker; on the other, Cantor, Frege, and Russell.

What makes this difference of view significant from an epistemological point of view is the general intellectual motive underlying it. Here indeed two fundamental views stood opposed and they far transcended the sphere of pure mathematics. For what was at stake was no longer the concept of the object of mathematics but the universal question of how knowledge is actually related to "objects" and what conditions it must fulfill in order to acquire "objective meaning." We place this systematic problem in the forefront because only so is it possible to obtain a sure orientation with respect to the various conflicting trends in the number problem of the mathematics of the nineteenth century.

The first basic view of knowledge from which one can start out is that all knowing has to fulfill a representative function. It refers to a being and fulfills its role the more completely as it succeeds in expressing the definitive nature and essence of this being. To show the truth of an idea, therefore, is to specify the objective substrate to which it corresponds. Without that it would remain suspended in thin air, and might be no more than a subjective illusion. The correspondence between concept and thing, the *adequatio intellectus et rei,* is thus the supreme postulate that must be complied with in every case—no matter whether we deal with mathematical or empirical conceptions. These differ according to their origin and content but not in respect to their mode of dependence upon their corresponding objects. Even mathematical thought can never be a mere cogitation, for no bounds could be set to such a process; given free rein, it might pass over into pure fantasy. Hence even in pure mathematics we cannot speak of "free creations" of thought with-

---

14. See P. Natorp, *Die logischen Grundlagen der exakten Wissenschaften* (Leipzig und Berlin, B. G. Teubner, 1910), Kap. iii, S. 105.

out endangering its content of truth. There must always be a *fundamentum in re:* it must be related to some given objective factual content with which its ideas correspond and which it will bring to expression.

The empirical sciences are concerned with the actuality of things, with their existence in space and time—a reality that is only accessible to us through sensory perception. Mathematics does not move in this circle of sensory existence, yet its truth, too, is firmly anchored in original being; in the reality or essence of things. This essential being can be apprehended only through concepts, yet abstract thinking in no way creates but only discovers it. In this sense even the pure form of mathematical reality is always related to a definite "matter," though this is not a sensible but a wholly "intelligible matter."

This conception of the affair contrasts with another, which may be called the functional view of knowledge.[15] Here, too, the relation of thought to object is the central point, but the theory establishes the possibility of this relation in another way and strikes out, as it were, in the opposite direction. For the object is not treated as a given fact but as a problem; it serves as the goal of knowledge, not as its starting point. This lies rather in the realm that is immediately accessible to knowledge, the realm of its own operations. No matter whether we are concerned with the ideal or the real, the mathematical or the empirical, with nonsensuous or sensuous objects, the first question is always not what these are in their absolute nature or essence, but by what medium they are conveyed to us; through what instrumentality of knowledge the knowing of them is made possible and achieved. This knowing is built up by stages; as the process advances the object becomes more and more sharply designated. We progress from general to particular, from abstract to concrete determinations, and try to show how the latter presuppose the former and are based upon them.

Applying this interpretation to number, we do not have the question here of seeking to understand the "nature" of number, which we can simply glean from the nature of things. The point is rather to keep in mind the general procedure by virtue of which there originates what we call number and from which it receives its whole significance. Once this process is understood in principle a definite field of operations is indicated, and this it is that we may

15. For the following I refer to the more detailed exposition in my *Substanzbegriff und Funktionsbegriff* (Berlin, B. Cassirer, 1910) ; *Substance and Function,* Eng. trans. by W. C. and M. C. Swabey (Chicago, Open Court Publishing Co., 1923).

venture to call the realm of numbers. To be sure, we are here only at the very beginning of the problem, not at the end, for it must be shown next how the function of number, thus defined and derived, is related to the other basic functions of knowledge; how it must cooperate with them and somehow permeate them to bring about that universal lawful order, which, according to this interpretation of knowledge, constitutes the fundamental character, in fact, the proper definition, of "reality."

We have sharply contrasted these two fundamental views, but with no desire to maintain that in the development of the theory of number during the nineteenth century mathematicians were always aware of this antithesis as such or ever stated it precisely. Purely mathematical discussion seldom had either occasion or opportunity to go back to this epistemological root of the problem, but even so the theoretical difference was sensed as an underlying motive in all arguments about the nature of number. These turned out to be amazingly close to contemporary investigations along very different lines into the nature of space. From a theoretical standpoint the main problem was fundamentally the same in both cases: what is meant by mathematical "existence," and how can there be any meaningful question about the proof of such existence? For with regard to the view represented by Cantor, Frege, and Russell, the fact is that every concept must correspond with something real if it is to have any objective validity whatsoever, and that the task of the logical deduction and justification of the concept can be none other than that of the producing and characterization of this reality. As regards Cantor, he expressly ties up with the scholastic distinctions, often speaking consciously the language of scholastic "realism." Just because of that he could not be satisfied to regard number as a universal principle of knowledge or to see in it an original intuition, in the sense of intuitionism, a "free doing." A principle, in the sense of a true beginning, is for him never an action but always simply "being," since every function demands final verification by and establishment on some sort of substrate. From these metaphysical or theoretical premises, the content and development of Cantor's theory followed logically. Implicit in it was the idea that the concept of sets must become the real foundation, the logical and factual antecedent of the number concept. It is in sets, in the plurality of existing objects (an existence which is of course that of pure essence, since it is conceptually, not sensuously, given), that number first attains its substantial footing and hence its significance and truth. The cardinal number designates a definite attribute that is attached to sets and can be derived from them by abstraction; it is the expression of what Cantor called the "power" of sets. "Every set of clearly differentiated things can be regarded as a unit in itself, of which those things are component parts or constituent elements. If one abstracts from the constitution of the elements as well as from the order in which they are given, one obtains the cardinal number, or power of a set." [16]

Frege, too, saw the only chance for a logically satisfying explanation of number in the closest possible association of its nature with the nature of the concept. He also had recourse not so much to the meaning of the concept as to its extension. Every concept denotes such extension in this wise: out of the totality of being a certain class of objects is selected that possess the characteristic given in the concept. Now it remains only to decide wherein consists the property of being that we want to express when we attribute number to certain things. For this it is only necessary to make clear what condition must be fulfilled before two sums can be declared to have the same "number." So the concept of numerical equivalence, and the criterion of the same, which is one-to-one correspondence, are prior to the number concept: "The number that belongs to the concept *F*," as Frege defines it, "is the content of the concept 'of number equal to the concept *F*.' " [17] Independently of Frege, and by a very similar route and from identical intellectual motives, Russell arrived at his own definition of number as a "class of classes." Thus the number 2 is nothing other than the totality of all existing pairs, the number 3 nothing other than all the triads. Russell also had a preference herewith for the extensional definition of the class over the intensional, seeing in the class only the aggregate of single and independent elements.[18]

Wholly different was the course of those mathematicians who took as their point of departure the ordinal number. They regarded "order" not merely as a property and, as it were, an appendix of number but as the truly fundamental and constitutive principle of number. For them numbers did not "exist," as is the case of those who started with sets and the power of sets as something given in themselves, which had the *supplementary* possibility of being arranged in a fixed order. On the contrary, the individual number

16. Cantor, *Zur Lehre vom Transfiniten*, S. 12.

17. Frege, *Die Grundlagen der Arithmetik*, S. 79 f.

18. Russell, *The Principles of Mathematics* (Cambridge, 1903), chap. vi. For Russell's and Frege's interpretations of the relationship of class to number see Wilhelm Burkamp, *Begriff und Beziehung. Studien zur Grundlegung der Logik. IV. Studie: "Klasse und Zahl in der Begriffslogik"* (Leipzig, F. Meiner, 1927), S. 182 ff.

represents nothing but a *cut*, a particular place in a universal order structure; and this structure determines the character and essential nature of the number. This determination was thus transformed from an absolute into a purely relative one; but this relativity could not possibly be regarded as a limitation upon the "objective" character of number, for it actually formed the only adequate expression of it. The relationship comprised all being and all the truth that we could sensibly attribute to number.

From this first insight springs that general reversal, that new total orientation of the problem of knowledge, which may be called the purely "functional" view, in contrast with the "conceptual realism" of Cantor, Frege, and Russell. To characterize it simply as nominalistic would be insufficient and misleading. Many of its advocates, to be sure, come close to doing so with their great emphasis on the fact that where numbers are concerned we are dealing not with a system of things but with a pure system of signs. But for a genuine mathematical nominalism, such as was first established in modern philosophy by Leibniz, all mathematical thinking and reasoning must stick to signs and always stay within that realm, whereas these signs in the functional sense are not empty but very meaningful signs. The meaning given them is not determined by looking out on the world of things but rather by considering the world of relations. The signs express the "being," the "duration," the objective value of certain relations, and hence they indicate "forms" rather than material things. The theory of number thus appears as one chapter in a general theory of forms, yet it loses nothing in its significance thereby but actually gains. Instead of becoming an idle game of signs it proves to be the *terminus a quo*, the very beginning and first matter of all objective knowledge; the theory begins with pure number relation in which there is nothing given at the outset save the concepts of identifying and distinguishing. But number does not remain at this stage of pure conceptual identity and difference but adds thereto the concept of succession (sequence) of the serial order of what is given. On this one concept there is constructed, according to Leibniz and all mathematicians who have struck out in this direction, the whole of arithmetic.[19] In this derivation number remains throughout in the domain of pure mathematics and in its foundations there must be no admixture of reference to the field of its application, the things that are counted. Yet it is by no means iso-

---

19. For Leibniz' attitude toward mathematical nominalism see "Meditationes de cognitione, veritate et ideis," *Die philosophischen Schriften* . . . , ed. Gerhardt, IV, 422 ff.

lated thereby; on the contrary, number stands at the threshold of a series of relationships which, further pursued and conceived more concretely, should lead finally to the determination of "reality" and be included in it.

Mathematical theory was not here concerned with a survey of the total system of these relational forms but had to be satisfied with making certain of the way to do so and explaining the first steps in a logically unobjectionable way. In so doing, the ordinal theory started from an ordered series of discrete elements and then went on to show how it was possible thence to arrive at number as the expression of plurality; the cardinal number of a set. That the same cardinal number is proper to every finite set, no matter what the arrangement of its individual elements, had to be shown by special proof.[20] The concept of 1 as the first member of the set and the general relation of ordering are of course presupposed herewith; but even though it be assumed that this restricts the theory from the standpoint of formal logic, none of its epistemological value is lost. For unless one is willing to accept an infinite regress, the critical examination of knowledge must always come to a halt at certain primal functions that are neither capable nor in need of an actual "deduction." Indeed it is difficult to understand why only logical identity and difference, necessary elements in the theory of sets, are admitted as ultimate functions of this sort, whereas numerical unity and numerical difference are excluded at the outset from this realm. A truly satisfactory deduction of the latter from the former has not been successfully made in the theory of sets, and there remains always the suspicion of a concealed vicious circle in respect to all attempts in this direction.

The basic philosophical idea upon which the ordinal theory rests in essentials has been characterized in the simplest and most pregnant manner by Dedekind. For the construction of the whole realm of number nothing more is required than the "ability of the mind to relate things to one another." On the basis of this single function, and without the admixture of any such alien notions as that of measurable quantities, it is possible to attain first to the series of so-called natural numbers and thence to all extensions of the number concept: to the originating of zero and of negative, fractional, irrational, and complex numbers. The number concept is and remains herewith "an immediate issue of the laws of pure thought"; since the basic function of thinking is precisely "to relate things

20. See, for example, Helmholtz, "Zählen und Messen," *Philosophische Aufsätze zu Ed. Zellers,* S. 32; and L. Kronecker, "Über den Zahlbegriff," *ibid.,* S. 263 ff.

to things, to make one thing correspond with another or to represent one thing by another"—a function without which thinking would in general be impossible.[21]

It was one of the most important advances made by mathematical thought in the nineteenth century when the system of real numbers was first successfully constructed with logical rigor. Weierstrass recognized this construction as one of the essential postulates of mathematics that must be complied with if there is to be advance.[22] Yet the work was not to be accomplished without great internal friction. Doubts arose again and again, though originating less often in the realm of mathematics itself than in that of the philosophy of mathematics where they were long familiar. Dedekind declared in the work cited above that it was one of the most marvelous achievements of the human mind, that man without any representation of measurable quantities could mount through a finite system of operations of sheer thought to the creation of the realm of pure and eternal number.

But what is meant by the word "creation" used in this connection? Is the realm of the real number to be abandoned to subjectivity and hence to caprice because it is explained as the product of a human creation? Are we not turning our backs upon that certainty of "being" given us in the "natural numbers" only to lose ourselves forevermore in a world of our own fictions? All these misgivings are summed up in the well-known phrase of Kronecker: Whole numbers were made by God; all the others by man.[23]

It is obvious from the way this proposition is put that the objection was more ontological than mathematical. Since the early days when the Pythagoreans discovered in number not only the supreme principle of knowledge but actually the expression of the real nature of things as very "being itself" this objection has never been silenced. We know what a profound shock the discovery of irrational numbers was to Greek mathematicians. Plato saw a problem not only for mathematics but for παιϲεια, the whole culture of mankind. In a familiar passage of the *Laws* he declared that whoever was ignorant of irrationals was not worthy to be called a Greek. But the

---

21. R. Dedekind, *Was sind und was sollen die Zahlen?* (2. unveränd. Aufl. Braunschweig, F. Vieweg & Sohn, 1893), S. vii ff.

22. For further details see A. Pringsheim, *Vorlesungen über Zahlen und Funktionenlehre,* Erste Abteil. (Leipzig und Berlin, B. G. Teubner, 1916), Bd. I.

23. On the contrast between Weierstrass and Kronecker in this respect see Klein's *Vorlesungen über die Entwicklung der Mathematik im 19. Jahrhundert,* S. 284 f.; also M. G. Mittag-Leffler, "Une page de la vie de Weierstrass," *Congrès International des Mathématiciens* (2e éd. Paris, Gauthier-Villars, 1902), p. 131 ff.

mathematical thinking of antiquity never advanced to the idea of
a continuous series of numbers. On the basis of its philosophical assumptions there could be incommensurable quantities and relations
but not irrational numbers. One of Euclid's propositions states explicitly that incommensurable quantities are not related to one another as numbers are.[24] An absolute meaning was always associated
with natural whole numbers, which assured them, so to speak, of a
sort of privileged being. But this conception lost its hold when the
transition took place from the ontological to the purely methodological foundation of number, as happened, with growing emphasis and ever clearer conviction, in the modern philosophy
of mathematics. For here the relationship is quite reversed. Even
whole numbers are a case of being self-subsistent, "being-to-itself"
and "existing-through-itself." As ordinal numbers they signify nothing but positions in an ordered series, and hence have no other being
and no other meaning than those that come to expression in their
many-sided interrelationships. Once this fundamental character of
number is recognized and raised to the dignity of a general principle, there are no further difficulties about the extension of the domain of numbers. For now it is no longer a dubious and essentially
hopeless attempt to add to the already given a class of new things
that were supposed to have originated in pure thought. The task
rather is simply that of advancing from a system of relatively simple
relationships to more complex systems of relations and of creating
for them appropriate symbolic expressions. This action is not a matter of arbitrary subjective choice; it develops rather out of the objective problems of mathematical thinking itself, for it is the simple,
fundamental operations of counting and computing, followed consistently and given general actual application, that lead to those
complex systems of relations of which the new numbers are the expression.

This was made fully clear in Dedekind's deduction of irrational
numbers, where they appear not so much as new forms which have
some peculiar absolute nature, but rather as a section we single out in
the system of rational numbers, as cuts, by which this system is divided
into classes A_1 and A_2, and in such a way that every number a_1 in
the former is smaller than every number a_2 in the latter. The proof
for the "existence" of the irrational numbers is then limited solely to
establishing, first, that an infinite number of such cuts exist which
are not generated by rational numbers, and second, that we can

24. For further details see H. Hankel, *Zur Geschichte der Mathematik in Altertum
und Mittelalter* (Leipzig, B. G. Teubner, 1874), S. 111 ff.

reckon with these irrationals in exactly the same way, that is to say, that we can apply to them all the known arithmetical operations in exactly the same manner.[25]

But a firm foundation for irrational numbers can be found herein only if one accepts beforehand the basic presupposition upon which Dedekind's deduction apparently rests. This is that in numbers we have to do not with symbols of things but with symbols of operations, and that even the so-called "natural" numbers are nothing other than operational symbols. Then the advance beyond them would not mean a creation out of nothing but is explicable in the simplest way as a continuous extension of the realm of operations that occurs when, to relations already at hand, "relations of relations" and so on are added. If it is a question of postulates here, to which the new kinds of number owe their existence, they are never postulates as to any "objects." The only postulate is that our concept of the domain of number be so inclusive that it becomes a self-contained structure. Whenever we make any combination with the single elements of this domain, in accordance with the fundamental rules of calculation, we are supposed to consider the result in its turn as an item belonging to the whole system and possessing therein its own definite significance. It appears that we may ignore certain conditions that are valid within the system of whole numbers and accordingly seem to be inherent in the nature of number as such without loss of certainty; rather do we gain certainty of another and more general kind. As the process is continued the fundamental and deeper strata of the number concept emerge, what is permanent, constant, and necessary separating off from the relative and the fortuitous.

The system of whole numbers is not only ordered but is of such a sort that every number has an immediate predecessor and an immediate successor, with the exception of zero, which has no predecessor. But this rule is broken even for the system of rational numbers, for in this case, since the system is compact throughout, no one of its elements has any other that immediately precedes or follows it. The number continuum that comes into being with the admission of irrationals exhibits still other structural conditions, but it proves to be connected with all the previous numbers in so far as one essential remains in force; here, too, when we consider two elements, a and b, it is unequivocally established which is the larger and which the smaller; which precedes and which follows. But that

25. Dedekind, *Stetigkeit und irrationale Zahlen* (2. unveränd. Aufl. Braunschweig, F. Vieweg & Sohn, 1892), § 4.

even *this* determination may be given up without the essence of number disappearing is shown by the transition to imaginary numbers, which no longer can be ordered from the standpoint of larger or smaller, and for which even the relation, "between," has lost its meaning.

From the point of view of the theory of knowledge the order in levels that is the outcome of all this may be compared in a certain sense with the situation already encountered in an entirely different field, when we analyzed the problem of space. There, too, it appeared that the various geometries offered different aspects of the spatial order, and that in progressing from one to the other we found this order more clearly defined; so that in passing from metric to affine and projective geometry and thence to analysis situs we were able to grasp more and more general and "essential" characters.[26]

When the development of the theory of numbers is understood in this sense the new numbers, and especially the irrational and the imaginary, lose all the metaphysical mystery that has been time and again sought in them ever since their discovery. Yet the miracle of arithmetic seems no less but perhaps even greater than before. For the fact that in so simple a basic relationship as the mere following in a series there lie contained such other rich and complex systems of relations is a circumstance ever and again calculated to arouse philosophical wonder. To be sure, in order to unearth these treasures a certain basic power and tendency of mathematical thinking was requisite. The complex systems had to be made accessible by continually devising new symbols for them. On the basis of these symbols mathematics gained the ability to operate with the complex in the same way as with the simple structures. Even the latter were not strictly or absolutely simple, for as soon as they were analyzed they turned out to be totalities of relations that depended upon definite structural conditions. These totalities are treated mathematically as *one* object and provided with one sign, and only by virtue of such concentration does one achieve a scientific consideration and treatment of them. The higher stages carry this fundamental process further by acquiring the power, through the creation of new symbols, to make a synopsis of more and more complex contents and render them capable of determination. In this respect, too, the mathematical thinking of the nineteenth century far surpassed that of earlier periods, and for the first time became master of its subject.

The new orientation thus acquired is best shown, as far as the

26. See Chap. I, p. 33.

theory of numbers is concerned, by the manner in which the concept of the imaginary was introduced and established. For the great mathematicians of the seventeenth century imaginary numbers were not instruments of mathematical knowledge but a special class of objects upon which knowledge had stumbled in the course of its development and which contained something that was not only mysterious but virtually impenetrable. When Leibniz told Huyghens he had found that two complex quantities added together could give a real quantity the latter replied that the observation was astonishing and wholly new, and that there was something mysterious, something incomprehensible in it.[27] Leibniz himself often betrayed an agnosticism about imaginary numbers that was generally alien to him and contrary to the spirit of his philosophy; for he once designated them as an extraordinary hybrid, "an amphibian between being and nonbeing." [28] The apparent mystery was first completely resolved by Gauss, when he answered the question in the simplest way with his geometrical argument and proof. Calculation with imaginaries now appears as merely a calculation with pairs of numbers, in which it must be shown by special proof that the basic axioms of algebra such, for example, as the associative law of addition and the commutative law of multiplication retain their validity. In this sense Cauchy [29] explained an imaginary number as a "symbolic expression" (*expression symbolique ou symbole*) that is nothing other than a statement of two equations between two real quantities. Hamilton also explained and justified calculations with complex numbers as operations with pairs of numbers.[30] All this contained an important methodological suggestion not only with respect to the imaginary numbers themselves but also for all other extensions of the domain of natural whole numbers, for it could be universally shown that the new kinds of numbers here introduced are always defined through a system of numbers of an earlier variety and that their meaning is exhausted therein.

But the introduction of complex numbers shows in a very special and striking way the methodological significance pertaining to every extension of the theory of numbers, for the fruitfulness of the im-

27. C. Huyghens, "Briefe an Leibniz," *Leibnizens mathematische Schriften,* ed. Gerhardt, Erste Abteil. (Berlin, A. Asher & Co., 1850), II, 15.

28. For the interpretation of imaginaries by the mathematics of the seventeenth century see Klein, *Elementarmathematik,* I, 61 ff.

29. Cauchy, *Cours d'analyse de l'Ecole Royale Polytechnique* (Roi, Debure frères, 1821), première partie, chap. vii.

30. W. R. Hamilton, "Theory of Conjugate Functions, or Algebraic Couples," *Transactions of the Royal Irish Academy,* XVII (Dublin, P. D. Hardy, 1837), 293 ff.

aginaries was not confined to the domain of algebra but showed itself in the fact that the whole logical structure of mathematics appears henceforth in a new light. Things that had seemed previously to be merely standing side by side now are conceived of in their mutual relations with each other and their systematic interdependence. Imaginary numbers were called for only by algebraic problems in the sixteenth century, by the so-called irreducible case of the equation of the third degree.[31] Geometrical applications did not follow until much later. Not until the beginning of the eighteenth century did the new idea of the "imaginary point," introduced by Poncelet, make headway.[32] It was explained very precisely that without this expansion a geometry could never be constructed to rival analysis in universality and rigor, a prophecy amply fulfilled. A wholly satisfactory and coherent structure of projective geometry was achieved only when Staudt,[33] in his *Geometry of Position* and his *Contributions to a Geometry of Position*, gave a purely geometrical meaning to the imaginary point, plane, conic section, and so on, instead of merely taking them over from the formulas of analysis, as had been formerly done.[34] But the full significance of imaginaries did not become apparent until Riemann made the concept of the function of a complex variable the basis for a theory of algebraic functions, in his dissertation "Basis for a General Theory of the Functions of a Complex Quantity" (1851). With the completion of Riemann's work by Weierstrass, analysis won sovereign mastery over the whole domain of mathematics in the second half of the nineteenth century.[35] The use of complex numbers in vector analysis then showed how extremely fruitful the concept of imaginaries could be in the natural sciences as well; in calculations with vectors there was revealed, to use Weyl's expression, "a wonderful harmony between the given and reason." [36]

Thus in the course of centuries there had come about not only a change in the conception of imaginaries but a complete reversal. What had been regarded originally as something impossible or as a sheer riddle, upon which one gazed in astonishment without be-

31. For details see Hankel, *Zur Geschichte der Mathematik*, S. 372.

32. J. V. Poncelet, Introduction, *Traité des propriétés projectives des figures* (Paris, Augustins, 1822), S. xix ff.

33. *Geometrie der Lage* (1846); *Beiträge zur Geometrie der Lage* (1856–60).

34. A summary of Staudt's theory of imaginaries is given by Klein, *Vorlesungen über die Entwicklung der Mathematik im 19. Jahrhundert*, I, 136 ff.; and *Elementarmathematik*, II, 133 ff.

35. For historical details see Klein, *Vorlesungen über die Entwicklung der Mathematik im 19. Jahrhundert*, I, 246 ff.

36. H. Weyl, "Philosophie der Mathematik," *Natur* . . . , S. 55.

ing able to understand it, developed into one of the most important tools of mathematics; into a means to survey mathematics as a whole and to reveal it as a complete organism.

In such examples one recognizes how with every forward step in mathematical thinking new realms have opened up without its ever having to pass outside the field of its original intellectual material. To be sure there is in this connection one of the most difficult problems of the mathematical theory of knowledge, for the possibility that this thinking might remain wholly confined within its own sphere and yet could acquire ever new and strictly objective knowledge therein, seems more and more problematical. Modern mathematics has tried very different ways of solving this problem, advocating almost every view from a naïve realism that treated the content of mathematical thought as real things to an extreme nominalism that saw in it nothing but "marks on paper."

On the one hand, the rigorously logical character of mathematical propositions was emphasized to the extent that these were regarded as identical statements, through which the whole system of mathematics would eventually be reduced to one single, colossal tautology. What value such a tautology might hold for knowledge and what thought was supposed to gain by moving thus in its own narrow circle was not revealed.

On the other hand, it seemed as though every tie that one sought to impose upon thought endangered the ideal nature of pure mathematics and made it dependent upon alien authority. The stronger it became in its own right during the nineteenth century and the more completely the dominion of pure analysis extended to include all its branches, the more it felt obliged to repudiate this external rule.

Georg Cantor explained that one can speak of the meaning of the reality or existence of whole numbers, finite as well as infinite, in two ways. First, they may be regarded as real in so far as, by definition, they occupy an entirely distinct place in our understanding, are distinguished in the clearest manner from all other components of thought, and thus modify definitely the content of the mind. This kind of reality he called *intrasubjective*, or immanent. But secondly, reality can also be ascribed to numbers in so far as they "must be accounted an expression, or a representation, of occurrences and relations in the external world as it confronts the intellect"—in so far as the various classes of numbers are representatives of something that actually presents itself in the material and intellectual worlds. This second sort of reality Cantor called *transsubjective*, the "transient" *reality* of whole numbers. According to him there is a sort of pre-established harmony between the two forms of being: a concept characterized as existent in the first sense always possesses a transient reality in certain relationships, even, in fact, in an infinite number of them, the ascertaining of which is, of course, mostly a problem for metaphysics, and is besides one of the most difficult problems.

But mathematics may go its own way, untroubled by all this. To develop its ideas it need take into account solely their immanent reality and therefore is not under the slightest obligation to prove their transient reality. "Because of this fortunate position, which distinguishes it from all the other sciences," wrote Cantor, "it deserves to be called *free mathematics*, a name that I should bestow in preference to the customary *pure mathematics*, if I had any choice in the matter." [37] But the next theoretical problem resulting therefrom was how to construe this freedom to form concepts, which is the undeniable natural and inalienable right of mathematics, so that it cannot be confused with subjective caprice. Merely invoking the law of contradiction is not enough, for not all that is free of inner contradiction has proved its right thereby to be a part of mathematics. Accordingly there must be another criterion and another sort of deduction introduced for all "existential proofs" of mathematics.

Kant explained philosophical knowledge as the rational knowledge of concepts and mathematical knowledge as that derived from the construction of concepts and he based his proof on this explanation, that by its very nature mathematics is not mere analysis but must be a synthesis. There was a mighty argument in modern mathematics about the justification of this distinction but by and large it has been fruitless, for the writers have neither used the expressions "analysis" and "synthesis" in a uniform and unequivocal sense nor even succeeded in agreeing on what Kant meant after all by these terms. The "transcendental" distinction that is here referred to was generally misunderstood, and criticized as a psychological distinction.[38] For Kant himself the distinction belonged to the sphere of neither psychology nor formal logic; indeed, he went so far as to say that the explanation of the possibility of synthetic judgments is a problem that does not concern general logic in the least

37. Cantor, *Grundlagen einer allgemeinen Mannigfaltigkeitslehre,* § 8, S. 19.
38. For further details see E. Cassirer, "Kant und die moderne Mathematik," *Kant-Studien* (Berlin, Reuther & Reichard, 1907), XII. 1 ff.

and, in fact, that logic would not even be acquainted with the very name of the thing.[39] What Kant meant is that the fundamental character of the synthesis at which mathematics aims comes to light not so much in the formation of concepts and judgments as in the building up of the mathematical world of objects. The formation of the objects of mathematics is constructive, and hence synthetic, because it is not concerned simply with analyzing a given concept into its characteristics, but because, starting from certain determinate basic relations, we advance and ascend to ever more complex ones, where we let each new totality of relations correspond to a new realm of "objects."

The development of the realm of numbers fully confirms *this* meaning, which Kant associated with the idea of mathematical synthesis. There can be no question that the concept of the whole number includes all those features from which the notions of rational, irrational, and complex numbers were later derived. Such essential stipulations of the concept as this, that every whole number has an immediate predecessor and successor, had to be abandoned in order to achieve the other number systems. These were acquired not by stopping to consider the single elements of the original realm of numbers but by advancing to a contemplation of whole fields, in which new relations were discovered.

Calculation with the "new" numbers could only be understood and cogently explained by not regarding them as new elements added to the original series, or as somehow having independent and real existence, but by recognizing them as mere symbols of certain systematic relationships within the original realm. Thus, for example, the mystery of the existence of irrational numbers disappears when, with Dedekind, we explain them as cuts, that is to say, see in them no more than a systematic division of rational numbers into two classes. Similarly it appears that a positive or negative real number can be explained simply as a pair, a/a', of absolute numbers, and that calculation with imaginary numbers also only implies operating with pairs, a, β, of real numbers. For every combination, for every new synthesis, there arises a corresponding new object, which in a strictly methodological sense develops out of preceding ones but in no way coincides with them logically.

When the idea of synthesis is thus understood the claim of modern logistic to have completely ousted synthesis from the realm of mathematics and proved the wholly analytical character of mathematical

39. I. Kant, *Kritik der reinen Vernunft* (2. Aufl.), S. 193.

ideas is recognized as untenable.[40] After it had appeared to pursue a wholly different course for a time the development of modern mathematics has in this respect turned back remarkably toward certain positions taken by Kant. Transcendental logic did not undergo modifications similar to those imposed on transcendental aesthetic by the discovery of the non-Euclidean geometries and their various forms of space.

Among modern mathematicians it is Otto Hölder in particular who calls the construction of a mathematical world of objects the characteristic and fundamental feature of the mathematical method, emphasizing that it is as distinctive for arithmetical as for geometrical thinking. According to Hölder all mathematical thought starts with self-formed or synthetic ideas, and the essential for mathematical proof, for deduction, is not the ordinary rule of the syllogism but the manner in which these synthetic ideas are employed. In geometry or mechanics they are based on presuppositions, that is, on fundamental concepts derived from experience or intuition (point, straight line, plane, angle, force, mass) and assumptions resting on these. "But there are also concepts that originate in the absence of such special presuppositions merely on the basis of certain general logical operations of placing and removal, of grouping and simultaneously keeping separate, of correspondence and ordering as, for example, numbers, groups, and permutations." The whole numbers are the simplest of these concepts, because they are derived from purely elementary functions of placing and combining; but other syntheses are associated with them, which in constant connection with one another constitute the totality of mathematical relations and therewith all mathematical objects, though in the later stages the earlier ones would not be simply repeated. Hence mathematical conclusions cannot be referred to the logical process of subsumption. They do not depend upon the ordering of individuals under class concepts or the subordination of classes under each other, but upon a concatenation of relations according to a logically original and independent principle that is in no sense referable merely to the principle of identity and contradiction.[41]

Even the development of the theory of sets, the starting point for the logistic foundations of the theory of numbers, comes under the same principle. "Sets of one and more dimensions," wrote Weyl,

40. In opposition to Kant, Louis Couturat tried to sustain this thesis, "La Philosophie des mathématiques de Kant," *Les Principes des mathématiques* (Paris, F. Alcan, 1905), Appendix, p. 235 ff.

41. O. Hölder, Einleitung und "Das Wesen dieser Beweise," *Die mathematische Methode* (Berlin, J. Springer, 1924), S. 1 ff., 22 ff.

"constitute a newly derived system of ideal objects above the realm of objects originally given; it is developed therefrom by a *mathematical process*, as I like to say. In fact, I believe that in this sort of concept formation one has what is characteristic of the mathematical way of thinking." [42]

But with that, intuition, which logistic had presumably cast out of pure arithmetic and left far behind, has regained its rights. Almost all trends in modern mathematics agree that in any derivation of number concepts there can be no recourse to empirical intuition, that is, to intuition of concrete things. But "pure" intuition of number had to come more and more into the center of attention when scholars were convinced that the theory of sets could not meet the demands made upon it. The discovery of its paradoxes marks a definite breach and a turning point in the epistemology of mathematics. Here occurred the first attacks of the intuitionists against the firmly entrenched system of classical analysis. The chasm between the finite and the infinite, apparently filled in by the theory of sets, said Weyl, opened up again into a yawning abyss. The treatment of natural numbers by this theory may be of great value for systematic mathematics but it should not try deceitfully to hide the fact that it is actually founded upon the intuition of repetition and the series of natural numbers.[43]

Brouwer and Weyl, the advocates of intuitionism, thought that the crisis in fundamentals brought about by the antinomies of the theory of sets could be resolved only by a return to general principles. They insisted that it was self-deception to think that in the foundations of number they could dispense with the factor of "ordered sets" and replace it with something different and more original. According to Weyl, modern investigation into the foundations of mathematics, which had now overthrown the dogmatic theory of sets, has confirmed the idea that the pure concept of order is not deducible and shown that the ordinal numbers have primacy over the cardinal.[44]

Once more algebra was defined as the science of pure time in the sense of William Hamilton and in conformity with a fundamental idea of Kant. The objection so often raised, that not number but only the psychological act of counting presupposes time, by virtue of its subjective existence and meaning, seems not to be valid if the definition be understood in accordance with both Kant and Hamilton. The

---

42. H. Weyl, *Das Kontinuum* (Leipzig, Veit & Co., 1918), Kap. i, § 4, S. 15.
43. *Ibid.* See especially Poincaré's attacks on "Cantorism," "Les Mathématiques et la logique," *Science et méthode* (Paris, E. Flammarion, 1924), II, chap. iii, 152 ff.
44. Weyl, *op. cit.*, S. 28.

latter left no doubt that he wished to emphasize in time only the element of ordering or ordered sequence and not the element of change, or the succession of psychic acts or events. Therefore he defined algebra as the "science of pure time or *order in progression*." [45]

If this fundamental view be adopted algebra can be established in full rigor but its rational character does not in this case imply a complete merger with logic. Its specific laws are neither impugned nor annulled thereby, and still less is all analysis transformed into one colossal tautology. This view was advocated and pushed home most energetically and characteristically by Poincaré, who declared that even the simplest calculations are invariably governed by a unique "logic," which is in no way comparable to that of the syllogism but requires the application of an entirely different principle. In proving the elementary truths of arithmetic and setting up the associative and commutative laws of addition or the commutative and distributive laws of multiplication, one must go back to this principle of so-called "complete induction." But wherein lies the actual justification for this principle itself? It appears that the procedure here employed is not of empirical origin, neither can it be deduced from the basic laws of logic, if deduced be understood to mean acquired by the ordinary process of deductive inference. We begin by showing that a certain theorem holds good for the number 1; proceed to show that if it be valid for any number n — 1, it is valid also for the following number n; and in this way convince ourselves that it is true for all whole numbers. This method of proof by recursion, which forms the root of every arithmetical calculation, we cannot fail to recognize as mathematical deduction in its simplest and purest form. The distinguishing feature of the procedure is that it contains an infinite number of hypothetical syllogisms compressed, as it were, into a single formula.

Such an achievement, which affords a survey of the infinite series of numbers at a glance, appears not to be possible with the type of induction employed in the empirical sciences. There we start from the consideration of a single case; go on to prove many cases; in order finally, by an ever precarious process of inference and with a sort of sudden jump, to conclude with an assertion that is supposed to apply to "all cases." Experience could show only that a certain proposition is true for the first ten, or hundred, or thousand numbers but it could never assert anything about the limitless series of numbers.

On the other hand, there is no help in an appeal to the basic principles of logic, the law of identity or the law of contradiction. The latter principle would suffice in the case of a restricted number of

45. Hamilton, *op. cit.*, pp. 293 ff.

conclusions, for it would always allow us to develop as many syllogisms as we wished.

But when we have to include an endless number of deductions in one single formula, when we are face to face with the infinite, the principle of contradiction falls down just as experience proves itself to be insufficient. This rule, then, which is unattainable either by experience or by analytical proof, is the exemplar of a synthetic judgment a priori. Why does this judgment force itself upon us with irresistible evidence? Precisely because it asserts nothing about the nature of things but only about an original faculty of the mind. For the mind recognizes its capacity to repeat a certain act continually, once it has become convinced of the possibility of such an act. But the mind does have an immediate intuition of this possibility; experience only affords the opportunity to employ it and so to become conscious of it.[46]

The constructive nature of pure mathematics, the fact that it possesses its ideas and therewith its "objects" only in so far as it is able to produce them from an original principle, is here fully recognized in contrast with the viewpoint of the theory of sets, where the set was regarded as something "given." Even Weyl insisted that "complete induction" introduces an entirely new and peculiar element into mathematical demonstrations unrecognized in Aristotelian logic, and that therein lies "the real soul of the art of mathematical proof." [47]

This constituted a highly important step in the theory of knowledge. Those trying to establish a purely logical foundation of number, constructing it solely from logical constants, had indeed attained considerable formal rigor, but in so doing had lost sight almost entirely of the theoretical problem. Number was raised so high above the world of perception that it was hard to understand how, without prejudice to its purity, it could be related to the empirical world; indeed, even become a specific principle of knowledge therein. It was intuitionism that first succeeded in constructing a bridge, and Felix Klein, too, acknowledged this fact. What the formal foundation of arithmetic has done, he explained, is to divide into two parts a vast problem that was too complex to be attacked as a whole and to make the first of them capable of being handled, viz., the purely logical task of setting up independent basic propositions or axioms and the

---

46. H. Poincaré, "Sur la nature du raisonnement mathématique," *Revue de métaphysique et de morale*, II (Paris, Hachette et Cie., 1894), 371 ff.; *La Science et l'hypothèse*, p. 19 ff.

47. Weyl, *op. cit.*, S. 28.

investigation of their independence and freedom from contradiction. "The second part of the problem, which has more to do with the theory of knowledge and the question of the basic application of those principles to real relationships, is not taken in hand at all though naturally this, too, must be settled if the foundations of arithmetic are to be firmly established. This second part is in itself a problem of the utmost profundity, the difficulties of which lie in the general theory of knowledge." Once the problem has been put in this way it becomes evident that pure mathematics will have to pass beyond its own frontiers. Its logic must broaden itself to the logic of the exact science of nature.

V

The Goal and Methods of Theoretical Physics

N O SINGLE realm of learning is so closely related to the general problem of knowledge, and none has exerted such a strong and lasting effect upon its historical development, as mathematical physics. Between theoretical physics and epistemology there is not only constant reciprocation and uninterrupted collaboration, but there seems to be a sort of spiritual community. In our discussion of the problem of knowledge we have been able to follow this association step by step from its inception at the very dawn of modern scientific thought and to see how it has become increasingly closer throughout the centuries. From the Renaissance on nearly all the great natural scientists have endeavored to maintain it.

Galileo was more than creator of the science of dynamics and a leader in the conflict over the Copernican world view. He never would have been able to erect the new physics and astronomy had he not been guided by a new definition of what scientific knowledge can and should be. It was his philosophical conception of truth that opened the way to his establishment of physics and the reform of cosmology.[1]

Kepler, too, had been the first to formulate exact laws of nature in his theory of planetary motion, and he was also a pioneer in purely methodological respects, having proposed in his published vindication of Tycho Brahe the first really precise definition of the meaning and function of scientific hypotheses.[2]

And Newton, also, included in his great work a special section in which he sought to bring the concept formation of physics under certain rules and to determine its object and limits. He reflected not only on the goal of natural science but on its methods as well, and the rules of reasoning in philosophy go side by side with the mathematical principles as a necessary and integral part of his system.[3]

Thus philosophy is tied up with all the efforts of research and it also brings them into unity. It attempts to represent them systematically and then critically to justify them. Kant's *Critique of Pure Reason* grew out of this ambition. It aimed to seal the covenant, as it

---

1. See E. Cassirer, "Galilei," *Das Erkenntnisproblem* (Berlin, B. Cassirer, 1922), I, Zweites Buch, Kap. ii, 377 ff., and "Wahrheitsbegriff und Wahrheitsproblem bei Galilei," *Scientia,* LXII (1937), 121 ff., 185 ff.

2. "Kepler," *op. cit.*

3. Newton, Introduction, *Philosophiae naturalis principia mathematica,* Book III.

were, that had existed between philosophy and mathematics ever since the Renaissance. This was not to be regarded merely as historical fact; it should be understood and explained as something necessary and inescapable.

This tendency was faithfully preserved, strengthened, and deepened by nineteenth-century science, though of course there were many and prominent investigators who were not only out of sympathy with it but actually saw serious danger in it. They wanted to restrict empirical science to facts and thought it could most surely be done by avoiding all subtle epistemological reflection and speculation. But although this naïve realism recommended itself to natural scientists as the only suitable way for them to think, still it never succeeded in keeping them within the proposed limits. On the contrary, every advance into the world of new facts was accompanied by problems that appeared to be soluble only on the ground of a theoretical analysis of knowledge, and it became increasingly clear that this analysis was no mere supplementary task to be passed along to philosophy after the conclusions of research had been reached. The questions to be answered had not been imposed upon natural science from without but had arisen from within during the course of its own investigations. Empirical science itself would have to take them firmly and resolutely in hand if it meant to master them.

This is what actually happened and to an unprecedented degree. From the middle of the nineteenth century onward the demand for reflective criticism in the natural sciences was urged with ever mounting emphasis. Works of an epistemological character occupy a significant place in Helmholtz' writing,[4] and he himself maintained that critical examination of the sources of knowledge is one of those philosophical tasks that no generation can evade with impunity. Heinrich Hertz proved himself at once a physicist and a disciple of Helmholtz by prefacing his book on the principles of mechanics with a general discussion of the characteristic and distinctive nature of scientific knowledge.

The necessity for such considerations had already been recognized then in respect to the cosmology of classical physics, but it was felt far more when this world view was unsettled by the crisis regarding fundamentals brought about through the general theory of relativity and the development of the quantum theory. Then problems arose that had never before been encountered, at least in the domain of nat-

---

4. See the collection of Helmholtz' articles on the theory of knowledge. *Hermann v. Helmholtz Schriften zur Erkenntnistheorie,* hrsg. und erläutert von P. Hertz und M. Schlick (Berlin, J. Springer, 1921).

ural science. Heisenberg declared that the latest advances in atomic physics shatter all belief "in the objective course of events in space and time, independent of any observation," and said that physics will never return to this conviction in its original form, though it had been the heart of classical theory.

This poses a question that the great investigators of the seventeenth and eighteenth centuries, Galileo and Kepler, Huyghens and Newton, d'Alembert and Lagrange, not only had never raised but probably would have regarded as inadmissible or impossible. Nevertheless it is evident that physics, though it raises such a question, has in no way renounced the idea of objective reality, nor has it succumbed to any sort of radical skepticism. But just as little should there be any blurring of the line that separates the theory of knowledge from natural science. The "modern theories," Heisenberg expressly stated,

have not originated from revolutionary ideas brought into the exact sciences from without, so to speak; rather they are naturally forced upon science as it attempts to carry out logically the program of classical physics. . . . It is manifest that experimental investigation is always the necessary pre-condition of theoretical knowledge, and that significant progress is made only under pressure from the results of experiment, never through speculation . . . The change that has come to pass in the foundations of exact science has been necessitated by experimental investigation." [5]

Limitation of space does not permit us here to follow in detail the course of these researches. Elsewhere [6] I have attempted to describe how they affected the establishment and systematization of the general theory of knowledge; hence I shall not return to the question here but merely select one definite problem that concerns not so much the content as the form of modern physics. For even in the conception of its form, too, a deep-seated change is encountered in the second half of the nineteenth century and the opening years of the twentieth. Now not only does the picture of nature show new features, but the view of what a natural science can and should be and the problems and aims it must set itself undergoes more and more radical transfor-

5. W. Heisenberg, *Wandlungen in den Grundlagen der Naturwissenschaft* (6. Aufl. Leipzig, S. Hirzel, 1945).

6. For classical physics see *Substanzbegriff und Funktionsbegriff* (Berlin, B. Cassirer, 1910); for the special and general theory of relativity, *Zur Einstein'schen Relativitätstheorie* (same publisher, 1921); for the quantum theory, *Determinismus und Indeterminismus in der modernen Physik*, "Göteborgs Högskolas Årsskrift," XLII (1936), No. 3.

mation. In no earlier period do we meet such extensive argument over the very conception of physics, and in none is the debate so acrimonious. Even classical physics did not have this conception ready at hand; on the contrary, one of its first tasks had been to create the concept and then to defend it in constant battle with the Aristotelian-scholastic view. But this conflict was waged on a compact and united front in the conviction that reason and experience would be able to penetrate the nature of reality and progressively reveal it. The *ontological* significance of the physical theories was never seriously challenged, however widely these differed from each other in content.

In the nineteenth century, however, there came a sudden change. The realism of natural science was supplanted by a phenomenalism that disputed not only the possible existence of a solution but even the meaning of the problems that had been set up by physical thought. When Mach or Planck, Bolzmann or Ostwald, Poincaré or Duhem are asked what a physical theory is and what it can accomplish we receive not only different but contradictory answers, and it is clear that we are witnessing more than a change in the purpose and intent of investigation. This new orientation in physics has slowly and steadily been brought to completion. Its logical consequences have been much less noted and emphasized than the concomitant revolution in the content of scientific ideas, in the concepts of space, time, and matter, and in the formulation of the law of causality.

Yet from the standpoint simply of the theory of knowledge the former development is hardly less consequential and pervasive than the latter, for it is always highly significant when a science, instead of directly and resolutely seeking its object, suddenly deserts this "natural" attitude for another; when it feels compelled to inquire into the nature of its object and into its own concept, and into the very possibility of the science itself. At such turning points in research it is clear that reflection gains a wholly different status and must be conceded a much more important role in the upbuilding of science than during more naïve periods. Indeed, the earlier ingenuous attitude had been lost beyond recall when this period of development came to a close; no great investigator any longer tries to evade the questions that here press upon him or to refer them to the court of "philosophical thinking." Everyone has to decide them independently, and his general conclusions almost always bear the stamp of his own scientific principles as well as that of his concrete research.

In the eighteenth century and until the middle of the nineteenth there was no serious doubt but that the ideal of knowledge to which physics was pledged once for all was the ideal of Newtonian science. Its fundamental concepts, which had been exposed to such grave doubts when they were first introduced, had not only lost more and more of their paradoxical character but were regarded as essential to any accurate understanding of nature, and there was a universal and prevailing effort to transfer to all other fields the type of thinking that Newton had made so influential in mechanics. At first it had seemed as if natural phenomena promised to conform to this expectation the more fully and exactly they were understood. They appeared to arrange themselves without difficulty in the general scheme set up by Newton in his theory of gravitation. Yet internal friction was never lacking throughout this development. In the field of thermodynamics the explanations connected with the second law of the theory of heat and with the idea of entropy led more and more constantly to the view of the distinction between reversible and irreversible processes as a basic feature in all natural events which cannot possibly be eliminated. Planck said, in his Leyden Lecture of 1908,[7] that this distinction, with better right than any other, could be made a preeminent basis for the classification of all physical phenomena and might eventually play the chief role in any cosmology of the physics of the future. Likewise in the development of the theory of electricity, the Faraday-Maxwell field concept, which was steadily proving itself a true and indispensable instrument of knowledge, stood in sharp contrast at the outset with the Newtonian idea of force. Yet, on the other hand, the form taken by Coulomb's law of magnetic and electrical phenomena seemed to show a perfect correspondence between them and the phenomena of gravitation, so that even in this realm the concept of "action at a distance" might assert its claims.

Thus it appeared not only permissible but obligatory to put this concept of force at the center of all interpretations of nature. This was most plainly and decisively done in the introductory observations of Helmholtz in the first formulation of the law of the conservation of energy. Here Newton's action at a distance was not only recognized as valid for the field in which it had been discovered but elevated to the dignity of a general axiom for the understanding of nature. All operations in nature are to be traced to attractive and repulsive forces, whose intensity depends only upon the distance between the mutually interacting points, for only thus is it possible to give full validity to the highest law of scientific investigation, the law of causality. The demand for a consistent explanation of events is never

7. M. Planck, "Die Einheit des physikalischen Weltbildes," *Wege zur physikalischen Erkenntnis* (2. Aufl. Leipzig, S. Hirzel, 1934), S. 7 ff.

satisfied so long as we have not penetrated to the ultimate causes which operate according to an immutable law and therefore produce the same effect at all times and under the same external conditions.

The appointed . . . task of physics is thus to refer natural phenomena to unchangeable attractive and repulsive forces, whose intensity depends upon distance. The solution of this problem is at the same time the prerequisite for a thorough understanding of nature. . . . So if theoretical science is not to stop halfway on the road to comprehension it must bring its views into accord with the postulates set up regarding the nature of the simple forces and their consequences. The work of science will have been completed only when phenomena have been traced back to the simple forces, and when it can be shown also that the given account is the only possible one admitted by the phenomena. Then this would have been proven to be the necessary way of interpreting nature, and it would be the one to which objective truth should be ascribed.[8]

If this program, advanced by Helmholtz in the middle of the nineteenth century, could have been realized it would have furnished a cosmology that would have been equally satisfying from both empirical and epistemological standpoints. Of course it would have been necessary to put up with the absurdity that seemed to reside in the idea of action at a distance, but once the idea was accepted for this purpose an extremely simple and self-consistent system of physics would have been attained. All the complexity and all the qualitative differences of natural phenomena would have been brought ideally under one common head.

It was easy to overlook the fact that this simplicity had been merely postulated, not empirically proved. As far as the popular materialism was concerned there were no scruples of that sort to hinder its constructions and proofs, for it had apparently grown out of natural science, though in truth it was actually but a remnant and later offshoot of dogmatic metaphysics. We need not go into the materialistic controversy here as it raged in the second half of the nineteenth century. Its origin and historical development have been exhaustively described by Friedrich Albert Lange.[9] Most of the doctrines that he analyzed so minutely, however, have left no permanent trace in either scientific or philosophical thought. Neither the opponents nor the defenders of materialism were theoretically equipped for the battle they attempted to fight. Often both thesis and antithesis stood on the

8. Helmholtz, Einleitung, *Über die Erhaltung der Kraft,* Ostwald's "Klassiker der exakten Wissenschaften" (Leipzig, W. Engelmann, 1889), I, 6 f.

9. F. A. Lange, *Geschichte des Materialismus* (Leipzig, J. Baedeker, 1887).

same ground. How thoroughly skepticism and dogmatism were permeated by the same spirit is seen especially in the sort of criticism and refutation of materialism found in du Bois-Reymond, which could not help at every turn affirming implicitly just what it seemed explicitly to oppose and deny. Du Bois-Reymond meant to show the objective limits set for all knowledge of nature and to prove that there are definite realms of being that this knowledge can never penetrate, realms which remain world riddles, and for which not *ignoramus*, "we do not know," but *ignorabimus*, "we never shall know," are the right dicta.[10]

The sole basis for this assertion, however, is the assumption that mechanism represents the sole trustworthy and possible route to understanding, and that outside it there can be no salvation for natural science. Still far in the future lay the notion that the questions of science itself could ever compel a transformation of the mechanistic cosmology. Even the more rigorous thinking of philosophy yielded place to this idea slowly and with reluctance. At first philosophers sought to follow the same path as Helmholtz and held that a complete and adequate understanding of nature could be reached only through an explanation of its mechanism, but then they wanted to establish the special position and pre-eminence of this sort of explanation on a priori and not solely empirical grounds. For this there was nothing else to do but define and form the general concept of cause in such a way that all natural phenomena would necessarily be reduced to pure phenomena of motion. This tendency appears most clearly in Wilhelm Wundt's *The Axioms of Physical Science and Their Relation to the Causal Principle* (1866). A comparison of his train of thought with the introductory remarks in Helmholtz' treatise on the conservation of energy shows how science, austere and aloof from the popular catchwords of the quarrel over materialism, conceived the problem. Wundt's book alone suffices for an insight into the deeper epistemological motives that underlay adherence to the mechanistic explanation of nature.

As the first of his six axioms of physics Wundt formulated the proposition that all cause in nature is concerned with motion. This theorem, to be sure, cannot be derived immediately from experience, which seems rather to contradict it, since all changes in objects that are open to direct observation have to do with their perceptible qualities, and as such these present an irreducible complexity and variability. Were we entirely dependent on the information furnished

10. E. du Bois-Reymond, *Über die Grenzen des Naturerkennens: Die sieben Welträthsel* (3. Aufl. Leipzig, Veit & Co., 1891).

by our senses, therefore, every change in nature would have to be described by the statement that an object, that is, a collection of perceptible characteristics, had disappeared and that another object with qualities partly different had taken its place. That we do not stop here in our *scientific* interpretation of nature, but can refer the event to a fixed substrate and say that the identity of the object has been preserved during its various modifications, is not because of experience but primarily because of reflection over the evidence given by our senses. In this first step beyond mere observation all the following ones are implicitly included and from it they can be logically developed. The principle of identity—understood as a physical not as a logical principle—compels a transition to the mechanistic view and shows how this is not a fortuitous but a necessary factor in all our interpretations of nature.

Observation forces us to assume two objects, whereas thought will admit but one . . . The struggle would be endless were it not terminated by observation itself. There is one single case where an object does change before our eyes and yet still remains the same, and this is the case of motion. Here the change consists merely in alteration of an object's spatial relationships to other objects. Thus a difference in position is the only imaginable change in objects during which they remain identical.

If we would be saved from a flood of experiences or from Heraclitus' river of becoming, without consequent denial of becoming itself and a retreat to the motionless being of Parmenides, there remains but one escape: "We must trace every change back to the only conceivable one in which an object remains identical: motion." [11]

Here was a sort of transcendental deduction of the mechanistic view of nature that might have seemed highly satisfactory and convincing at first glance, since this explanation appeared to flow as a simple corollary from the chief fundamental concepts of all natural science: those of matter and causality. Grave doubts over its validity could not arise until scientific thinking ventured to undermine these basic ideas and until it broadened its criticism to include the ideas of matter and cause themselves, which lay at the very roots of classical physics. But such a venture was possible, of course, only when experience itself prompted and even demanded it.

11. W. Wundt, *Die physikalischen Axiome und ihre Beziehung zum Causalprinzip. Ein Kapitel aus einer Philosophie der Naturwissenschaft* (Erlangen, 1866), S. 125 ff.; and *Die Prinzipien der mechanischen Naturlehre* (2. ungeänd. Aufl. Stuttgart, F. Enke, 1910), S. 178 ff.

In Planck's lecture before the Königsberg meeting of the Deutscher Verein Naturforscher und Ärzte in 1910 he described the various historical stages of this process, tracing the particular empirical motives that had compelled physics to change its attitude toward the mechanistic view and placing in the foreground the problem concerning the mechanics of the luminiferous ether. The more exactly its nature seemed to be understood, the more had it proved to be the "truly woebegotten child of the mechanistic view." For while the existence of a material luminiferous ether is a postulate of the view, the behavior of the ether certainly contrasts very strangely with that of all other known matter. Every barely imaginable suggestion and combination had been exhausted in an effort to establish its constitution until finally, after all endeavors had failed, a change in the whole intellectual orientation was effected and investigators began to submit to critical proof the assumption of its existence instead of continuing to examine into its nature. No longer did they ask about the constitution, the density, the elastic properties of the ether, or about its longitudinal waves, and so forth; they began to inquire what relations must subsist among the forces of nature when one says it is impossible to demonstrate any of the properties of matter in the luminiferous ether, and to wonder whether on general principles the ether would have to be denied that material substantiality and identity which earlier theory had to assume.[12]

But however impressive and decisive all these empirical considerations were they might not have sufficed alone to shake the firmly constructed edifice of the mechanistic theory without the aid of other motives, which originated in purely methodological opinions on the scientific character of mechanics itself. Gustav Kirchhoff had already abandoned all claims that the mechanistic view could furnish an explanation of natural phenomena. He saw as its goal and object merely a complete description of the motions occurring in nature, given in the simplest possible fashion. His definition played an important role in theoretical discussions of the concept and task of natural science.[13] It was regarded as a significant innovation, and many experimentalists and thinkers regarded it as a complete break with the tradition of classical physics.[14] From a purely historical standpoint,

---

12. For further details see M. Planck, *Die Stellung der neueren Physik zur mechanischen Naturanschauung* (Leipzig, S. Hirzel, 1910); see also *Physikalische Rundblicke* (Leipzig, 1922), S. 38 ff.

13. G. Kirchhoff, *Vorlesungen über mathematische Physik* (2. Aufl. Leipzig, B. G. Teubner, 1877), I, 1.

14. K. Pearson, "Cause and Effect—Probability," *The Grammar of Science* (2d ed. London, Adam and Charles Black, 1900), chap. iv, pp. 113 ff.

however, such a belief was hardly justified, since even in the debates about the Newtonian theory of action at a distance a similar definition had been reached. The first followers of Newton had disarmed criticism by saying that theoretical physics had no business to offer an explanation of the inner possibility of happenings in nature and that in this matter only a description should be striven for and attained.[15]

The decisive feature in Kirchhoff's definition, however, lies in another quarter. There had been no doubt in the eighteenth and nineteenth centuries that there is a sort of hierarchy of existence, which science must trace and copy in its structure of knowledge. In his Preface to the *Encyclopédie* and his *Elements de philosophie*, d'Alembert sketched this hierarchy from the simplest to the most complex phenomena. Beginning with logic, it proceeded to algebra and geometry, and finally reached in mechanics the first science of reality. That all other branches of natural science—astronomy, optics, hydrostatics, and empirical physics in its entirety—were erected on this foundation and wholly dependent on it for their validity was thought to be beyond dispute. But just toward the end of the nineteenth century serious doubts respecting this notion began to arise, because of the new problems with which physics was faced in thermodynamics, in optics, and in the theory of electricity. Is there really such a firmly established "lower" and "higher" in the order of natural events, and is it so certain that the only secure base for this imaginary pyramid is mechanics? If the task of theoretical physics is not to settle the nature of things; if it must be satisfied instead with description, with a systematic classification of phenomena, at least it is not restricted either in its methods or in the path that it may pursue. Here is no unilateral relationship of dependence as in the connection between "cause" and "effect"; no logical "earlier" or "later." On the contrary, pure correlation rules, whose simplest expression is to be found in the mathematical concept of "function." Once the physicist's idea of force has been recognized as merely a special case of the function concept, all necessity disappears of conceding to mechanical forces any sort of exceptional position and there is no need to treat the phenomena of motion as "better understood," or "simpler," than any other phenomena.

This line of thought could be pursued in two different directions according to the particular concept of knowledge and reality from which one started. Scientific phenomenalism takes it for granted first that all reality with which natural science has to do is nothing but

15. For other examples see Cassirer, *Das Erkenntnisproblem*, II, 404 ff.

sensory reality. The *esse est percipi*, "to exist is to be perceived," is here the obvious point of departure. What would be the relationship of physics to mechanics on this assumption, and if one explains accordingly that color, sound, heat, pressure, space, time, and so on, as immediately experienced by the senses, are the true and only objects of physics, whose task is consequently nothing else but studying the manifold ways in which these elementary data are associated? The answer to this question was what Mach set out to give in his theory of knowledge. This is strikingly apparent even in one of his earliest works, in which there was already a fully developed program that he consistently held to and extended in his later writings.[16] What distinguishes his analysis and lends it a special significance at the outset is the fact that it stressed emphatically the difference between the claim to give a causal interpretation of nature and the postulate of the mechanistic view. We have seen that the boundary line between these two questions was obliterated by Helmholtz as well as by Wundt, both of whom endeavored simply to derive the axioms of mechanics from the general principle of causality. The aim of Mach's inquiry was to show why any such attempt must remain forever fruitless. The law of causality demands nothing more than certainty and determinateness in what happens; it says nothing, however, about one realm of events being in principle of a higher order than all others. Hence it is absolutely impossible to prove that all strict and actual causality must be of mechanical nature.

If there is any proposition in physics directly connected with the general principle of causality, as representing in a measure a concrete expression of it, this very general proposition alone is the one in question, viz., that work cannot be obtained from nothing, and not the other proposition that all causes in nature are mechanical ones. This principle of the conservation of energy, that is to say, the conviction that so-called perpetual motion is impossible, must indeed be deeply rooted, for it can be shown to have colored the thought of mankind long before it was explicitly formulated by science. This fact Mach endeavored to prove by examples from the history of mechanics, especially by the way in which the law of the lever and the fundamental laws of hydrostatics were deduced and formulated by Archimedes and Stevinus.

At first glance it may appear very surprising that the whole argument should have then assumed a very different character—that its center of gravity should have shifted from the systematic to the his-

16. See the early lecture, *Die Geschichte und die Wurzel des Satzes von der Erhaltung der Arbeit* (Prag, J. G. Calve, 1872), S. 27.

torical problem. But Mach took this step with full awareness of its implications and without relinquishing in the least his general theoretical convictions. "There is a special classical education for the student of nature," he wrote, "which comprises a knowledge of the history of his science. Let us not lose track of the guiding hand of history. It has made everything and can change everything."

Here speaks an adherent of the modern theory of evolution, who is convinced that there can be no such thing as truth in itself. What a given proposition means and is, and how far it is objectively valid, can be determined only by tracing its origin and development. All truths, the logical and mathematical as well as the physical, have had their beginning and their growth, and none of them can advance the claim to be superior to and untouched by the stream of time as an "eternal truth." Every abstract theory has its roots in primitive and instinctive experiences which have forced themselves upon man in daily intercourse with his environment and which become more impressive throughout the centuries. From such beginnings, from the disappointment repeatedly suffered in consequence of attempts to get work out of nothing, man learned that perpetual motion is impossible. This persuasion cannot be grounded in mechanics, for it was felt long before the science had been developed. Tracing this sentiment and its origin back through history, we come to the real root of physical principles and discover at the same time why these principles have nothing to do with any sort of reflection on the nature and ultimate grounds of natural occurrences. Reflective thought and abstraction come only at the end, never at the beginning of science. They merely combine into formulas the precise results from thousands and thousands of single cases. Hence it is dangerous to base all physics on a mechanistic view and set this up as an axiom of the science. For whatever one may think of its value, it is a relatively late product after all, with no direct logical evidence in its favor, and it owes its plausibility to purely empirical, and to this extent accidental, factors. Mechanics is concerned with the physical world, that is, with what is given us in visible and tangible qualities, but we are not entitled, and nothing compels us, to give this series of qualities any privileged position in our cosmology. No such distinction is recognized in immediate experience, where qualities of all sorts intermingle and are seen to be indissolubly blended. There are other sensory perceptions entirely analogous with that of space, wrote Mach: the series of sounds, which corresponds to a space of one dimension. As a phenomenon it is exactly similar to the order of qualities that are seen or felt, and thus there is no reason, unless undemonstrable metaphysical assumptions are introduced, why it should not be given the same ontological value as the other. Yet we do not in fact think of everything as sound and represent molecular phenomena in terms of musical pitch or tonal relationships, though we have as much right to do so as to think of them in terms of space.[17]

The only safe course here is to remain within the ambit of appearances themselves and describe them simply as they present themselves, without seeking groundless explanations. Physics recognizes only the dependence of phenomena upon one another, and this can be established directly without any circuitous interpretations or hypothetical substratum. Even space and time require no special form of intuition for their defining; on the contrary, they can be reduced purely to determinations of content alone which in no way transcend sensory items like color, sound, and pressure.

As we recognize what we call time and space only through certain phenomena, spatial and temporal determinations are achieved only by way of other phenomena. When, for example, we express the positions of the heavenly bodies as functions of time, that is, of the earth's angle of rotation, we have merely found out that these positions depend upon one another . . . The same is true of space. We know the situation with respect to space through an effect on the retina, on our optical or other means of comparison, and actually the x, y, and z in the equations of physics are no more than convenient terms for these effects. Thus spatial determinations are also determinations of some phenomena through other phenomena. The present effort of physics is directed toward representing every phenomenon as a function of other phenomena and certain positions in time and space. If in the equations above we make substitutions in this fashion for the temporal and spatial positions we have the result simply that every phenomenon is a function of other phenomena.[18]

Here we reach the point of view that Mach later called phenomenological physics, in contrast to mechanistic physics.[19] The science seems to have entered upon a new phase in its theoretical development, a phase that has often been regarded not only as a significant step forward but as a final and conclusive one. Yet one opponent after another has appeared, even within physics itself. Noted investigators like Boltzmann and Planck have rejected it vigorously,

17. Mach, *loc. cit.*
18. *Ibid.,* S. 34 f.
19. Mach, "Der Gegensatz zwischen der mechanischen und der phänomenologischen Physik," *Die Prinzipien der Wärmelehre* (Leipzig, J. A. Barth, 1896), S. 362 ff.

seeing in it an unjustifiable restriction of the concept of physical knowledge.[20] It may be said however that in one respect the new interpretation far surpassed the views that had ruled physics for so long and influenced its whole development. Mach might well have boasted that his elimination of the metaphysical idea of matter had freed the science of a long series of imaginary problems. He explained that the only real constant in things is the set of definite equations or relations, so that if actual substantiality is to be ascribed to any element of experience it must be ascribed to these constant relations. But then it will be necessary to expel all the naïve ideas of matter with which this concept has been commonly associated throughout the history of physics.[21]

In the first half of the eighteenth century these naïve ideas had not yet lost any of their force. For every separate class of phenomena a special material agent was assumed, and the number of these "imponderables" increased more and more. In addition to material light and material heat, magnetic and electrical matter was recognized. The theory of electricity had to struggle longest with this sort of notion and reached full scientific stature only after it had taken strides forward to emancipate itself. Whereas Franklin believed that one highly tenuous substance, which is distributed throughout all nature, is responsible for electrical phenomena, it was necessary later to postulate two different substances of opposite polarity in order to reconcile the facts of positive and negative electricity. The conflict between the one-fluid and the two-fluid theory lasted for many years without either side realizing the hypothetical nature of the electrical substance.[22] Sir Oliver Lodge, for example, continued to ascribe complete physical reality to it. Electrical waves, he declared, must be "waves of something," and the existence of this something was as certain as that of any physical object. "The evidence for the ether is as strong as the evidence for the air." [23]

It was this sort of thinking that Mach opposed so incessantly, hoping to strike it down by his criticism, but he was thereby driven far beyond his proper methodological goal, for his theory of knowledge recognized only one dimension of reality, that of the simple data

---

20. L. Boltzmann, "Über die Unentbehrlichkeit der Atomistik in der Naturwissenschaft," *Populäre Schriften* (Leipzig, J. A. Barth, 1905), S. 141 ff. Planck, "Die Einheit des physikalischen Weltbildes," *op. cit.,* S. 1 ff.

21. Mach, "Der Substanzbegriff," *op. cit.,* S. 422 ff.

22. For details see Rosenberger, *Die moderne Entwicklung der elektrischen Prinzipien* (Leipzig, 1898).

23. O. Lodge, *The Ether of Space* (London and New York, Harper & Bros., 1909), pp. 17 ff.

of the senses such as colors, sounds, odors, and so on. These were the essential components out of which reality is built, and behind these elements no others were to be sought. Thus all that went beyond the establishment of sensory facts incurred the suspicion of "transcendence," and a sharp dividing line could no longer be drawn between the assumptions of physical theory and those of metaphysics. The obliteration of this boundary, especially striking in Mach's criticism of atomic theory, robbed his opinion of the greater part of its fertility. Boltzmann [24] rightly objected that he had not protested in the name of metaphysics or speculative natural philosophy against the restriction demanded by such phenomenological physics, but in the name of mathematics. As a matter of fact it was an extraordinary blunder, from an epistemological as well as a historical standpoint, for Mach to call modern atomic theory an attempt "to make a notion as thoroughly naïve and crude as that which holds matter to be absolutely unchanging the fundamental tenet of physics." [25] Even the atomism of antiquity was far removed from such naïveté, since it was in fact a sharp criticism of sense perception upon which this atomism was based and which was its starting point.[26]

Mach's restriction of phenomenological physics could be the more easily overlooked, however, since in other respects it was undeniably characterized by great methodological fertility. It freed physics of the burden of imponderables and limited its task to a knowledge of the laws associated with natural events. It did not have to depend upon definite ideas of substance for an exact formulation of these laws: the permanence of relations replaced the permanence of matter. In this connection the discovery of the principle of conservation of energy was an important circumstance; furthermore, in a purely methodological respect it represented a turning point in physical theory. Whereas Humboldt still continued to associate this principle directly with the mechanistic view of nature and endeavored to deduce it therefrom, Robert Mayer chose another path. He saw in the equivalence between heat and mechanical energy the nucleus of the principle, but had no intention of interpreting that as an identity. He wanted explicitly to leave out of consideration any question as to the nature of heat. All that is known with certainty,

24. L. Boltzmann, "Ein Wort der Mathematik an die Energetik," *Populäre Schriften*, S. 104 ff.

25. Mach, *op. cit.*, S. 428.

26. On the epistemological assumptions in the atomism of antiquity see P. Natorp, "Demokrit," *Forschungen zur Geschichte des Erkenntnisproblems im Altertum* (Berlin, W. Hertz, 1884), S. 164 ff.

he believed, is merely that heat, motion, and kinetic energy can be converted one into the other in conformity with fixed numerical relationships; but there was reluctance to infer from this that kinetic energy and motion are identical, and no less reluctance in drawing a similar conclusion for heat. Thus Mayer was well justified in distinguishing sharply between his theory and all hypotheses of natural philosophy. "It would certainly have to be called a backward step," he wrote, "if an attempt were to be made to construct a world a priori. But when one has succeeded in connecting the innumerable events of nature with each other and deriving a supreme principle therefrom, then it is no ground for reproach if, after this has been carefully tested, it is used as a sort of compass to guide the investigator safely forth on the sea of particulars." [27]

These remarks by a discoverer of the law of conservation of energy foreshadow clearly and precisely the trend of philosophical thought that was later to bring the new science of energetics into general recognition and acceptance. At first glance the vehemence of its struggle with mechanics during the last decades of the nineteenth century is astonishing, for when the law of the conservation of energy is considered only as to content it is found to hold nothing that would fall outside the views of mechanics or radically contradict them. This, the first law of thermodynamics, did not constitute the same difficulty for the mechanical view of nature as was the case with the second law and the idea of irreversible phenomena which followed from it. Historically, too, the law of the conservation of energy developed out of the principle of the conservation of kinetic energy as formulated in mechanics by Huyghens and Leibniz. Thus there was no real opposition between the assertions of energetics and those of mechanics, and it would have been just as reasonable to make the law of the conservation of energy supreme and deduce from it the mechanical axioms of the conservation of energy as, conversely, to make the mechanical view a basis for deducing the law of the conservation of energy. Planck chose the former course, expressly emphasizing, however, that the rights of the second were by no means to be gainsaid thereby.[28]

But toward the end of the century the situation underwent a complete change. After Ostwald's lecture at Lübeck in 1895,[29] the con-

27. R. Mayer, "Die organische Bewegung in ihrem Zusammenhange mit dem Stoffwechsel," *Die Mechanik der Wärme,* Zwei Abhandlungen (Leipzig, W. Engelmann, 1911), S. 9 ff.

28. M. Planck, *Das Prinzip der Erhaltung der Energie* (Leipzig, B. G. Teubner, 1887), S. 135 ff.

29. W. Ostwald, *Die Überwindung des wissenschaftlichen Materialismus* (Leipzig, Veit & Co., 1895).

flict between mechanics and energetics was waged with a vigor that seemed to exclude any chance of reconciliation between these two fundamental views. Both parties believed not only that they were in possession of scientific truth but that they were defending the only possible and solely justifiable concept of science.

"In the Lübeck controversy of 1895," says Georg Helm, who described thoroughly all its various phases,

the question was not really about atomism or about the plenum or about discrepancies in thermodynamics or about the grounding of mechanics upon energetics, for these were all mere details. In the final analysis it was about the principles of our knowledge of nature. Opposing the omnipotence claimed by the mechanistic method of reproducing experience there appears a new procedure that allows of far more immediate description yet at the same time attains the generality of concept which is indispensable for every useful theoretical interpretation of nature. If one regards energetics as having such a broad scope (and that is the only way one can do justice to what it is trying to do), the decision is easy. The choice is simply between scholasticism on the one hand and energetics on the other.[30]

Not since the controversies over the validity of Newton's idea of force acting at a distance had minds been so engaged and agitated by a dispute over method. The very manner in which the battle was waged makes it clear that it was not primarily concerned with empirical results, since there was no difference of opinion between the two sides in respect to the authenticity and fundamental significance of the law of conservation of energy. Instead there was the feeling in both camps, just as in the polemic between Leibniz and Newton, that it was again a matter of principle; the argument was over definitions of the concept and the task of scientific knowledge.

There were prominent investigators who took their stand with classical mechanics, and who were convinced like Huyghens that one must either explain a phenomenon on mechanical grounds or abandon once for all any hope of understanding it. Energetics made this mode of apprehension wholly inadequate and inadmissible. Ostwald's lecture on the conquest of scientific materialism introduced a real iconoclasm, whose first commandment was: "Thou shalt not make unto thee any graven image, or any likeness of anything. . . ."[31]

In order to understand this opposition it is necessary to go back to its roots in the theory of knowledge. The conflict was essentially between two different motives, each one indispensable in the construction of the edifice of scientific knowledge. The exclusion of either was not to be thought of, though there was room for argument as to which should be accorded the central position and real supremacy. At times the concept of space, at other times the concept of number, took the lead. Galileo said that truth lies open before us in the great book of nature, but that only those can find it who are familiar with the characters in which it is inscribed. These are of a geometrical kind: lines and angles, triangles, circles, and other figures. No natural process can be understood unless it can be expressed geometrically. In modern philosophy this ideal of knowledge had received its logical justification. In Descartes it was the idea of extension that possessed the character, above all other ideas, of being clear and distinct. The physical object must be completely reducible to spatial determinations if any exact knowledge of it is ever to become possible. Matter was thus transformed and taken up into space, and all changes in it had to be traced back to purely spatial changes. Geometry and mechanics were accordingly declared the true and only foundation for physics, an idea that remained in almost full force until the middle of the nineteenth century. Then, however, an intellectual movement set in that may be compared in a way with the arithmetization of mathematics, which occurred at the same time.[32] The center of gravity of theoretical scientific knowledge began to shift, number taking the position formerly conceded to space, which made the previous mechanistic schemata of doubtful value. Ought it not to be possible to determine natural phenomena mathematically without such schemata and thus to gain a rigorous knowledge of them? Robert Mayer had already asked this question and answered it in the affirmative. He explained that it was enough to connect the different natural processes with one another without changing them qualitatively and thus abolishing their obvious dissimilarities, but yet in such a way that the connection would be subject to general quantitative rules and that the transition from one province to another would occur always according to fixed and constant numerical relationships. The ascertaining of these numerical equivalents would then be the sole aim of the empirical interpretation of nature, and all beyond that would be at best only a work of supererogation. Once strict numerical relationships have been discovered between the various classes of natural phenomena, all that can be expected and demanded of knowledge has been attained, and over and above this we cannot go. "Precise delimitation of the natural

32. See above, Chap. IV, p. 59.

limits of human inquiry is an end that has practical value for science, whereas the attempt to penetrate by hypotheses to the inner recesses of the world order is of a piece with the efforts of the alchemists." All our reliable and established knowledge of natural events is contained in our mathematical knowledge: "One single number has more real and permanent value than an expensive library of hypotheses." [33]

In its further advance energetics held to this view and endeavored consistently to broaden it. With Rankine, who was the first to speak of a science of energetics, its development from the standpoint of the theory of knowledge was already in view. He emphasized that research in physics could set up a twofold goal and strike out into one of two paths. Either it could try to get behind events and discover their underlying substratum or remain content with a classification of appearances in order to determine solely their common factors and the fixed relationships between them. The second plan appeared preferable from a methodological standpoint, since it did not involve the necessity of leaving the firm ground of experience and introducing assumptions that could not be proved. Instead of attributing the various kinds of physical phenomena to motions and forces no instances of which are ever given but which are merely inferred, it would suffice to stop at simple comparison and eventually reach principles that hold equally for all cases and so represent the ultimate discoverable relationship between facts.[34] In such statements Rankine had no intention of disputing the mechanistic view of nature as a whole; indeed he himself even set up a definitely mechanistic hypothesis on the intrinsic nature of bodies.[35] But though he did not deny himself such hypotheses, he wanted to define their limits more sharply than they had been set in the past. The later development went far beyond this view, and it was thought finally possible to build up a natural science which would be wholly free of hypotheses. But not all the proponents of energetics could hold strictly to this position. Helm rejected with decision the idea that energy is an indestructible substance shifting from place to place and declared such a notion entirely useless and unwarranted,

---

33. R. Mayer, "Mayer an Griesinger," *Kleinere Schriften und Briefe* (Stuttgart, J. G. Cotta'schen Buchhandlung, 1893), S. 222 ff.

34. W. J. M. Rankine, "Outlines of the Science of Energetics," *Miscellaneous Scientific Papers, Proceedings of the Philosophical Society of Glasgow,* III (London, C. Griffin & Co., 1881), No. 4 (1855), 209.

35. For details see Helm, *op. cit.,* S. 110 ff.

For Rankine's place in the history of energetics see A. Rey, "L'Energetique de Rankine," *La Théorie de la physique chez les physiciens contemporains* (Paris, F. Alcan, 1907), II, chap. i, 49 ff.

since energy is never more than an expression of relationships. "For general theoretical physics," he emphatically stated,

there exist neither atoms, nor energy, nor any kind of similar concept, but only those experiences immediately derived from direct observation. Therefore I believe the most valuable feature of energetics to be that it is far better able than the older theories to adapt itself straightway to experience and I see in attempts to attribute substantial existence to energy a hazardous departure from the original clarity of Robert Mayer's views.[36]

But other noted champions of energetics were much less cautious here. Ostwald often spoke of energy as though it were to be taken not only as *an* actuality but as *the* actuality, the thing of things and the source of all dynamic effect. Even in this respect he would not place it over matter, of which we never have a direct but only an indirect knowledge, whereas of energy we have direct perception.

What we hear originates in work done on the ear drum and the middle ear by vibrations of the air. What we see is only radiant energy, which does chemical work on the retina that is perceived as light. When we touch a solid body we experience mechanical work performed during compression of our finger tips and, in suitable cases, of the solid body itself . . . From this standpoint the totality of nature appears as a series of spatially and temporally changing energies, of which we obtain knowledge in proportion as they impinge upon the body and especially upon the sense organs fashioned for the reception of the appropriate energies.[37]

In our representation of the role of energetics and phenomenological physics as a whole in the theory of knowledge of the nineteenth century there appear, apart from differences among individual thinkers in developing their fundamental ideas, some positive accomplishments and also some obvious limitations in them. The fruitfulness of the movement lay, above all, in resolutely dispensing with all ontological elements in physics. The metaphysical idea of substance was attacked in all its various forms, and the scientific object was resolved into a system of relations and functional connections.[38] In this respect J. B. Stallo's book, *The Concepts and Theories of Modern Physics*, published in 1881, was of special importance. The German edition was introduced with a preface by

36. Helm, *op. cit.*, S. 362.
37. Ostwald, *Vorlesungen über Naturphilosophie* (Leipzig, Veit & Co., 1902), S. 159 f.
38. For details see Cassirer, *Substanzbegriff und Funktionsbegriff*, chap. iv.

Mach, who praised the work because it had recognized and definitely removed the scholastic, metaphysical elements that still clung to the older physics.[39] Of course Stallo did not stop here, but on the strength of his theoretical convictions furiously attacked certain empirical theories besides, such as the kinetic theory of gases and the entire theory of the atomic constitution of matter, professing to see even in these nothing but a hidden metaphysics. This onslaught was possible only because Stallo had slipped imperceptibly from logical criticism of the concept of substance to an entirely different problem. In his attempt to be a consistent empiricist he became a psychologist who strove to confine physics to the realm of "phenomena of consciousness." His own thesis of the relativity of all knowledge attained thereby a wholly different character. The proposition that "objects and their properties are known only as functions of other objects and properties," and that in this sense relativity is necessarily predicated of all objects of knowledge, was transformed into this other, quite distinct, proposition, that what is present in the mind in the act of thinking is never a thing but always a state of consciousness, and so, in the final analysis, even physics has to do only with the description and classification of such states of consciousness.[40] This psychologism is the hereditary malady, so to speak, of all "phenomenological physics": the phenomenon, in the sense of the object of physical knowledge, is resolved into a series of elements and states of consciousness.

There was nothing original in the idea that an object is nothing absolute but consists entirely of relationships: The *Critique of Pure Reason* had enforced the point again and again and with the strongest possible emphasis. "Matter," said Kant,

is *substantia phaenomenon*. Whatever is intrinsic to it I seek in all parts of the space that it occupies and in all effects that it exerts, which, after all, can never be anything but phenomena of the outer sense. Thus I have nothing absolute but merely something comparatively internal which, in its turn, consists only of external relationships. But what appears to the mere understanding as the absolute essence of matter is again simply a fancy, for matter is never an object of pure understanding; but the transcendental object that may be the ground of this appearance called matter is a bare Something, whose nature we should never be able to understand even though someone could tell us about it. . . . The observation and analysis of phenomena press toward a knowledge of the se-

39. J. B. Stallo, *Die Begriffe und Theorien der modernen Physik* (Leipzig, J. A. Barth, 1911), S. xii.

40. Stallo, *ibid.*, Kap. ix, S. 126 ff.

crets of nature and there is no knowing how far they may penetrate in time. But for all that we shall never succeed in answering those transcendental questions that reach out beyond nature, though all nature were to be revealed to our gaze.[41]

In respect to the exclusion of these transcendental questions, phenomenalistic physics took exactly the same position as the critical philosophy of Kant. The difference between them is not the thesis of the relativity of knowledge but the way in which physics seeks to establish this thesis. The foundations of the phenomenalism ultimately go back not to the logic of physics but to anthropological and psychological considerations, which appeared to demand that what we call an object of knowledge be reducible to an aggregate of simple sense data, a mere "bundle of perceptions." For Kant, however, the object, even when understood as object of "appearance," was never such a "rhapsody of perceptions." It depended rather upon a "synthesis" into which the pure concepts of the understanding entered as necessary conditions.

But in trying to eliminate even these conditioning factors and to make of physical experience a mass of sense data, the chief defenders of energetics became more and more deeply involved in contradictions. The underlying reason was that Mach and other champions of energetics, while attacking mechanism in physics, still remained wholly in bondage to its assumptions so far as their psychology was concerned. It was and remained a psychology of elements. It was only Gestalt psychology that caused any change in this respect, by virtue of the concept of "wholeness" (*Ganzheit*), which when it gained acceptance in physics as well as in psychology placed the two sciences in a new relationship.[42] Before this clarification came to pass the phenomenalistic view was in constant peril of being limited by its sensationalistic concept of physical knowledge. This danger was especially apparent in criticisms of the atomic idea, which was regarded with the most profound distrust at best as a purely fictitious and auxiliary hypothesis that must be dispensed with as speedily as possible once its service had been rendered. The escape from such a narrow sensationalistic system was not due to considerations of the theory of knowledge but to imperative demands from within physics itself. The wholly empirical proofs of atomism eventually broke down the last stronghold; they had been accumu-

41. Kant, *Kritik der reinen Vernunft* (2. Aufl.), S. 333 f.
42. See Wolfgang Köhler, *Die physischen Gestalten in Ruhe und im stationären Zustand* (Braunschweig, Philosophische Akademie Erlangen, 1924).

lating one after the other—Boltzmann's establishment of the kinetic theory of gases, the investigations on Brownian movement, Helmholtz' proof of the atomic nature of electricity, and Laue's discovery of crystal diffraction. Even Ostwald, who had been the most active champion of the battle against atomism, had to give up in the end, declaring that experimental proof of the atomic structure of matter had at last been attained.[43]

But although such a transition from "hypothesis" to rigorous physical "theory" had been possible, the relation of hypothesis to theory had to be examined anew from a purely epistemological standpoint and the connection between the two more firmly established. The purely abstract features encountered everywhere in physics throughout its development could not be treated merely as convenient experiments; they had to be recognized and confirmed in their distinctive character. Even when one continued to speak of the fundamental concepts of theoretical physics as symbols, in order to avoid from the first any danger of ontological interpretation, there was a necessity of attributing to these very symbols themselves a theoretical meaning and therewith an "objective" content. Far from being merely arbitrary additions to what was given by direct observation they became essential factors with which alone an organization of the given, the fusion of the isolated details into the system of experience, was possible.

The first great physicist actually to complete this turn of affairs and at the same time to grasp the full measure of its philosophical implications, was Heinrich Hertz, with whom began a new phase in the theory of physical methods. In order to understand the change and assign to it its rightful place in the history of physical thought, one should really examine it in connection with Hertz's experimental investigations. In his *Researches on the Propagation of Electrical Force* he had applied himself to the testing of Maxwell's theory of light. He succeeded in producing experimentally the electromagnetic waves that Maxwell had described in theory, and demonstrated that they possess all the known properties of light, such as reflection, refraction, interference, and so on. Thus the question of the nature of light, which had occupied physical speculation for so long and given rise to two opposing theories—the wave theory and the emission theory—was clarified. The electromagnetic theory, according to which electrical waves differ from heat and light waves only in their length, was speeded on its way to final victory.

43. W. Ostwald, *Grundrisse der allgemeinen Chemie* (4. Aufl. 1909).

But it might have been argued that one riddle had merely been substituted for another, since the nature of electromagnetic phenomena was no more easy to understand than that of optical phenomena. An objection like this can be disposed of only by proving that it contains a significant misunderstanding of the meaning and purpose of a physical theory.[44] It was such a challenge, no doubt, that led Hertz to the reflections later set down with systematic rigor in the introduction to his work *The Principles of Mechanics*. Maxwell himself, still feeling the need of a mechanistic statement and interpretation of his theory, had successively constructed a number of entirely different models of the ether.[45] But Hertz no longer asked which of these was the "right" one. He declared that Maxwell's electromagnetic theory of light was nothing but the system of Maxwellian differential equations, and that no objective content need be sought in it over and above that already expressed there.[46] When we can develop deductively determined consequences from Maxwell's theory and find them verified by experiment, said Hertz, then the proof of its validity is furnished and no more is possible, nor is there any point in trying to achieve more. This view is fully presented and justified in the following preliminary observation:

It is the first and, in a way, the most important task of natural science to enable us to predict future experience so that we may direct our present activities accordingly. . . . But our procedure in deriving the future from the past, and thus achieving the desired foresight, is always this: We set up subjective pictures or symbols of the external objects, and of such a type that their intellectually necessary consequences are invariably symbols again of the necessary consequences in nature of the objects pictured . . . Once we have succeeded in deriving symbols of the desired kind from the totality of past experience we can develop from them in a short time, as from models, consequences that would appear in the external world only after a long time, or as a result of our own manipulations . . . The symbols of which we speak are our ideas of things; with these objects they have one essential conformity, which lies in fulfillment of the practical demand we have mentioned above, but it is not necessary to their purpose that they have any further sort of resemblance to things. In fact we do not even know and have no way of discov-

44. Planck, *Das Wesen des Lichts* (2. unveränd. Aufl. Berlin, J. Springer, 1920).

45. See Poincaré, "La Théorie de Maxwell et les oscillations Hertziennes," *Scientia* (November, 1907).

46. H. Hertz, *Untersuchungen über die Ausbreitung der elektrischen Kraft* (Leipzig, J. A. Barth, 1892), S. 23.

ering whether our ideas correspond with objects in any other way than just this one fundamental relationship.[47]

At first glance these remarks seem to contain nothing different from and to prove no more than what had been emphasized by phenomenological physics in its various aspects. They appear to confirm Mach's theory, that transformation and adaptation are an integral part of all scientific thinking. By adaptation to relationships in the external world certain ideas take form in the mind, and each fresh experience adds a new feature until finally a more complete correspondence is achieved between these ideas and external phenomena.[48] Upon closer examination, however, it turns out that the concept of symbols is employed by Hertz in quite another sense, and that it has a function to fulfill in the construction of physical theory that is entirely different from the one assigned by Mach. For the latter, the "reality" that the physicist has to describe is only the sum of simple sense data: sounds, colors, smells, tastes. Theory accordingly will better accomplish its task the more completely it succeeds in conforming to these data and expressing them simply as they exist, without arbitrary changes or addition. Even the general propositions of a theory can serve no other purpose. They always refer ultimately to an individual in the Aristotelian sense; they point to individual facts and endeavor to express them in all their concrete precision, in their *here* and *now*. They cannot, of course, dispense with general terms, but these are only convenient mnemonics, providing the dissimilar and the complex with one linguistic sign and so making it more easily reproducible. Hence wherever general concepts or principles are encountered in a physical theory they are but convenient devices for expression.[49]

Because the capacity to comprehend and remember details is limited, the material must be arranged in order. For instance, if we knew for every period of time the space traversed by a falling body we might be well content. But what a prodigious memory it would take to carry the pertinent table of s and t in our heads! Instead of so doing we employ the formula $s = \dfrac{gt^2}{2}$, that is to say, the principle by which we can find

47. Hertz, *Die Prinzipien der Mechanik in neuem Zusammenhange dargestellt* (Leipzig, J. A. Barth, 1894), S. 1 f.
48. Mach, "Über Umbildung und Anpassung im naturwissenschaftlichen Denken," *Populär-wissenschaftliche Vorlesungen* (3. verm. und durchges. Aufl. Leipzig, J. A. Barth, 1903), Kap. xiv, S. 243 ff.
49. Mach, "Die ökonomische Natur der physikalischen Forschung," *Populär-wissenschaftliche Vorlesungen,* Kap. xiii, S. 215 ff.

the appropriate s for any given t, and this provides a complete, convenient, and compendious substitute for the table. This principle, this formula, this "law" has not one iota more of factual value than the isolated facts taken together, its worth lying merely in its convenience. It has utilitarian value.[50]

As an empiricist Hertz was certainly not inferior to Mach, as the whole nature and tenor of his research shows, and for him too there was not the slightest doubt that every idea employed by physical theory would eventually have to be confirmed by concrete observation. But he was convinced that not every single element of a theory is susceptible or in need of such verification. This is only necessary for the whole; for an entire system of theoretical propositions. Thinking was thereby given an entirely different significance and assured of a much wider scope than in Mach's doctrine, which held that the validity of any definite idea can be proved only when it is identified as a copy of a definite "impression." The fundamental concepts of physics, according to Mach, are the product of and the passive impressions left by the effects of objects upon the sense organs, whereas for Hertz they are the expression of a highly complex intellectual process—a process in which theorizing holds full sway in order to attain to its goal through experience and therein to find confirmation or justification. Accordingly Hertz held fast to the possibility and necessity of a "pure natural science" in the sense of Kant—an idea that Mach and the phenomenalistic physics which he represented could only reject with horror.

Hertz begins with an entirely free sketch of thinking, with a comprehensive system of physical concepts and axioms which are introduced at first as pure hypotheses only in order to compare their consequences with the concrete facts of reality. "Experience remains wholly foreign to the considerations in the first book," he wrote regarding the definitions of time, space, and mass with which he prefaced his system of mechanics. "All the statements there set down are a priori judgments in the sense of Kant. They rest on the laws of inner intuition and forms of the inner logic of the person stating them, and have no connection with his external experience other than these intuitions and forms may have with it." [51] Thus for Hertz the fundamental concepts of theoretical physics were patterns of possible experiences, whereas for Mach they were copies of actual experiences.

50. Mach, *Die Geschichte und die Wurzel des Satzes von der Erhaltung der Arbeit*, S. 31.
51. Hertz, *op. cit.*, S. 53.

The logic of physics received herewith a new and highly characteristic form. Above all it appeared that fundamental concepts are not established from the first with entire precision but may vary freely within certain limits. Hertz undertook an audacious alteration in the system of classical mechanics when he ventured to banish its central and basic idea and substitute other abstract definitions for it. Classical mechanics, whose various stages of development are signalized by the names of Archimedes, Galileo, Newton, and Lagrange, was founded upon the ideas of space, time, force, and mass, with force introduced as the antecedent and independent cause of motion. The complete system seemed wholly to satisfy all possible demands for logical rigor, and from its basic concepts the principles and laws of motion were strictly deduced in perfect order. Yet more exacting criticism was able to discern certain difficulties and inconsistencies that could not be removed within the confines of the system. These logical discrepancies justified and encouraged the attempt to carry out the reform that was proving more and more urgently necessary, not only in regard to details but respecting the whole system itself. Then investigators were led to that second representation of mechanical events that set up energetics in place of the Newtonian system. The start was made here also from four independent basic concepts, whose relations to one another were supposed to form the content of mechanics. Two of them, space and time, are mathematical in character while the other two, mass and energy, were introduced as physical realities that are present in given amounts, indestructible, and not susceptible of increase. The idea of force did not appear among these elements but was brought in, if at all, as a mathematical artifact and somewhat as though it were a simplification or an ancillary item that was unnecessary though it might prove convenient. But even this system, Hertz meant to show in detail, was not absolutely satisfactory and had certain serious flaws. Thus the way was open for his real task, which was to prove that besides the system of Newton and that of energetics there was possible a third constructive view of the principles of mechanics. This differed radically from the others in starting with only three independent basic concepts: time, space, and mass. This "third picture" allowed, as the work of Hertz demonstrated, a thoroughly consistent development of all the fundamental laws established by classical mechanics. It could not conflict with any of the basic phenomena and therefore was just as "true" as either of the first two representations. But it was more satisfactory and more to the point because it had definite methodological advantages in so far as it contained, in addition to the essential features, a smaller number of relations that were supernumerary or without any content and thus as a whole it was simpler.[52]

Through this attitude, expressed in his *Principles of Mechanics*, Hertz originated a demand that went far beyond the problems in question. The task of physical theory was now posed in another way. In the view represented by Mach and Ostwald the relation of physical theory to physical facts had hardly yet become a problem. Theory was defined merely as an adaptation to facts and hence as a simple reproduction of them. Accordingly a physical law or principle had no independent cognitive value comparable to that of immediate perception, and certainly none above it. It merely repeated in abridged form, as a convenient verbal summary, the knowledge that perception furnished directly, and consequently better and more faithfully. A law is no more than a catalogue of isolated facts, a principle no more than a register of laws. The implication of this was the strange corollary that the necessity of thinking in general concepts and laws did not represent a special virtue of the human mind but actually originated in its weakness. An intellect broad and inclusive enough to grasp all details as details would require no such roundabout method—nor would there be any "science" for it. "If all single facts, all separate phenomena, were as directly accessible to us as we demand that knowledge of them be," Mach expressly declared, "science never would have arisen." [53]

If physical theory had actually no aim other than to describe definite, individual facts as faithfully as possible, it would have to be confessed that so far it had accomplished this task very poorly, for even in its most important theorems it not only turns its back upon these facts but directs its gaze upon something "that has never occurred." The law of inertia proposes to describe the motion of a body that is not acted upon by any external forces, though the assumption that such a condition is ever realized in nature is absurd. Whence this urge to pass from considerations of the real to considerations of the unreal, even of the impossible? Is there any sense in entertaining such notions as that of an "ideal gas," or a "perfectly black body," when we are aware that these correspond with no empirical facts? Mach's theory actually did not dispute the right to introduce ideal elements like these into physics, for they form an integrating part in the "experimental thinking" without which physics, as Mach emphasized, cannot complete its edifice.[54] Yet from the stand-

---

52. Hertz, Einleitung, *op. cit.,* § 1–3, S. 5 ff.

53. Mach, *op. cit.,* S. 31 f.

54. Mach, "Über Gedankenexperimente," *Erkenntnis und Irrtum* (Leipzig, J. A. Barth, 1905), S. 180 ff.

point of his general theory of knowledge it is doubtful in the extreme whether experimenting with mere thoughts of things rather than with the things themselves is ever justifiable.

The Hertzian system of mechanics represents experiment of this sort in the grand manner, for it resolved upon a free variation of the basic concepts of mechanics in which even its once fundamental idea, the idea of force, was sacrificed. The spontaneity inherent in all theory was herewith brought out into clear view. To be sure, the freedom was not to be unbridled license, for a theory can be proved valid only through the fact that its inferences lead to results that correspond with experience. But it was shown that no single component of any theory of nature, such as the idea of force or that of mass, can be separated out in order to seek an objective correlate for it and thence to decide as to its validity and truth. The process of verification was proved to be much more complex. It was no longer demanded of the single concepts hypothetically set up in a theory that they should reproduce concrete and empirically demonstrable facts; their part was really performed when it could be shown that in their totality, in their mutual interrelations, they represented a symbol of reality in such a way that "their intellectually necessary consequences" would always be "symbols of the necessary consequences in nature of the objects represented."

A continuation and development of this train of thought is to be found in Poincaré's investigation of the nature of scientific concepts and hypotheses.[55] Here the problem was broadened in so far as it related directly to Poincaré's interpretation of the meaning of mathematical hypotheses. In respect to the non-Euclidean geometries he wished to show that in establishing a system of mathematical axioms we are not bound to experience, in the sense that we can draw from experience a decision as to which of the various systems, all equally possible from the standpoint of logic, corresponds to "real" space. Experience is unable to give such a decision, and accordingly the "truth" of any one geometry cannot depend upon it. No geometry is "truer" than another, though one may be more suited to the purpose of experience or, in other words, prove a more useful instrument for a systematic description of its given facts.[56]

But this freedom in forming ideas and hypotheses, according to Poincaré, does not stop with mathematics. It must be extended to physics in so far as this science, in the form of theoretical physics, makes use of mathematics and so actually becomes the same type of

55. H. Poincaré, *La Science et l'hypothèse* (1902); *Science et méthode* (1909); *La Valeur de la science* (Paris, E. Flammarion, 1905).
56. See above, pp. 43 f.

knowledge. The "scientific fact" of physics differs from "brute fact" precisely in this respect, that it is not limited to the information from perception but expresses the data in the new language of mathematical symbols. Only so is a transition from one kind of fact to the other made possible.[57] This reasoning shows how the axioms of physics are connected with the world of facts; no one axiom can be asserted to be in itself the simple description of any isolated fact given in experience. That every physical principle owes its establishment to the stimulation which we have received from experience is true beyond all question, but the universality attributed to the principle can never be derived from experience alone. The raising of any principle to universality is always a free act of scientific thought. In this fundamental point of view Poincaré agrees with what Hertz said, that the symbols we construct for ourselves of external objects not only depend upon the nature of these objects but owe their form to "the inner logic of the one making the assertion." This logic calls for another and closer connection between phenomena than what meets us immediately in observation. It teaches us that we must reconstruct the conditioned assertions, which are all that we are entitled to make on the ground of observation, in such fashion that they take on the character of absolutely universal and to that extent unconditioned assertions. According to Poincaré this reconstruction is the truly basic feature in the formation of all physical theory, and it has become more and more apparent in the modern development of the science.

The older physics was for the most part a physics of symbols in *this* sense: it tried to represent the nature of every object or event investigated in a corresponding mechanical model, whose single items passed as replicas of the details and properties of the object. Modern physics has increasingly renounced this procedure, and from a physics of literal pictures has become a physics of principles. Its development in the nineteenth century was signalized by the discovery and precise formulation of several principles, such as Carnot's principle, the principle of the conservation of energy, the principle of least action, and so on. A principle is neither a mere synopsis of facts nor solely an epitomization of single laws. It contains in its meaning the claim of "always and universally," which experience as such is never warranted in making. Instead of deriving a principle directly from experience we use it as a criterion of experience. Principles constitute the fixed points of the compass that are required for

57. For further details see Poincaré, *La Valeur de la science,* troisième partie, chap. x, § 3, p. 221 ff.

successful orientation in the world of phenomena. They are not so much assertions about empirical facts as maxims by which we interpret these facts in order to bring them together into a complete and coherent whole.

Poincaré insisted that the selection of these reference points is not imposed on us by objects but originates in the free choice of theoretical thinking, though he definitely refuted the extreme nominalistic and skeptical conclusions that many followers wished to draw from his premises.[58] Freedom in the construction of physical hypotheses and theories is not caprice, in his opinion, for the relationships expressed in them are subject to constant verification by experience and are confirmed in their objective validity by it. Only the language of physical theories and the symbols applied to experience proved to be variable factors, but this changeableness does not exclude the continuity and the logical coherence of these theories; on the contrary it turns out to be a means of actually keeping them intact.

This symbolic character of all physical knowledge was emphasized by Duhem even more strongly than by Hertz or Poincaré himself. Duhem thought it pure theoretical naïveté to believe that even a single proposition made in physics can be regarded as describing a result of direct observation. No judgment in theoretical physics ever relates directly to those "elements" in which Mach, in his "phenomenological physics," saw the essence and meaning of all reality. Duhem's criticism of this interpretation is more searching than that of either Hertz or Poincaré, for he proceeds on the assumption that if physical sensationism is ever to be displaced the lever should be applied more fundamentally. What the Machian system could not adequately explain was not primarily the general principles but rather the particular statements of physics. Between the two types of assertion there is not the wide gap ordinarily assumed. They are inseparably bound together and in some measure have an ultimate solidarity. As far as meaning and truth value are concerned, the judgment of fact cannot be divorced from that of principle, for there is not a single factual conclusion that does not contain an implicit assertion of principle. Every judgment concerning an individual case, in so far as it purports to be a proposition in physics, already includes a *whole system* of physics. It is not true, therefore, that the science consists of two strata, as it were: simple observation and the results of measurement being in the one, theories built upon these in the other. Observation and measurement prior to all theory,

58. See especially *La Valeur de la science*, p. 213 ff.

and independent of its assumptions, are impossible. Nothing of the sort is ever given as a fact; it is rather a theoretical abstraction which upon critical analysis turns out at once to be pure illusion.

The distinction between "brute fact" and "scientific fact" was drawn still more rigorously by Duhem than by Poincaré. Between the two there is a difference not only in degree but actually in kind. No physical proposition, be it ever so simple, is to be understood merely as a sum of observed facts, an aggregate of such observations as are carried out in everyday life. On the contrary, ordinary observations and those of physics move on entirely different planes and belong therefore in wholly different spheres. When a physicist imparts the results of an experiment undertaken to discover or test a definite law of nature, he cannot give them in the form that he would employ in presenting the series of sense impressions received during the course of his experiment. The latter would be a psychological report but in no way a presentation of his experimental findings. The scientific statement would not describe the ocular, auditory, or tactile sensations of an individual observer in a particular physical laboratory but would state an objective fact of quite another sort—a fact that could be made known, of course, only if an appropriate language, a system of definite symbols, had been created for its communication. What is told is not that while making his readings the observer suddenly noticed one or another sensation within himself, but that an electric current of given intensity passed through a magnetic field, or that the pressure, volume, and temperature of a gas varied in this way or that under certain experimental conditions. In order to understand the meaning of this evidence, in order to define exactly what an electric current is, or pressure, volume, or temperature, mere reference to the data of simple observation is never adequate. On the contrary, it is realized upon closer examination that the very use of such terms involves highly complex theoretical assumptions, and that a whole system of physical judgments is therefore implied. Every time instruments of measurement are employed there is presupposed a theoretical designation of the phenomena in terms of such judgments. In order to give a strict explanation of what is meant by the *volume* or the *pressure* of a gas it is necessary to go back not only to the principles of arithmetic and geometry, but to the axioms of general mechanics as well as to the most abstruse theories of hydrostatics, electricity, and so on. "What a physicist gives as the outcome of an experiment is not a report on the isolated facts that he has ascertained but an interpretation of these facts, or in other words their transposition into an ideal, abstract, symbolic world constructed on theories that he regards as established." A law of physics is a symbolic relationship, whose application to concrete reality demands a knowledge of a whole system of theories which one assumes to be valid.[59]

This granted, it will be realized that the process of verification of a theory signifies something other than what empiricism in its usual form admits, and it is a much more complicated process. The decisive experiment, which Bacon called the *experimentum crucis*, becomes impossible, since the theoretical can never be separated from the factual in such a way that the former stands on one side and the latter on the other. Inasmuch as even the simple determination of a physical fact implies a whole set of theoretical statements and is significant only in relation to this whole, the truth or falsity of a physical theory can never be determined by measuring it against the world of facts as though this represented self-contained reality independent of all assumptions of the theory. A theory can be tested only by means of another theory; a physical system can never be compared with the "exact" data of observation if we wish to discover its truth value but only with another system, with a whole set of theoretical principles and theorems.

This is the same view that we encountered in the writings of Hertz and Poincaré, but it gains a special importance and more precision in Duhem. It is generally assumed that every hypothesis employed by physics can be accepted on its own merits and separately tested by experience, and that after its value has been established by manifold and varied experiments it will receive its final place in the system. But this is not true. Physics is not a machine that can be taken apart. One cannot test every piece individually and wait until it has stood this sort of testing before putting it into the system. Physical science is a system that must be accepted as a self-contained whole, an organism of which no single part can be made to work without all the others, even those farthest removed, becoming active—some more, some less, but all in some precise degree. When the functioning is blocked in any way the physicist must try to guess from the behavior of the whole which part is at fault and in need of repair, with no possibility of isolating and testing it separately. Given a watch that will not go, the watchmaker removes all its parts, examining them one by one until he finds which was out of place or broken, but the physician cannot dissect a patient in order to make a diagnosis; he must guess at the seat and cause of the disease merely

---

59. P. Duhem, *La Théorie physique* (Paris, Chevalier et Rivière, 1906), deuxième partie, chaps. iv, v, p. 233 ff.

by studying a disturbance that affects the whole body. The physicist resembles the latter when he has a defective theory before him which he has to improve.[60]

The word *symbol*, which both Hertz and Duhem had to employ in order to establish their views of the nature of physical theory, itself contains plenty of new epistemological difficulties. Hertz did not hesitate to call the symbols of physics "inner illusions" (*innere Scheinbilder*). But the question arises immediately how these "illusions" can bring us nearer the truth; how it is possible by their aid not only to combine present experiences but even to make valid hypotheses about an unknown future. The problem of induction now looms once more with all its difficulties and appears capable of solution only if we accept with Hertz the supposition that "there is a certain accord between nature and our minds." Experience teaches that the postulate can be met, he explained, and therefore such a rapport actually exists.[61]

But here we run the risk of being caught in that well-known epistemological circle that Hume disclosed in his criticism of the theory of causality: the axiom of the "uniformity of nature" is derived from experience, yet it appears to be the necessary presupposition of the validity of every inductive inference. The difficulty can be met in a certain sense if the concepts of physics are regarded as nothing but direct models or reproductions of objects, for while even in this case there is no necessity of any identity between prototype and copy, still a high degree of similarity between the two may be asserted, on the strength of which the one may be substituted for the other in practice. But the strictly symbolic character of physical concepts puts an end to this similarity, too, for the signs have a wholly different structure from that which they indicate and belong, as it were, to an entirely different world. For symbols in the sense employed by Hertz and by Duhem no connection with reality, such as was demanded by earlier theories, is either necessary or possible. Here a particular symbol can never be set over against a particular object and compared in respect to its similarity. All that is required is that the order of the symbols be arranged so as to express the order of the phenomena.

This conception made its way but slowly and against strong opposition. The mechanistic view of nature demanded that every hypothesis shall be capable of verification by direct observation and the demand would not be satisfied until all the various details of the

60. Duhem, *op. cit.*, p. 307 f.
61. Hertz, *op. cit.*, S. 1.

picture had been completely filled in. "I am never content," wrote William Thomson,

until I have constructed a mechanical model of the object that I am studying. If I succeed in making one, I understand; otherwise, I do not. Hence I cannot grasp the electromagnetic theory of light. I wish to understand light as fully as possible, without introducing things that I understand still less. Therefore I hold fast to simple dynamics for there, but not in the electromagnetic theory, I can find a model.[62]

And even Maxwell himself, who contributed most to the supplanting of this older view, was at first still in the toils of it. "The complicated structure that Maxwell ascribed to the ether in the earliest version of his theory," remarked Poincaré, "made his system strange and repellent. One could almost believe that one were reading the description of a factory, with its cogwheels, its drive shafts bending under the strain of transmitting motion, its governors, and its belts." [63] The renunciation of this way of making things plain in sensible form came reluctantly, but when it was made the surprising result emerged that physics was thereby nearer its real goal of unification.

The last step in this direction was the development brought about by the general theory of relativity and the quantum theory. It required a far greater sacrifice in regard to the sensible representation of nature but brought the fullest measure of compensation for this sacrifice. The general theory of relativity showed that even the hypotheses upon which geometry is founded are not fixed once and for all, but are subject in principle to the same sort of variations as those that can be observed in the axioms of physics. There resulted a solidarity of the geometrical and physical principles, yielding a theory not composed of distinct and separate elements but an integrated one where the principles mutually penetrate each other, and this total theory can be compared with experience and either corroborated or rejected.[64]

Previously it had been necessary only to concede logical possibility to the non-Euclidean geometries, which were without sensible representation and consequently, it was believed, without any relevance to physics, so that the new geometry and physics were kept absolutely apart. Now this barrier, too, fell with the construction of

62. W. Thomson, *Lectures on Molecular Dynamics and the Wave-theory of Light* (Baltimore, 1884), p. 270.

63. Poincaré, "Théorie de Maxwell . . . ," *Scientia* (November, 1907), p. 7 f.

64. See Chap. III, p. 53.

the Einstein theory of gravitation, which explained how all former definitions of the space-time continuum by means of rigid measuring rods, watches, light rays, and paths of inert bodies might satisfy the laws of Euclidean geometry in narrow and restricted fields, but that on the whole a more comprehensive theory of space needed to be set up.[65]

The progress of the quantum theory exhibits the same characteristic process of transformation. The first models of atoms seemed to satisfy the demand for sensible representation in the most gratifying way. They were believed to afford a more or less direct *view* of the atomic world, and the microcosm appeared in exactly the same form as the macrocosm. The atom became a planetary system in which the planets were electrons revolving around a central body, the nucleus.[66] But the simplicity of this picture was lost as the theory developed, and it was Niels Bohr himself, one of the earliest creators of the atomic model, who warned against overvaluing it as a representation. In his essay of 1925, "Atomtheorie und Mechanik," he expressed the conviction that the general problem of the quantum theory was not concerned with a modification of mechanical and electrodynamic theories that could be explained on the basis of ordinary physical concepts but involved a radical denial of the space-time ideas by means of which a description of natural phenomena had previously been attempted.[67] Atomic physics cannot be constructed "without resignation of the wish for sensuous presentation." [68]

Quantum mechanics achieved herewith a character wholly different, in epistemological respects, from that of classical physics and mechanics. It required the development of new symbolic methods. Heisenberg relied on a new algebra, for which the commutative law of multiplication was not valid and in which the symbolic character of the theory was strikingly evident in the appearance of imaginaries in the law of commutation.[69] So the quantum theory retained indeed a mathematical schema, but this could not possibly be interpreted as

65. For details see Max Born, "Die allgemeine Relativitätstheorie Einsteins," *Die Relativitätstheorie Einsteins und ihre physikalischen Grundlagen,* "Naturwissenschaftliche Monographien und Lehrbücher," III (2. umgearb. Aufl. Berlin, J. Springer, 1921), 218 ff.

66. For details see, for example, A. Sommerfeld, "Das Wasserstoffspektrum," *Atombau und Spektrallinien* (4. umgearb. Aufl. Braunschweig, F. Vieweg & Sohn, Akt.-Ges., 1924), Kap. ii, S. 73 ff.

67. N. Bohr, "Atomtheorie und Mechanik," *Atomtheorie und Naturbeschreibung* (Berlin, J. Springer, 1931), S. 22.

68. "Wirkungsquantum und Naturbeschreibung," *ibid.,* S. 64.

69. W. Heisenberg, *Die physikalischen Prinzipien der Quantentheorie* (Leipzig, S. Hirzel, 1930), S. 48, 78 ff.

a simple connection of objects in space and time. On the other hand, it was Schrödinger's hope, in his doctrine of wave mechanics, to be able to achieve an even closer union with space-time intuition. But here, too, new problems immediately arose, since the wave process is not embedded in the three-dimensional space of coordinates but in an extended space, where the number of dimensions is equal to the number of degrees of freedom in the system and thus essentially different from three-dimensional, ordinary space.[70]

So Heisenberg insisted,

the atom of modern physics can be symbolized only through a partial differential equation in an abstract space of many dimensions. . . . *All* its qualities are inferential; no material properties can be directly attributed to it. That is to say, any picture of the atom that our imagination is able to invent is for that very reason defective. An understanding of the atomic world in that primary sensuous fashion . . . is impossible.[71]

But here we stop, having already passed beyond the limits of our purely historical discussion.[72] The problems that now emerge do not yet lend themselves to simple historical review, for they are still in flux. They have been touched upon here merely because they show that the advance of physical thought which had led to the recent revolutionary results of atomic physics has been proceeding more steadily, on the whole, than is generally realized. Physics would hardly have accepted the consequences of the new theories, which conflict so strikingly with the findings of direct observation, had it not been encouraged and enabled to do so by a change in the idea of knowledge that had grown out of the classical system. In this fact we see how the concrete work of research, and reflective thought on the theory of knowledge which accompanied it, have constantly interacted and stimulated each other in important and fruitful ways.

70. For details see Bohr, "Das Quantenpostulat," *op. cit.*, S. 50; and Reichenbach, "Ziele und Wege der physikalischen Erkenntnis," *Handbuch der Physik* von Geiger und Scheel (Berlin, J. Springer, 1929), IV, 77.

71. W. Heisenberg, "Zur Geschichte der physikalischen Naturerklärung," *Wandlungen in den Grundlagen der Naturwissenschaft* (6. Aufl. Leipzig, S. Hirzel, 1945), S. 36.

72. For a statement of the epistemological problems of modern atomic physics see Cassirer, *Determinismus und Indeterminismus in der modernen Physik*, S. 1–265.

PART II

THE IDEAL OF KNOWLEDGE AND ITS TRANSFORMATIONS IN BIOLOGY

VI

The Problem of Classifying and Systematizing Natural Forms

THAT biology deals with a specific and distinct subject, that the world of the living is distinguished from the world of the nonliving by characteristic differences—this is a conviction that not only forces itself immediately upon the attention but from time immemorial has been inspired and defended by both science and philosophy. Yet many years went by before its consequences for the problem of biological knowledge were understood.

It would hardly be going too far to maintain that this problem was first discovered by Kant, but even he was slow to see it in sharp outline and formulate it precisely. As a critic of reason he began by inquiring into the possibility of a mathematical natural science, which for him embraced at first the whole of natural knowledge. That there could be a view of nature belonging to an entirely different type of knowledge seems to have been explicitly disputed by Kant. In his *Metaphysical Elements of Natural Science* (1786) he declared that the scientific and the mathematical views of nature were one, and that in any particular theory there was only as much real science as there was mathematics. A few years later, however, he attained a different orientation. The *Critique of Judgment* (1790) marked a decisive break when it asserted the autonomy and the methodological independence of biology without giving up its connection with mathematical physics. Herewith there was posed a new question, which biological research, no matter what its school or trend, could not in the future neglect.

Philosophy prior to Kant had sought to get around this question in one way or another by trying to force physics and biology into some sort of unity. Either physics was based on biology or biology on physics. The former was the position taken by Aristotle, for whom vital phenomena were the center of interest; they determined his general idea of development, and from them he drew the categories of his science: "matter," "form," "potentiality," and "actuality." But the modern age brought about a sharp reaction. Descartes expected and demanded of the *mathesis universalis* that it should include all the problems and phenomena of biology and make them accessible to scientific treatment. Even Leibniz, too, who as a metaphysician returned to the Aristotelian concept of entelechy, held as a critic of knowledge the same opinion. He eliminated the notion of "plastic forms" from the view of nature and demanded that every natural phenomenon be explained mathematically and mechanically, according to the same laws.[1] To abandon this principle would be to sink back immediately into the obscurities of the Schoolmen.

This being the state of the problem until the end of the eighteenth century, it was a bold and significant step that Kant took when he determined to extend his critical revision of the foundations of knowledge to this field, and to redefine the boundary between biology and mathematical natural science in accordance with the general aspects opened up by his critique of reason. The approach to the question was not easy to make. For a modification of the "critical" concept of "object" was required, and that modification had to be so made, moreover, as not to endanger or disturb the foundations laid down in the *Critique of Pure Reason*. The dogmatic and metaphysical idea of object must, as before, be guarded against and rejected; yet, on the other hand, the new critical transcendental concept of objectivity must be extended. This had nothing to do with the existence of "things in themselves," but solely with the order of appearances. A strictly lawful connection of phenomena is possible only, as the *Critique* had shown, when they are brought under definite rules. And these empirical rules presuppose the universal "principles of the understanding" which Kant called the "analogies of experience." Only on this basis of the concepts of substance, causality, and reciprocity is that "context of experience" that we call "nature" possible. The object with which biology is concerned would disappear from nature's ambit if it contradicted, in any respect, these universal conditions of natural knowledge. Every object of nature must in principle conform to this set of conditions.

In his *Metaphysical Elements of Natural Science* Kant intended

---

1. See G. W. Leibniz, "Considérations sur les principes de vie, et sur les natures plastique," *Die philosophischen Schriften von Gottfried Wilhelm Leibniz*, ed. Gerhardt (1885), VI, 539 ff.

to show how from these general presuppositions Newton's concrete cosmology followed, as presented in his *Mathematical Principles of Natural Philosophy*. The principles and laws that were here set up served Kant to some extent as the constitutional laws of empirical knowledge. If biology is not to be a "state within a state," it must conform to these laws on all points. But how is an "autonomy" of biology to be attained in this way, a self-legislation that will not appear simply foreign to the principles upon which mathematical physics is founded? Kant meant to give the solution of this question in his *Analysis of the Concept of Purpose*. There is no question, he thought, of banishing the idea of purpose from biology, since the prime feature of the biological problem would thereby be overlooked. The concept of an organism cannot be grasped unless there is included in it the element of purposiveness: "An organized product of nature is that in which all is reciprocally end and means." [2] The question that now remains, and upon whose decision our interpretation of the scientific character of biology rests, is this: What sort of methodological value may be ascribed to the concept of purpose? Has it the value only of human analogy (*ex analogia hominis*) or that of an analogy with nature (*ex analogia universi*)? Does it express a basic feature of *reality* where "reality" is thought of solely as empirical, as "reality of appearance," or is it merely a subjective point of view under which we comprehend certain definite phenomena?

The difficulties in the interpretation of the *Critique of Judgment* come from the fact that when the question is so put no simple answer can be given. Not that Kant was obscure or uncertain, but rather because his philosophy had undergone a complete change in respect to the meaning of "subjective" and "objective," a change which no longer allowed those concepts to be regarded as proper members of a logical disjunction. Kant did not proceed from the existence of things as "things in themselves," but only analyzed the knowing of them. His philosophy "renounced all claim to the proud title of an ontology that presumes to furnish a priori synthetic judgments of things in general in a systematic doctrine"; it was modestly content with being an "analysis of the understanding." The concepts that appear in such an analysis cannot claim to be more than principles for the explanation of phenomena.[3] They should teach us how to "spell out phenomena in order that we may be able to read them as experiences." This was just as true for the

---

2. Kant, *Kritik der Urteilskraft*, ed. K. Rosenkranz, "I. Kants Sämmtliche Werke" (Leipzig, L. Voss, 1838), Teil IV, § 65, S. 260.

3. Kant, *Kritik der reinen Vernunft* (2. Aufl.), S. 303.

idea of cause as for that of purpose, for even causality, even "the principle of reason," was no longer, as with Leibniz, a metaphysical principle that revealed the nature and ultimate origin of things. It showed us only how to complete a "synthesis of appearances according to concepts," and on the basis thereof to achieve objective knowledge; that is to say, knowledge of an objective order of the phenomena in space and time. Accordingly the term "objectivity" can never mean anything more in Kant's system than a predicate that is ascribed to certain *kinds of knowledge*. So the problem is reduced to that of the relation between the mode of causal knowledge and that of the knowledge of purpose. The issue which had divided metaphysics from earliest times, whether purposeful or "intelligent" causes govern things, or whether everything follows a "blind" necessity, had therefore lost all meaning for Kant. He asked simply whether it was possible and rational, at one and the same time, to conceive of phenomena as obedient to natural law, that is, to refer them to the universal dynamic principle of causality, and to regard them also from the point of view of purpose and organize and arrange them accordingly.

The *Critique of Judgment* aims to prove that there is no antinomy whatsoever between these two *forms of order* in knowledge. They cannot contradict one another because they relate to problems in distinct fields that must be carefully kept apart. Causality has to do with knowledge of the objective temporal succession of events, the order in change, whereas the concept of purpose has to do with the *structure* of those empirical objects that are called living organisms. To appreciate this structure as such in its characteristic and specific form does not mean that we must desert the general domain of causality in order to explain it or catch at some sort of superempirical or supersensuous cause. It is enough if we recognize a special kind of being—that of "natural forms"—and understand it in its systematic order as a unified self-contained structure. Biology can assert no more, as long as it stays within the limits indicated by this critical philosophy, than that the living world is just such a structure. It considers nature under the aspect of a whole so formed that it determines the properties of its various parts. Then nature ceases to be a mere aggregate and becomes a system.

In the *Critique of Judgment*, Kant wanted to prove that such a point of view is not only justified but absolutely necessary even if, from inner methodological reasons of the system, he makes a strict distinction between this necessity and that which we must ascribe to a mathematical natural science. The necessity in the latter case has a "constitutive" significance, whereas that of the former is only "regulative"; but this does not mean that one of the two factors in the construction of knowledge can be reduced to the other and dispensed with. The concept of purpose can never be struck out of the whole of natural knowledge and absorbed into the idea of cause. For even if it is not an independent principle for the *explanation* of nature, still the approach to one of her most important domains would be barred without it, and the *knowledge* of phenomena would therefore be incomplete and defective. Kant limited the principle of purpose to this role of taking *cognizance* of nature, which must be distinguished from mathematical knowledge of it. We can never adequately understand organized beings and their inner possibilities, and indeed we cannot even apprehend thereby that they exist and how they exist merely through the mechanical principles of nature.[4] Here the principle of purpose functions, however, not as a mysterious power in the original ground of things but rather as a rule for gaining knowledge, so that it has at any rate a "regulative" significance. "The concept of purposive combinations and forms in nature is at least, then, *one principle more* for bringing the appearances under rules, where the laws of mechanistic causality do not suffice." [5]

Thus, in Kant's opinion, the question of the objective *truth* of the principle of purpose can only be answered when one has freed the concept of such truth from all its metaphysical associations and understands it in a critical or transcendental sense alone. In consequence Kant had to reject both solutions of the problem of purpose that had been offered in the earlier metaphysics. And the negative thesis was no better than the positive one, so far as both remained at the dogmatic level in their formulation of the question. In the history of philosophy the positive thesis was represented by Aristotle, the negative by Spinoza. And until then there had seemed to be no way of escaping a choice between these alternatives. Even the scientific biologist had ultimately to make his decision, and in regard to his use of the concept of purpose become either an Aristotelian or a Spinozist.

Aristotle ranked the "formal causes" above the "material causes." Purpose is the true and original essence and universal moving principle. Whoever wants to study nature must go back to the supreme cause. The operations of this cause can no longer be described in purely mechanical terms. This God is the ἀκίνητον κινοῦν; he moves the world without being in material contact with it and without him-

<hr>

4. *Kritik der Urteilskraft,* § 74.
5. *Ibid.,* § 60, S. 240 f.

self being moved by it. He acts merely through his own being, by his all-embracing presence, and not by force and impact.

Spinoza vigorously opposed this view. When Aristotle said that God moves all things in the same way as does a "beloved object," (κινεῖ ὡς ἐρούμενον) his very metaphor betrayed the highly dangerous origin of the Aristotelian concepts of form and purpose. The usage of these concepts in metaphysics and science revealed itself to be simply a case of anthropomorphism. Until this is destroyed there can be no really universal interpretation of nature. Far from being a supreme objective principle, purpose is rather a typical expression of a specifically human limitation and restriction. It is not knowledge but sheer obscurantism, nothing but an escape and a mask for our ignorance. There is only one way to stop this flight from reality and to tear this mask away. Mathematics is the thing that can free us from the deceptiveness of the idea of purpose. We do not ask about the "purposes" of triangles, circles, or squares, but absorb ourselves in the contemplation of their pure being. Without the help of mathematics, said Spinoza, man would never have escaped from the toils of anthropomorphism but would have remained in the realm of sheer "imagination" instead of rising to the level of rational knowledge and even that of "philosophical intuition."

It is the distinctive characteristic of Kant's achievement that he rejected the solutions of both Aristotle and Spinoza. This holds when one considers not only the position he took in regard to philosophy but also that in regard to the science of his time, for even in this respect there was no example that he could have directly followed. There had been such an example in the case of his *Critique of Pure Reason*. In deducing his system of synthetic principles he had had constantly before his eyes a definite scientific achievement in which these principles were incorporated. He had before him in Newton's *Principia* the first great system of natural philosophy whose foundations appeared to be secure. His "transcendental analysis" referred to this system and inquired into the "conditions of its possibility." Its goal could be regarded as achieved if the "special laws of nature" that Newton had derived from a few general principles could be interpreted as "specifications of general laws of understanding." But nothing of the sort was possible in biology, for the science was only in the earliest stages of its development at the end of the eighteenth century. When the biology of Kant's time is compared with that of the present day one sees not only that it was far from any *solution* of its problems but that even its own *task*, its concept and its problem, had not been explored with nearly the same sure judgment as was the case with the mathematical physics of the time. Here Kant had to seek and find his way alone. But on *one* important and central point it is clear, nonetheless, that even in treating this problem he was not simply speculating in empty space. He proceeded, as before, from the definite scientific form which the science of biology in his day had taken; and he asked how that kind of structure of science is "possible," that is, on what universal transcendental conditions it rests. In disclosing this problem he was led to one of the most remarkable and distinctive problems of the critical theory of knowledge, a problem that had not been stated in this form by any logician or biologist.

From the time of Aristotle there had been one point of contact and even more, an inner bond between logic and biology. Aristotelian logic was a logic of class concepts, and such concepts were an indispensable means to the knowledge and scientific description of natural forms. This primacy of class concepts was still unchallenged in the biology of the seventeenth and eighteenth centuries, whereas in mathematics the signs of a transformation and a new intellectual orientation were already apparent everywhere. The logic of relations had been pushing the logic of classes into the background ever since Leibniz, and it was constantly gaining in significance. Meanwhile, biology had just witnessed in the *Systema naturae* (1735) and *Philosophia botanica* (1751) of Linnaeus one of the greatest scientific triumphs of the class concept. A systematic division of the natural forms had been achieved that surpassed every previous attempt in its clarity and precision. At one stroke the manifold variety of these forms, which were incapable of being seen in any one view, were classified as members according to a regular scheme. The whole of animate nature was constructed according to genus and species, class and order, and every individual was assigned its determinate place in the whole scheme.

But just here arose a question which Kant put to himself and discussed exhaustively, in the first introduction to his *Critique of Judgment* (which he later suppressed because of its great scope, replacing it with a shorter version): What justifies us in seeing nature as a whole that assumes the form of a logical system and is capable of being treated as such? Whence comes this harmony between natural forms and logical forms, and upon what is it based? The concepts of genus and class are purely logical, and therefore a priori, and it is by no means self-evident that we can apply them to experience and in a sense rediscover them there. Here there is presumably an agreement between nature and our understanding, which the *metaphysician* may explain by assuming a common source for both and a consequent "pre-established harmony," but which to the *critic* of knowledge remains largely a riddle. The problem can be solved only by discovering some sort of justification, or "transcendental deduction," for this particular thesis. But the form of deduction that Kant had given in the *Critique of Pure Reason* for the causal principle and the other synthetic principles, completely deserts us here. The causal principle and the others could be proved objectively valid and firmly established against skepticism of the sort Hume had proposed by showing that they are the necessary conditions for all possible experience, and that without them there can be no empirical order of phenomena whatsoever in space and time. They were thus explained as presuppositions, as "constituents" of the concept of nature in general: *If* we think of nature, we must necessarily think of it as subject to the rules expressed in these supreme principles. But nothing like this holds for our concepts of class and genus. It is no contradiction to imagine a nature that obeys the rules of connection according to law, as they are specified in the principles of substance, cause, and so on, and that in other respects discloses an *irreducible diversity* in the manifold of its appearances, a diversity that would never permit us to order them according to genus and species. Such a "nature" would still be a cosmos, and no chaos, since it would still be subject to *universal laws*. But it would be no longer possible to connect *particular* beings in such fashion that they appear as an ascending order which has its members related to each other by certain affinities. Every particular could here stand alone, in a sense; and to be known at all it would have to be apprehended and described simply by itself. Such a nature appears to us, of course, as an illusion: we cannot *believe* in the possibility of any such disparateness of the forms of being. But critical philosophy cannot be content with any such "belief," in the Humean sense. It must seek out the principle for such a belief, on which it depends. Kant chose to designate it "the principle of formal purposiveness," and explained that it was not, like the universal principles of substance and causality, a law of the pure understanding, but a principle of the "reflective judgment." It prescribes no law for the *content* of appearances, but it points the way for our *study* of or our reflection upon appearances. It contains a rule that holds not so much for the natural objects themselves as for our research into them. In so doing we must always make the presupposition that nature as a whole not only behaves according to law, but also discloses a thoroughgoing organization in

all details as well, and that definite relations of greater or less similarity, or closer or more remote affinity, prevail among all the various
forms.

We presuppose this relationship, without being able to prove it
a priori, but no such proof is necessary as long as we remember and
keep firmly in mind that we are dealing not with an objective principle but with a "maxim." Whether this maxim turns out to be reliable,
whether or not a perfect classification of natural forms according
to class and order, family and genus, is attainable, experience alone
can teach us. But we should not have discovered such a system in nature had we not first *sought* it. The search is not something we are
compelled to by the objects; it expresses a peculiar command of the
reason. For reason addresses itself to nature, "to be taught by her,
certainly, but not as a pupil who accepts anything that the teacher
chooses to say, but rather as a judge invested with the power to require the witness to answer the questions put to him." [6] Our concept
of the species and the genera of natural forms should not, however,
be taken dogmatically but must be understood in the critical sense. It
asserts nothing about the metaphysical structure of being, but is a
question we address to nature, the satisfactory answer to which only
the subsequent course of our experience can give.

Kant used a noteworthy expression for this interpretation when
he spoke of an "adaptation" of nature to our understanding or to
the rules of our faculty of judgment. We find that nature "favors"
the effort of our faculty of judgment to discover a systematic order
among her separate forms, and, so to speak, meets it half way. The
question is how one could hope by comparison of perceptions to attain to empirical concepts of that which is common to different natural forms, if nature (as it is possible to think), because of her very
different empirical laws, had imposed such a great dissimilarity on
them that comparison would be entirely or in large part futile, so far
as bringing out any harmony and hierarchy of species and genera
is concerned.

Any comparison of empirical ideas in order to know empirical laws and
accordingly the *specific* forms and, through their comparison with
others, the *generically similar* forms in natural objects—all such comparison presupposes this: that in respect to her empirical laws nature
has observed a certain economy that to our judgment appears fitting,
and an understandable uniformity, and this presupposition as a principle of a priori judgment must precede all comparison.

6. *Kritik der reinen Vernunft,* S. xiii.

The reflective judgment thus proceeds with given appearances, in order to bring them under the empirical concepts of certain natural things, not schematically but *technically,* not just mechanically, as it were, as an instrument under the direction of the understanding and the senses but *with art.* The judgment orders the appearance according to the universal, though at the same time indeterminate, principle of a purposive arrangement of nature in a system, as if nature were something favorable to our judgment in the conformity of her particular laws . . . to the possibility of experience as a system. Without some such presupposition we cannot hope to find our way in a labyrinth of the multiplicity of possible separate laws.[7]

It is generally recognized that this principle of "formal purposiveness," and the conclusions Kant drew from it as to "the adaptation of nature to our judgment," are among the most difficult problems in the interpretation of Kant.[8] But a reliable clue can be obtained at once if we bear in mind that here, too, he started out from the problem as he found it in the science of his day, and that he was seeking to fathom it and throw as much light as possible upon it. One can say that in establishing the principle of formal purposiveness he spoke as the *logician* of Linnaeus' descriptive science, just as in the *Critique of Pure Reason* and the *Metaphysical Elements of Natural Science* he had appeared as logician for the Newtonian system. He tracked down the hidden problem contained in Linnaeus' work.

Linnaeus was not only a brilliant observer but an indefatigable and inexorable logician as well, and it was said of him that he was possessed at times by a veritable mania for classification. The urge to codify and arrange phenomena has never been so strongly developed in any other great naturalist.[9] But much as his system advanced descriptive botany there is something questionable about it from an epistemological point of view, and Linnaeus himself was by no means insensible of the doubt. What have we gained when we have succeeded in making such a survey of the plant world after the manner of his system? Are we moving then in the realm of things or, which is more probable, in the realm of mere names? Is the binary nomenclature there introduced ever any more than a simple aid to

---

7. First Introduction, *Kritik der Urteilskraft,* "Werke," ed. E. Cassirer, V, 194.

8. For further details see H. W. Cassirer, "The First Introduction to the Critique of Judgment," *A Commentary on Kant's Critique of Judgment* (London, Methuen & Co., Ltd., 1938), S. 97 ff.

9. See E. Nordenskiöld, "Linnaeus and His Pupils," *The History of Biology,* trans. by L. B. Eyre (New York and London, Alfred A. Knopf, 1929), Pt. II, chap. vii, pp. 203 ff.; and E. Rádl, *Geschichte der biologischen Theorien in der Neuzeit* (2. gänz. umgearb. Aufl. Leipzig und Berlin, W. Engelmann, 1913), Teil I, S. 253 ff.

memory that may be subjectively useful but takes us no deeper
into the nature of things? Linnaeus never denied that his system was
an "artificial" one, realizing that his classification by stamens and
pistils emphasized but one single factor, whereas to gain a "natural
system" required the consideration of all the organs of a plant together. It was such a natural system that he expressly designated
as the highest goal of botany, and he continued to work toward it as
long as he lived without ever achieving it.[10] So he really distinguished
between the natural and artificial orders, and meant to attribute to
the latter a certain value for purposes of diagnosis of the natural
forms; but the artificial order cannot be treated as knowledge.[11]
Thus a problem was indicated that determined the course of future
investigation. Is there any possibility—so the question now ran
—of advancing beyond Linnaeus, and what criterion have we by
which to judge that we are on the right path and that our classifica-
tions are not mere verbal cloaks but pertain to real objective differences?

The first great biologist to give a precise answer and establish a
theory that was intended to solve the problem was Cuvier. Like Linnaeus he shifted the center of importance for biological research to
morphology. Philosophy, as it happens, was not wholly without a
share in the development of Cuvier's scientific convictions, even
though he relied entirely upon empirical investigation and condemned all philosophical speculation on nature. He seems to have
been stimulated by Kant's philosophy during his student years.[12]
Like Schiller, he received his earliest education at the Karlsschule, in
Stuttgart, where he seems to have come into touch with the philosophical movements in Germany through Karl Friedrich Kielmeyer,
his teacher in biology. The decided phenomenalism in his view of
nature is especially Kantian. That is why the theory of development
seemed to him incapable of being carried through because even in
the formulation of its problem it overstepped the limits within which
every theory of nature is confined. We cannot answer the question
of the nature and origin of life and must be content with seeing as
completely as we can the existing life forms in their systematic relationships. We must always direct our gaze to the whole if we are to
reach an understanding of particulars and individuals. For it is just

10. For further details see Nordenskiöld, *op. cit.*, pp. 213 ff.
11. "Ordines naturales valent de natura plantarum, artificiales in diagnosi plantarum." C. v. Linne, "Ratio operis," *Genera plantarum* (editio sexta Holmiae, L. Salvii,
1764), pp. 1 ff.
12. For an account of Cuvier's life and education see Nordenskiöld, *op. cit.*, pp.
331 ff.

this irreducible coherence of whole and part that constitutes the essence of organic nature. In this connection the definition of the organism given by Kant in his *Critique of Judgment* will be especially remembered.[13] The organism is no mere collection of parts, for even in its separate parts we can find the form of the whole. Cuvier's idea of the type served to advance this thesis. It was the indispensable instrument of his empirical research. We can never understand the world of living beings if we are to lose ourselves in the contemplation of its variegated and multiform character, for in the absence of fixed outlines and guiding principles it has no conceivable pattern. The task of biological investigation is to discover these and classify the different forms of life in accordance with them; and here there is no better and more trustworthy guide than comparative anatomy. For Cuvier this was not simply a separate empirical discipline, related to others and equal to them in rank; it expressed rather the methodological ideal that all biological knowledge must strive to approach. Thus he established a general trend in research that persisted long after his own time, and is apparent even today—as, for example, in Johannes von Uexküll's *Theory of Life*. "The theory of living things is a pure science, and has but a single goal: investigation of their structural plan, their origin, and their activities." [14] The idea of a structural plan originated with Cuvier. There is no creation of nature, howsoever lowly it might appear to be, that does not exhibit and adhere strictly to such a plan in the arrangement of its various parts, down to the very last detail. For this reason it is useless to restrict biology to the study of individual phenomena and try to retain it there.

Lamarck declared, referring to Buffon's sharp criticism of the system of Linnaeus, that every system is somewhat artificial, since only individuals exist in nature and the categories under which they are arrayed are only products of thought.[15] To Cuvier such a view was inadmissible. Biology would not be a science unless it advanced from the particular to the general. But it was purely structural relationships rather than laws of process as these are formulated by physics and chemistry which he sought. He never doubted for a moment that there were such relationships, and that they could be understood as surely as the laws of these sciences, for the order of

13. See G. Cuvier, Préface and première leçon, *Leçons d'anatomie comparée,* éd. Dumèril et Duvernoy (2e éd. Paris, Crochard, 1835), I, v ff., 6.

14. J. v. Uexküll, *Die Lebenslehre* (Potsdam, Müller & Kiepenheuer, und Zürich, O. Füssli, 1930), S. 1.

15. See Buffon's Introduction, *Histoire naturelle.* For details of his attack on Linnaeus see E. Rádl, *op. cit.,* Teil I, Kap. xi, § 3, S. 275 ff.

living things is no less rigorous and no less general (than that obtaining in the world of the nonliving).[16] All life is organized throughout and is therefore not merely a random collection of parts but a closed system with a kind of inherent and characteristic necessity. Once we have succeeded in coming to know the chief and fundamental types of organisms—and comparative anatomy offers a certain means of acquiring this knowledge—we should know not only what actually exists but also what things can or cannot so exist.

Thus along with inductive knowledge there appears a form of "deduction" which is not denied to biological knowledge and, indeed, according to Cuvier, constitutes one of its distinguishing characters. For the comparative anatomist, if one part of the skeleton of an animal is given him, can reconstruct the whole animal, since every part is related to every other part and all are in a relation of constant interdependence. From a bird's feather he can deduce the shape of the bird's clavicle, and vice versa. Cuvier did not hesitate to equate the laws of biological structure, in respect to certainty, with those of mathematics or even of metaphysics. In the process of life, he explained, not only do the various organs subsist simply side by side but they react upon one another and work toward one common end, whence it followed that some of them are mutually exclusive of each other whereas others mutually aid each other. "Upon this mutual dependence of function and reciprocal aid are based the laws that determine the relations of their organs, laws that have a necessity equal to that of metaphysics or mathematics." [17]

Only experience, of course, can show what special relations and dependencies exist among the various parts of an organism, but their constancy suggests that they must have a definite and sufficient cause. Here observation provides empirical laws that become almost as reliable as laws of reason if they are based upon experiences sufficiently repeated; so that anyone who found even the trace of a cloven hoof, for example, can infer that the animal which had left this vestige of itself had been a ruminant.

We cannot explain these relationships, of course, but we may and must assume that they are no mere play of chance. As the equation of a curve contains all its characteristics, and as each of these can be used to derive the equation and with it all other properties, so a nail, a scapula, a femur, or any other bone by itself will give information regarding the teeth and conversely. One who knew the laws of nature's organic economy and

16. Supplied by translator—text deficient.
17. Cuvier, *Leçons d'anatomie comparée,* I, 50.

applied them with understanding could start with such a fragment and from it reconstruct the whole animal.[18]

The dentition of the carnivora, with its long canine teeth and dissimilar molars, was just as essential to them as were molar teeth to the herbivora; and not only could it be shown equally for all other characteristics that they were possessed by certain natural classes, but we could understand why this should be so.

These distinctive utterances on the part of Cuvier indicate clearly the difference between his ideal of biology and that of Linnaeus. At first glance the two investigators seem to be very close together in their whole methodological attitude. Both were rigorous empiricists and tireless observers, who rejected all speculation on the origin and nature of life and strove for nothing other than a complete knowledge of its phenomena. But the method of acquiring this information was understood in a different sense. Linnaeus was satisfied in general to identify plants, to select one feature, as simple as possible, that would facilitate their identification, whereas Cuvier's system of types was no longer really concerned with single characteristics: it was their relationship one to the other that was for him the decisive and determining factor. The individuality of an organism is not to be expressed in terms of any one special property, but depends upon the correlation obtaining among all its parts. Hence it follows that if biology were to reach its goal and realize its empirical ideals, it could not dispense with rational factors but must retain them for the development of its own rational methods. Its course did not lead simply from the particular to the general; even in considering each separate part it must presuppose the whole, the general in the particular. This holds for the single organism and for the whole living world as well, where likewise nothing stands alone but every being is related to every other one. Thus the knowledge of a single form, if it is really to penetrate to the heart of the matter, always presupposes a knowledge of the world of forms in its entirety. Systematic biology, therefore, as understood and practiced by Cuvier, was no mere device of classification and arrangement that can be easily apprehended, but a disclosure of the very framework of nature herself.

Hence follows Cuvier's claim to the objective validity of his concept of the type. Certainly he was not caught in any naïve realism, for he did not treat the type as though it were a sensibly distinct thing. Its validity and truth lay in its indispensability as a principle

18. Cuvier, "Principe de cette determination," *Discours sur les révolutions de la surface du globe* (5e éd. Paris, C. G. Dutour et E. d'Ocagne, 1828), p. 95 ff.

of classification, and here Cuvier had chiefly and exclusively in mind
the position in the scale of existence. Type had to do only with being:
the causal order, the order of happening was outside his purview. The
relations which he recognized were pure relations of contiguity, not of
sequence, and the laws to which they led were not laws of succession
but of coexistence. Yet without such a knowledge of being, which precedes and underlies it, the science of development would not be possible. From this one can understand how physiology must depend on
anatomy, and can only be completed as a science after anatomy has
been perfected.[19]

For this purpose it was above all necessary, however, that physiology should hold strictly to the concept of form as such—so instrumental in comparative anatomy—and let it stand in its strictly precise meaning. It was from his deep-rooted conviction of this that
Cuvier was led to oppose so strongly all his life the attempts to relax
this concept and make it more flexible and elastic in form. If one
examines his attack on the first exponents of a "theory of evolution"
more closely, his underlying intellectual motive becomes clear at once.
He did not want to exclude the question of the evolution of organisms
from the field of biological investigation, nor did he lack all interest
in problems of the history of life. The very opposite is the case, for he
was the first to establish the systematic study of the early history of
living forms, and he based the principles of his comparative osteology
as much on the examination of fossils as on that of the living specimen.
He even applied to fossils his theory of correlation, explaining that
the entire animal, its way of life, its environment, and so on, could be
reconstructed from one single bone. In his *Investigations on Fossil
Bones* (1812) he became, indeed, the founder of scientific paleontology.

But even in these investigations on the early history of living
organisms he still held fast to his general thesis. He wanted to identify
the stable and enduring forms, and distinguish them clearly one from
the other. He conceived of evolution not as a slow and steady process,
not as a sheer stream of life, a flowing transition in which the outlines
of all forms were abolished, but thought that it took shape and became
accessible to our knowledge only when divided into sharply distinct
epochs. His geological theory of "catastrophe" rested entirely upon
this view. In the development of the earth and of its organisms there
was not gradual unfolding; at bottom there was only a disappearing
of the old and an emergence of the new. The old and new were connected by analogies, but a real identity never obtained. Even the ani-

19. Cuvier, *Leçons d'anatomie comparée,* I, 57 f.

mal world of a past epoch was never connected with our present world by any actual relationship but was of a wholly different type. The desire to arrange all forms of life in one single, ascending series Cuvier regarded as pure fantasy.

To do justice to his theory historically it is necessary to remember that in his contest with the first defenders of the theory of evolution he took his stand not upon dogmatic but upon methodological grounds. He defended the "constancy of types" not as an ontological or theological dogma but as a methodological principle. In the argument with Geoffroy Saint-Hilaire there appears in classical purity and clarity the antithesis in modes of thought which Kant had described in the *Critique of Pure Reason* and endeavored to trace back to "reason itself." He distinguished between two different "interests" of reason, one having to do with "homogeneity," the other with "specification." Both led to the setting up of distinct principles, which were commonly understood as ontological propositions, as statements about the nature of things, whereas in truth they were nothing but maxims that should indicate the way of inquiry.

When merely regulative principles are regarded as constitutive they can, as objective principles, well be in conflict with each other; but when they are taken simply as maxims there is no real opposition, only a different interest on the part of reason. . . . This is how it is possible for one reasoner to follow the interest of multiplicity (according to the principle of specification), and another the interest of unity . . . Each one thinks that he derives his opinion from an insight into the object, yet he bases it solely upon a greater or less dependence on one of these two principles, neither of which rests on objective grounds but only on the interest of reason, and hence might better be called maxims than principles. When I see intelligent men quarreling with one another over the characteristics of mankind, or animals, or plants, or even of substances from the mineral kingdom, and see some assume, for example, that there are distinct national characters based on descent, or even assume that there are decided hereditary differences among families, races, and so on, whereas others are convinced that in these individuals nature has provided an identical soil and that all differences depend upon external factors, I need only consider the subject under dispute to realize that it is far too obscure for either side to speak from an immediate understanding of it. Nothing is involved here but the twofold interest of the reason, one side taking seriously or affecting one interest, and the other side the other interest, whence comes the difference in the maxims respecting the variety or uniformity of nature, which might well be reconciled but, so long as they pass for objective insights, bring about strife and delay truth for a long time, until some means has been found to unite the conflicting interests and thus satisfy reason.[20]

Here Kant described in detail half a century, in fact, before it broke out, the famous quarrel between Cuvier and Geoffroy Saint-Hilaire. The latter fought with extreme bias for the interest of "rational unity," declaring that all distinctions into class and species were nothing but pure fiction. "From this standpoint," he wrote, "there are no different animals. One fact alone dominates; it is as if a single Being were appearing." [21] All that was for Cuvier simply fantastic. He rejected in a most decided way all the notions that many naturalists had formed—he had in mind particularly Buffon, Bonnet, and Lamarck—of a gradation among living forms that would permit their assemblage in one series. Such a sequence might be possible within one definite type, but there was no transition between the various related types. No matter how the vertebrates and invertebrates were arranged, it would never be feasible to place at the end of the one series and the beginning of the other two animals similar enough to serve as a connecting link between these two great classes.[22] What had been brought forward on that score therefore was sheer aesthetic trifling that came to nothing when brought face to face with the facts.

Even in his memorial lecture on Lamarck, delivered before the Académie des Sciences, Cuvier spoke in the most extreme way for this view. "A system resting upon such foundations," he said on this occasion, "might please the fancy of a poet, and a metaphysician might derive from it a wholly different group of systems; but it cannot survive for a moment the scrutiny of anyone who has dissected a hand, a visceral organ, or even a feather." [23] For every single animal type, for vertebrates, for molluscs, for arthropods, for radiolaria there was a definite structural plan characteristic of it. To wipe out

20. Kant, *Kritik der reinen Vernunft,* ed. K. Vorländer (Halle, a. d. S., O. Hendel, 1899), S. 556 f., 694 ff.

21. See Nordenskiöld, *op. cit.,* p. 342.

22. Cuvier, *op. cit.,* I, 59.

In a critical review of Charles Singer's *Short History of Biology* (Oxford, 1931) in *Lychnos,* Nils von Hofsten said that in his opinion Cuvier was fundamentally no nearer the theory of the origin of species than Buffon. But he offered no proof for this view, and among the sources themselves I can find no support for it. See N. v. Hofsten, "Rezension von C. Singer's *A Short History of Biology,*" *Lychnos: Lärdomhisotriska Samfundets Årsbok* (Stockholm, Almquist & Wiksell, 1937), II, 548 ff.

23. G. Cuvier, "Eloge de M. de Lamarck," *Mémoires de l'Académie Royale des Sciences de l'Institut de France,* XIII (Paris, Didot frères, 1835), 20 f.

their differences would be to abandon all possibility of accurately describing nature. The thought of a uniform scheme to include animals of all sorts was no more than an empty notion.

Cuvier's fundamental ideas on the task and methods of descriptive natural science were taken over into botany by Candolle, who wanted to show that the views advocated by Cuvier for the animal kingdom held for plants as well. For him too the central point was the principle of correlation of the parts of the organism. He emphasized particularly that it held for the two chief systems of the plant: the reproductive and the vegetative systems.[24] Only on such a foundation is it possible, according to Candolle, to advance from an artificial to a natural system—a goal which, as he insisted, Linnaeus also had held continually in view.[25] The significance of Candolle's work for our problem, too, is the fact that he not only prepared the outline for a natural system of this sort, but also reflected on the principles on which one had to rely in such an undertaking. He wanted to give a theory of natural classification modeled, as he explicitly emphasized, "on the principles of logic." [26] At the heart of this logic of biology there is the question, too, of the objective validity of the concept of species. This was affirmed by Candolle no less decisively than by Cuvier, and supported by the same arguments. Pure nominalism, as embraced by Buffon and by Lamarck, the view that there are only individuals in nature and that classes and species are simply names, was opposed as dangerous skepticism.[27] Of course species are not independently existing things but they are the expression of constant relations, and not simply ascribed to nature by us but found there on the basis of observation. The idea of a "scale in nature," of a single connected series of living things rising by imperceptible degrees from the lowest form of life to man, must really be given up; it is only a metaphor, a "factitious image." [28]

The task is to see nature not just as a vague whole but in its clear and precise outlines, and it was a task worthy of the naturalist. His function would be far better served, continued Candolle, if he adhered to the principle of the invariability of species instead of being lured away by questionable analogies to the notion of their mutability.

24. For further details see Nordenskiöld, pp. 436 ff.
25. A. de Candolle, "Théorie élémentaire de la botanique ou exposition des principes de la classification naturelle et de l'art de décrire et d'étudier les végétations," *Introduction à l'étude de la botanique* (Paris, Libraire Encyclopédique de Roret, 1835), Tomes I, II. (I quote from the German translation by Joh. Jac. Roemer, Zürich, 1814.)
26. Candolle, *ibid.*, II, S. 96 ff.; cf. S. 182.
27. *Ibid.*, S. 188.
28. *Ibid.*, S. 227 f.

The chief requirement of any systematic description of nature is that it be based on an examination of *all* organs, though in doing so one should not attribute the same significance to each one. In appraising their importance the investigator must be guided only by the object and not betrayed into thinking that what lies nearest, and is most accessible to observation, is at the same time of greatest consequence. The measure of significance should not be drawn from our technique of observation but sought in the life processes of the plants alone. Not all organs are equally important or equally lasting; the main thing always is to be sure of their position in the hierarchy of systems in the whole organism and to formulate this as definitely as possible.[29]

As a clue to this Candolle found the concept of "symmetrical design" useful. Though not always immediately accessible to observation, being often concealed by such fortuitous conditions as atrophy or deformity, it would not escape the attentive gaze of the experienced naturalist. All organized beings are by nature regular, and it is only the various obstacles to their development that cause the appearance of irregularity. Here the philosophic eye of the investigator must learn to penetrate from semblance to reality. The symmetry of the various parts, which is the essential object of the naturalist's study, represents nothing other than the united whole, which comes to light in the relative ordering of its parts.[30]

From a general epistemological point of view all this is obviously in closest relationship with Cuvier, whose concept of type finds its direct counterpart in Candolle's concept of symmetry. In both cases the salient problem for biology is that of classification. But the scientific ideal of classification itself has now broadened and deepened, as compared with Linnaeus' ideal of identification. It makes other and higher demands and thereupon discovers itself face to face with new problems, which biological thought attempted to cope with only later.

29. *Ibid.,* S. 67, 91 ff.
30. *Ibid.,* S. 114.

VII

The Idea of Metamorphosis and Idealistic
Morphology: Goethe

GOETHE'S theory of metamorphosis has profoundly affected the development of biology. In no other field of natural science have his ideas exerted so deep and fruitful an effect, and it was his good fortune to have the support of prominent investigators during his lifetime. The magnitude of his accomplishment is no longer in doubt today; opinion on this is well-nigh unanimous. But it is much more difficult to fix his just place in the history of biology, for he can be definitely assigned to no school or line of thought. All his research was stamped with his own personality and his own individual cast of mind, and he himself declared that he "belonged to no guild," and wished to remain "an amateur to the end." [1] He fought nothing so strongly as attempts to "proscribe" any method of research.[2] This exceptional position later had the result that as the significance of his theories became more and more widely recognized almost all schools endeavored to appropriate them and interpret them in their own sense. Whereas there had formerly been an inclination to regard him as a purely speculative natural philosopher, empirical research now claimed him with increasing frequency for its own.[3]

Yet even within this circle it is difficult to place him. In the second half of the nineteenth century, in the golden age of Darwinism, it was thought that no higher praise could be bestowed than to call him a "Darwinian before Darwin," but this verdict has long since been abandoned and today the sharp and irreconcilable differences between Goethe's conception of evolution and that of either Darwin or Spencer are apparent. Nothing has yet been decided, in a precise and positive sense, about this issue. In any event, it is generally recognized that he must be numbered among the forerunners and pioneers of the evolutionary theory. He himself has brought this fact

1. J. W. Goethe, *Zahme Xenien,* I, "Werke" (Weimar, H. Böhlau, 1890), III, 243.
2. Goethe, *Maximen und Reflexionen,* ed. M. Hecker, "Schriften der Goethe-Gesellschaft" (Weimar, Goethe-Gesellschaft, 1907), XXI, No. 700, 154. "The most dangerous prejudice is that which would put any branch of scientific research under the ban."
3. A. Hansen, *Goethes Metamorphose der Pflanzen* (Giessen, A. Töpelmann, 1907); and *Goethes Morphologie* (Giessen, A. Töpelmann, 1919).

home to us by his passionately active part in the controversy between Geoffroy Saint-Hilaire and Cuvier. He believed that his own
cause was at stake. "The matter is of the highest significance," he
said to Soret, "and you have no conception of how I feel about the
report of the meeting of the Paris Academy of Sciences on July 19.
We now have in Geoffroy Saint-Hilaire a powerful ally for the principle of permanence . . . This event is of untold value to me, and I
have every right to rejoice over the final and sweeping victory of a
cause to which I have devoted my life, and which at the same time is
pre-eminently my own." [4]

Nevertheless, when the content and intellectual motives of Goethe's
view of nature are more carefully examined they are found to be
not fully in agreement with the notion of evolution espoused by
Lamarck and by Geoffroy Saint-Hilaire. Even with respect to them
he represented a peculiar and independent view, and when traced
back to its real sources and basic intellectual purposes this view stands
much closer to that of Cuvier than Goethe himself consciously realized. For with Goethe, too, the concept of type held a dominant position, and without it he could not have proposed and developed his
theory of metamorphosis. He never renounced this idea of type,
though he modified the version of Cuvier and Candolle in a highly
significant way, a modification which marks a turning point and reversal in the current of biological thought.

To Cuvier or Candolle "type" was an expression of definite and
basic constant relationships in the structure of living things that
are fixed and unalterable and upon which all knowledge of them
depends. They follow rules no less inviolable than the purely ideal
figures of geometry. Candolle insisted that the disposition of the
parts was the most important factor for the establishment of the plan
of symmetry of a plant. Likewise K. Ernst von Baer explained the
type as the "positional relationship of the inherent elements and
the organs." [5] But this point of view was not Goethe's. He did not
think geometrically or statically, but dynamically throughout. He
did not reject permanence, but he recognized no other kind than that
which displays itself in the midst of change, which alone can discover it to us. In the connection and indissoluble correlation between
permanence and change he sought the distinguishing characteristic
of the "ideal way of thinking," which he himself had adopted and

4. W. F. v. Biedermann, Zu Soret, 2. August 1830, *Goethes Gespräche* (Leipzig,
F. W. v. Biedermann, 1910), IV, 290 f.; V, 175 f.
5. K. E. v. Baer, *Über Entwickelungsgeschichte der Tiere* (Königsberg, Bornträger,
1828), Teil I; Teil II (1837).

which he contrasted sharply with the analytical method that had prevailed during the eighteenth century.[6] The "ideal mode" of thought, according to Goethe, is that which allows the "eternal to be seen in the transitory," and he said that through it we should be raised gradually to the proper viewpoint, "where human understanding and philosophy are one." [7] Philosophy seeks the unchanging, the enduring, that which transcends space and time; but "we humans are appointed to live with extension and movement." [8] We have life only in a colored reflection of life, and existence is not comprehensible or accessible to us except as it unfolds itself before us in change. This peculiar intermingling of being and becoming, of permanence and change, was comprehended in the concept of form, which became for Goethe the fundamental biological concept. Form is akin to type, but the geometrical fixity of the type is no longer suited to the form. The difference is that form belongs to another dimension, as it were. For the type, as Cuvier and Candolle thought of it, a three-dimensional model could be made, not as something abstracted from individual forms but actually just a model by reference to which the connections and spatial relationships that uniformly recur in countless single organisms could be studied. But true biological form could never be adequately understood simply in this way, for here we are on another plane. Form belongs not only to space but to time as well, and it must assert itself in the temporal. This could not consist in merely static being, for any such condition of a life form would be tantamount to its extinction.

> *Es soll sich regen, schaffend handeln,*
> *Erst sich gestalten, dann verwandeln;*
> *Nur scheinbar steht's Momente still,*
> *Das Ewige regt sich fort in allen:*
> *Denn alles muss in Nichts zerfallen,*
> *Wenn es im Sein beharren will.*[9]

6. For further details see Cassirer, "Goethe und das 18. Jahrhundert," *Goethe und die geschichtliche Welt,* Drei Aufsätze (Berlin, B. Cassirer, 1932), S. 27 ff.

7. Goethe, "Aphoristisches zu Joachim Jungius Leben und Schriften," *Naturwissenschaftliche Schriften,* "Werke," Zweite Abteil., Bd. VII: "Zur Morphologie" (Weimar, H. Böhlau, 1892), Teil II, 120.

8. Goethe, *Maximen und Reflexionen, op. cit.,* XXI, No. 643, 141.

9. Goethe, *Gedichte, Eins und Alles,* "Goethes Werke" (Weimar, H. Böhlau, 1890), III, 81.

> First it must stir in self-creation,
> Shaping itself for transformation,
> And merely seems at moments still.
> The Eternal energizes all;
> Each into nothingness must fall
> If preservation be its will.

It is remarkable how everything developed logically and consistently from this one original and basic concept of Goethe. It gave him the great theme of his view of nature, which recurs again and again in countless variations. Thus he could well have entitled his studies on morphology *The Formation and Transformation of Organic Beings.* "Here may be the place to remark," he said in his review of the discussion between Cuvier and Geoffroy Saint-Hilaire,

that this is the easiest way for the naturalist to make his first acquaintance with the value and importance of laws and rules. If we see at the outset the regularity of nature we are apt to think that it is necessarily so, and was so ordained from the very first, and hence that it is something fixed and static. But if we meet first with the varieties, the deformities, the monstrous misshapes, we realize that although the law is constant and eternal it is also living; that organisms can transform themselves into misshapen things not in defiance of law, but in conformity with it, while at the same time, as if curbed with a bridle, they are forced to acknowledge its inevitable dominion.[10]

As a comparison with the earlier botany will show, this view not only extended the content of previous descriptions of nature to an extraordinary degree but set up a new ideal of knowledge and thereby gave a new meaning and direction to scientific observation itself. "The period in botany that began with Goethe," says Hansen, a modern investigator, "bears about the same relation to the preceding period of Linnaeus as the era of chemistry bears to that of alchemy." Goethe was, he continued, the first "rational empiricist" in the field of botany, whereas Linnaeus was nothing but a Schoolman who believed that plants had been created simply for man to register and classify.[11]

Goethe himself would not have approved of this harsh and biased opinion. He placed no small value on the taxonomic labors of Linnaeus; he thought them indispensable, and never failed to acknowledge his great indebtedness to them. On a journey undertaken in November, 1785, he wrote to Frau von Stein that he had taken the *Philosophia Botanica* with him, and now hoped at last to be able to study it without interruption.[12] It was not wholly theoretical considerations that prevented him from remaining a disciple of Linnaeus, but rather his own special feeling for nature and for life. He said

10. Goethe, "Principes de Philosophie zoologique, discutés en Mars 1830 au sein de l'Académie Royale des Sciences," *Naturwiss. Schriften,* "Werke," VII, 189 f.

11. Hansen, *Goethes Metamorphose . . . ,* Teil I, S. viii, 125 ff.

12. *Goethes Briefe* (Weimar Ausgabe), VII, 117.

of himself that the eye was the organ with which he investigated the world, and that he felt himself "born to see, appointed to look." From this standpoint he developed his ideal of knowledge, *scientia intuitiva* or intuitive knowing, invoking Spinoza, whose fundamental ideas, of course, underwent a characteristic change at his hands, for Goethe transformed the metaphysical intuition of Spinoza into an empirical intuition. He wrote to F. H. Jacobi, after having read his *Lehre des Spinoza in Briefen an Moses Mendelssohn:*

When you say that we can only *believe* in God, I reply that I lay great stress on *seeing*, and when Spinoza says of *scientia intuitiva: Hoc cognoscendi genus procedit ab adaequata idea essentiae formalis quorundam Dei attributorum ad adaequatam cognitionem essentiae rerum,*[13] these few words encourage me to devote my whole life to reflecting upon things that I may hope to grasp and of whose "formal essence" I may hope to form an adequate idea, without worrying in the least over how far I shall get and what is in store for me.[14]

For this task of seeing nature he in nowise rejected the method of classification. It seemed indispensable to him, in accordance with his own saying, that in order to find a way into the infinite one must "first distinguish and then unite." [15] But he was not searching for a mere survey or a "pure theory" of nature; he wanted to understand her throughout and penetrate to her very heart. "What does all our communion with nature amount to, indeed," he said, once more referring to the difference between Cuvier and Geoffroy Saint-Hilaire, "if we busy ourselves with analyzing only single material portions, and do not feel the breath of the spirit that dictates the role of every part and restrains or sanctions all excess through an immanent law?" [16]

Neither Linnaeus' concept of species nor Cuvier's idea of type could make this "breath of the spirit" perceptible, or this "immanent law" intelligible. Consequently Goethe had to strive to go beyond them both if nature were not to remain forever a riddle to him. His greatness as an investigator, however, lies in the fact that he did not give way to his poetic imagination in so doing, but discovered a form of conception of his own, appropriate to his way of observ-

---

13. "This kind of knowing proceeds from an adequate idea of the formal essence of certain attributes of God to the adequate knowledge of the essence of things." Spinoza, *Ethic,* Bk. II, Prop. XL, Schol. 2.

14. An Jacobi, 5. Mai 1786, *Goethes Briefe,* VII, 214.

15. "Atmosphäre," *Gedichte,* III, 97.

16. An Eckermann, 2. August 1830, *Goethes Gespräche,* V, 175.

ing nature and created his own theory of method, which put biology as a science on a new foundation.

In an account of his botanical studies he described the transformations they had undergone, which gives us a direct insight into his inner motives.

So with others like myself, contemporaries of Linnaeus, I was appreciative of his sweep of view and marvelous accomplishments. I had surrendered myself to him and to his theory with perfect confidence but gradually I came to realize, without knowing it, that there was much to make me dubious at least, if not to hold me back on the road upon which I had set out. Were I now to bring the circumstances of those days into clear consciousness, I should have to be pictured as a born poet, who was studying how to form his words and expressions so that they would apply accurately and justly to each object as it actually existed. One who approached the subject that way would adopt a terminology already established and have in his memory and at his disposal a certain . . . number of nouns and adjectives, so that when confronted with any sort of organism he would be able, by skillful selection, to give it a suitable name and classify it . . . Now even though I could understand the necessity for this procedure, whose aim it was to achieve familiarity with plants by describing certain external characteristics in a generally accepted nomenclature . . . I found that the chief difficulty in such an attempt at a precise application was the variability of the organs of the plants. When I discovered on the same stem first roundish, then notched, and at last virtually pinnate leaves, which next contracted, grew simpler, changed to small scales, and finally disappeared altogether, I lost the courage to drive in fixed stakes between them or even to draw any lines of demarcation. The problem of defining genera with fixity and arranging the species under them appeared to me insoluble. Attentively I studied what was to be done, but how could I hope for accurate identification when even during the lifetime of Linnaeus many of his designated "genera" had already been separated and broken up and, what is more, the classes themselves actually done away with? It seemed to follow from this that even that most acute of men, highly gifted with genius though he was, could only become master of nature in the gross. Though my reverence for him was not in the least diminished there did arise in consequence of all this a peculiar conflict within my own mind.[17]

Goethe came out of this predicament by setting up his theory of the metamorphosis of plants. We need not concern ourselves here

17. Goethe, *Naturwiss. Schriften,* "Werke," VI, 115 ff.

with its content, but only with its place in the development of the biological ideal of knowledge. Goethe's theory is the most remarkable, and perhaps a unique, example of a "born poet" penetrating into a definite field of empirical research in natural science and making himself fully master of it without forsaking for a moment his truly poetic nature. That there should come from his efforts not only an artistic picture of nature, but that permanent objective results should be secured and new and fertile methods of research discovered can be explained by the cast of Goethe's genius and the way in which his various powers reacted on one another and maintained a nice balance. Observation and thought, fantasy and emotion, all worked together in this achievement, and it is hardly possible to say which of these was actually foremost. Kant wrote that genius, in the aesthetic sense, is the "formative principle in the mind." "But what this principle makes use of when it animates the mind, the stuff it uses, is whatever stimulates the powers of the mind to a purposive activity, that is, to a self-maintaining activity, and one which further strengthens those very powers of mind themselves." [18] Such a free play of the intellectual faculties, upon which, in Kant's opinion, every great work of art depends, is to be observed in the development of Goethe's view of nature. All his forces participated, and each gave ample scope to the others. One single great feeling, his dynamic sense of life, permeated the whole. But mere feeling was not all; everything must be made clear to perception, elevated to firm and certain form. This was not to be attained by way of pure concepts, for these could only separate, not truly unite. To the analytical work of the concept, which is indispensable, there must be joined the synthetic work of the imagination. This is how the transition can be made from mere "conceptions" of nature to "ideas" of nature. But throughout all this there must prevail a most careful and faithful attention to the proper functioning of the imagination. Only so can we be certain that we have not been building in a vacuum or chasing after empty shadows.

It was in this way that Goethe arrived at his idea of the "ancestral plant," whose existence he thought confirmed because "the spirit of the actual is the true ideal." [19] How could this or that organism be recognized as a plant, were it not that all plants are formed according to one pattern? "With this pattern, and the key thereto, one can still discover plants *ad infinitum* which must be consistent with the pattern; that is to say, they might exist even though they do not, and hence they are not merely poetic shadows and apparitions but

18. Kant, *Kritik der Urteilskraft*, § 49.
19. Biedermann, Äusserung Goethes zu Riemer (1827), *Goethes Gespräche*, III, 484.

have intrinsic truth and necessity. The same law," he continued, "is capable of application to all other living things." [20] "Fundamentally there is an inner and original community in all organization," and he emphasized the fact that this "includes the animal world too," but, on the other hand, the "differences in form result from necessary adaptations to the environment and one may rightly assume at the same time both an original difference and unceasingly progressive transformation in order to explain the variations as well as the constant appearances." [21]

Thus Goethe could not relinquish the idea of "type," for he regarded any description of nature as impossible without it, but he rejected the idea when it meant, as with Cuvier, setting up rigid and insurmountable barriers between different classes of organic beings. All the higher organisms are created according to an original pattern which varies more or less only in respect to the least stable parts of the organism, which is ever changing and developing through propagation.

Would it be impossible, then, once we recognize that the creative force has engendered and developed the more complete organisms according to a universal plan, to make this ancestral form evident, if not to the senses at least to the mind, and to work out our descriptions in conformity with it as a norm, and further, since it had been reached by abstraction from the forms of the various animals, to trace the most dissimilar forms back to it again? Once one has grasped the idea of this type, however, he will see quite well how impossible it would be to set up a single order as a criterion. An individual cannot serve as a standard for the whole, and so we must not seek the model for all in any one. Classes, orders, species, and individuals are related as cases are to a law; they are included under it, but do not constitute it. [22]

Thus the dogma of the invariability of species was abandoned; yet Goethe, believing in the ancestral form that appears to the mind but not to the senses, was very little disposed to go over to a theory of organic evolution in the sense of Lamarck or Darwin. He had set up an independent ideal of biological knowledge, that of "idealistic morphology," which has to be understood and appreciated in its unique character.

The uniqueness was long unrecognized because those who sought to make his ideas intelligible looked for analogies, which obscured

20. Brief an Frau von Stein, 8. Juni 1787, *Goethes Briefe,* VIII, 232 f.; *Italienische Reise,* "Werke," XXXI, 147.
21. Goethe, "Die Skelette der Nagetiere," *Naturwiss. Schriften,* VIII, 253.
22. Goethe, "Entwurf einer vergleichenden Anatomie," *ibid.,* VIII, 73 ff.

rather than clarified their meaning. Only in the past few decades has there come a change. Science has been gradually learning to see Goethe's fundamental concepts with his own eyes, instead of measuring them by the standards of others.[23] There are two dangers here that must be carefully avoided. It is customary either to regard his theory as a thesis in natural philosophy that rests almost wholly on speculative grounds, or to seek its meaning and value in the purely empirical. Goethe was as little a natural philosopher in the sense of Schelling, however, as he was an empiricist after the fashion of Darwin. There prevails in his writings a relationship of the "particular" to the "universal" such as can hardly be found elsewhere in the history of philosophy or of natural science. It was his firm conviction that the particular and the universal are not only intimately connected but that they interpenetrate one another. The "factual" and the "theoretical" were not opposite poles to him, but only two expressions and factors of a unified and irreducible relation. This is one of the basic maxims in his view of nature. "The highest thing would be," he said, "to realize everything factual as being itself theoretical. The blue of the sky reveals the fundamental law of chromatics. Look not only for something behind the phenomena, for these are themselves the theory." [24] This sounds like the language of a strict empiricist, who might be satisfied with a simple description of phenomena and not raise any question as to their "causes." Yet, on the other hand, there was for Goethe no experience that stands entirely by itself and is to be regarded as a detached entity. "Time is governed by the oscillations of a pendulum, the moral and scientific worlds by oscillations between ideas and experience." [25]

Thus experience must swing one way toward the idea, and the idea back again toward experience if any knowledge of nature is to arise. There is no question which of the two is of greater value, or whether one is superior or subordinate to the other. Here a per-

23. In my *Freiheit und Form; Studien zur deutschen Geistesgeschichte* (Berlin, B. Cassirer, 1915), IV, 271 ff., I have endeavored to present in detail the full significance of the idea of metamorphosis for Goethe's whole view of life and the world.

In the biological literature the originality of and methodological justification for idealistic morphology have been clearly set forth by Adolf Naef in particular (*Idealistische Morphologie und Phylogenetik. Zur Methodik der systematischen Morphologie* [Jena, G. Fischer, 1919]). See also Adolf Meyer, *Ideen und Ideale der biologischen Erkenntnis* (Leipzig, J. A. Barth, 1934).

The term "idealistic morphology" was coined by E. Rádl in his *Geschichte der biologischen Theorien in der Neuzeit* (Leipzig, W. Engelmann, 1905, 1909). At the time he did not do full justice to Goethe's accomplishment, but as a result of Hansen's presentation (see p. 137) his judgment was substantially modified in a second edition.

24. Goethe, *Maximen und Reflexionen, op. cit.*, No. 575.

25. Goethe, "Zur Morphologie," Verfolg, *Naturwiss. Schriften*, VI, 354.

fectly reciprocal determination holds. "The particular always underlies the universal; the universal must forever submit to the particular." [26] The relation between the two, according to Goethe, is not
one of logical subsumption but of ideal or "symbolic" representation. The particular represents the universal, "not as a dream and
shadow, but as a momentarily living manifestation of the inscrutable." [27] For the true naturalist one "pregnant instance," not countless, scattered observations, exhibits the "immanent law" of nature.
For this relationship neither "deduction" nor "induction," as they
are ordinarily called, is a pertinent and adequate expression. Goethe
was always violently opposed to the deduction of a theory of nature,
in the sense of a derivation from abstract mathematical principles,
and there was no way for him to come to an appreciation of Newton's *Philosophiae naturalis principia mathematica*. But neither
could he subscribe to Bacon's inductive method and he once went
so far as to say that he "had never permitted himself induction."
His reproach to Bacon was that "single cases received too much
prominence," and that "before one could achieve the simplification
and the conclusion by induction, even the kind that Bacon recommended, life would have gone and one's powers would have been con-
sumed." [28] To the genius "one case is as good as thousands" provided he can detect in it the law that governs the whole.

Only if one is fully cognizant of this peculiar relation between
"idea" and "appearance" is it possible to understand clearly the
position that Goethe's theory of type and metamorphosis takes in the
history of biological thought, which he influenced very strongly and
even transformed. Nevertheless he did not "found a school," and
nothing actually like his fundamental view can really be found in
any philosophical thinker or in any empirical investigator. Cuvier's
idea of type, as we have seen, bears an explicitly deductive character
and biology was sometimes brought by that, as far as its purely
logical character is concerned, very close to mathematics. Cuvier's
fundamental principles were designed to effect the special task that
he, as an empirical investigator, had set himself, and his highest goal
was that of comparative anatomy. What he really sought was the
statics of vital phenomena. Accordingly he regarded the natural
forms as stereometric forms, with fixed and invariable structure. Once
this structure were apprehended it is evident that although the vari-

26. *Maximen und Reflexionen*, No. 199, S. 35.
27. *Ibid.*, No. 314, S. 59.
28. "Zur Farbenlehre," historischer Teil, *Naturwiss. Schriften*, III, 236.

ous groups of organisms are sharply separated and none can be traced back to another, there is within each group a merely apparent diversity, a mere congeries of unrelated modifications. Here all things hang together rather like the links in a chain. Hence it makes relatively little difference at what point observation is begun, for we can be sure of obtaining the whole of the chain in every case, thanks to the strict law of correlation. As every property of a geometrical figure, such as a circle or a parabola, can be employed to derive its analytic equation, and this leads to all other properties of the curve, so in biology a similar process of derivation can be used, once the concept of type, which can be acquired only through observation, has been thoroughly understood. Thus "necessity of connection" was not confined to mathematics or logic according to Cuvier but extended over the structural theory of living things and hence into descriptive natural science.[29] In considering biological forms, therefore, it was always justifiable to employ mathematical illustrations, since these are more than metaphors or analogies; indeed, they will yield a glimpse into the objective architecture of living organisms.

According to Candolle botany has to search into the symmetry of plants just as crystallography does into the symmetry of crystals. This view was carried farthest by Nees von Esenbeck, who sought to trace all forms of life, and especially plants, to geometrical ground plans.[30] He was among those investigators who were most strongly influenced by Goethe's theory of metamorphosis, and Goethe said of him that he had had the largest share in spreading abroad a convincing view of plant structure that agreed with nature.[31] Esenbeck's own basic tendency was not the same as that of Goethe, for the latter did not think of forms in space but of forms in time. His "ideal way of thinking" aimed to see "the eternal in the transitory," and it could not be satisfied, therefore, with whatever could be gathered from quiescent stereometric form. And it was just as impossible in his opinion to conceive of the phenomena of life arithmetically, through purely numerical relationships. "Numbers," he said to Riemer, "like our poor words, are but attempts to understand and give expression to appearances—they are forever inadequate approximations." [32] And to Zelter he wrote that he had from the first avoided all nu-

29. See the citation from Cuvier's *Discours sur les révolutions de la surface du globe.* Above, pp. 130–131.

30. For further details see Rádl, *op. cit.* (1909), Teil II, S. 23.

31. Goethe, "Zur Morphologie," Verfolg, *op. cit.,* VI, 255.

32. Goethe, "27. März 1814 an Riemer," *Goethes Gespräche, November 1808 bis September 1823,* ed. Biedermann (Leipzig, Biedermann, 1909), II, 223.

merical symbolism, from the Pythagorean down to that of the latest mathematical mystic, as "formless and unrewarding." [33] No less did he feel himself compelled to reject all mechanical models based solely on arithmetic and geometry.

When Link, the botanist, in his *Elementa philosophiae botanicae* (1824) interpreted Goethe's theory in the sense that the "oscillations of nature" are found not only in mechanical movement like that of the pendulum and of waves, etc., but also in living bodies and the periods of life,[34] Goethe spoke dubiously of this interpretation and seeming praise of his theory, "since where formation and transformation should actually have been under discussion, it is only the final vague, sublimated abstraction that is trotted forth, and the most highly organized life is associated with the most general sort of natural appearances that are completely devoid of form and body." [35] The type itself is a being that is only perceived in its development, a permanence that exists only as it comes to pass. Thus Goethe spoke of the "modality and flexibility" of the type, which is paradoxical enough when its original meaning is recalled to mind: he described the type, indeed, as a "real Proteus." [36] While we hold fast to the permanent, he went on, we must learn at the same time to change our views with the changeable and become acquainted with its manifold variability, so that we may be ready to pursue the type through all its changes and never let this Proteus slip away from us.[37] Thus alone can we penetrate to the true harmony in nature, which is to be heard only in the eternal rhythm of life. Each creature is but "one single note, a nuance, in a great harmony, which must be studied as a whole, otherwise each individual thing is but a meaningless item." These were the words Goethe wrote to Knebel when he sent him the manuscript that contained his discovery of the intermaxillary bone in man. It was from this standpoint the manuscript had been written and this, in reality, was the underlying interest that lay concealed in it.[38]

But here is the chief problem by reference to which Goethe's whole conception of things is to be adequately characterized. Does Goethe mean, when he rejects the rigid spatial form and thinks in

---

33. Goethe, "12. Dez. 1812 an Zelter," *Goethes Briefe, Mai 1812–August 1813,* "Goethes Werke" (Weimar, H. Bölaus Nachfolger, 1900), XXIII, 197.

34. Link, *Elementa philosophiae botanicae* (1824).

35. Goethe, "Zur Morphologie," *op. cit.,* VI, 261 f.

36. *Ibid.,* S. 313.

37. Goethe, "Einleitung in die vergleichende Anatomie," *Naturwiss. Schriften,* VIII, 18.

38. An Knebel, 17. November 1784, *Briefe,* VI, S. 390.

terms of temporal forms and rhythms, to commit and to restrict biology to the consideration of empirical events alone? Must he, because he would not conceive of life in mathematical terms, become the historian of life? Those who saw in him the pioneer and forerunner of the Darwinian theory of the origin of species have answered this question in the affirmative. But a general objection can be made to this view. Goethe rejected in the most decisive fashion not only all "mathematicism" but every form of "historicism" as well. He thought very little of history as a science; he explained that what is given there could make no claim to be regarded as the actual truth. About everything historical there was something of a wondrously uncertain nature; the best that could be attained was symbol or legend.[39] Would he entrust biology, the one firm basis for his view of the world, to such an uncertain factor; was the question of the genesis and temporal development of life of such burning interest to him? This is actually not the case. The theory of metamorphosis has nothing to do with this question of the historic sequence of the appearances of life. It is quite separate from every sort of "theory of descent" not only in its content but in the posing of the question and in method.[40] Goethe's concept of "genesis" is dynamic, not historical; it connects widely unrelated forms, demonstrating how they are constantly intermediated, but it aims to set up no genealogical trees of the species. The transformation by virtue of which various parts of the plant, its sepals, petals, stamens, and so on, originated from the one common archetype, the leaf, is an ideal, not a real genesis. "It is not a broadening but a deformation of the sciences," said Kant, "when their boundaries are allowed to run together." It would be such a deformation if we were to confound Goethe's biological idea of knowledge with that of Darwin or Haeckel. Today the clarification in this field has at last come about, and the special type of knowledge to which idealistic morphology belongs has been made plain. Naef wrote that ". . . idealistic morphology has been, in the history of the science, the presupposition for the introduction of phylogenetics . . . and what is more still, it must be put in the forefront even today on logical grounds." [41] And Schaxel declared that comparative anatomy, raised by Goethe to an independent science at the end of the eighteenth and the beginning of the nineteenth century under the name of *morphology*, was "per-

---

39. An Zelter, 27. März 1824, *Briefe*, XXXVIII, 92. For further details see Cassirer, *Goethe und die geschichtliche Welt.*

40. For the details of this difference see Hansen, "Metamorphosenlehre und Deszendenztheorie," *Goethes Metamorphose* . . . , Teil I, S. 103 ff., 367 ff.

41. Naef, *Idealistische Morphologie und Phylogenetik.*

haps the most magnificent statement of a problem" concerning the organism that had been attempted since the time of Aristotle.[42]

But its magnificence cannot, of course, permit us to overlook its inherent limitations. This one particular problem could be posed so sharply and definitely only by avoiding other problems, whether it was because the time was not ripe for handling them or because they had to be considered in general as insoluble according to the presuppositions of Goethe's own view. Only time brought these questions to light, and this has placed the problem of knowledge in biology on new ground and fundamentally altered the biological ideal of knowledge.

42. Schaxel, *Grundzüge der Theorienbildung in der Biologie* (Jena, G. Fischer, 1922), S. 22.

VIII

Developmental History as a Problem and a Maxim

THE PROBLEM of the origin and development of organisms has occupied philosophy since its earliest beginning. Few questions were so calculated to arouse philosophic "wonder." The first attempts at a theoretical answer are found in the Ionian natural philosophy, and curious and naïve though they may appear some historians have not hesitated to ascribe to Anaximander "a foreshadowing of the modern theory of evolution." [1]

Aristotle went far beyond these primitive beginnings by putting the problem of developmental history on a firm empirical basis, treating it at the same time in the truly universal spirit of his philosophy. His *De generatione animalium* made him the founder of comparative embryology. Many of the facts to which he there alluded were only rediscovered and confirmed in the nineteenth century. In few fields of research has that union of keen observation and speculative thought that distinguished Aristotle revealed itself so brilliantly, and his authority here remained quite unshaken even when the Renaissance built up a new view of nature sharply opposed to the Aristotelian Scholastic physics.

In his struggle against scholastic physics, Descartes referred to Harvey, and praised him for having first opened the way, with his discovery of the circulation of the blood, for the mechanistic view of nature. But Harvey was still a thoroughgoing Aristotelian; indeed, Aristotle's science, to which he owed his comparative methods and his ontogenetic views, seems to have been one of the factors that led him to his great discovery. Reviewing the development of embryology during the seventeenth century in his history of biological theories, Rádl described Harvey as the "foremost disciple of Aristotle," and explained that the adversaries of the immortal English investigator could reproach him because his theory was completely encased in "Aristotelian armor." [2]

In the second half of the seventeenth century the discovery of the spermatozoa marked a decisive empirical advance, but it also gave occasion for the strangest speculations. Thus spermatozoa were

1. T. Gomperz, *Griechische Denker* (Leipzig, Veit & Co., 1896), I, 45.
2. E. Rádl, "Embryologie," *Geschichte der biologischen Theorien in der Neuzeit*, Teil I, S. 134 ff.

pictured in Leeuwenhoek's *Arcana naturae detecta* as homunculi with heads, trunks, hands, and feet.[3] But the marvels of microbiology disclosed by the microscope not only stimulated imagination in the highest degree; they fructified, too, the strictly systematic thinking of philosophy. Leibniz, for example, liked to refer, for the basis of his idea of the monad, to the discoveries of Malpighi, Swammerdam, and Leeuwenhoek.[4] The century deluded itself with the vain hope that the telescope and the microscope would not only raise human knowledge to a new plane, but that the chasm between the infinitely great and the infinitely small could be bridged at last. "It is certain," wrote Leibniz, in sketching the foundations of natural right, "that the capacities of mankind have been immeasurably increased in our time. The heavens themselves have drawn nearer and our eyes have become sharper, so that we can peer into the heart of things; the picture has been magnified a hundred times, and we behold new worlds and new species that amaze us, either because of their magnitude or their diminutive size." [5]

In biology itself, Caspar Friedrich Wolff's *Theoria Generationis* (1759) first brought about the triumph of the theory of epigenesis, which immediately showed itself superior to the older preformation and "box-in-box," or *emboîtement*, theories. Here the ideas of Leibniz continued to exert an influence, but they were developed in a sense opposite to his own. "Whereas the evolutionists borrowed only Leibniz' superficial ideas," concluded Rádl, "and thought that the organism develops from a pre-existing form by mere increase in size, others such as Needham and later C. F. Wolff, had a deeper grasp of the concept of the monad, which develops through its own inherent power . . . The historical sources of Wolff's epigenetic theory were, first, Leibniz . . . with his theory of the monad, and secondly Needham, who attempted to apply this idea to embryonal development." [6]

Goethe agreed wholeheartedly with Wolff's theory, believing that he recognized a comrade in arms. Of course he did not forget to draw the boundary, in terms of method, between the empirical trend of Wolff's research and his own "idealistic" morphology and he coined an expression that was illuminating and characteristic of his whole manner of reflecting on nature. Wolff, he said,

3. For details see Rádl, I, 173.
4. See, for example, G. W. Leibniz, *Die philosophischen Schriften von Gottfried Wilhelm Leibniz,* ed. C. J. Gerhardt (1880), IV, 480; *Système nouveau de la communication des substances, aussi bien que de l'union qu'il y a entre l'âme et le corps.*
5. G. W. Leibniz, "Juris et aequi elementa," *Mitteilungen aus Leibnizens ungedruckten Schriften,* ed. G. Mollat (Leipzig, H. Haessel, 1893), S. 19.
6. Rádl, *op. cit.,* I, 242 f.

makes it a fundamental maxim of all his research to assume, grant, and assert nothing but what he can see with his own eyes and demonstrate to others at any time. That is why he always tries to penetrate to the very beginnings of the formation of life by microscopic research, so as to trace organic embryos from their earliest appearance through all their development. However excellent this method is—and he has accomplished so much with it—still this admirable man has not realized that there is a difference between seeing and seeing; that the eye of the spirit and the eye of the body have to work continually in a vital union because otherwise there is danger of seeing and yet entirely overlooking what is there.[7]

Wolff's investigations were wholly concerned with ontogenesis, but once his findings had been accepted they necessarily led over to phylogenetic problems, and the two fields drew constantly closer until their separation became hardly perceptible. The principle that ontogenesis is actually but a recapitulation of phylogenesis had already been advanced. Meckel, the first to defend it, was an adherent of Wolff and had paved the way for it with a German translation of one of Wolff's Latin embryological treatises. As early as 1821 Meckel had mentioned a "similarity between the evolution of the embryo and that of the animal order," and suggested that in their development the higher animals must pass through the forms of the lower and more simple ones.[8] But this "biogenetic law," in the form here stated, did not take its place immediately in the science of the nineteenth century, for the real founder of modern embryology, Karl Ernst von Baer, did not recognize the principle as so conceived but vigorously attacked it. In his work on the developmental history of animals,[9] which contains fundamental investigations on the origin of the ovum in mammals, including man, von Baer of course recognized that there was an ascending sequence of organisms, but he rejected the notion that in their development the higher members actually pass through all the stages of the subordinate and more simple forms. He rested his case on the Aristotelian version of development, according to which this one progressive differentiation is a case of advance from the "universal" to the "particular." Features common to its group are completed in the embryo before those that are in-

7. Goethe, "Zur Morphologie. Entdeckung eines trefflichen Vorarbeiters," *Naturwiss. Schriften,* VI, 155 f.

8. J. F. Meckel, *System der vergleichenden Anatomie* (Halle, Rengerschen Buchhandlung, 1821), 6 Bde. See also Oskar Hertwig, *Das Werden der Organismen* (2. Aufl. Jena, 1922).

9. Baer, *Über Entwickelungsgeschichte der Tiere,* Teile I, II.

dividual to it; first the characteristics of the type develop, then those of the class, the order, the family, the genus, and the species. Only with the rise of the Darwinian formulation later did there grow out of this ideal concept the real prototype of developmental history, and with it Haeckel's thesis that ontogeny is an abbreviated and incomplete recapitulation of phylogeny.[10] Different animals may look alike during their development, of course, and the younger the embryos are the more difficult are they to distinguish from one another. But similarity is not identity. The differences upon which Cuvier had founded his theory of type are not effaced by development, and the essential properties of one animal group can never appear in the fully developed members of another: gill respiration, for example, which makes a fish a fish, is never encountered at any time in the embryonic stages of mammals or birds.[11]

The discussion had reached this point when there entered an investigator, Mathias Schleiden, who had been led to it not, as Meckel was through anatomy or as von Baer, through zoology, but through the efforts he had been making toward the establishment of botany on new scientific foundations. As a scientific thinker Schleiden presents a curious figure, differing from the traditional type in both personality and the course of his life. Even what he accomplished has been very differently judged and evaluated. But it is incontestable that his discovery of the significance of the nucleus and his introduction of the cell theory into botany were of epochal importance, even though his idea of the cell does not correspond entirely with the modern view.[12] But hardly less remarkable and penetrating was his view of the method of botany. This he explained fully in a long introduction to his book on the elements of botany,[13] and said in his preface that he placed the highest value on the hints suggested there. Before one can pursue a definite aim in research one has to be clear about the road he proposes to follow. The wrong road can never lead to truth, for the mind's activity naturally conforms to certain rules, which one can never break without falling into irreparable error. To read only these sentences from Schleiden's introduction is to

10. Haeckel, *Generelle Morphologie der Organismen* (Berlin, G. Reimer, 1866). For the distinction between von Baer's theory and this view see Schaxel, *Grundzüge der Theorienbildung in der Biologie*, S. 28.

11. For details on von Baer's idea of the relations between ontogeny and phylogeny, see Rádl, *op. cit.*, II, 60 ff., and Nordenskiöld, *op. cit.*, English trans., pp. 363 f.

12. For the difference between the two see Tschulok, *Das System der Biologie in Forschung und Lehre* (Jena, 1910), S. 99 ff.

13. M. J. Schleiden, *Grundzüge der wissenschaftlichen Botanik nebst einer methodologischen Einleitung als Anleitung zum Studium der Pflanze* (Leipzig, W. Engelmann, 1842), S. 6 ff., 39, 55 f.

realize that here a disciple of Kant is speaking. Indeed he confessed to being an "adherent with all his soul" of Kant's philosophy, especially as he had learned it through Fries. In the name of that philosophy he raised the strongest protest against natural philosophy and dialectics. One must not abandon himself to the "fantastic and childish dreams" of Schelling or the arrogant presumption of Hegel. What had astounded their thoughtless followers and been praised as philosophical profundity was without real scientific content; for to make certain of it one has, above all, to know from what source of knowledge a tenet has been derived, and whether it has been appropriately deduced. The school of Wolff and Kant was infinitely superior in this latter respect to those of the present, and for science there remained no other course than to return to this starting point.

It is obvious that Schleiden was striving for nothing less than the setting up of a theory and critique of science. The value of this critique consists chiefly in this—that it was not content with general and abstract propositions but aimed to translate the insights gained at once into deeds. Historically too Schleiden's influence seems to lie principally in this direction. "Not through his accomplishments as an investigator," said Julius Sachs, "but through what he demanded of science, through the goal that he set up and defended for its superiority over the trivial aims of the textbooks, did he win for himself the greatest merit. He paved the way for those who were capable of really great work . . . From now on anyone who had anything to say must take heed, for he would be measured by an entirely different standard than before." [14] Schleiden made causal inquiry into the plant world the basic and principal goal of botany. All else was purely preparatory and subservient to this task, and in the most drastic and radical terms he demanded the conversion of "biotaxy" into pure "biophysics." [15] Only so, in his opinion, could biology be converted to a true science, to a body of knowledge that would be on a plane with physics and chemistry in both value and objective significance. For science is never a mere collection of facts, but rather a theoretical working over and mastery of them. Everything merely classificatory, and indeed even the merely descriptive or historical, does not deserve the name of science. "If botany cannot assert its right to be called a theoretical science, it is naught but the trifling of an idle curiosity." In putting forward this ideal Schleiden

---

14. J. Sachs, *Geschichte der Botanik vom 16. Jahrhundert bis 1860,* "Geschichte der Wissenschaften in Deutschland," Neuere Zeit (München, R. Oldenbourg, 1875), XV, 202 f.

15. For the difference between the two see Tschulok, *op. cit.,* Kap. ix, S. 174 ff.

obviously approached very closely to Kant, who had asserted that in all knowledge of nature there is only as much real science as there is mathematics. Botany should be treated as a branch of physics, which, in its turn, should be traced back to mathematically demonstrable explanations. So even the method of botany should in principle be nothing other than that of physics: observation and experiment, induction and hypothesis, must be the chief instrument of knowledge here as well as there. Mere classification did not count; it is merely the hod carrier for those who are building true and legitimate science. It should be regarded only as a transitional stage, and to accept it as something conclusive would be to take a "hopeless view of science." Even Linnaeus himself was never guilty of this, continued Schleiden, and his pupils and adherents would have failed in their appreciation of his real genius if they ever meant to keep botany at the stage of mere classification.[16] Until we succeed in tracing appearances back to physical and chemical laws the whole field of research lies entirely unexplored.[17]

Schleiden well understood, of course, that these laws could not take the abstract mathematical form assumed by those of theoretical physics. He wanted to establish botany as an inductive, not a deductive, science, and this aim occupied such a prominent place in the foreground of his thought that he finally expressed it in the title of his book, calling it, from the second edition onward, *Die Botanik als induktive Wissenschaft*. According to Kant, whom Schleiden followed in this respect as well, the distinction between the deductive and inductive sciences is not that the former rest upon universal principles and the latter merely present the factual. The distinction lies rather in the character of these principles: the deductive are concerned with "synthetic principles" of "constitutive" value, the inductive with "maxims." And here the question must be put—what maxims must we make fundamental to botany in order to set it on its sure way to science? Schleiden's answer was that only developmental history offers these maxims. The nature and significance of an organism can be understood only through the history of its development or through the manner in which the complex finished creature grows out of the primitive germ. Even classification of plants is not possible by a mere comparison of individuals but only through their complete developmental history. If we do not possess this clue, we only fall into an unsteady groping about and random guessing without the guidance of principle. The truly natural view of plants is to

16. Schleiden, *op. cit.,* S. 72 ff.
17. *Ibid.,* S. 49.

be gained only by regarding them as a continuous series of forms
and conditions that develop out of one another.[18]

In this sense developmental history was set up as the "real heuristic
maxim of botany." [19] Some have wondered about this conception at
times and regarded it as an unnecessary superstructure to Schleiden's
main thesis. Sachs remarked that it might be considered superfluous
for Schleiden to bring forward developmental history as a maxim,
instead of showing that it really presented itself as a fact of inductive research.[20] But this observation betrays a failure to understand the true character of Schleiden's theory of knowledge. He
wants to keep all metaphysics and speculation on natural philosophy
at a distance from science, but when he aims to establish botany on
the basis of pure induction he understands it in the sense of Kant and
of Fries, his masters in philosophy. In order rightly to understand
his own teaching concerning method, therefore, one must have in
mind not Baconian induction but the other type which Apelt, another pupil of Fries, had thoroughly developed and established. For
Apelt had distinguished explicitly between *empirical* and *rational*
induction and taught that the latter followed a law entirely different from the law of expectation of similar cases. It was this "rational
induction" that Schleiden desired to introduce into botany and he
emphasized, as did Apelt later, that it always requires a "leading
maxim." [21] Botany, therefore, as little as any other theoretical science, could dispense with a universal element.

Every natural science falls naturally into two parts, general and special,
in accordance with the nature of the problem and the course of the investigation. On the general side we start from empirically given particulars
and rise by continued investigation to the supreme principles, the fundamental concepts and laws. Here our problem is to discover these concepts
and laws. In the case of the special part we assume that they have already been discovered and according to the principles of classification
and the order defined by them we work further and further down until
we reach the individual organism. Now the problem is to arrange the
whole mass of individuals under those ruling principles and to define them
thereby.

Thus developmental history was proposed as an intellectual tool,
a *precept*, that should teach us how to probe ever more deeply into

18. *Ibid.*, S. 62, 100 ff.
19. *Ibid.*, S. 107.
20. Sachs, *op. cit.*, S. 204.
21. E. F. Apelt, "Empirische und rationelle Induktion," *Die Theorie der Induction*
(Leipzig, W. Engelmann, 1854), § 6, S. 41 ff.

the structure of the organism. But Schleiden never believed for a moment that he had reached the ultimate goal; on the contrary, he was convinced that such a goal would contradict the true character of empirical investigation. Nothing, he thought, is more harmful to the organic natural sciences than to treat them as a complete system down to the last detail, instead of regarding them as a first step toward an infinitely remote goal. Developmental history ought to bring us nearer to this goal. But it should be conceived not as dogma but as the proper heuristic maxim of botany; it is "at once the sole and the richest source of new discoveries, and will remain so for many years." [22]

It is remarkable and significant how clearly Schleiden, on the basis of the methodological schooling which he owed to the Critical Philosophy, set forth the general program of developmental history that was not to be carried to its proper completion until later. The very idea of development, of course, had to undergo a thorough and characteristic *change of meaning*. There could be no stopping at the "formation and transformation of organic forms" as taught by Goethe (physics and chemistry too had once been declared the only guiding stars of biological research). What had been glimpsed in the idea of plant metamorphosis was now to be empirically established and experimentally confirmed. It became increasingly evident that idealistic morphology was passing into an *experimental morphology*. Hofmeister's discovery of the alternation of generations provided an entirely new concept of development, and now for the first time there became possible a consistent version of sexual propagation throughout the whole vegetable kingdom.[23] At the same time the methodological superiority of developmental history over systematic biology became clearly apparent. If the course of development in plants, which had been assumed to differ radically in the flowering and the nonflowering, was as completely similar as Hofmeister's observations showed, it was evident that the apparent features alone would never suffice for an understanding of the actual relationships, and that recourse must be had to other criteria, which developmental history alone could provide.[24]

With the problem so stated, biology was compelled to give up the

22. Schleiden, *op. cit.,* S. 107.

23. W. Hofmeister, *Vergleichende Untersuchungen der Keimung, Entfaltung und Fruchtbildung höherer Kryptogamen* (Leipzig, F. Hofmeister, 1851). For further details see Sachs, *op. cit.,* S. 214 ff.

24. For details see C. v. Goebel, *Einleitung in die experimentelle Morphologie der Pflanzen* (Leipzig und Berlin, B. G. Teubner, 1908), S. 2; "Die Grundprobleme der heutigen Pflanzenmorphologie," *Biologisches Zentralblatt,* XXV (1. Februar 1905, Leipzig, G. Thieme, 1905), 66.

notion of a "wholly passive" observation of nature and to make an effort at eliciting the phenomena instead of merely describing them.[25] This was far removed from the goal of idealistic morphology, for Goethe had been convinced that nature's secret could never be wrung from her "with levers and screws." But Goebel attempted a logical development of the new concept in his *Organographie der Pflanzen*. He proceeded from the view that if metamorphosis were a truly fertile principle of knowledge, it must be regarded not only as ideal but real; as not only conceptual but an actual transformation.[26] This change could be fully understood however only if it could be imitated, that is to say, if forms of life could be produced instead of simply observed. The ideal of the manipulation of nature (*encheiresis naturae*), rejected and derided by Goethe, was now to become a complete and literal truth. Schaxel said of Klebs, an investigator of this school, that the results of his research were reminiscent of the mechanical ideal of an engineer of the organic, for he had written that in the modern state of causal morphology the main problem was "to produce at will, through a knowledge of circumstances, as many as possible of the formative processes of plants." [27]

Here developmental history is obviously no longer a maxim of research, as with Schleiden; it is constructed, rather, on the dogma of strict mechanism. However, the hope that the future of biology would be determined by this dogma was not fulfilled. On the contrary, this position was actually instrumental in precipitating a reaction through which the thesis of the autonomy of life, opposed by Klebs, was to be reinstated and supported with new arguments.

But before embarking upon a description of this movement we must turn our attention to still another group of problems. Experimental morphology had developed its ideas pre-eminently in the field of ontogenesis and its fundamental concept of metamorphosis, in the main, was oriented and defined ontogenetically.[28] The problem had to take another turn as soon as phylogenetic considerations entered in, and it actually began to appear, in its new form, as the real nucleus of all biological investigation whatsoever. With this shift of emphasis in the system of biological knowledge, every one of the individual concepts, too, received a new accent. The first impulse to this transformation was provided by Darwin's *Origin of Species*, published in 1859, with whose appearance, consequently, both empirical research and the logic of biology entered upon a new phase.

25. See Goebel, *Einleitung* . . . , S. 25.
26. Goebel, *Organographie der Pflanzen* (Jena, G. Fischer, 1898), Teil I, S. 4.
27. G. Klebs, *Willkürliche Entwicklungsänderungen bei Pflanzen* (Jena, 1903); see Schaxel, *op. cit.*, S. 49.
28. See, for example, Goebel, *Organographie* . . . , S. 8.

IX

Darwinism as a Dogma and as a Principle of Knowledge

THE CONFLICT over Darwinism as a *Weltanschauung*, which was waged so long and so bitterly, is stilled today. One no longer expects the theory to answer in one word all the problems of biology, and still less does one see it as a key that will open the doors of metaphysics to a solution of all the world's riddles. The exuberance with which it was greeted by its first disciples and the passionate opposition directed against it by its adversaries have long since given place to more tranquil criticism. When we undertake critically to distinguish the content of the theory from the special form imposed by the period in which it was first advanced, attention must be given above all to the methodological side of the problem.

The question is not what gains in material insight the theory brought with it, but to what extent it altered the concept and the task of biological knowledge. Haeckel liked to compare Darwin's reform of biology with the reform of cosmology achieved by Copernicus three hundred years earlier. He thought one of its chief virtues was that it removed the last traces of anthropomorphism from science and provided it with a really universal point of view.[1] Here emphasis was placed not so much on the content of the doctrine, some particular theorem, as on the fact that it changed biology's whole frame of reference. Is this claim warranted? And what is the essence of the transformation?

The manner in which Darwin discovered, established, and propounded his theory is a model of genuinely inductive research and proof. His *Origin of Species* would remain a classic of inductive logic even if one considered only its form. Darwin started from some detached concrete observations made on a surveying expedition aboard the *Beagle* when he was twenty-two years of age. Three classes of phenomena particularly struck him: the way in which closely allied species appeared and replaced one another in South America as the expedition made its way southward; the near relationship between

1. E. Haeckel, *Natürliche Schöpfungsgeschichte* (8. umgearb. und verm. Aufl. Berlin, G. Reimer, 1889), S. 17, 35 u.ö.

species inhabiting the islands off the coast and those native to the Continent; and, finally, the close relationship between the surviving and the extinct species of edentate mammals and rodents. "As I pondered these facts and compared them with some similar phenomena," he wrote in a letter to Haeckel,

it seemed to me probable that closely related species might spring from a common ancestral stock. But for some years I could not understand how each form could be so admirably adapted to its environment. Thereupon I began to study systematically the domestic animals and cultivated plants, and perceived clearly after a time that the most important modifying force lay in man's power of selection and in his use of selected individuals for breeding . . . When, by a fortunate chance, I then read Malthus' *Essay on Population* the idea of natural selection suddenly rose to my mind.[2]

But more than two decades passed before the idea had taken shape sufficiently for Darwin openly to propose it. He demanded first that it meet all empirical tests, which were carried out with the utmost patience and in infinite detail. His book shows how he collected one stone after another, as it were, carefully examining each for flaws and fitting it to others until at last the whole edifice stood complete. Every single argument was subjected to the most minute empirical criticism, in which all possible objections were raised and their refutation attempted. The theory and its indirect inferences were broadened until often they seemed boldly to transcend the facts of observation, but Darwin was conscious of the obligation to verify every detail over and over again by comparison with the facts, and only when this examination had been completed did he feel himself on firm ground. Even then he spoke with great caution, denying himself all speculative views. But at the end of the work we detect his deep inner satisfaction over the fact that science had at last succeeded in coming upon a clue to that "secret of secrets," the origin of species.

Thus, from the war of nature, from famine and death, the most exalted object which we are capable of conceiving, namely, the production of the higher animals, directly follows. There is grandeur in this view of life, with its several powers, having been originally breathed by the Creator into a few forms or into one; and that, whilst this planet has gone circling on according to the fixed law of gravity, from so simple a beginning endless forms most beautiful and most wonderful have been, and are being evolved.[3]

2. Letter to Haeckel, October 8, 1864. See Haeckel, *ibid.*, S. 119 f.
3. Charles Darwin, concluding words of the *Origin of Species*.

Haeckel's *Generelle Morphologie der Organismen* (1866) and his *Natürliche Schöpfungsgeschichte* (1868) were separated by only a few years from Darwin's work, and the goal of both books was nothing less than the provision of a crowning piece for the structure that Darwin had erected. He saw himself as the successor of Darwin and the most loyal among his disciples. But in his conception and defense of the "natural history of creation" Darwin's thesis came to assume a wholly different aspect, not in content of course but in method. All critical doubt, all the careful weighing of evidence for and against the thesis, disappeared. "Evolution," declared Haeckel in his preface, "is henceforth the magic word by which we shall solve all the riddles that surround us, or at least be set on the road to their solution. But how few have really understood this password, and to how few has its world-transforming meaning become clear!" [4]

Haeckel himself made unlimited use of the "magic word," convinced that no problem of human knowledge would be able to resist its spell. The empirical source of the theory was given the greatest possible prominence, but it sometimes appears to have been forgotten entirely in Haeckel's own conclusions. Nothing in the theory was for him merely hypothetical or probable; everything bore the stamp of strict apodictic or mathematical necessity. This kind of necessity was asserted even for those elements of the theory that were most difficult and most problematic. "The origin of new species by natural selection or, what is the same thing, through the cooperation of inheritance and adaptation in the struggle for existence, is consequently a mathematical necessity of nature that needs no further proof." [5] The doctrine of descent gives us not only a detailed acquaintance with all the phenomena of life; but in addition a satisfactory answer to every question regarding the "why" of these phenomena. And these answers are of a purely mechanical and causal nature. They show that natural, physicochemical forces alone are the causes of phenomena which had been customarily ascribed to the immediate influence of supernatural creative powers. It was this elimination and overcoming of all teleological considerations that Haeckel believed to be Darwin's great act of emancipation, one comparable with the achievement of Copernicus. Now for the first time there was feasible a treatment of nature from which all anthropomorphic features had been stripped away. The idea of purpose had been driven out of that last refuge from which even Kant's

4. Haeckel, Vorwort, *op. cit.*
5. *Ibid.*, S. 150 f.

critique had been unable to dislodge it. The "Newton of the grass blades," whose possibility Kant had disputed, had appeared at last in Darwin, and his theory of selection had solved the riddle that Kant had believed insoluble.[6]

But from the standpoint of the critique of knowledge a whole series of further questions immediately presses forward for attention. It is manifest that Haeckel's philosophy of nature had not renounced anthropomorphism or anthropocentrism at all but rather advocated and proclaimed it most decidedly. For everywhere he was trying to grasp and understand the "meaning" of natural events by tracing them back to their ultimate "physical" causes. Herewith the mechanical explanation of the phenomena of life, which Haeckel regarded as the chief merit and real triumph of the theory of selection, collapses of its own accord. For the explanation is only accomplished by inserting into matter the living phenomenon ready made, rather than by deriving it from matter. The monism of Haeckel was a naïve hylozoism because he believed that all forces, the purely physico-chemical equally with the organic, were ultimately from the primal life force. This is especially clear in his later writings, which increasingly renounced biological empiricism and appealed instead to a "psychological unity of the organic world," the recognition of which was hailed as the most brilliant advance that psychology, aided by the theory of evolution, had made in the second half of the nineteenth century.[7]

But even as early as 1875 Haeckel had developed his doctrine of "cell souls" and "soul cells," and of the "perigenesis of the plastidule," in which inheritability was attributed to the "memory of the plastidule," and variability to the "mental capacity of the plastidule."[8] The reversion to anthropomorphism could not be more clearly or strikingly shown. The progress that Darwin had aimed at was almost turned to retrogression, for even the theory of evolution itself seemed now to be interpreted in the sense of Lamarck rather than in that of Darwin. Lamarck had started from psychological categories in setting up his theory. The changes in the organic world were, according to him, conditioned by the fact that certain needs are developed that guide the activities of the organism

6. *Ibid.,* S. 95.

7. Haeckel, "Stufenleiter der Seele," *Die Welträtsel* (Bonn, E. Strauss, 1899), Kap. vii, S. 125 ff.

8. Haeckel, *Gemeinverständliche Vorträge und Abhandlungen* (2. verm. Aufl. Bonn, E. Strauss, 1902). Bd. I: "Über Zellseelen und Seelenzellen," 171 ff.; II: "Über die Wellenzeugung der Lebensteilchen oder die Perigenesis der Plastidule," 31 ff.

in a definite direction, until finally the new function leads to the formation of a new organ.[9] Far from being dismissed, teleology was here raised to the dignity of a supreme explanatory principle that openly usurped the place of causality and made any further causal investigation unnecessary. There appeared too that type of "teleological mechanics" which Pflüger summed up in the phrase: "The cause of every need in a living organism is at the same time the cause of satisfaction of that need." [10]

The later development of "psycho-Lamarckism" carried this principle to an extreme, teaching that all purposeful activity seen in the living world traces back not only to psychic but even to "intelligent" factors. "There cannot be several principles sharing in the explanation of the purposive," but we must realize "that purposiveness can be brought into existence only by a principle that exercises judgment, and when the assumption is made that there is one such principle, all other theoretical efforts at explanation must be eliminated as pseudoteleology." Here "animism" was not only defended but asserted to have a "logical necessity," since a rational phenomenon can be explained only by referring it to a rational cause.[11] A teleology without psychology was thus not merely rejected but declared contradictory, a *contradictio in adjecto;* for "the connection of various sensitivities in one subject is the condition of all judgment, and judgment, in turn, the condition of all teleology." [12]

Similar views are repeatedly encountered in the subsequent literature on Darwinism, even in the most convinced adherents of it, though they are not expressed so undisguisedly. Boveri, for example, wrote that a theory of mere chance would not adequately account for the origin and maintenance of adaptation to an environment; a "desire" for the adaptation to be achieved and an "endeavor" to preserve it must be assumed in addition: "It must rather be taken for granted that there is in the organism a feeling of the particular utility of any characteristic offered it by sheer accident." [13]

Certainly Darwin himself would not have approved of such reversions to Lamarckism, for although he recognized the French zoologist as his predecessor he decisively rejected his philosophy of

9. J. B. P. A. Lamarck, *Philosophie zoologique* (Paris, Duminil-Lesueur, 1809), I, 5 ff.

10. E. Pflüger, "Die teleologische Mechanik der lebendigen Natur," *Archiv für die gesammte Physiologie*, XV (Bonn, M. Cohen & Sohn, 1877), 76.

11. A. Pauly, *Darwinismus und Lamarckismus* (München, E. Reinhardt, 1905), S. 16 ff.

12. Pauly, *op. cit.*, S. 145, 163.

13. T. Boveri, *Die Organismen als historische Wesen* (Würzburg, H. Stürtz, 1906), S. 9, 25 ff.

nature. In a letter to Hooker he called the "tendency to evolution," as conceived by Lamarck, sheer nonsense. He thus appears to have been thoroughly in earnest about the elimination of teleology.[14]

But when we pose the question as to what all this means for a critical theory of knowledge, we must first be clear about what sort of "purposive explanation" is discarded by Darwin's theory, to be replaced by something different and better. Haeckel consistently represented the situation as if all pre-Darwinian biology had substituted purposive causes for efficient causes and so stopped at merely apparent explanations. But a glance at history has shown us how little truth is found in this interpretation. Ever since Kant's *Critique of Judgment* and his criticism of the "physicotheological" proof for the existence of God, that naïve form of teleology had been shattered in the realm of scientific biology as well as in the popular philosophy of the eighteenth century. Its weaknesses had been recognized long before the time of Darwin. Goethe rejoiced to let his agreement with Kant on this point be known and called it an "immeasurable service" that Kant should have brought us deliverance from "absurd final causes." [15]

The sort of notion that a living being is created from without for certain ends and that its form is determined thereto by some primal purposive force has already retarded the philosophical treatment of natural things for many hundred years, and still retards us, though a few have strenuously opposed it and shown what obstacles it throws in our way . . . It is, if the expression be allowed, a trivial sort of notion that is trivial as all trivial things are, for the simple reason that it is on the whole so convenient and satisfactory for the human mind.[16]

In the field of ontogeny too the demand for a strictly causal inquiry had been raised to the dignity of a principle long before Darwin. Here Schleiden went so far that he tried to explain even the most complex reciprocal effects of bodies in space and time, as they appear in organic phenomena, by the simple relations between corpuscular attractions and repulsions either at a distance or during contact. He thought that the reduction of such phenomena to the mathematically determinable laws of motion was the goal of all "descriptive" natural science.[17]

That "purpose" as an independent force, a special motive power

14. E. Nordenskiöld. Eng. trans., *The History of Biology*, pp. 463 f.

15. An Zelter, 29. Januar 1830, *Goethes Briefe*, XLVI, 223.

16. Goethe, "Versuch einer allgemeinen Vergleichungslehre," *Naturwiss. Schriften*, VII, 217 f.

17. See pp. 154 ff.

in nature equal or superior to physicochemical forces, was "a stranger
to natural science" had been more and more clearly recognized ever
since Kant's *Critique of Judgment*.[18] The actual problem awaiting
solution after that was quite a different one: whether the "category"
of purposiveness could assert its role as a peculiar "principle of order" in scientific description and presentation or whether it had
become superfluous and should be eliminated once and for all. But
to this question Darwinism did not return the answer so often read
into it. One may always regard it as the peculiar merit of Darwinism
that it carried through a strictly unitary causal explanation, with
no assumption of any special type of causality equal or superior to
the physicochemical. But that it has finally overcome the purposive
way of looking at things, that it has succeeded in dispensing with
all concepts of purpose in scientific research, is something which cannot be asserted if one even attends only to its most general logical
structure. Here the concepts of purpose have their secure place; they
prove themselves to be not only admissible but absolutely indispensable. Not only the answer that Darwinism yields but even its formulation of the problem is indissolubly bound up with the purposive idea.
The concepts of "fitness," "selection," "struggle for existence,"
"survival of the fittest"—these all have plainly a purposive character and they exhibit a theoretical organization quite different from
that of the concepts of the mathematical sciences. The constant use
that Darwinism makes, and must make, of these concepts would alone
suffice to show that in opposing a definite form of metaphysical teleology it in no way renounces "critical teleology."

Indeed, one can go even further and assert that no earlier biological theory ascribed quite so much significance to the idea of
purpose, or advocated it so emphatically, since not only individual
but absolutely *all* the phenomena of life are regarded from the
standpoint of their survival value. All other questions retreat into
the background before this one. But this is by no means true of the
earlier biology. The interest of "idealistic morphology" was centered on the *form* of life and its changes of form, both of which it
endeavored to understand by pure observation and without asking
whether anything like conscious aim or inherent "striving toward a
goal" ever disclosed itself. Goethe wanted to content himself with
this "real illusion," this "living play" of the formation and transformation of organic natures, and he sought no other meaning than
that contained in, and directly revealed to, observation. "Nature and

18. *Kritik der Urteilskraft,* ed. Rosenkranz, § 72, S. 280.

art," he explained, "are too sublime to aim at purposes, nor need they; for relationships are everywhere present, and relationships are life." [19]

Darwinism chose from the totality of all these relationships but *one* group of them alone for attention, asking only: What has survival value for the individual and the species? Value for selection is glorified as the real, in fact, the only criterion, by which the meaning of every vital phenomenon is to be discerned and by which alone it can be understood. In this sense the critics of Darwinism have rightly emphasized that its disciples, who boasted of having overthrown the idols of purposiveness, were "the greatest teleologists of all" both in their fundamental concept of life and in the conceptual language they used.[20] In the effort to discover some utility and survival value for every organ and every characteristic they were often led to wholly untenable hypotheses.[21] They overlooked or else they denied the fact that there is an independent and purely morphological study of living beings that sees in them quite other features than merely adaptation and purposive connection. In this respect Darwin expressed himself far less dogmatically than many of his adherents. He attached great importance to Naegeli's remark that the most important characteristics of plants, indispensable for the identification of phyla, classes, orders, and families, were of no recognizable use to them and thus of no value for selection.[22] Regarding this statement Darwin said in his *Descent of Man* that he had probably given too much weight to natural selection in earlier editions of *The Origin of Species*, and conceded that he had not paid sufficient attention at first to the existence of many structural relationships that, as far as could be judged at present, seemed neither beneficial nor injurious; indeed, he declared this to be "one of the greatest oversights" that he had discovered in his work up to then. Curiously enough he explained his tendency to biased emphasis on the factor of usefulness by saying that he had retained too strong a belief in teleology.

19. An Zelter, 29. Januar 1830, *Goethes Briefe,* XLVI, 223.
20. See Oskar Hertwig, *Das Werden der Organismen* (3. Aufl. Jena, 1922).
21. See E. Ungerer, *Die Regulationen der Pflanzen; ein System der teleologischen Begriffe in der Botanik* (Berlin, J. Springer, 1919), S. 247; and Ludwig v. Bertalanffy, *Theoretische Biologie* (Berlin, 1932), I, 14.

E. Rádl, too, insisted that the Darwinians were practical teleologists, though they attacked teleology theoretically and rebuked their opponents. *Geschichte* . . . , Teil II, S. 556.

22. C. Naegeli, *Entstehung und Begriff der naturhistorischen Art* (München, Königl. Akademie, 1865).

I was not, however, able to annul the influence of my former belief, then almost universal, that each species had been purposely created; and this led to my tacit assumption that every detail of structure, excepting rudiments, was of some special, though unrecognised, service . . . hence if I have erred in giving to natural selection great power, which I am very far from admitting, or in having exaggerated its power, which is in itself probable, I have at least, as I hope, done good service in aiding to overthrow the dogma of separate creations.[23]

These are important words for they show with what critical clarity Darwin himself, as contrasted with many of his uncritical adherents, judged his own work. His emphasis was on the facts of evolution, not on his particular explanation of them. These facts may be accepted and conceded in their entirety without any obligation to draw therefrom the epistemological and methodological inferences of the earlier Darwinism.[24] Then it was believed that the question of phylogenesis had replaced and made superfluous all other biological questions. The establishment of genealogical trees seemed almost the only, or at any rate the chief, goal of biology. Its former divisions, "biotaxy" no less than "biophysics," lost their methodological autonomy through such uncompromising Darwinism.

Schleiden had already declared in 1842 that the older systems of classification were mere tools, of no intrinsic value for knowledge. Now the sentence pronounced on them was even more severe: they were rejected as sterile scholasticism. "The theory of Linnaeus," wrote J. Sachs, "was wholly the fruit of scholasticism, whereas the essential point in Darwin's theory of evolution is that scholasticism no longer has any place in biology." The figurative affinity that was assumed has now become a real blood relationship. When the "natu-

23. Darwin, *The Descent of Man* (2d ed. revised and augmented, New York, Appleton, 1909), Part I, chap. ii.

24. The best presentation of the *modern* status of this question from a methodological and epistemological standpoint seems to me to have been given by J. B. S. Haldane, in his *Causes of Evolution* (New York and London, Harper & Bros., 1932), pp. 6 f., 152 f. He accepted evolution in its entirety as a purely historical thesis regarding the origin of species. "When one has made acquaintance with such series of related types," he wrote, "any hypothesis other than evolution becomes fantastic" (pp. 6 f.). As for questions about the "causes" of evolution, he insisted that these be put with great critical caution. A certain role must be granted to the factor of "selection," even if it is by no means the only one. Furthermore, according to Haldane, evolution is not to be regarded as a simple, rectilinear, ascending series that finally culminates in man; it is more like a zigzag with many divagations, retrogressions, and blind alleys. The dogmatic "idea of progress" held by Haeckel and other early Darwinians is thus abandoned. "Degeneration," said Haldane, "is a far commoner phenomenon than progress . . . If we consider any given evolutionary level we generally find one or two lines leading up to it, and dozens leading down" (pp. 152 f.).

ral system" was thus recognized as only a model for the genealogy of the vegetable kingdom, the old problem was solved.[25]

But this belief in the supremacy of phylogeny was gradually shattered by subsequent criticism which accepted the facts of evolutionary history but no longer regarded it as the "magic word" destined to solve all the problems of biology. Not only was a place made for morphology in the system but it was emphasized that only on a basis of rigorous morphological investigation could the problems of ontogeny be stated and coped with. The "logic of morphology" became more and more significant; and in philosophical respects, too, it was perceived to be an independent problem and treated as such.[26] Even those who had retained a phylogenetic viewpoint and insisted that it must always remain one of the most important problems of biology to discover how organisms had arrived at their present state, now declared themselves in favor of maintaining strict methodological boundaries between the various departments of research. They explained that "morphological primacy" must be preserved at all costs, since otherwise the description of nature could not be so framed as to provide a useful foundation for research in ontogenesis.[27]

Modern experimental morphology was wholly at one with Darwinism in so far as it likewise regarded a purely causal investigation of the processes of the organism as the essential aim of biology, but in order to define its position and procedure it had to work out clearly its specific difference from the phylogenetic point of view. "Our concept of metamorphosis," said Goebel, "is primarily ontogenetic and therefore something that can be conceived and proven experimentally. Phylogenetic considerations may enter in, but that it is not justifiable to speak of metamorphosis in a purely phylogenetic sense is shown by the simple fact that the theory of metamorphosis is older than that of evolution, and would survive even though the latter had to be abandoned." [28] According to this view phylogenesis can never lead to the first causes of events. What it had achieved up to then, in Goebel's opinion, was more like a product of poetic fancy than one of exact research working with reliable proofs. The theory advanced by Haeckel, that there is no explanation for morphological phenomena other than the actual blood relationship among organisms, was thus abandoned.[29]

25. Sachs, *Geschichte der Botanik,* S. 12, 115, and elsewhere.

26. The most searching examination of this problem is that of Adolf Meyer, *Logik der Morphologie im Rahmen einer Logik der gesamten Biologie* (Berlin, 1926).

27. A. Naef, *Idealistische Morphologie und Phylogenetik,* S. 62 ff., 25 ff.

28. C. v. Goebel, *Organographie der Pflanzen,* Teil I, § 8.

29. E. Haeckel, *Generelle Morphologie der Organismen,* II, 290 f.

The modern exponents of the theory of evolution proposed questions that can almost be called "transcendental" problems in Kant's sense. Before starting any individual research they wanted to inquire "according to what precisely conceived presuppositions and principles any phylogenetic research in general is possible." Only by settling this preliminary question, they believed, could the earlier naïve phylogenetics be transcended and the doctrine of evolution raised to the rank of a science that is conscious of its special task and its methodological limitations.[30] In respect to the problem of knowledge as a whole there arises still another question which compels us to look far beyond the domain of biology. How was it possible for evolutionary history to attain to such value and significance in the biological thinking of the nineteenth century that all else disappeared beside it—all other interests and problems being swallowed up, as it were. Was it merely the weight of the empirical proofs advanced by Darwin that caused the scale to turn? It is known how incomplete his material was at first, and how disappointing the findings of paleontology still are when it comes to the reconstruction of an ascending series of organisms. That such lacunae should have been readily and cheerfully overlooked, however, is explained by a deep-seated characteristic of general intellectual history in the nineteenth century.

This century presents the first encounter and first reckoning between the two great ideals of knowledge. The ideal of the mathematical sciences, which had engrossed and dominated the seventeenth century, was paramount no longer. Since the time of Herder and romanticism another mentality and spiritual force had been opposing it with increasing vigor and conviction. Here, for the first time, the *primacy of history* was proclaimed by both philosophy and science. The eighteenth century had not been a stranger by any means to historical thought as such, and the traditional reproach that the period was completely unhistoric is not justified; but real "historicism" had no place there, for that was almost entirely a product of the nineteenth century.[31]

Hegel's system provided the appropriate metaphysical foundation for and expression of historicism. This new way of thinking, thanks to the Darwinian doctrine, penetrated into biology. It may seem strange at first sight that anyone should want to establish any

30. Naef, *op. cit.,* S. 2 ff.

31. For details see E. Cassirer, "Die Eroberung der geschichtlichen Welt," *Die Philosophie der Aufklärung* (Tübingen, J. C. B. Mohr [P. Siebeck], 1932), Kap. v, S. 263 ff. For the genesis of historicism see the admirable presentation by Ernst Troeltsch, *Der Historismus und seine Probleme* (Tübingen, J. C. B. Mohr, 1922).

connection between the conception of development in Hegel and that
of Darwin, for the two concepts appear to have hardly more than
the name in common. Could there be a wider chasm than that between Hegel's dialectic, where reality is derived from "thought
thinking about itself," and the method employed by Darwin in pro-
pounding and establishing his theory? Yet in entire disregard of this
fundamental difference, one of the best known expositions of the
Hegelian philosophy has not hesitated to make it very nearly approximate to the theory of evolution. Kuno Fischer closed his great
history of modern philosophy with a presentation of Hegel's system,
which he regarded as the very pinnacle of philosophic thought, and
declared that the basic principle of Hegel's doctrine was "the idea
of world development" and he then endeavored to show how it had
finally conquered not only philosophy but natural science as well.
That which Hegel had begun as a thinker, Darwin had completed as
an empirical investigator; they were the expression and witness of
the same spirit, which was none other than the spirit of the nineteenth
century itself.[32]

This thesis can be maintained, of course, only if one wholly dis-
regards all the discrepancies between the foundations and basic views
of the two systems. One thing however is unmistakable: that an entirely different position in the whole of natural knowledge had been
made for historical thought by the Darwinian theory and its far-
spreading influence. Neither the ideal of an exact natural science nor
idealistic morphology nor even Goethe's theory of metamorphosis
provides anything analogous. All of a sudden history came to occupy
the center of the stage, and there was the belief that with its help
even the problems of pure classification and of physiology could be
solved. What sometimes made the knowledge of this connection of
things difficult was the failure of the exponents of the new idea to
see clearly the critical position which they had reached in scientific
thought. With Darwin, Rádl said, there first appeared the magnificent thought "that one could not possibly conceive of the true
nature of an animal by any analysis, be it ever so profound, or by
any comparison with other forms, however comprehensive, because
there lies hidden in the organism traces of the past that only
historical research is able to reveal." But the significance of this
new solution was not grasped. Just as Columbus did not realize that
he had discovered another continent but continued under the delusion that he had found only a new route to lands already known,

32. K. Fischer, "Hegels Leben, Werke, und Lehre," *Geschichte der neueren Philosophie* (Heidelberg, C. Winters Universitätsbuchhandlung, 1901), VIII, 219 ff.

so the Darwinians were not the founders of a new science of *historical morphology* but on the contrary simply took over the old morphology, "explaining" it in terms of evolution, the struggle for existence, adaptation, inheritance, etc., and trying to deck out its ideas in a phyletic form. Essential factors of all *true* historical study, such as strict chronology or "dating," were totally neglected.[33]

This criticism of the *method* of Darwinism is no less significant than the criticism of its content, directed against it by so many of its opponents.[34] One of its most noted achievements from an epistemological point of view is that it opened to natural science a new *dimension* of thought, so to speak, by showing that scientific and historical concepts are far from opposed but rather mutually supplement and need one another. But the theory could fight for the rights of historical thinking and make a place for it in natural science only by transforming it, in a certain sense, and giving it a different meaning. Instead of recognizing the true role of historical thought, Darwinism imposed tasks that were quite foreign to its nature and which it was not competent to fulfill. Historical *description* was supposed to perform at once the whole duty of "explanation": insight into the *evolution* of organisms was to open the way forthwith to the understanding of all problems relating to their structure and physiology. Thus Boveri, for example, declared that *all* the properties of living things could be comprehended at one stroke, through the single assumption that taxonomic relationships were true blood relationships, and accordingly that the theory of evolution contained "the final solution for the problem of variations." He overlooked the fact that there is not merely one problem of variation in the organic world; there are many such problems of very different kinds, and each must be treated and solved by special methods.[35] Nevertheless, after the introduction of Darwin's theory, one could never again question or forget that the historical study and investigation of living things, in accordance with such a system of methods, could claim separate and independent rank, and deserved "a place in the sun" of natural science. "Today," Boveri could rightly say, "the idea of the historically evolved is the fundamental tone, as it

33. Rádl, *op. cit.*, Teil II, S. 326 f.

34. For the criticism of its content, which need not be gone into here, see especially Oskar Hertwig, *Das Werden der Organismen;* Alb. Wigand, *Der Darwinismus und die Naturforschung Newtons und Cuviers* (Braunschweig, F. Vieweg, 1874 und 1877); and Gustav Wolff, "Beiträge zur Kritik der Darwinschen Lehre," *Biologisches Zentralblatt,* X (15. September 1890, Erlangen, E. Besold, 1891), S. 449 ff.; also *Leben und Erkennen* (München, 1933).

35. A. Meyer, *Ideen und Ideale der biologischen Erkenntnis.*

were, that constantly accompanies the biologist's thinking; it is the standard to be universally applied, and serves him just as the law of the conservation of energy serves the physicist." [36]

The change that had taken place is clearly apparent when one thinks back to the theory of knowledge and the general theory of science characteristic of the eighteenth century. Even this theory had not been oriented in such a narrowly rationalistic way that the claim of the historical to be regarded as knowledge was unrecognized or denied, and even the strict rationalism that is met with in the system of Christian Wolff, for instance, conceded the historical its comparative rights. Each separate scientific discipline, according to Wolff, consists of a historical and a rational part. The former contains pure "truths of fact," in the sense of Leibniz; the latter traces these back to universal truths of reason. From the former we receive the answer to the question concerning the "what"; from the latter that to the question of the "why." The one is concerned with the knowledge of empirical phenomena in their particularity, their here and now, the other with deducing them from their "sufficient reason." In the eighteenth century this view had entered, too, into the mode of presentation of the various sciences and formed for them a settled framework of procedure. Thus C. G. Ludwig, for example, insisted in his manual of botany that there are two different ways of considering natural bodies. One, the more superficial, leads to their classification; whereas the other, penetrating to the heart of things, teaches us their origins and the changes of their different parts. The former is the *physical* method, the latter, the *historical* method; hence there is a historical as well as a physical side to the three kingdoms in nature.[37] Generally speaking, the school of Wolff divided botany into three subordinate disciplines: historical, physical, and medico economic, all of which were usually represented as coordinate and of equal value throughout.[38]

Darwinism broke with this long tradition once and for all. The historical, barely tolerated previously, was not actually to *supplant* the rational, for there is no rational explanation of the organic world save that which shows its origins. The laws of *real* nature are historical laws, and only through their discovery is it possible to escape a bare logical schematism and get back to the actual causes of phenomena.

36. Boveri, *op. cit.,* S. 9, 32.

37. C. G. Ludwig, *Institutiones historico-physicae regni vegetabilis* (Leipzig, 1742). For details on Ludwig's system of botany, see Tschulok, *Das System der Biologie,* S. 25 ff.

38. See Tschulok, *ibid.,* S. 28, 153.

But if we study the biological literature of the second half of the nineteenth century we realize, of course, that the transition to this new appreciation of the "historical" was not effected so smoothly as it appears by any means. Just at the important and critical places, the old opposition would break out again and again. The process may be seen with special clarity in a thinker and investigator like Driesch, who from the very beginning withdrew himself from the "historical" trend of his day. He was the typical metaphysician of biology, seeking to answer only questions of "being," never questions of "becoming." He was not only unfamiliar with history but actually hostile to it and he could never bring himself to admit that it had any definite scientific value.[39] Far from regarding it as a central point or even as a direction of biological research that was entitled to equal rights, he could see in it only a perverted tendency and he vigorously opposed it. He declared "it can be a matter of complete indifference to us that just such and such forms have been realized on this earth and have succeeded one another in time—wholly indifferent, that is, to general, to theoretical natural science, which finds the idea of history, associated as it is with particular times and places, alien." [40]

Here "eternal truths" are once more sharply opposed to the mere "truths of fact," beyond which phylogenetics as such could never go. But objections to such a view as Driesch's were not lacking, and there was repeated endeavor to attack the standard which was here being applied to biological reality, and even to turn the tables on the position. Thus Bütschli wrote:

Entirely apart from the fact that we study nature not only to learn the laws governing her phenomena but also, and more generally, to know the world wherein we live and by which we are surrounded, one may well ask *why* our attention should be engaged, after all, by sciences of orderly events which for the most part appear as mathematical equations that are of but little interest in themselves: *why* are these regularities not a matter of indifference to us? . . . The reason why is just this, that we can draw conclusions from them, either for our own practical ends or for an understanding of what is transpiring at present in nature and what has happened in the past. Exactly the same would be true, too, of laws to be experimentally discovered in the physiology of development: these are not a matter of indifference to us but are of the greatest interest, and

39. For Driesch's deprecatory attitude toward everything historical, see Troeltsch, *Der Historismus und seine Probleme, op. cit.,* III, 663 ff.

40. H. Driesch, *Die Biologie als selbständige Grundwissenschaft* (2. durchaus umgearb. Aufl. Leipzig, W. Engelmann, 1911).

it is because they have made it possible for us to grasp the organic forms as they have evolved historically.[41]

Once again we confront an alternative often before met with in history, and particularly within biology itself in the quarrel between Cuvier and Geoffroy Saint-Hilaire. Science is not satisfied with sheer observation of particular phenomena or establishing general laws, but speaks in the name of a distinct "interest of reason" which it has at heart and means to urge. Controversies of this sort, as Kant emphasized, are incapable of being decided in such a way that one side is proved right or wrong.[42] Critical philosophy must be content with understanding and safeguarding both the empirical and the rational interests instead of pronouncing a judgment in favor of either party. For they are only exclusive of each other *as dogmas*, but when they are conceived as principles and directives for knowledge they can supplement and yield results for each other. In the controversy over Darwinism the thesis of evolutionary history was just as often dogmatically asserted as it was dogmatically attacked, and it was long before it came to be understood as a "maxim" of research, as a regulative principle of biological knowledge.

41. O. Bütschli, *Mechanismus und Vitalismus* (Leipzig, W. Engelmann, 1901), S. 53 f.
42. See the quotation from the *Critique of Pure Reason,* S. 694 f., pp. 133–134.

X

Developmental Mechanics and the Problem of Cause
in Biology

THE FIRST adherents of the Darwinian doctrine to dis-
seminate it abroad lived in the proud and happy belief
that human knowledge had at last succeeded in penetrating
into a domain which had previously defied all efforts. The mystery
of life seemed to have been revealed at last and faith in miracles
driven from its final refuge. No longer were the phenomena of life
to constitute a "state within a state"; they were subject to the strict
laws that govern all natural phenomena without exception. Not only
the "problem of variations" but even that of "cause" in biology
seemed finally solved, and in both cases it was by means of the same
surprisingly simple premises.[1] The theory of the origin of species
was as significant for the understanding of the organic world as
the law of gravitation had been for that of the inorganic, and Haeckel,
as we have seen, claimed the same mathematical certainty for both.[2]

At times it seemed as if the purely inductive origin and character
of Darwin's theory had been almost forgotten, or relegated entirely
to the background. In his *History of Botany* Julius Sachs wrote that
the decisive advance of the theory consisted in its discovery of the
principles of variation and natural selection, as principles from
which the facts of biology flowed as "necessary effects of known
causes." Thus Darwin had not introduced any previously unknown
presuppositions but had deduced "the most important and irrefutable of his propositions directly from the facts of both the natural
system as then established and morphology." [3]

How did this "deduction" fare once attention was centered not
simply on the mere program of the theory but on its actual fulfillment? Had Darwin already set foot in the promised land of an
exact causal explanation of the phenomena of life or had he merely
pointed to it from afar? How long the way would be appeared evident the more one turned to the examination of the individual phenomena. Here, perforce, the problems of heredity took first place,

1. See the remarks of Boveri, above, p. 172.
2. See above, p. 162.
3. For details see W. Johannsen, *Elemente der exakten Erblichkeitslehre* (2. Aufl.
Jena, 1913).

for upon the theory of heredity hinged the fate of the entire position. And here, too, came the first and almost insurmountable difficulties. When Darwin had set up his hypothesis, the inheritance of acquired characteristics was still generally accepted as a fact, so that inheritance to him was a simple process of transmission through which certain individual characteristics were impressed, so to speak, on the descendants. Within orthodox Darwinism this idea was first criticized and sharply rejected by Weismann, though his own positive views, and in particular the assumption of special minute units for the different organs and tissues, proved also to be mistaken. But the modern theory has put a definite end to that traditional conception of inheritance.[4] In order to achieve a really exact science of inheritance, the ground of which had already been laid by Galton,[5] it was necessary to abandon one after another of the presuppositions upon which Darwin had proceeded. Here Mendel proved to be the real leader, though the theory he proposed remained almost unknown at first and had to be rediscovered just toward the turn of the century by Correns, Tschermak, and De Vries independently. A modern investigator in this field has remarked that the scales would fall from the eyes of a selectionist as he pondered over Mendel's laws; in a flash he would realize the true meaning of stability of type, variability, and mutation, and these things would be nebulous mysteries no longer.[6]

Before there had been any really close analysis the process of heredity could be conceived only as an undifferentiated whole, but such a view of it was very far from being a causal explanation of the phenomenon in the true sense. The explanation consisted of nothing more than the introduction of an "inheritance capacity" that was suspiciously reminiscent of the old occult qualities. The "ability to transmit," according to Haeckel, is a fundamental property of every living thing. "Not only is the organism able to pass on to its descendants such characteristics as form, color, and size, which it in turn has inherited from its progenitors; it can also transmit variants of these qualities that have been acquired during its lifetime through the influence of external factors like climate, nutriment, and so on, as well as of habits and training." [7] To Weismann's criticism he retorted

4. For more details, see Johannsen, *op. cit.*

5. F. Galton, *Hereditary Genius: An Inquiry into Its Laws and Consequences* (New York, Appleton, 1870); *Natural Inheritance* (London and New York, Macmillan, 1889).

6. W. Bateson, *Mendel's Principles of Heredity* (Cambridge University Press, 1930); see Johannsen, *op. cit.*, S. 395.

7. E. Haeckel, *Natürliche Schöpfungsgeschichte* (9. umgearb. Aufl. 1898), S. 140.

that comparative anatomy and ontogeny, physiology and pathology furnished proofs by the thousand for the transmission of acquired characteristics. Other Darwinians even spoke of "daily experience" proving such capacity of the organism to impart by heredity.[8] How little value there was in the proof by everyday experience was shown the moment one went into the rigorously experimental science of heredity which opened the way to strictly quantitative methods of investigation.[9]

But before this happened sheer fantasy had free rein and was in nowise diminished by the fact that the idiom of physics and chemistry was preferred to that of the older natural philosophy. In his "perigenesis theory" of the year 1876, Haeckel attempted a mechanistic explanation of the elementary processes of development, and particularly of heredity. He assumed that in all propagation not only was the special chemical constitution of the plasson or plasma peculiar to the begetter carried over to the begotten but with it the special form of molecular motion associated with its physicochemical nature. At the same time the plastidule was described as a "molecule with a soul," and the assumption made that its motions (attraction and repulsion) were connected with sensation (desire and aversion) as were those of the atoms composing it.[10] In such an elaboration of the Darwinian theory Haeckel's assertion that the theory had first introduced "exact thinking" into biology appears curious indeed.[11]

The reaction could not fail to come and it led, in purely methodological respects, to a highly remarkable and significant result. Though in the first enthusiasm aroused by the theory of evolution it was assumed to have virtually settled *the causal problem in biology*, now the conviction grew steadily stronger that the question had not even been *stated* by the theory of descent in its usual form and that in order to do so one would have to go over to another foundation. It was the merit of the new science of "developmental mechanics," especially as founded largely by Wilhelm Roux, that it was the first to have seen this problem and expressed it clearly. Whereas Haeckel had insisted that Darwin had found the "real, efficient causes" of the endlessly complex forms encountered in the organic world, Roux did not hesitate to convert this statement into its opposite, for he stated that

8. See Haeckel, *ibid.*, S. 192; Boveri, *Die Organismen als historische Wesen,* S. 11.

9. Erwin Baur, *Einführung in die experimentelle Vererbungslehre* (Berlin, Bornträger Brüdern, 1911); and V. Goldschmidt, *Physiologische Theorie der Vererbung* (Berlin, 1927).

10. Haeckel, *Über die Wellenzeugung der Lebensteilchen oder die Perigenesis der Plastidule* (1876); see also *Natürliche Schöpfungsgeschichte,* S. 200 f.

11. Haeckel, *Generelle Morphologie . . . ,* S. xiii f.

despite all the advances made by phylogeny a knowledge of the *causes* underlying development was still entirely lacking, and that in order to obtain this knowledge the lever would have to be applied at another place.[12] For there was a great difference between simply following an event in its temporal course and being able to distinguish the separate states of this course, on the one hand, and on the other, understanding it *causally*. Here we are dealing not with the study of merely factual questions, for indeed the empirical validity of Darwin's theory seemed to Roux as firmly established as it did to Haeckel, but rather with the *epistemological* question of what is meant by the idea of cause and under what conditions the concept may be employed in biology.

The starting point for the discussion was the "fundamental biogenetic law." To Haeckel this proposition, that embryonic development epitomizes racial development, that ontogeny is a short and rapid recapitulation of phylogeny, was no mere statement of fact that could be verified by empirical observation; he claimed for it a validity not inferior to that of the most rigorous laws of physics, the universal laws of motion, and he believed it to be the most important universal law of organic evolution.[13] Not until later was it shown that the individual does not *exactly* repeat the history of the race. In its modern "critical" form this law is far more complex; there is no reason to see in it anything more than the expression of an empirical regularity, something far removed from that "necessity" ascribed to it by Haeckel. "In ontogeny there are no end-stages of ancestors repeated," said A. Naef, "nor is there any palingenesis in the sense of F. Müller and Haeckel, nor any xenogenesis, either . . . In the modern formulation this empirical regularity is all that the so-called fundamental biogenetic law amounts to and of course it is not a true law but only the consequence of one." [14]

Two other scientists, His and Goette, had already protested against Haeckel's view. They made a sharp separation between the phylogenetic and the physiological way of thinking and insisted that a real causal explanation of the facts could be obtained only through the latter. Development must be studied as a physiological process and it would be understood in a causal sense only when each later stage could be connected with the next preceding one in accordance with definite laws. A physiological study of genesis was much more

12. Haeckel, *Natürliche Schöpfungsgeschichte,* S. 5, 25 f.; W. Roux, *Die Entwicklungsmechanik: Ein neuer Zweig der biologischen Wissenschaft* (Leipzig, W. Engelmann, 1905), S. 4 f.

13. Haeckel, "Studien zur Gastraea-Theorie," *Generelle Morphologie* (Jena, H. Dufft, 1877), Heft II, S. 70.

14. A. Naef, *Idealistische Morphologie und Phylogenetik,* S. 58 ff.

important, in every instance, than all the phylogenetic speculation.[15]

Roux was a pupil of Goette and started directly from his position. But he felt much more strongly the need and the responsibility not only to use concretely the method of research but to make it clear in an abstract sense as well, and to define its precise place in the totality of natural knowledge. Hence he made genuinely philosophical investigations into the concept of biological "causality" and the course of research into causes in the realm of vital phenomena. Bacon's idea of "dissection of nature" is recalled by the remark of Roux, that "the method universally employed by causal anatomists," upon which biology must necessarily be based, should not be restricted to the use of material implements like knives, stains, or measures, for it was just as important to carry on an accurate "intellectual anatomy," which consists in the exercise of analytical causal thinking. Thanks to this "intellectual anatomy," the two factors that in earlier Darwinism had merged vaguely into one now appeared clearly separated. The question concerning the "why" was strictly distinguished from that of the "what." Not even the most complete description of a phenomenon of life or the fullest history of its origin could ever afford a reliable proof of a causal relationship.[16] A wholly different procedure must be adopted, for which the exact science of physics would provide the model. A physicist in search of the law governing a definite event could never treat this occurrence as an unanalyzable whole. When Galileo wanted to discover the laws of falling bodies or the law of trajectories he had to identify both phenomena as complexes of elementary components and not simply as they presented themselves to immediate observation. Every one of these components must be studied in itself and understood in its conformity to law before the law of the *whole* occurrence could be expressed. This analytical and synthetic method, as developed in classical physics, was obviously the pattern that Roux was striving for in biology. Only in this way, according to him, can the decisive step be taken which may transform biology from a purely historical into a causal discipline. The knowledge of the causes of development can only come by way of analytical experiment, but for this in turn, if it is to be fruitful, analytical *thinking* must precede it. The numerous individual forms must be traced back to a progressively decreasing number of con-

15. W. His, *Unsere Körperform und das physiologische Problem ihrer Entstehung* (Leipzig, F. C. W. Vogel, 1874); A. Goette, *Entwicklungsgeschichte der Unke* (Leipzig, L. Voss, 1874). On His and Goette as pioneers in developmental mechanics, see Nordenskiöld, *The History of Biology,* English trans., pp. 531 ff.

16. W. Roux, *Gesammelte Abhandlungen über Entwicklungsmechanik der Organismen* (Leipzig, W. Engelmann, 1895), I, 23; and II, 75.

stantly formative modes of causal action. "It is the duty of the anatomist, the morphologist, . . . to strive for *complete* knowledge of the development of organic forms and not to hold arbitrarily that the idea of the Logos in this field has been exhausted with a mere discussion of the relations between individual and phylogenetic development." [17]

Phylogenetics pure and simple can never take the place of the inquiry into causes; and it is much more important that this search for the determining causes of events shall be made only after ascertaining the facts. It was in this sense that developmental mechanics was proposed as the science of the causes underlying development, that is, the "true causes," the individual formative powers and the combinations of these powers. The sole reliable method of research is that of *analytical experiment*. But if one has already taken "the fundamental biogenetic law" to be by itself an adequate explanation of embryonic development, then it is a case of confusing the work of two entirely different principles of knowledge.[18] Roux expected the "Newton of biology" to arise in physiology, never doubting that such a one would come, though he was far from the opinion of Haeckel that Darwin was already playing that role. The Newton to come would be able to construct the whole organism from that of its separate parts, though he would not be so fortunate as to be able to refer it simply to three laws and components of motion.[19]

There can be no doubt that this analytical clarification of the problem marked a significant advance in regard to method. The "historical" no longer coincided wholly with the "rational" but was clearly and distinctly separated from it. But which of the two deserved first place in the development of biology was still a moot question. Oskar Hertwig was strongly opposed to any assertion of the primacy of a physical and physiological mode of explanation over the purely descriptive and historical, and explained that biology would lose its individual character and abandon the specific individuality of its subject matter if it recognized such a primacy. For the characteric feature of the organism is precisely this, that it cannot be regarded as an abstract system of forces which can be reduced to elementary "components" and reconstructed from them. Whoever proceeded in this fashion would possess in the end only the residual fragments of the system. After all, the object that biology studies is

17. *Ibid.*, S. 27, 32, 39, 50; for Galileo's "resolutive and compositive" method see Cassirer, *Das Erkenntnisproblem*, I, 381, 398, 409.

18. Roux, *op. cit.*, II, 53 ff., 75 f.

19. *Ibid.*, II, S. 29.

an individual formation, the "cell" with its "disposition." To us this formation can be only something that already exists; it cannot be referred to something else, something more simple, and thus be causally and analytically "explained." The attempt to do so would result only in self-deception. Pure description and historical study cannot really be dispensed with; the investigator into the so-called causes actually does nothing more than translate the findings of the descriptive scientist into another language and pretentiously apply to what he discovers by analysis the one little word "force." [20]

In this controversy over the method of description and the method of causal analysis, Bütschli adopted an intermediate position. He allied himself with Roux so far as to insist that real insight into vital phenomena is not to be gained by simple observation or description but by experiment alone. Thus the knowledge that ova and spermatozoa are single cells, and that development depends upon continuous cell division did not strictly deserve, according to him, to be called *knowledge* of life processes. This knowledge can be attained only if we are able to follow clearly the course of these processes, and, further, in some way or other to produce them experimentally or to copy them analytically. Thus Bütschli sought to throw light on the structure of protoplasm, by preparing artificial inorganic "foams" in which, as in a sort of model, he studied the movements of the protoplasm. So in processes that run their course under known conditions in non-living matter which is of a known nature, and that are more or less similar to what is observed in the most simple organisms, he tried to trace the course of these processes of life.[21]

But, of course, analogy is not identity, and a model is not the object itself. The specificity of the life processes is not done away with by such comparisons, however instructive and fruitful they prove to be. Bütschli's experiments do not allow us to answer with a simple Yes or No the question whether the causal analytic method or the descriptive method is the more suitable one for biology. The right and the duty of research to analyze each intricate vital process into its simplest terms and to study these separately is certainly unchallenged. Nowhere should this analysis of causes be halted. But when it is prosecuted to the limit it comes eventually to a point where it must give way to the purely descriptive account. For every explanation in

20. O. Hertwig, "Mechanik und Biologie," *Zeit- und Streitfragen der Biologie* (Jena, G. Fischer, 1897), Heft II, S. 35 ff., 59.

21. O. Bütschli, *Mechanismus und Vitalismus*, S. 18, 62 ff., 93. For the foam theory, see his *Untersuchungen über mikroskopische Schäume und das Protoplasma. Versuche und Beobachtungen zur Frage nach den physikalischen Bedingungen der Lebenserscheinungen* (Leipzig, 1892).

developmental mechanics, as Bütschli emphasized, has to start from a given base: the fertilized ovum and its special complex of conditions. "But how is this complex of conditions . . . of the fertilized ovum to be explained? *Here the explanation of developmental mechanics ends,* for this ovum and its particular complex of conditions is something that has had a historical development and is to be understood only with reference to the evolution of those organisms that throughout the history of the earth have aided in its production." In this sense all causal study, all tracing of the connection between causes and effects in biological research, must invariably end with the recognition that both procedures are indispensable to theoretical understanding. Descriptive ontogeny provides only a statement of changes in form; the explanation of the efficient causes or conditions upon which these changes depend is to be derived only from causal analysis and the experiments based upon it.[22]

This was an important clarification of the problem of knowledge in biology, in so far as a strict separation is effected between the two factors that had been confused throughout in the earlier Darwinism. The "historical" has its rights in every explanation of the phenomena of life but it does not contain forthwith the whole explanation and it cannot answer every question of "why."

All natural sciences, said Naef, in a critical summary of the state of the problem, seeks to explain the phenomena before it, in other words, to discover their causes. A complete explanation of the facts of nature requires two constituents, first a historical, second, a dynamic one. The historical element consists in the fact that every condition presupposes an antecedent condition, or "primordial cause"; the dynamic factor consists in this, that each condition has arisen from its antecedent condition through the action of *forces,* and we then assume that universal *laws of nature* hold for this passage from one condition to the next one following, that is to say, for the working of these forces.[23]

The sharp distinction between these two constituents cannot be obliterated by asserting that even to state that there are physical "forces" is, after all, only to *describe* certain matters of fact. Hertwig in his debate with Roux had recourse to the position that even *mechanics,* which Roux considered the model of genuinely causal thinking, could provide no real explanation of the phenomenon of motion but was, according to the familiar definition of Kirchoff, only a

22. Bütschli, *Mechanismus und Vitalismus,* S. 54, 66. Italics by Cassirer.
23. Naef, *op. cit.,* S. 37.

"description" of it.[24] But Roux could rightly disregard this objection, for Kirchoff's definition of the concept had been intended only to guard against false *metaphysical* expectations arising from mechanics and to free the science from the question about the "ultimate grounds" of phenomena, in terms of some "essence" of the moving forces. The term "description" in Kirchoff should not be understood in such a way as to efface the boundary line between the mathematical demonstration of an event and the simple account employed in biology. The "description" in differential equations would always be something different from the purely sensible representation of concrete matters of fact: physical and biological descriptions belong, as it were, to different levels.[25] Roux remarked, in this connection, that when Kirchoff offered his definition of mechanics he never could have suspected what confusion, in purely methodological respects, he was to introduce.[26]

But this controversy had still another side, which referred to an even deeper stratum of thought. It was the expression of an intellectual struggle that not only took place in biology but can be traced throughout the whole history of modern philosophy. Bacon and Descartes had both begun by promising man "dominion over nature." With Bacon it was to be obtained through the method of induction, which, properly developed, would enable mankind to govern nature even while obeying her. In the case of Descartes the leadership was assigned to mathematics, which, far from restricting itself to abstract speculation about figures and numbers, would provide us with the first true knowledge of reality and make us the "masters and possessors of nature." And life too could not escape this dominion, for life contains nothing that eludes the rigorous laws of mathematics and mechanics. We shall bring it the more into our power the more we succeed in analyzing it into its simple conditions and intellectually reconstructing it in terms of them. Now the "intellectual anatomy" which Roux wanted to introduce into biology was nothing other than the renewal and continuation of this double Baconian-Cartesian ideal of knowledge. But from ancient times quite a different view had stood in opposition to it. Among investigators of life there had always been those who resisted this "dissection of nature," because they thought that it would drive life out of nature and leave only her dead body. Life, they said, cannot be understood in this way, by abstract analy-

24. See above, pp. 89 f.
25. See Hertwig, *op. cit.*, S. 45 ff.
26. W. Roux, *Für unser Programm und seine Verwirklichung; Die Entwicklungsmechanik, ein neuer Zweig der biologischen Wissenschaft* (Leipzig, W. Engelmann, 1905).

sis; it must be seen and felt as a whole. Against that "analytical universal" then is arrayed the "synthetic universal." This was another case of the opposition between the "discursive" understanding and the "intuitive" understanding. In the most profound chapters of his *Critique of Judgment* Kant had studied this antithesis and tried to throw light on its ultimate reasons.[27]

Historically, the antithesis is to be seen in its classical form in the relation of Goethe to Newton. Goethe wanted to drive out that spirit of *mere analysis*, not only from biology but from physics as well. "Physics," he wrote, "must describe itself as something distinct from mathematics. It must live in perfect independence and, with all its capacities for sympathy, respect, and devotion try to penetrate into nature and her hallowed life, quite unconcerned about what mathematics produces and does." The life of nature can be envisaged and interpreted only from the standpoint of human life, but such an interpretation itself can succeed only to the extent that we preserve the existence of man, like that of nature, in all its purity and completeness and resist all attempts to dissect and dismember it. For these reasons Goethe was inclined to distrust all experimenting on nature. He ascribed a greater truth value to simple observation than to those artificial contrivances of "levers and screws" with which we attempt to wrest from nature all her secrets. Hence he declared that the microscope and the telescope really confuse the "pure sense of man," who does not need such intervention to establish truly harmonious relations with nature and particularly with the living world. "Man in himself, in so far as he makes use of his normal senses, is the best and most exact physical instrument that there can be, and the greatest evil of modern physics is that we have separated the experiments, as it were, from the man himself and want . . . to understand nature merely through what is disclosed by some artificial apparatus." [28]

So far as this attack on "artificial apparatus" applied to physics, it was doomed to defeat from the outset. But in biology its after-effects persisted for a long time, nor were they limited to purely negative results but actually bore some lasting fruit.[29] Even here it was not possible to *suppress* experiment; but Goethe's admonition served well by pointing up the *methodological difference* between the unaided observation of nature and "artificial" experiment. No less a person than one of the founders and pioneers of modern physiology,

27. Kant, *Kritik der Urteilskraft,* § 77 ff.

28. Goethe, *Maximen und Reflexionen,* XXI, No. 573, S. 124; No. 502, S. 108; No. 706, S. 156.

29. E. Cassirer, "Goethe und die mathematische Physik: Eine erkenntnistheoretische Betrachtung," *Idee und Gestalt* (2. Aufl. Berlin, B. Cassirer, 1924), S. 33 ff.

Johannes Müller, followed his lead, acknowledging himself a disciple of Goethe and also accepting his critical limitation of experiment. No one will see in Müller an *enemy* of the microscope or of experimentation; on the contrary he was the very one to introduce experimental physiology into Germany, and among his pupils were Schwann and Virchow, du Bois-Reymond and Helmholtz.[30] Nevertheless it was he who explained that "quiet, simple observation leads one to the heart of problems," whereas it remains a "dangerous game to busy oneself with merely preparatory measures" and to "surrender oneself to an untrustworthy instrument." For "what else is observation except perceiving the essential in the midst of changes, separating what is inherent in the mutable from what is accidental there; whereas experiment, grabbing here and there, often enough shows a tendency to jumble together, helter-skelter, the essential with the accidental." In his own defense of the purely descriptive method of biology, O. Hertwig expressly invoked this passage.[31]

But Roux did not stand alone here, for he represented a definite trend of research that had sprung from the Cartesian ideal of natural science and had enjoyed a continuous and consistent development. Among the physiologists of France it had no more constant advocate than Claude Bernard himself: "The only way to reach truth in the science of physiology is the experimental way." [32] And Roux, too, thought this the fundamental maxim for all genuine knowledge of nature. He believed that causal-analytical thinking and experiment have a solidarity, as it were, and cannot be separated from each other: the former must prepare the way for the latter, which alone decides whether the way taken has been the right one and leads to the goal. Roux emphasized that this division of roles between thought and experiment in no way impugned the significance of description for biology, and that its rights should not be curtailed. For there was such a thing as *purely descriptive experiment*, which could also be called "formal analytical experiment." It operates without the intention of calling forth any reaction from the object and without making use of any that might happen to occur. Its purpose is solely to bring the event formally under a closer scrutiny. To this

30. For J. Müller's achievements and his place in history, see du Bois-Reymond's memorial address, 1860, *Reden* (2. vervollständigte Aufl. Leipzig, Veit & Co., 1912), I, 135 ff.

31. J. Müller, *Zur vergleichenden Physiologie des Gesichtssinnes des Menschen und der Tiere* (Leipzig, C. Cnoblich, 1826), S. xix ff.; see Hertwig, *Mechanik und Biologie,* S. 80 ff.

32. C. Bernard, *Leçons sur les phénomènes de la vie* (Paris, J.-B. Baillière et fils, 1878), I, 17.

class of experiment belonged the first experiments of Pflüger and Roux on frog's eggs, the purpose of which was to find out whether the direction of cleavage into the first two blastomeres bears a definite relation to the plane of symmetry of the future animal. It turned out that they coincide entirely, or almost entirely, in three quarters of the cases. Purely descriptive in itself, this was later converted into a causal experiment by the elimination of one causative factor, namely, gravity. Pflüger found that gravity determines which region of the egg shall give rise to the spinal cord, and that this occurs entirely without reference to the kind of egg material at the site. By a suitable arrangement of his experiment Roux was then able to eliminate the effect of gravity with no interference to the normal development of the egg, and it was thus shown that no regulating directive effect by gravity is necessary for the determination of the median plane. From this followed the important inference that all the factors which determine the form characteristic of an organism are contained in the fertilized ovum itself, and that development is therefore to be interpreted as a "self-differentiation." Developing organisms are, in substance, "self-contained complexes of activities that are determining and productive of form," for whose actual realization only the nutritive materials and regulating energies are provided from without.[33]

Roux himself drew no vitalistic conclusions whatsoever from this result but held rather closely to his mechanistic system. It was Hans Driesch, a pupil and collaborator and likewise working toward the ideal of developmental mechanics, who was led by his own experiments to draw conclusions that resulted both in the overthrow of this ideal and in Driesch's proposing and establishing the doctrine of the "autonomy of the organic" in a quite new sense.

33. Roux, *Die Entwicklungsmechanik*, S. 21, 32 ff. An exhaustive description of Pflüger's experiment was given by Roux in his *Beiträge zur Entwicklungsmechanik des Embryo* (1884); *Gesammelte Abhandlungen*, II, 256–276. For his rotation experiments, see Roux's article, "Das Nichnöthigsein der Schwerkraft für die Entwicklung des Froscheies," *Archiv für Entwicklungsmechanik der Organismen*, XIV (13. Juni 1902, Leipzig, W. Engelmann, 1902), 300 ff.

XI

The Argument over Vitalism and the Autonomy of Living Organisms

EVEN ONE who had been familiar with the development of biological thought in the nineteenth century would hardly have been able to foresee the movement of *vitalism* that set in during its last decade and continually gained in intensity and sweep. Until then vitalism had seemed to be losing ground. Of course it had never been banished entirely from philosophy, though a sharp critic had arisen there in the person of Lotze.[1] In science the idea of a "vital force" had long since been wholly discredited. Du Bois-Reymond ridiculed this "maid-of-all-work," who at one time had been supposed capable of settling all problems, and he insisted that the field allotted to the "vital force" was shrinking daily. In chemistry the cudgels were taken up by Liebig.[2] It soon became clear that through the advance of empirical investigation vitalism was losing the very positions formerly believed by its advocates to be impregnable.

Whereas it had once been thought that the difference between the animate and inanimate worlds could be defined in terms of matter, and that the existence of a specific 'vital substance" might some day be demonstrated, hope disappeared in 1828 when Woehler succeeded in synthesizing urea from inorganic compounds. And further, after the principle of the conservation of energy had been discovered, the concept of "force" offered no support to those wanting to secure some exceptional position for the phenomena of life. It could no longer be doubted that the transformation of energy obeys the same general laws in both living and nonliving matter. Those who favored vitalism showed no disposition then to question or reject the universality of the laws of energy; on the contrary they took pains to prove that it was wholly compatible with their own basic view.[3] When Verworn had

1. R. H. Lotze, *Allegemeine Pathologie und Therapie als mechanische Naturwissenschaften* (2. verbess. Aufl. Leipzig, Weidmannsche Buchhandlung, 1848); "Leben, Lebenskraft," *Handwörterbuch der Physiologie,* ed. R. Wagner (Braunschweig, F. Vieweg, 1842), I, ix ff.

2. E. du Bois-Reymond, *Über die Lebenskraft* (1887); *Reden,* I, 23; J. Liebig, *Die organische Chemie in ihrer Anwendung auf Physiologie und Pathologie* (Braunschweig, F. Vieweg, 1842), S. 200.

3. See especially H. Driesch, *Naturbegriffe und Natururteile* (Leipzig, W. Engelmann, 1904).

ascertained, as he expressed it, that "recent calorimetric investigations have shown that in the adult animal . . . a complete dynamic
equilibrium prevails; in other words, exactly the amount of energy
entering the body as chemical forces with the food is released from the
organism during its activities," the methods taken earlier to establish a privileged place for vital phenomena had to be abandoned.[4]
Thenceforward, if one wanted to assert such a position he had to seek
other arguments and other points of departure.

That *developmental mechanics* should have occupied the foreground in Driesch's earliest writings as well as that his thesis was
directly connected with it is at first glance very surprising. Roux had
introduced mechanics as a new branch of biology, whose eminent task
would be to prove that biology and physics were completely one with
each other. For vitalism to enter this field therefore and claim it for
its own was to attack the enemy in his strongest position. Roux himself had persistently repulsed all such attempts. Although he recognized an "anatomy" of the formative vital processes, he admitted it
only in so far as the specific activities of living organisms result from
their complex physicochemical composition, seeing in any explanation that appealed to causes other than the mechanical only "philosophical assumptions due to perplexity," that were valueless to natural science because they could not be tested by experiment.[5] But when
we take his work as a whole and consider the special methodological
foundations which he provided for it, we find that even his strictly
mechanistic program finally reached its definite limit, which is plainly
seen in his very *definition* of an organism. If the analogy between
biology and physics were to be complete, an organism would have
to be reducible simply to a system of active forces and it would be,
like any nonliving body, a sum of single material particles. If differential equations are set up for the motion of such particles, we must
be able to derive from them the general laws governing all phenomena
down to their last details. But here we come immediately upon a
fundamental difference which concerns not the laws of motion as such
but rather the *elements* with which biological research deals. In the
system of mechanics the elements are entirely uniform, none showing
any qualitative difference from the others. Every material particle is
by "nature" like the others; it has simply a numerical value. But in
the study of organic phenomena we can never achieve such a reduction
to homogeneous number, for here we encounter a specific difference

4. M. Verworn, *Allgemeine Physiologie* (4. Aufl. Jena, G. Fischer, 1903), S. 47.

5. W. Roux, *Die Entwicklungsmechanik,* S. 17; and "Das Wesen des Lebens," *Kultur der Gegenwart* (Dritte Abteil., IV), I, 183.

in the elements themselves, a difference of "form." In trying to describe an organism and to trace its development we must always reckon with this form and with an original "disposition" in the organism. Here certain specific causes are always governing, alongside the external conditions, and these Roux called "determination factors," since they give a determinate direction to what occurs. Fish, amphibian, or inverterbrate eggs in the same brook or pool, and eggs of various birds in the same incubator, all develop differently, in spite of a similar environment, and *typically* so, that is to say, they develop into beings each of its own class, genus, and species.[6]

This concept of a "typical occurrence" was characteristic of Roux's research and indispensable to it, but when he adopted this concept he had already taken leave of a strict mechanism. There was no place for such a view in the mechanics of Descartes, Galileo, or Newton—and it could not have been wrought out of their systems. It was rather the Aristotelian concept of "form" that obtained here, for only within the framework of that conception is it possible to speak of a "force" and "energy" and an original and specific "disposition" of the organism that achieves complete fulfillment in the course of its development. Certainly Roux was far from drawing any of the *metaphysical* conclusions that Aristotle had drawn from such premises, but in purely methodological respects this first step seemed to him not only significant but decisive for his entire system. Once the concept of potentiality is introduced and recognized, all the other questions and answers of developmental mechanics receive a new meaning and, so to speak, a changed prognostication. Even the interpretation of the experimental findings now goes in an entirely distinct direction, since it will be dictated by the interest in showing how the "outer" and "inner" conditions mutually respond to and determine each other.

From now on *developmental* mechanics speaks in something like another language, far removed from the usual language of mechanics and possessed of its own dictionary and its own syntax. We can follow the formation of this language step by step with the working out of Roux's system. Eventually the organism becomes more and more sharply differentiated in respect to its intrinsic and distinctive character and it is identified with a wide profusion of special functions. Roux insisted that when we want to designate this peculiar character we can never stop with the ascertaining of particular items which are purely material in character. There is no more a chemical definition of life than there is a static and physical one. Life is *activity*, and in

6. Roux, *Über kausale und konditionale Weltanschauung* (Leipzig, 1913), S. 48.

a sense only a functional definition of it is possible. Roux distinguished nine "typical spontaneous activities" of the organism: variation, elimination, ingestion, assimilation, growth, movement, reproduction, hereditary transmission of characteristics (inheritance), self-formation, and self-preservation. Only through such a complex system of functions, "self-activities," can an organism exist and be recognized as an organism. "Knowledge of this autonomous activity," Roux explained, "has not brought us any closer to the nature of living things. We know only that the organism has an individual identity, hence a so-called inwardness. The spontaneous activities in their totality effect the preservation of the living being." But to them must be added one final factor, in which all these activities in some measure culminate. The ability to survive requires above all "self-regulation with regard to its own form," the capacity to compensate for those external disturbances by which the organism is constantly threatened, and to restore itself always to its own characteristic form.[7]

Roux believed that in establishing all this he had not passed beyond the boundaries of what is strictly observable. The autonomous activities of the organism are, according to him, not conclusions of inference but rather the straightforward phenomena themselves that force themselves upon our observation. Without them a vital process could not even be described. But here an objection arises to which Roux's theory was open and one which involved it in a noteworthy epistemological discussion. From the standpoint of observation is there any justification for or even possibility of discriminating between "inner" and "outer," as was done in the theory; between what the organism performs of its own accord and the influences exercised upon it by external causes? Is all this still properly natural science, or has it not already become metaphysics? Verworn in particular raised these objections and he was led to conclude that so far from carrying out his mechanistic program Roux had actually been unfaithful to it from the very first. His scientific ideal had been to lead biology out of its purely descriptive stage into that of strictly analytical, causal thinking. But Verworn reproached him for having missed the main point by neglecting to give any clear and definite answer to the question of what "causal thinking" really is. Had Roux endeavored to do so he must surely have perceived that his distinction between inner and outer causes was a sheer fiction. Such a distinction can be maintained only from the standpoint of some metaphysical concept of cause, not from that of empirical causation. What is given

7. Roux, *Die Entwicklungsmechanik,* S. 226 ff.; see also "Das Wesen des Lebens," S. 173 ff.

us empirically is never more than the dependence of particular phenomena upon others, and we can only establish the fact that upon the appearance of the one the other is given in a certain way; but we lack any criterion for deciding which of the two is first, that is, the cause, and which is the effect. "Causalism" which until then had held sway in scientific thinking—and also burdened it continually with insoluble problems—must be changed into a pure "conditionalism," as Verworn expressed it. We can only ascertain the *conditions* under which an event occurs, never its so-called causes. But all conditions as such are equivalent to one another, since each is equally necessary for the end result, and if any one of them be lacking the result does not come about. So it is not possible to select *one* condition out of the whole complex and pronounce it "the essential one," superior to any others. Such distinctions are understandable in the superficial observation of everyday life where on many occasions we have but one particular factor in view, but in science they have neither value nor significance. Hence in the interest of serious work we must eliminate the idea of cause as a principle of explanation and replace it with that of condition. The only scientific view of nature is that of "conditionalism" and it is far superior to "causalism." When we come to such a conclusion, continued Verworn, there is no longer any occasion for our distinguishing between supposedly "inner" and "outer" causes of a phenomenon of nature. And therewith that concept of "disposition," upon which Roux had built, is conclusively dispatched. What is generally referred to as "organization" is not itself a fact of experience but only a "mystical" component that has penetrated into science, whose most important duty indeed is to eliminate all such notions.[8]

Roux took vigorous issue with such an interpretation of his efforts and with the criticism of his results. He stoutly maintained that from the standpoint of developmental mechanics or "causal morphology" it was not only possible but necessary to distinguish between the two factors that underlie activity. Both sorts are equally necessary, of course, to produce an effect but this by no means implies that they are of equal value. *Equal necessity* does not mean the sheer *equivalence* of all factors. On the contrary, they are clearly unequal. There is a difference between the "determining" factors of the organic occurrence and the "realizing" factors which help the former to attain their completion.

But here appears, even in Roux, that sharp contrast of which Driesch later spoke as the difference between the organic event and the

---

8. Verworn, *Kausale und konditionale Weltanschauung* (Jena, 1912), and *Die Erforschung des Lebens* (Jena, G. Fischer, 1911).

merely "cumulative" event. Thus, for example, Roux himself turned on Pflüger's view according to which "the fertilized egg bears as little essential relationship to the subsequent organization of the animal as snowflakes do to the size and shape of the avalanche that under appropriate conditions develops from them." [9] Roux answered, saying that the organism is truly a formation existing in its own right, not by virtue simply of any particular specific property that marks it out, but by the whole set of functions in which its power of self-preservation consists. Hence we call the other factors which, as we say, "act" on the organism the "outer" ones, but we do not say, conversely, as we ought to do from the standpoint of a pure conditionalism, that the living being "works on" these "outer" factors, for example, oxygen.[10]

In theory Driesch intended at first only to bring into complete and explicit clarity all the factors that were involved in Roux's conceptions of "typical development," "autonomous completion," "self-regulation," and "functional adaptation," and to draw the unavoidable conclusions from them. He wanted to bring the conception of *developmental mechanics* logically to its dialectical conclusion, so to speak. He believed it contained some constituent elements that were essentially irreconcilable with each other. According to Driesch, anyone who has thoroughly grasped the idea of "development" in its proper sense and has thought it through, must necessarily be led beyond mechanics. And conversely whoever clings to mechanics as the only source of knowledge must consistently deny all development in its real and typical sense. "When developmental mechanics advances the concept of self-regulation," as Schaxel put it, "it is in danger of negating both development and mechanics." [11] This was precisely the idea about which all Driesch's thinking had been incessantly turning from the first. He had set out very early to explain the regulatory processes in the organism in such a way as to harmonize with all the known facts and to penetrate to the ultimate causes whose formulation, in his opinion, was the object of philosophical thought. The whole complicated structure of conceptions which he reared was designed to that end.

The regulatory processes constituted the really crucial point for any mechanistic theory. This was recognized before Driesch, and,

9. E. Pflüger, "Über den Einfluss der Schwerkraft auf die Teilung der Zellen und auf die Entwicklung des Embryo," *Archiv für die gesammte Physiologie* . . . , XXXII (Bonn, E. Strauss, 1883), 64. Cf. Roux's work in opposition to Verworn, *Über kausale und konditionale Weltanschauung* (1913), S. 43 f., 59.

10. Roux, *ibid.,* S. 46.

11. Schaxel, *Grundzüge der Theorienbildung in der Biologie,* S. 45.

indeed, all the criticism of Darwinism and polemic against it had been increasingly concentrating on this point. Gustav Wolff had claimed that no such theory of mere accident, like Darwin's theory of natural selection, could ever bring us any nearer to the understanding of the regulatory processes. It could never explain how such a complicated organ as the human eye, for example, could ever arise, or how it could restore itself after an injury. Symmetrical and "homodynamic" organs could never be conceived as the outcome of accumulated chances; this very accumulation itself would remain always an inexplicable riddle and a real miracle.[12] And Bleuler calculated that the probability of a fortuitous occurrence of the location of cornea, lens, vitreous humor, and retina would amount at the best to approximately $1:10^{42}$, and that for the origin of the whole organ completely "adapted" to its purpose this value would have to be multiplied by thousands of fractions of the same order of size for every one of its parts.[13] Wigand, too, declared that herein lay the "crucial test" of Darwinism. If it does not succeed in explaining the simultaneous origin or transformation of two or more organs of the same sense, for example, two eyes or ears, and in making their reparative power understandable by means of chance variations and selection, then the theory must necessarily break down altogether, for "no Parthenon can be built merely by tossing stones together." [14]

Wolff based his view on his own experiments with the marine snail, *triton*. When the crystalline lens was removed it was *naturally* replaced after a time by a completely new one, but not in the same way as the original lens had developed in the embryo.

The embryonic lens originates from the ectodermal layer of the skin, the regenerated lens from the epithelium of the iris, the so-called optic cup, which comes from the embryonic *Anlage* in the brain. That a tissue entirely foreign to the new function should be drawn upon in this forming of a substitute seems an even more drastic procedure, for it is extraordinary that the material for a lens, the most transparent tissue in the body, should be derived from the most opaque tissue, the black pigmented layer of the iris.

12. G. Wolff, "Beiträge zur Kritik der Darwinschen Lehre," *Biologisches Zentralblatt*, X (15. September 1890, Erlangen, E. Besold, 1891), 449 ff.; and "Erwiderung auf Herrn Prof. Emery's 'Bemerkungen' . . . ," *ibid.*, XI, 321 ff.

13. E. Bleuler, "Mechanismus-Vitalismus-Mnemismus," *Abhandlungen zur Theorie der organischen Entwicklung* (Berlin, J. Springer, 1931), Heft VI. See also L. von Bertalanffy, *Theoretische Biologie*, I, 60 f.

14. Alb. Wigand, *Der Darwinismus und die Naturforschung Newtons und Cuviers;* cf. H. Driesch, "The Covert Presumption of All Theories of Descent," *The Science and Philosophy of the Organism* (London, A. and C. Black, 1908), I, 253 ff. and *Der Vitalismus . . .* , S. 141.

This seemed, then, a striking proof of what Wolff called the "primary purposiveness" of the organism, that is, a function which could not have been acquired in the course of time but must have been present from the first. For here it is a matter of the repair of an injury that the animal had seldom, if ever, suffered during its lifetime and to which, therefore, it could not have in any way gradually adapted itself. The loss of a lens alone does not happen to a triton under natural conditions, and more extensive eye injury, combined with a loss of the lens which is not severe enough to cause total destruction of the whole organ, is very rare to say the least.[15]

Driesch began in the same way with a comprehensive study of the phenomena of regeneration and regulation [16] but soon drew some conclusions that led him far more deeply into metaphysics than ever had been the case before, within the confines of empirical research, during the nineteenth century. His experiments on the eggs of the sea urchin constituted the point of departure, but he ventured at once upon a very bold explanation. The results of experiment had shown that perfectly normal organisms could develop from embryos which had suffered from very severe injury produced by the experiment: thus when the embryo was bisected an entirely normal larva of half size developed, and when embryos were crushed between glass plates so as to disarrange their cells completely, the wholly abnormal positional relationships did not necessarily exclude the formation of a normal, whole organism. No confusion resulted in the system. The embryo with misplaced cells remained an autonomous whole, and followed the usual course of development undisturbed.[17] The conclusion drawn was that since the formative power at work is not interfered with by division, separation, or displacement, it must be a "something" without spatial character and to which no definite position in space can be assigned, but Driesch hesitated to characterize this "something." In earlier writings he had not scrupled to call it frankly a "soul," and to explain that the soul accordingly is an "elemental factor of nature." [18] Later he modified the expression, in order to avoid introducing the idea of a consciously purposeful activity and spoke not of a soul but of a something-like-a-soul, a "psychoid." It was, of course, not a psyche but it could be spoken of only in such psychological terms. He

15. Wolff, "Entwicklungsphyiologische Studien I: Die Regeneration der Urodelenlinse," *Archiv für Entwicklungsmechanik der Organismen,* I (Leipzig, W. Engelmann, 1895), Heft III, 380 ff.

16. Driesch, *Die organischen Regulationen* (Leipzig, W. Engelmann, 1901).

17. Driesch, "The Experiments on the Egg of the Sea-Urchin," *The Science and Philosophy of the Organism,* I, 59 ff.; trans. from the German, *Die Philosophie des Organischen* (1909).

18. Driesch, *Die Seele als elementarer Naturfaktor* (Leipzig, W. Engelmann, 1903).

found the most suitable expression finally in the Aristotelian concept of "entelechy," which now became for him the innermost key to the whole biological system of things. The entelechy is the formative power of the organism, different from the physicochemical forces and not to be set on the same level with them. All merely physical or chemical factors are but means employed by the organism; they do not make life, though they are used by life and enlisted in its service. No machine of any kind and no sort of causality which depends upon spatial configurations can explain what is done daily and hourly by the organism. "Is it possible to imagine that a complex machine, unsymmetrical in the three planes of space, could be divided hundreds and hundreds of times and still remain intact?" [19]

Of course entelechy was not conceived as something given immediately to us in perception; it could only be *conceived*, since it does not belong to the sensory world, which is the world of space. Yet its reality is nonetheless indisputable, for it discloses itself directly in its effects. These are of a very peculiar sort, to be sure, and not on the same level of convertibility with physicochemical energies. That the latter come under the definite laws of conservation of energy, which cannot be suspended even by the entelechy, Driesch firmly believed. But although it is unable to alter the amount of energy in a dynamic system, still a "nonmechanical agency" like entelechy can have the capacity of diverting one or another of its elements and thereby changing the *direction* of the forces and movements. In this way an occurrence that would be entirely possible according to the laws of the inorganic world can be "suspended" by the entelechy. Here we are face to face with an activity that has no parallel in the world of the nonliving, since it is nonspatial, intensive, and qualitative rather than spatial, extensive, and quantitative. Yet both these diametrically opposed modes of activity relate to one and the same object—the chain of temporal and spatial events that we call "nature." For entelechy, though in itself it is not spatial and does not act within space, still "works itself *into* space." It relates to nature in space and is a factor of this nature.[20]

With these propositions Driesch wanted to establish biology as an independent fundamental science. But as we read them we get the impression that he has gone far beyond anything that *science* could establish and prove. The expedient of suggesting that while the soul

---

19. Driesch, *The Science* . . . , II, 78 (German original, II, 78); see *Der Vitalismus als Geschichte und als Lehre,* S. 221.
20. Driesch, *Philosophie des Organischen,* I, 139 ff., 229; II, 181 f., 207, 239 f. and elsewhere.

can neither increase nor decrease the sum total of motion in the universe it can still alter the direction of motion had been proposed by Descartes; but Leibniz had already countered it by showing that even this would be impossible without the expenditure of a definite amount of energy. From the very beginning this point was one of the weakest in Driesch's theory, and it was seized upon by his critics without delay.[21]

Still, however one may regard his theory or disagree with its metaphysical implications, there is no denying that through his experiments and the questions that he raised in connection with them, Driesch contributed greatly to defining the characteristic methodological *principle* and *problem* of biology. This was the most outstanding result of the theory. What it means has been variously construed, however, by the historians of modern biology. Nordenskiöld saw no more in the system, after all, than a detailed and long-winded analysis of concepts, in the course of which Driesch was led further and further into abstract speculation. One is reminded, it was said, of the palmy days of Hegel's philosophy, especially as Driesch's definitions and characterizations of the processes of life are hardly equaled for obscurity and unintelligibility.[22] But Rádl reached a quite different opinion in his history of biological theories. He stated that among philosophers Driesch stood next to Kant, and might be called his successor, for unlike other biologists he was not a mere empiricist but strove rather toward "pure natural science," whose propositions should be universal and secure against all doubt.[23] Yet to this it may be objected, at the outset, that for Kant the "pure" part of natural science is identical with its mathematical part, and that Kant explicitly restricted science to those mathematical principles of natural philosophy whose universal validity Driesch's vitalism contested with equal explicitness. But it was above all in this matter of the relationship between natural knowledge and metaphysics that Driesch not only failed to follow Kant but struck into a path that led in a dramatically opposite direction.

Of course Driesch himself believed that he was faithful to Kant's critical principles and he liked to designate his own system as "critical idealism."[24] He insisted that without continually being in touch

21. Julius Schultz, for example, showed that there could be no suspension without energy. Göttingen, 1909.
22. E. Nordenskiöld, *The History of Biology*, pp. 608 ff.
23. E. Rádl, *Geschichte der biologischen Theorien* . . . , II, 532 f.
24. Driesch, *Naturbegriffe und Natururteile*, S. 27; *Philosophie des Organischen*, II, 204, and elsewhere.

with the theory of knowledge natural science could not possibly be fruitful.[25] Nevertheless it is a fact that in his central theory of entelechy he not only breaks with Kant's critical idealism but actually does away with it altogether. When Kant discussed the relation of causality and purposiveness, of mechanism and teleology, it was not a question of delimiting with respect to each other two different systems of forces or absolute ontological powers. Kant declared the problem of the nature and relations of such ultimate powers to be insoluble, and emphasized that even in stating such a problem both science and common sense became entangled in a net of antinomies. He treated the purpose concept and the causal concept solely as principles of knowledge, as modes of knowing; and if he contrasted the two it was only to distinguish them sharply and clearly from each other in accordance with the methodological interest which each one represented and the function it must fulfill in the construction of natural science. Both principles serve only to make possible the "exposition of the appearances," and each one does it in a different way. Causality is a constitutive, synthetic, fundamental principle and is the indispensable condition of "the possibility of nature in general." Whatever escapes it must fall clean outside the realm of nature, for nature is "the existence of things so far as they are determined in conformity with universal laws." The possibility that there might be such universal laws that are not strictly causal laws, nor consequently of a mathematical and physical sort, was never once considered by Kant. On the other hand, he insisted that these causal laws alone cannot enable us to become even *acquainted* with that special realm of the phenomena confronting us in organic nature, to say nothing of completely "explaining" them. Here is the role of that other *principle of order*, which we call purposiveness. This principle is indispensable to the investigation of the phenomena of life but it remains, nevertheless, simply a maxim of the "reflective judgment," and not something real that exists in itself and acts by itself.[26]

It was precisely at this point, however, that Driesch reversed the problems. Where Kant had seen only two *points of view* from which we undertake to explain phenomena, Driesch saw a relation of two fundamental and ultimate powers, one of which takes the other into its service and employs it for its own ends. The "entelechy" is abstracted from the realm of spatial existence; it is something not sensible but supersensible. As such it is, as Driesch himself often makes plain, first describable only in negative terms, and analysis leads to nothing but

25. Driesch, *Die Biologie als selbständige Grundwissenschaft*, S. IV.
26. See above, pp. 119–120.

negative results. It is no "force, it is not an intensity, it is not a constant, it is just—'entelechy.' " [27] There is just as little hope of finding anything analogous to it in the realm of consciousness. When we call it a "psychoid," a something that is like a soul, we should not forget that it belongs as little to the psychic world as to that of inanimate nature. Thus neither "entelechy" nor a "psychoid" can be represented in idea, for whatever is thus capable of representation is really spatial.[28]

But this mere "system of negations" which Driesch, as a logical analyst, sought to display, changed for him as metaphysician into a positive system, and, even more, it became the *ens realissimum*, the most real of all being. The entelechy does not exist in space nor does it belong to nature and to natural science, but for those very reasons we must see in it the actual well-spring of nature, that in which "the power and seed of all activity" discloses itself.[29]

Johannes von Uexküll chose another way of establishing vitalism. He thought himself wholly in agreement with Driesch, in his fundamental conviction, and regarded him as his most loyal ally and comrade in arms. Nevertheless a real difference obtained between the two in respect to their general methodology and philosophy. This is evident even in their respective points of departure and in their empirical foundations and it appears even more plainly in the general theoretical system of concepts that each one individually used in the interpretation of his empirical findings. Driesch started from *physiology*, which he had always considered the systematic center of biology. But Uexküll was above all *an anatomist* and upheld the ideal of his science in its classical purity, in this respect recalling Cuvier, whose modern successor he seemed to be. The concept of "anatomical type," in the form laid down by his great predecessor, permeated and dominated all his thinking. Thus he was far less inclined than Driesch to draw metaphysical conclusions, though by no means opposed in principle to doing so. "The science of living beings," he wrote, "is a purely natural science and has but one goal: investigation of the structure of organisms, their origin, and their functioning." [30]

The emphasis of Uexküll in this statement was not, however, upon the *development* of the organism, as with Cuvier and his disciples, but upon its *being*, and the center of gravity was shifted accordingly

27. Driesch, *Philosophie des Organischen*, II, S. 206 ff., 252, Eng. trans., pp. 204 ff., 250.

28. *Ibid.*, S. 331, Eng. trans., p. 328; cf. *Der Vitalisms* . . . , S. 243.

29. Driesch, *Philosophie des Organischen*, II, 263 ff., Eng. trans., pp. 260 ff.; *Der Vitalismus* . . . , S. 228 ff.

30. J. v. Uexküll, *Die Lebenslehre*, S. 9.

from the dynamics of living beings, that is, from physiology and phylogenetics, to the *statics* thereof. If we ever succeed in obtaining a complete picture of the organism in that aspect, we can then construct a theory of all its functions. Logically too the concept of structure serves as a surer starting point, because it at once prescribes a definite direction for research and furnishes biology with an Archimedean fulcrum, as it were.

While Driesch in his conception of entelechy wanted to demonstrate a specific autonomy of function, Uexküll started from the autonomy of *form*. What is called the "form" of an animal or plant is, he believed, so little a material thing that it can be grasped only conceptually—it is quite insensible or incapable of representation. It stands fully determinate before us, in plastic clarity, yets its determinateness is not that of a corporeal object. The real analogue to the concept of biological form is not to be found in the world of material things or processes with which physics is concerned, but must be sought elsewhere, in the pure relationships of *geometry and stereometry.*

Structure is not a material thing: it is the unity of immaterial relationships among the parts of an animal body. Just as plane geometry is the science not of the material triangles drawn on a blackboard with chalk but of the immaterial relationships between the three angles and three sides of a closed figure . . . so biology treats of the immaterial relationships of material parts united in a body so as to reconstitute the structure in imagination.[31]

With that view the program of "idealistic morphology" was being thoroughly resurrected. When biologists in the middle of the century thought they could overthrow this theory and replace it with something better, they had, in Uexküll's opinion, strangely deceived themselves. Both the Darwinians and those working on developmental history had mistaken the decisive and essential factor, and from this mistake in principle emanated all their subsequent materialism and mechanism. "When the whole complex of natural phenomena was traced to only two factors, energy and matter . . . the third factor, form, was simply overlooked." [32]

We have seen in Cuvier how his geometrical and static idea of type determined the methodological character of biology in a very peculiar way and in a certain sense transformed it. Without ceasing to be a strictly empirical science it was now possible for biology to advance to

31. *Ibid.,* S. 9.
32. *Ibid.,* S. 19.

conclusions of a universal and "rational" sort. Deduction was no longer absolutely out of the question, even if it had to assume a special form to correspond with the nature of its object.[33] A similar development can be traced in the case of Uexküll. He too wanted to draw far-reaching conclusions from the anatomical type to which an animal belongs, and he insisted that these conclusions would have perfect certainty. Once we have clearly explored the structure of an animal in all its features the whole being and mode of existence of the animal is revealed. We know its characteristics and its activities; we look into its "inner life" and we see its environment, for whatever it undergoes from the outer world depends strictly upon the way it is able to accept and act on external stimuli. An animal can receive only those impressions for which it is prepared by its structure and can react to stimuli only in so far as it possesses the appropriate organs. Every creature has its own private world of perception and activity, prescribed once for all by its structure, by its type of receptors and effectors. Hence we realize that every action of an organism implies an endless chain of functions connecting the agent and its environment. This starts from the outer object in the form of one or more stimuli that affect the receptors. In the animal's body these are combined into a network of perceptions, to spread thence into a network of mechanisms that imparts to the effectors a definite kind of movement. This completes the circle that Uexküll called "the circle of functions." Every animal is closely bound up with its environment through such functional circles, of which a number are recognizable for almost every organism and which can be named by reference to their corresponding objects, such as prey, enemy, sex, habitat. . . . Here it is obviously erroneous to speak of an "adaptation to the environment" in the Darwinian sense, for to do so is to convert into a process which requires time something that is actually determinate and indispensable *from the first* to the survival of the animal. If it is the inner structure that creates the environment by its own activity, one should *not* say that an animal is more or less adapted to the environment. Only thanks to itself alone is each animal completely adjusted to its surroundings. Furthermore, it appears that the "things" of the animal's environment are just those that pertain to its life, things carved out, so to speak, from the totality of being by the operation of the animal's own specific structure. "The protoplasm that made an earthworm made it for an earthworm's activities, and set it in an earthworm's world."

Uexküll emphasized that an epistemological problem lay concealed in this biological problem. The biologist must rid himself of the no-

33. See above, p. 138.

tion that his own human environment is the very same as that of the animals. "The biologist is required to analyze his world into its elements (which cannot be done without a fundamental epistemological study), for he must be able to establish which of the ingredients serve as 'reality' for the animals."

Thereupon all that seems to us so self-evident disappears: all nature, the earth, the heavens, the stars, yes, the very objects that surround us, and there remain, as world factors, only those operations that exercise influence upon the animal in accordance with its own structure. When this relationship of the organic structure to the external factors is carefully examined, a new world wholly different from ours is seen to surround every animal and constitute *its* environment.

This world is the fixed frame within which its life is confined and from which it cannot escape. "Every animal carries its environment about with it like an impenetrable shell, all the days of its life." [34]

Uexküll strongly emphasized that the *research into the environment* which he endeavored to introduce into biology as an independent method was not a causal investigation but purely one into *the existence of structure*. Hence the problem of purpose assumed a different form for him than that of Driesch. There was no need for him to introduce any special purposive "forces": it was enough to prove that the living world, in its totality as in its details, has a stable teleological *structure*. In this sense he preferred to speak of "structural character" rather than purposive character. Although at first sight this may appear to be only an insignificant change in terminology, it was actually based on a new *concern* that was characteristic of Uexküll's vitalism. Unlike other vitalists he did not have to appeal to special "superior forces," "entelechies," or "dominants," which stand above the ordinary physicochemical forces and interfere with their activities so as to guide what is happening in a certain direction. He could dismiss the causal problem of physics and chemistry if only it were recognized that causality is not the whole of science and that there is an independent problem of form, for which biology has to develop its own concepts and methods of thought. Once this was granted, the conflict between mechanism and vitalism was over so far as Uexküll was concerned. He was interested in the fact that there is a nonmaterial ordering, a rule of the living process that gives to organic matter whatever arrangement it may have. In speaking of this fact "we may use indifferently the terms 'structural character,' 'functional

34. Uexküll, *Umwelt und Innenwelt der Tiere* and *Theoretische Biologie* (2. Aufl.). Both published in Berlin by J. Springer, 1909, and 1928.

character,' 'harmony' or 'wisdom.' The terminology is of no consequence, only the recognition that there exists a natural power which
binds together according to certain rules. If biology does not recognize this power in nature, it remains an empty delusion." [35]

In Uexküll's opinion physics is entirely correct in seeking to explain all connections in the world in terms solely of causality, but
quite wrong if that means banishing every other mode of thinking
from science. "For causality is not the only rule at our disposal for
construing the world." [36] In this sentence Uexküll returned much
more nearly to Kant's position and his solution of the problem of purpose than Driesch had ever done. No objection to this view could have
been found in the *Critique of Judgment*.

But in his struggle against materialism and mechanism Uexküll is
related in another important aspect to the classical tradition of idealistic morphology. He held fast all along to the idea of an "inner
purposiveness," though he resisted all attempts to convert it into an
"outer purposiveness." The living world is not so ordered that the
various kinds of animals exist for each other and relate to each other
in such a way that the whole series finds its end in mankind—"end"
in the two senses of a terminus and a purpose. The relations that
here obtained are entirely different, for every organism has its center
of gravity within itself. This basic conception is found in the general
history of ideas and goes back to the philosophy of Leibniz. It was
thanks to the revolution in that philosophy that the conception of
purpose entered upon a new phase of its development. For Leibniz the
"formal" took the place of "material" purposiveness, and "harmony" replaced utility. Every monad is a world in itself, a self-
contained cosmos that mirrors the whole universe in its own way. But
all these individual worlds are united with one another through a pre-
established harmony, inasmuch as they are expressions of the same
universal order. Each one has its definite place and its definite rights
in the plan of creation. With these thoughts a new orientation had
come into the philosophy of the seventeenth and eighteenth centuries
and it affected all fields of knowledge. Its results are discernible in
the interpretation of history and the philosophy of history prior to
its influence in biology. Here it was Herder who helped the idea to
achieve its ultimate victory. He fought the naïve belief of the Enlightenment in progress and the view of man as the goal of creation, and of
the educated man of that century particularly as the goal of all
humanity. For Herder the meaning and value of the development of

35. Uexküll, *Theoretische Biologie*, S. 98, 144.
36. *Ibid.*, S. 81.

humanity could be comprehended only in the totality of all its forms.
Every type is necessary in its place, and every one is significant for
its own sake, not merely for the sake of something else. There are no
more privileged epochs than there are privileged nations. "All taken
together!" he cried to the science and culture of his time. "The quintessence of all ages and peoples! What nonsense." "Every nation has
its center of happiness within itself, just as every sphere has its center
of gravity within itself." [37]

This basic idea was transferred by Goethe from history to the living world in general. He, too, constantly emphasized how impossible
it would be to select any one single race, human or otherwise, from
the totality of life and set it up as the goal, the measure, the canon.
One single being cannot be a pattern for all.[38]

> Zweck sein selbst ist jegliches Tier, vollkommen entspringt es,
> Aus dem Schoss der Natur und zeugt vollkommene Kinder
> Alle Glieder bilden sich aus nach ew'gen Gesetzen
> Und die seltenste Form bewahrt im Geheimen das Urbild.
>
> .　　.　　.　　.　　.
>
> So ist jedem der Kinder die volle reine Gesundheit
> Von der Mutter bestimmt: denn alle lebendigen Glieder
> Widersprechen sich nie und wirken alle zum Leben.
> Also bestimmt die Gestalt die Lebensweise des Tieres
> Und die Weise zu leben, sie wirkt auf alle Gestalten
> Mächtig zurück. So zeiget sich fest die geordnete Bildung.
>
> .　　.　　.　　.　　.
>
> Diese Grenzen erweitert kein Gott, es ehrt die Natur sie
> Denn nur also beschränkt war je das Vollkommene möglich.[39]

37. Herder, *Auch eine Philosophie der Geschichte zur Bildung der Menschheit,*
"Sämmtliche Werke," ed. B. Suphan (Berlin, Weidmannsche Buchhandlung, 1891), V,
503, 509.

38. See above, p. 143.

39. For its own purpose alone each animal, perfectly finished,
　　Issues from nature's womb and produces symmetrical offspring
　　Each of whose members evolves in answer to laws everlasting,
　　Even the rarest of forms inscrutably following the standard.

　　　　　.　　.　　.　　.　　.

　　So on each of the children is radiant health in abundance
　　Bestowed as a gift by the mother: For none of their functioning members
　　Are ever opposed to the others but labor in common toward life.
　　Thus does its form determine an animal's manner of living
　　And manner of living in turn react upon every form
　　In the most powerful way. Thus the organized being is stable.

　　　　　.　　.　　.　　.　　.

　　These bounds are enlarged by no god; and besides they are honored by nature,
　　For perfection is only attained by virtue of such limitation.
　　　　　　　"Die Metamorphose der Tiere," in Goethe's *Gedichte* . . .

It is remarkable to see how exactly the plan and development of Uexküll's biology conformed in every particular with this view of Goethe. Here a very characteristic reaction emerges against Darwinism because of its prejudice in interpreting evolution as a "progress" from the lowest forms of life to man. In the case of Haeckel this belief in progress colored both his biology and his whole philosophy of life as well. But Uexküll warned of a complete reversal on this point. He created a new conception of "the biological universe," which he compared with that of the "astronomical universe": the latter "is but one world whose infinite space and everlasting time hold countless stellar mechanisms aimlessly revolving around one another; the biological universe presents a picture instead of thousands upon thousands of self-contained worlds that are related to one another according to a plan of unexampled grandeur." [40] Everywhere there is perfection in a sense, but the perfection of course is not that of all-power; it is rather the full and appropriate use of the means available. "The lowest and the highest forms of life are . . . equally perfect in respect to their microchemistry. Faced with this fact, all our attempts to explain the living being as a fortuitous concourse of matter come to naught." [41]

After having been stirred up afresh by Driesch's interposition the *vitalistic controversy* increased progressively in extent and violence. At the turn of the century it dominated virtually all biological thinking, and both philosophy and specialized research became more and more deeply drawn into its circle. Viewed merely in the light of external events the controversy seems not to have produced any results of permanent value, for when it was over the opposition of the two theses was just as downright and irreconcilable as ever. And after the same arguments had been repeated over and over again the two sides retired from the field, wearied at last by the reiteration. But the apparent draw contained, nonetheless, an important though indirect methodological lesson. When the documents of this whole discussion are reviewed one finds that in respect to *one* point, at any rate, some approach to common ground had been made, viz., in the statement of the *problem* of biology.

We shall attempt to make this clear without concealing from ourselves the fact that at present all is still in flux and that there can be no mention as yet of any conclusive and generally accepted outcome. Between the extremists of the two schools, who set up their theses

40. Uexküll, *Die Lebenslehre,* S. 157.
41. Uexküll, *Theoretische Biologie,* S. 92, 137.

dogmatically, no reconciliation was ever to be expected. One side stated not merely that life is to be conceived mechanistically but further, on the basis of this insight, that it can be controlled and produced mechanically in every last detail. This assertion was made especially by the experimental morphologists. To them a complete knowledge of living forms is achieved only when we have them "entirely in hand" and can create them at will. "Whereas until now developmental phenomena have always been regarded as necessarily dependent upon the innermost nature of the organism," wrote Klebs,

it will be shown in the future how variously the organism can be modified and often completely changed. Research must set itself the task of becoming master of every living formation through the knowledge of its conditions. Just as the chemist must understand the properties of a substance so well that he can demonstrate them at any time, the botanist must endeavor to manipulate plants with perfect certainty. This mastery of plant life will, I hope, characterize the botany of the future.[42]

But there was no reason to restrict this ideal simply to the vegetable kingdom, for it could be extended with the same right to the animal kingdom as soon as the factor was discovered that unites plant growth and animal movement. Jacques Loeb tried to bridge the gap here and to lay the foundations for a common dynamic of all vital phenomena.[43] Loeb was a pupil of Julius Sachs, whose experiments on tropisms had in his opinion been entirely conclusive. According to Sachs only one step would be necessary to transfer the results acquired in this field to the animal kingdom. We must make up our minds to treat everything which at first sight looks like independent activity and development as a complex of interacting tropisms, each one realizing itself in a purely mechanical way and being explicable by strictly mechanical laws. The thesis of animal automatism, introduced into modern philosophy by Descartes, has never been so rigorously and consistently carried out in Sachs's opinion as it was by Loeb. The system of active causes is certainly much more complicated, for whereas in the time of Descartes all could be referred ultimately to simple relations of pressure and impact, the tropisms of Loeb's theory are divided into an ever increasing number of separate kinds until at last there are as many of them as there are different physical stimuli. Thus there is, according to the theory, a geotropism, a phototropism, a chemotropism, a hydrotropism, a barotropism, an anemotropism,

42. G. Klebs, *Willkürliche Entwicklungsänderungen bei Pflanzen,* S. 23.
43. For details on the course of Loeb's scientific development, see Nordenskiöld, *op. cit.,* Eng. trans., pp. 605 f.

a rheotropism, and a goniotropism.[44] The process of fertilization can be completely explained solely in terms of physical and chemical concepts, as the movements of animals are explained, and it can actually be achieved by the application of purely chemical and physical agents. The "homunculus" problem was held to be completely solved, or at least solvable in principle. We have only to improve our experimental technique in order to generate life in the test tube. For the chemistry of the living organism is fundamentally identical with that of the laboratory and the factory. "I have the feeling," said Loeb in a lecture before the First Monist Congress at Hamburg in 1911, "that technical shortcomings of our young science are alone to blame for the fact that the artificial production of living matter has not yet succeeded." [45] He considered his own investigations into artificial fertilization to have solved completely the problem of the beginning of individual life and of death, for it seemed proven that it is possible to replace the fertilizing activity of spermatozoa with simple physicochemical agents.[46] No "form factor" need be introduced, and to speak of "structural character" is meaningless, since so much that is not to the purpose arises and then dies out. "Disharmonies and false starts in nature are the rule, the harmoniously formed systems only the exception." [47]

To this last argument an objection could be made on behalf of vitalism—that the structural or formative character ascribed to the processes of life is not at all identical with external purposive adaptation. Even to speak of "failures" in form is to assume the *concept* of form, just as truly as if we regarded form as having been achieved. Of course there is no illimitable adaptation to purpose in nature; there are processes that *destroy* as well as processes that maintain the wholeness of living beings. So vitalism considers its form factor or "wholeness" factor not as a potentiality which is quantitatively unlimited but rather as one of a peculiar quality which makes its appearance in the abnormal as well as in the normal organism.[48]

44. J. Loeb, *Der Heliotropismus der Thiere, und seine Übereinstimmung mit dem Heliotropismus der Pflanzen* (Würzburg, G. Hertz, 1890). A critique of Loeb's theory of tropism from a vitalistic standpoint is contained in Uexküll's *Die Lebenslehre,* S. 133 ff.

45. J. Loeb, *Vorlesungen über die Dynamik der Lebenserscheinungen* (Leipzig, J. A. Barth, 1906), S. 11; and *Das Leben* (Leipzig, 1911), S. 9.

46. Loeb, *Das Leben,* S. 17, 22.

47. *Ibid.,* S. 34 ff.

48. See G. Wolff's remarks on Bütschli, *Mechanismus und Vitalismus* (Leipzig, 1902), S. 31; also E. Ungerer, *Regulationen der Pflanzen, ein System der teleologischen Begriffe in der Botanik,* S. 45 ff.

Of course it has always seemed especially difficult for vitalism to draw a sharp line between a wholly descriptive concept of form and a metaphysical and transcendental concept of purpose, and to hold steadily to the distinction in the course of the discussion. An example is furnished in J. Reinke's system, where almost the entire gamut of possible interpretations is run through without any clear and precise methodological demarcation between them. On the one hand Reinke was content to establish the characteristic striving of the life processes toward a goal as a sheer *phenomenon* which distinguishes the facts of the organic world from those of the inorganic. In this sense he rejected the assumption of a special life force and even regarded it as a "highly naïve biological interpretation." "The vital principle is no force but the symbolic expression for a complex of innumerable strands whose product, adaptation to a purpose, is evident throughout." Hence vitalism should not become a dogma any more than mechanism, that is, not a conclusive doctrine, but it should remain as a *problem* for further analysis in which mechanistic principles of research should be employed. The highest quality of critical caution seems to obtain here in Reinke's thought. But close beside it is the demand for independent formative powers or "dominants," whose existence Reinke was unable to prove but nonetheless *postulated*. Though he would not strictly call them "intelligent forces," still he insisted that in their operation they are best compared with an intelligence.[49] Indeed, he went so far as to describe the guiding powers not only as "pilots of the energies" but even as "demons" that do not originate in energy and cannot be changed into energy and so are not subject to the laws of its conservation.[50]

In Bunge we meet with another interpretation and argument. He likewise emphasized strongly that even the most advanced causal knowledge will never satisfy the dream of mechanism or do away with the specificity of life processes. The further we go on this road the clearer and more unmistakably would the difference appear. The more minutely, diversely, and thoroughly we seek to investigate a living phenomenon, the more insight we gain into the fact that processes which seemed to have been completely understood and mastered actually defy all mechanistic interpretation. We must realize again and again the truth that there is a wide gap between the passive motions we find in inanimate nature and the active, genuine

49. J. Reinke, *Einleitung in die theoretische Biologie* (2. Aufl. Berlin, 1911), S. 64 ff., 195 ff.

50. Reinke, *Die Welt als Tat* (4. Aufl. Berlin, G. Paetel, 1905), S. 269; "Gedanken über das Wesen der Organisation," *Biologisches Zentralblatt,* XIX (Leipzig, A. Georgi, 1899), 1 Februar 1899, Teil I, S. 81 ff., 15. Februar 1889, Teil II, S. 113 ff.

movements of living things. "I maintain," said Bunge, "that all processes of life that *can* be mechanically explained are no more the real phenomena of life than is the motion of branches and leaves shaken by the storm or the movement of pollen blown by the wind from the male to the female poplar." [51]

So here too we stand on the ground of strict vitalism: the antithesis between the movement of life and that of inorganic nature is maintained in a thoroughgoing fashion. A wide gap separates passive motions from the activities of life. But Bunge would not close this gap by taking refuge in any special sort of superior guiding force. He gave the physicochemical explanation free scope, convinced that this was the surest way for it to arrive at an insight into its own limitations. Here then the problem is shifted to other ground and assumes a form different from that given it by either Driesch or Reinke.

It was Driesch's complaint that Bunge had not taken a clear and decisive stand: on the question of vitalism everything he had said seemed intended only "provisionally," because the mechanistic view was not yet satisfied.[52] But here Driesch did not do justice to Bunge's interpretation, for he overlooked the fact that the mechanistic explanation of the phenomena of life remained for Bunge something infinitely distant, which science could increasingly approximate but never reach. The assumption of a "vital force" would not help matters, for Bunge was convinced, as Kant had been, that this would be nothing but a "comfortable couch where reason was lulled to rest on the pillow of mysterious properties." Hence Bunge declared that nothing remained but to work on resolutely toward a physicochemical explanation, patiently hoping to solve the problem at last in this way. "The method is fruitful throughout, and we must try how far we can go with the help of physics and chemistry alone; the inner core that cannot be explored in this way will then emerge the more clearly and distinctly. So the mechanism of the present day drives us surely onward toward the vitalism of the future." [53]

Such a cautious and critical interpretation of the problem had been reached here that a reconciliation between the wholly dogmatic antitheses might now have become possible. Indeed there were prominent advocates of mechanism who were virtually of the same opinion as Bunge in purely *methodological* respects. They said that no halt should ever be called to physicochemical inquiry, but while they

51. G. Bunge, *Lehrbuch der physiologischen und pathologischen Chemie* (2. Aufl.), S. 8; cf. Bunge's lecture, "Vitalismus und Mechanismus" (Leipzig, F. C. W. Vogel, 1889), S. 3 ff.

52. Driesch, *Der Vitalismus* . . . , S. 143.

53. Bunge, *Lehrbuch* . . . , S. 8 f., 14; "Vitalismus und Mechanismus," S. 3.

would not abandon it they still did not believe with Loeb that the goal had already been attained or could be attained in a short time. Thus Verworn maintained, for example, that all their high expectations of an advancement of experimental research and employment of exact methods had been disappointed. The problem of life was as little capable of solution on mechanistic grounds as it had ever been. We know that respiration, circulation, digestion, and resorption follow the laws of physics and chemistry, but physiology had not yet succeeded in explaining the selective capacity of the cells. It was understandable, therefore, that the "old specter of life force" should continue to haunt science; but instead of welcoming it, we should continue to advance and to improve our methods.[54]

It will be readily understood that in the field of *experimental research* itself mechanism and vitalism did not face each other as irreconcilable opponents but were able to unite and work together toward common goals. Here there was no exclusive antithesis but a peculiar relationship of alternating methods. Vitalism continually reminded mechanism of its limitations but in so doing only spurred it on to renewed activity while, on the other hand, because of the criticism to which it was exposed, vitalism itself did not succumb to the danger of "sinking back tranquilly on the couch of indolence." It has been rightly emphasized that in the history of biology the greatest vitalists have always rendered outstanding service toward the explanation of the mechanism *within* the living organism. "The same Harvey who penetrated most deeply into the development of the embryo discovered the circulation of the blood, and brilliant examples in more recent times are Johannes Müller and Naegeli." [55]

Thus the further evolution of the antithesis between mechanism and vitalism did not really go counter to Kant's attempted solution of the "antinomy of judgment" in any way but rather confirmed it in all essentials. It is not going too far to maintain that in this respect Kant stood nearer to modern biology than he did to that of his own day, and that he anticipated a number of methodological problems which only later came to maturity. It had become increasingly clear that "form concepts" have a specific structure and must be retained, notwithstanding all the progress made in causal explanation. As a logician Kant wanted only to describe this distinction, of course; but as a critic of natural science he also wanted to establish a certain distinction *in value* between the two sorts of con-

54. Verworn, *Allgemeine Physiologie,* S. 29 ff., 45 ff.
55. R. Burckhardt, *Biologie und Humanismus* (Jena, 1907), S. 73 f.

cepts. He expressed that distinction when he ascribed to the causal concept a "constitutive" role and to the other a merely "regulative" role, thus declaring causality to be the central category of natural science and the concept of purpose or form to be but an "idea" or an "heuristic maxim." We need not follow out this discrimination made by Kant, since it depended upon the form of the problem in his own day, and the problem has undergone a fundamental change since then both in physics and in biology. To Kant and to the generation of his period, it was evident that science had found its real protagonist in Newton and that it must never forsake the ideal portrayed in his *Mathematical Principles of Natural Philosophy,* under penalty of falling from its high estate. Here was a kind of classical prototype or canon, by which all knowledge is to be measured for the future: Newton's science was Science. When Kant found, therefore, as a result of his critical analysis, that biology not only could never reach the Newtonian ideal but could not even strive toward it, and that it was absurd to hope for a "Newton of the grass blades," all this must have led to a certain amount of resignation on his part. He could dwell on the special rights and value of biology but could not assign it the same rank or the same objective value in the hierarchy of knowledge as mathematical and physical knowledge. The latter possessed, and would always possess, a true objectivity, and this distinction could be neither belittled nor disputed.

Such misgivings exist no longer, for a limitation of mechanism does not imply today a limitation of physics. For modern physics has gradually freed itself of the chains imposed on it by the mechanistic view and developed a new ideal of science. Its relation to biology, too, appears in a new light. Assured nowadays of its own complete independence physics may readily concede to biology a much greater degree of freedom than hitherto, since in so doing it is only guaranteeing a right which it continually demands for itself in its own criticism and reform of the classical system.

In conclusion, if we look once more at the latest phase of theoretical biology in the twentieth century, it seems as if the alliance between biology and physics in the sense indicated just above has already been effected. The controversy between mechanists and vitalists has slowly died out and no faction attaches to it the same importance as previously. In place of it the outlines of a combined view begin to define themselves with increasing clarity, and it will be neither a dogmatic mechanism nor a dogmatic vitalism. It has been called by J. S. Haldane, one of its originators, "holism" or "organicism." [56] A survey of the development of this concept during the past few decades, and of its systematic significance, has been recently published by Adolf Meyer, who sees in both mechanism and vitalism merely "worthy old ideologies" that no longer have any real theoretical vitality. "One cannot escape the impression," he wrote, "that these highly respected ideologies have fallen behind in the development of the special biological disciplines; in any case they have nothing more to teach those who pursue them." [57] Biology cannot become a well-organized science as long as it emulates the two ideals that are essentially foreign to it. "Vitalism negates the modern Galilean-Newtonian-Kantian ideal of a mathematical natural science and thereby robs biology of unquestionably fruitful possibilities of knowledge, while mechanism degrades it to a special and meaningless appendage of theoretical physics." But organicism proposes to combine the positive content of both in a higher synthesis which is superior to both. It urges with vitalism the autonomy of the organic with respect to the inorganic and it urges with mechanism the deductive continuity of the two realms of actuality. But this continuity takes another direction of course, for it is not a case of the higher being deduced from the lower but precisely the reverse.[58]

It is difficult to sift out the meaning of this view for the theory of knowledge since all is in flux, and even in the field of empirical investigation it cannot be said that the new ideas in themselves have led to any logical conclusion. Nevertheless, the theoretical biology of the past decade has begun to define the method and the goal with ever increasing clarity. Here we encounter chiefly the idea of "wholeness" as a special category of biological knowledge. The very name "holism" shows that this concept is beginning to be preferred to the older and traditional idea of purposiveness. The development of scientific biology in the nineteenth century may be generally characterized by the fact that it has accorded the "idea of the whole" an ever greater significance.

In theoretical physics this idea has led to the primacy of "field physics," for the field appears as a whole that is not merely to be put together from the separate parts, the electrons, but rather forms

56. J. S. Haldane, *The New Physiology and Other Addresses* (London, C. Griffin & Co., 1919); and *The Philosophical Basis of Biology* (London, Hodder & Stoughton, 1931).

57. A. Meyer, "Bios," *Abhandlungen zur theoretische Biologie und ihrer Geschichte, sowie zur Philosophie der organischen Naturwissenschaften* (Leipzig, 1934), Bd. I.

58. A. Meyer, *Ideen und Ideale der biologischen Erkenntnis*, S. ix ff., 34 ff., 89 ff.

the very condition for their existence. In psychology, similarly, it demands the transition from a psychology of separate elements to Gestalt psychology. Thus a factor has been selected and emphasized common to various branches of research and of equal importance for each, and it now remains only to determine what is the *specific* feature in the biological idea of wholeness. Here there appears once more the methodological significance of the study of the phenomena of regulation and regeneration.

In a work on regulation in plants, Emil Ungerer advocates replacing the earlier purposive view with that of wholeness, in order to disencumber biology from metaphysical problems that are of no significance for it and that have continually hampered its progress and deflected it from its real scientific goals. A profound study of the facts of regulation and regeneration enables us to recognize with special clarity a definite character of all organic occurrences. The thing is first of all to establish the sheer existence of this character and to describe it without inquiring into its causes or troubling about an "explanation." For that task of simple description, however, the "concept of wholeness" proves far more appropriate than that of "purpose," since all relationship to human will and comparison with it are entirely eliminated. We simply ascertain that a great series of organic processes, or most of them at least, run their course in such a way that the whole of their functions can be reconstituted within definite limits, if they suffer any disturbance. We need for the investigation of the phenomena of life nothing more than the vision of this "primal phenomenon" which we must abide by and allow to prove its worth. "There is no significance to the purposive view as such in the *theory* of the organism, but that character of maintaining wholeness *has* significance in the *realm of life* itself." To employ a teleological method in the study of living organisms means only that we examine the processes of life so as to discover to what extent the character of preserving wholeness manifests itself. This is essential for scientific knowledge of the phenomena and it is also fully adequate to it. To seek or desire more is to provoke conflicts and boundary disputes between biology and physics. Such disputes are at bottom illusory affairs, since they have nothing to do with the matter in question itself but only with the trespassing on both sides. Even the concept of "potentiality," which was introduced into biology by Aristotle and has ever since maintained its secure place therein, is not open to epistemological objections so long as one does not fall into the error of hypostasizing a special sort of *cause*. The expression "wholeness" has the advantage of being completely free from hypothesis. It contains nothing psychic, nor does it assert that the events of life must always proceed in such a way as to achieve the highest degree of purposiveness.

Ungerer specified three sorts of wholeness, and common to them all is the fact that the "maintenance of the organization" is always manifest in one particular aspect or other. It is exhibited either in the *form* of the organism which is repaired or restored, or in the *ordered connection* of all metabolic functions, or in the *coordinated activities* of a motor apparatus. All these factors, which Driesch had called configuration harmonies, causal harmonies, and functional harmonies come under the same heading and do not require for their understanding and scientific mastery a new class of "causes" which are entirely distinct from the efficient causes. A distinction between efficient and final causes is unnecessary here; yet the category of the "teleological" holds and asserts its place.[59]

All this is in the Kantian manner and leans on the *Critique of Judgment*, which Ungerer minutely analyzed in a work of his own, comparing the *Critique* with the results of modern biology. He arrived at the conclusion that the latest phase of biology more than any other prior to it has brought into currency the fundamental view which Kant had advocated.[60]

The modern movement called holism or organicism agrees in its general orientation with the methodological tendency of Ungerer, though of course not all investigators sympathetic with it have been as interested as he in working out the purely epistemological problem. But this point of view has been decidedly emphasized in a recent comprehensive account of theoretical biology given by an adherent of the new movement. In the introduction to his work on theoretical biology Ludwig von Bertalanffy has insisted that for every science the progress in conceptual clarity is no less important than that in purely factual knowledge.[61] This intellectual clarification requires a strict separation of the concept of wholeness from that of purpose. The former must be unconditionally retained, since it is the gateway, in a sense, through which we must pass if we are ever to arrive at the true problems of biology. Even in the very description of the

59. E. Ungerer, *Die Regulationen der Pflanzen; ein System der ganzheitbezogen Vorgänge bei den Pflanzen,* "Monographien aus dem Gesammtgebiet der Physiologie der Pflanzen und der Tiere" (2. Aufl. Berlin, J. Springer, 1926), Bd. X.

60. Ungerer, "Die Teleologie Kants und ihre Bedeutung für die Logik der Biologie," *Abhandlungen zur theoretischen Biologie* (Berlin, Gebrüder Bornträger, 1922), Heft XIV.

61. Bertalanffy, *op. cit.,* Bd. I.

phenomena of life a procedure is necessary which is quite different from the causal analysis of individual processes.

Of course we can describe such processes in the organism in a physico-chemical way, but *as life processes* they are not at all to be so characterized. The great majority, if not all, of the processes of life are ordered in such a manner that they are directed toward the preservation, repair, or restitution of the whole organism . . . Even the concept itself of an organ, for instance, that of vision or hearing or sex, involves function of which it is an instrumentality. Actually every textbook on biology is forever telling us of the functions performed by the heart, lungs, chlorophyll, achromatic spindle, reflexes, secretions and so on.

In establishing this idea that life is ordered toward wholeness we are simply concerned with a *phenomenon* that can be demonstrated by purely empirical methods. No theoretical skepticism can prevent our recognition of this "ordering" as something factually given. Skepticism can be directed toward the interpretation which science may venture to give to this basic phenomenon, and here Bertalanffy was emphatic that the concept of purpose is not the best means for the description of the actual facts because it leads almost unavoidably to false anthromorphic notions.

That phenomena in the organism are chiefly "whole-forming" or "system-forming" in character and that it is the task of biology to establish whether and to what extent they are so can hardly be a matter of dispute. Those who followed long custom and called this organization of life "purposive" were wont to ask what end or function an organ has. In their notion of purpose, however, they seemed to conceive of a will and an aiming at a goal, and this is a way of thinking with which the natural scientist is rightly out of sympathy. And so the attempt was then made to represent purposiveness as a merely subjective and unscientific way of looking at things. In fact, the idea of the wholeness of life, conceived of purposively, has been badly used many times, first in Darwinism, which in its endeavors to discover a use and survival value for every organ and characteristic, set up many an untenable hypothesis about adaptation, and secondly in vitalism, which saw in the situation a proof of the role of its vital factors.

But, in the opinion of Bertalanffy, the objections that can rightfully be raised against this false use of the concept of purpose do not touch the proper concept of wholeness at all. The knowledge of the "whole organization" of what occurs in the organism is knowledge of a unique kind, which cannot be made superfluous or replaced by the ascertaining of any causal connections. Once this is understood, then it is idle to argue whether one of the two forms of knowledge is higher than the other, and still more fruitless to reserve the term "science" for causal knowledge alone. It is a "dogmatic theory of knowledge" which asserts that biophysics, which deals with causal explanations, alone deserves the name of science. For organic wholeness and historicity likewise constitute essential traits of reality which one cannot argue away but must search into from every side, using the appropriate specific methods.

From this reasoning follows the attitude Bertalanffy took toward the earlier systems of vitalism. He thought their merit lay in the fact that they had put an end to the merely "summational" view of the living being. But vitalism was guilty of overstepping its bounds as soon as it went on to "explain" the organic wholeness by tracing it back to transcendental factors, and, in the last analysis, factors analogous to the psychic. "Psychism" in every form must be rejected. But the new "organismic biology" does not need that notion in any way. It puts in place of the idea of purpose the concept of organization and characterizes life by ascribing to it the property of a system. What we call "life" is a system arranged in hierarchic order. This order is the clearest, indeed the only, distinguishing feature of the life processes in contrast with the usual physicochemical processes. Hence Bertalanffy, like Ungerer, declined to choose dogmatically between mechanism and vitalism. The "organismic" view reconciles them and sets them in proper methodological balance, for it makes no objection to any attempts at explaining the life processes in a physicochemical way. But this position implies that one is conscious of the need of other means than those of the physical sciences if he undertakes successfully to deal with the problem of wholeness— and these other means are what the new theory intends to provide.[62]

From this outcome of the vitalistic controversy we can conclude the following as to its benefits and fruitfulness. The struggle between mechanism and vitalism has brought science no nearer to an explanation of the "essence of life." But it has compelled biology again and again to examine the question concerning *its own nature as a science* and thus to gain a clearer knowledge of its own specific task and of the methods of thought which are especially suited to its accomplishment.

62. See Bertalanffy, *op. cit.*, S. 11 ff., 36 ff., 65 f., 80 ff.

PART III

FUNDAMENTAL FORMS AND TENDENCIES OF HISTORICAL KNOWLEDGE

XII

The Rise of Historicism: Herder

IT IS a widespread and constantly recurring belief that the nineteenth century was not only a "historical" century but that precisely this feature is what distinguishes it from all earlier periods. Its chief title to fame has been seen therein, though not all voices have joined in the chorus of praise. Ever since the publication of Nietzsche's *Unzeitgemässen Betrachtungen* in 1874, the philosophical questioning of "historicism" has grown more and more severe and the theme of "the use or the drawbacks of history for life" has been discussed in the most diverse ways.

It is a mistake to believe, however, that historical thinking as such was discovered, and its specific value to knowledge first realized, by Herder and romanticism. The Enlightenment, generally discounted as unhistorical, was not only familiar with this manner of thinking but made use of it as one of the chief measures in the battle for its own ideals. Indeed, the slow and progressive "conquest of the historical world" ranks among the great achievements of the Enlightenment, which was led to pose new sorts of questions and even to shape the distinctive methods of historical knowledge that later times needed only to develop. Even aside from Giambattista Vico, who distinctly set his own "historical" ideal of knowledge in opposition to the mathematical and scientific ideal of Descartes, we find in the eighteenth century, in Montesquieu and Voltaire, in Hume, in Gibbon, and in Robertson the pioneers of modern historical thinking.[1]

1. In an earlier work I sought to demonstrate the course of the development in detail, and now have the satisfaction of seeing the original interpretation there developed confirmed by a prominent historian. Friedrich Meinecke moves the beginnings of

What characterizes and marks out the nineteenth century, therefore, is not the discovery of historical thinking as such, but the new
direction which it takes. Indeed, there is here a peculiar reversal, a
sort of "Copernican revolution," which gave the science of history
a new form. Just as Kant wanted to be regarded as the "Copernicus
of philosophy," so Herder may be called the Copernicus of history.
His achievements as a historian and as a philosopher of history are
a matter of dispute, however, so that if his work be regarded from
these two points of view alone there is danger of underestimating
his importance. As a philosopher of history he never succeeded in
establishing a unified and self-contained system. His manner of
thinking alternated between the two opposite poles of the "immanent"
and the "transcendent"; on the one hand proposing to explain history through the nature of man alone and to conceive it as an unfolding of "humanity," yet on the other being obliged to reach out
again and again toward a divine plan, an act of Providence. What
he wrote in history proper is of unequal value. Here only his *aperçus*
in the field of poetry are epoch making and fundamental. Generally
speaking, political history lay outside his purview, and the older he
grew the more disinclination he had for it. Measured by ordinary
standards, therefore, his role can easily be much undervalued. The
well-known book of Eduard Fueter, which discusses the development of historiography from the humanistic writings of the Italians
up to the present time, devotes only a very moderate amount of space
to Herder.[2] He is given hardly four pages, whereas others who cannot compare with him in intellectual significance are treated far more
extensively.

The picture changes immediately, however, when Herder is regarded from the point of view not of his achievement in the field
of history but of what he was striving for, what he desired and
claimed for history. It was in the novelty and the immense vigor of
this claim that his essential and incomparable merit lay. The first
person who thoroughly understood and appreciated his deserts was
Goethe, who was far more remote from the historical world than he
was from the world of nature, and who had no immediate insight into

---

historical thought back to the eighteenth century, and the entire first volume of his
work is given over to a description of them. See E. Cassirer, "Die Eroberung der
geschichtlichen Welt," *Die Philosophie der Aufklärung* (Tübingen, J. C. B. Mohr
[P. Siebeck], 1932), S. 263–312. F. Meinecke, *Die Entstehung des Historismus,* Bd.
I: "Vorstufen und Aufklärungshistorie" (München und Berlin, R. Oldenbourg, 1936).

   2. E. Fueter, *Geschichte der neueren Historiographie,* "Handbuch der mittelalterlichen und neueren Geschichte," Erste Abteil. (3. Aufl. München und Berlin, R. Oldenbourg, 1936).

it.[3] Goethe saw that a new type of historical thinking and perception had emerged which filled him with real enthusiasm and to which he could fully surrender himself. "I have received your books," he wrote to Herder in May, 1775,

and regaled myself with them. God knows how you make one feel the reality of that world! A compost heap teeming with life! And so thanks, and thanks again, . . . And I feel, too, the very essence of your being in these figures of the scene; you're not the curtain from behind which your puppets slip but the same eternal brother, man, God, worm, and fool. Your way of gathering gold, not by just sifting it out of the dirt but by having the dirt itself brought to life again in the form of plants, is ever close to my heart.[4]

This was the great experience Goethe shared through Herder, and we of today can still feel it in all its force. For him, who until then had so often seen history as only a "rubbish heap and a lumber room, or at best the activities of a ruler or a state," it was vivified in a flash through the magic of Herder's presentation; it ceased to be a mere chain of events and became a great inward drama of mankind itself.

To be sure, history had never been satisfied, even in the past, to represent merely the external course of events and apprehend their causal relationship. All the great historians, men like Thucydides and Machiavelli, wanted something different and something more. They wanted to make real the men who were behind all these happenings and who gave them their dynamic drive. Dilthey has very finely depicted how Machiavelli could be a great historian only because he had a new view of mankind and how he imparted this idea to the whole modern world.[5] But the man Machiavelli started from was the practical man of affairs, who is dominated by certain purposes and who deliberately sets about their accomplishment and chooses the means of so doing. With Herder, however, a new conception of history replaced this very practical view. Man is no longer seen exclusively, or even predominantly, as the man of achievement but as a man of feeling; and no longer in the sum of his acts but in the dynamics of his feelings. All his deeds, whether in the field of politics or philosophy, religion or art, represent but his outer side after all. His inner life discloses itself only after one has penetrated behind these to examine his nature, and this appears in more primitive guise,

---

3. E. Cassirer, *Goethe und die geschichtliche Welt.*
4. M. Morris, *Der junge Goethe* (Leipzig, Insel-Verlag, 1911), V, 30.
5. W. Dilthey, *Auffassung und Analyse des Menschen im 15. und 16. Jahrhundert,* "Gesammelte Schriften" (Leipzig und Berlin, B. G. Teubner, 1914), II, 24 ff.

more directly, more unconcealed, in his feelings than in his intentions and his plans. Here are discovered for the first time both the heart of nature and the heart of history, for "is not the essence of nature in men's hearts?"

The focal point of history shifted herewith. Events were significant only in so far as they were revelations and disclosures of human nature. All that had happened in the past became an allegory, for only in allegory could the nature of man be grasped and expressed. "Oh, to press forward along this road! What a goal! What a recompense!" cried Herder as early as 1769.

If I could venture to be a philosopher my book would be on the human soul, full of observations and experiences! I should like to write it as a man and for mankind! It would teach and discipline! . . . It would be living logic, aesthetics, history, and art! Develop a splendid art from every sense! Draw a science from every faculty of the mind! And make of them all a history of learning and science in general! And a history of the human spirit in general, throughout the ages and in all peoples! What a book! [6]

In Herder's work there is much of the unfinished, the merely begun or the unsuccessful, but he did reach the goal that he set himself at the age of twenty-five, and the laurels that he sought to win were gained in part. He did not make the discovery of the world of history but, in Goethe's words, he made that world a living thing; he breathed a new spirit into it, and it was endowed with new life.

Then all the norms of the historical life of man had to change accordingly. For Herder had by no means renounced such standards. The "historicism" which he championed was no unrestrained relativism that repudiated all values. He was saved from such relativism by his own highest ideal, the ideal of humanity, which remained for him a general and universally binding principle without which history had no unity or meaning. All the various nations and all the various epochs were but members in a series, only moments in the evolution of mankind toward its highest goal. Yet this goal was not simply some infinitely remote point never attained or attainable. It was present in actuality at every moment when genuine spirituality and a perfect human life shone forth. Every one of these moments came singly but each was not merely a passage to another or a means to another; each possessed, rather, its own unique content and intrinsic meaning, and its own incomparable worth. Thus Herder did

6. Herder, *Reisejournal von 1769*, "Sämmtliche Werke," ed. B. Suphan (Berlin, Weidemannsche Buchhandlung, 1878), IV, 368.

not deny standards by any means, though he rejected all those which made any single nation or any single epoch sacrosanct and a model for all the rest. Here he also went far beyond Winckelmann's view of antiquity. He could not assign any absolute value to Hellenism no matter how highly he regarded it as something eternal and never to be lost. There was nothing in history that was only a means, nothing merely utilitarian or without some sort of value in its own right. "I cannot persuade myself that anything in all the kingdom of God is only a mere means; all is at once means and end." [7] Therefore we should never ask what use any being in history is for the purposes of another since each is here for its own sake, and that is its value for the whole. No member in the order can be thought of without the others, yet none exists merely for the sake of another. "Egypt could not have been without the Orient, Greece depended upon the former, and Rome climbed to power on the backs of the whole world. Real advance, progressive development . . . Theater of a guiding end on earth (even though we are never to see the ultimate end) ; theater of the Godhead beheld only through the gaps and the fragments of individual scenes!" [8]

Yet none of these fragments was a mere fragment; the meaning of the whole lived in each one. The meaning given could be only in the totality of phenomena and this, too, only in the form of a sequence not seen all together. This "die and become" revealed for the first time the true content of history. It was in that very fragmentation and apparent annihilation of the particulars that their actual significance came to light. Whoever saw in history not the external course of events but instead sought out the soul of it, he alone could find this soul beneath all its disguises and masks. He would find it in the Olympic games of the Greeks as in the simple forms of patriarchal life; in the mercantile Phoenicians as in the warlike Romans. But "in the laurel wreath or the spectacle of consecrated herds, in merchant ships and in captured banners themselves, there is nothing—only in the hearts that craved these things and strove for them and then attained them and wanted nothing more—every nation has its center of felicity in itself alone, as every sphere has its center of gravity." [9]

"Is not the good distributed throughout the whole world? Simply because no one form of humanity and no one spot of earth could

<hr/>

7. Herder, *Auch eine Philosophie der Geschichte zur Bildung der Menschheit* (1774), "Sämmtliche Werke," V, 527.

8. *Ibid.,* S. 513.

9. *Ibid.,* S. 509.

contain it all, it was divided into a thousand forms, transformed—an eternal Proteus!—in every region of the world and in every century . . . and yet a plan of striving forward is always visible—my great theme." [10] With these words Herder had reached a significant turning point, for the modern view of the nature and value of history begins here. It is customary to see the beginning of this view in romanticism and to concede to Herder the role merely of pioneer and prophet of romanticism. But this view is without foundation. It is true that romanticism had a far more inclusive grasp of historical material than Herder and as a result saw more clearly into details, but in purely philosophical and historical respects the transition from Herder to romanticism marked a regression rather than an advance, for there was never again the magnificent universality of his view of history. At first a literary movement, romanticism grew more and more to become a religious movement, and as such it was again ensnared by that absolutism which Herder had combated and whose foundation he had intended to blast from under it. Romanticism not only espoused the cause of the Christian Middle Ages but saw there the lost Paradise of humanity for which it longed and to which it wanted to return. In this case "universality" was tied up with religion, while in the case of the liberal theologian, Herder, the universality was much freer and less committed, even with regard to Christianity. Of course Herder was not equally sympathetic with all epochs. He had his own definite inclinations and aversions; yet in his judgments he kept them critically in check and rarely gave them free rein. Wherever he was unable to admire he made a special effort to be just. In his early period the Middle Ages had seemed to him an epoch of "Gothic barbarity," in keeping with the monstrosities of Gothic and monastic taste. Even in his *Auch eine Philosophie der Geschichte zur Bildung der Menschheit* (1774) he did not retract this opinion in any important respect, though now he would not deny all justice even to this barbarity with all its consequences for life, thought, and belief. "The spirit of the age was interwoven and connected with the most diverse characteristics: valor and monasticism, adventure and chivalry, tyranny and magnanimity; it fused them into the whole that now seems like an apparition, like a romantic and adventurous interlude between Rome and our own times, though once it was nature, once it was reality." [11]

Still more remarkable, and at first sight highly ambiguous and

---

10. *Ibid.*, S. 511.

11. *Ibid.*, S. 523. For Herder's position on the Middle Ages see F. Meinecke, *Die Entstehung des Historismus*, II, 435 ff.

contradictory, was Herder's attitude toward the Enlightenment. He appeared as the resolute opponent of its pride of reason, that consciousness of our having come so wonderfully far that we can look down on all past epochs. He attacked the eighteenth century for having branded the word *philosophy* on its forehead and shut out every lifelike view of the spiritual and human circumstances of earlier times and spoiled all appreciation of them. But no matter how severe his hostility, he was frank and impartial enough to give the Enlightenment credit within its own sphere. It meant much to him as long as it was wise enough not to claim to be everything.

On this point he differed from Rousseau, to whom he was deeply indebted and who had exerted the greatest influence upon his development. Not without right has Herder been called "the German Rousseau." [12]

> *O Rousseau! den die Welt im Vorurteil verkannt,*
> *Das wahre grosse Mass des Menschen in der Hand,*
> *Wägst Du, was edel sei, wenns gleich das Volk verdammet;*
> *Du wägst das Kronengold, und was auf Kleidern flammet. . . .*
> *Du wägst es; es wird Staub! seht das sind Eure Götter!*
> *Ein Mentor unserer Zeit wirst Du der Ehre Retter.*[13]

Thus wrote Herder in one of his youthful poems.[14] But he felt the longing to return to a state of nature only in his earliest period, having soon overcome the historical and philosophical pessimism of those years. In the place of denial there appeared now the most determined affirmation. "With every age the human race has striven after felicity but in a different way; we in our time fall into extravagance, therefore, when, like Rousseau, we praise times that are no more and never were. Up, and preach the virtues of thine own times!" [15]

This goal, set for himself by Herder in the days of his early youth and overflowing productivity, was actually attained in his life work, fragmentary though it was in many respects. He became the "apostle

---

12. See H. A. Korff, *Geist der Goethezeit* (Leipzig, J. J. Weber, 1923), Teil I, S. 74 f.
13.   Oh, Rousseau, whom the world could never understand,
    Humanity's great scale unerring in thy hand,
    Thou weighest what is fine, though man may it condemn;
    Thou weighest golden crown, and glittering diadem. . . .
    Thou weigh'st them. They are dust! Look, to such gods ye bow!
    A mentor of our time, our honor's savior thou.
14. Herder, "Der Mensch," *Poetische Werke,* ed. C. Redlich, V, 256, "Sämmtliche Werke," ed. B. Suphan (Berlin, Weidmannsche Buchhandlung, 1889), Bd. XXIX.
15. See Korff, *op. cit.,* Teil I, S. 88.

of the virtues of his own period"; not in a moral or religious but in
a purely intellectual sense. He introduced his era to some of its own
most productive, most original, most profound forces, which until
then had slumbered, and in so doing he became a signpost for the
future as well. The historical thinking and writing of the years that
came after were frequently to choose ways and submit to tendencies
that were entirely different from his, yet wherever a living understanding and a spiritual interpretation of history are concerned it
is virtually essential to refer to Herder.

At first glance it seems as though there could not be a sharper
antithesis than that between Herder's subjective way of taking
history and Ranke's rigorous objectivism. Ranke's sole purpose was
to show "how it actually happened," and he would have preferred
"to blot out his own self likewise," so to speak, in order to let only
the historical events and mighty forces of the centuries be heard.
Such a course was impossible for Herder, whose method required
a sympathetic understanding of the inner lives of others. This sympathetic insight necessitated not the effacement of self but its enormous expansion and intensification. Herder would never renounce
his ego, and he never could deny it. Like Faust, he wished to enlarge
it to include the universe, and enjoy within himself that which is
apportioned to all mankind. Apart from this difference in personality
and fundamental tendencies, however, Herder influenced Ranke in
the most forceful way.[16] Ranke's famous remark that every epoch
belongs "directly to God," and that its value does not depend upon
what comes out of it but upon "its own existence, its own self," merely
repeats in a pregnant form the basic conviction for which Herder had
contended in his first important work on the philosophy of history,
Auch eine Philosophie der Geschichte zur Bildung der Menschheit.
And Ranke held closely to Herder's words when he wrote that all
generations of mankind are equally justified in the eyes of God, and
that even the historian must see things in this way.

There is no break in continuity, therefore, between the eighteenth
and the nineteenth centuries, that is, between the Enlightenment and
romanticism, but only a progressive advance leading from Leibniz
and Shaftesbury to Herder, and then from Herder to Ranke.

One would not detract too much from Ranke's achievement [said Friedrich Meinecke, in his memorial address on Ranke], if one were to say
that the very principles that made his historical writing so vital and

---

16. Friedrich Gundolf has insisted that it is even harder to imagine Ranke without
Herder than it is without Niebuhr. See F. Gundolf, "Historiography," *Philosophy and
History:* Essays presented to E. Cassirer (Oxford, Clarendon Press, 1936), p. 281.

so fruitful—feeling for the individual, for the inner forces that shape
things, for their peculiar individual development, and for the common
basis of life which brings all these together—were won through all the
efforts of the German mind during the eighteenth century. All Europe
helped . . . Shaftesbury gave valuable intellectual aid to the German
movement with his theory of inner form, while at the same time Leibniz
in Germany with his theory of the monad and his phrase "universal
sympathy" σύμπνοια πάντα kindled the fire which, long smoldering in the
young Herder, finally broke out when he adopted that expression from
Leibniz and discovered the individuality of nations, rooted in a common
and divinely related ground of all life.[17]

17. Meinecke, "Gedächtnisrede gehalten am 23. Januar 1936 in der Preuss. Akademie
der Wissenschaften," *Die Entstehung des Historismus,* "Beigabe: Leopold von Ranke"
(München und Berlin, R. Oldenbourg, 1936), II, 632 ff.

XIII

Romanticism and the Beginnings of the Critical Science of History. The Theory of Historical Ideas: Niebuhr, Ranke, Humboldt

THERE is no denying that romanticism fructified historical thinking to an extraordinary degree, and that this was one of its most important intellectual achievements. But the part that it had in the process is not easy to determine, and opinions on the actual significance of its influence are widely at variance. Even today these views and value judgments are in many ways sharply opposed. Thus two articles in a work on medieval and modern history arrive at exactly opposite conclusions. One article, by von Below himself [1] is an unqualified vindication, a "rescue," of romantic historiography. Everything achieved in the nineteenth century is attributed to romanticism and regarded as its spiritual outcome. Wherever history departed from those fundamental notions it was considered to be in danger of being led astray on some bypath such as materialism, or the sociological point of view, or the positivistic interpretation of history as developed in France under the influence of Comte. "Back to romanticism!" must be the battle cry of modern historiography. Von Below defended this position with great insight and clarity but at the same time with the utmost bias. The other article, by Fueter,[2] presents an entirely different picture, denying to romanticism any capacity at all for objective historical knowledge. Fueter argues that romanticism approached the world of history with definite, preconceived ideas and so never achieved an unprejudiced understanding of events. The theories of "national spirit" and organic development, the high regard for the unknown which was valued far above the known, all blinded at the outset those who held this view to important aspects of historical activity. The diversity and many-sidedness of the factors that determine history were never revealed to them. "Their dogmatically conceived theory, founded on a series of unproved assumptions and premature general-

---

1. G. v. Below und F. Meinecke, *Die deutsche Geschichtsschreibung von den Befreiungskriegen bis zu unsern Tagen,* "Handbuch der mittelalterlichen und neueren Geschichte," Abteil. I (2. Aufl. München und Berlin, R. Oldenbourg, 1924).
2. E. Fueter, *Geschichte der neueren Historiographie,* S. 418.

izations of romanticism, accorded ill with historiography, having been developed chiefly by men who had but little to do with history." The romantic historico-political doctrine in its unadulterated form was as good as useless.

What can we make of this sharp difference of opinion between two investigators like Below and Fueter, who had a thorough grasp of the development of modern historical thinking and had followed it in all its distinct phases? It becomes clear at once that Fueter's view is unacceptable as soon as one leaves the narrow field of historiography to glance at the development of the Geisteswissenschaften in the nineteenth century. The direction there taken showed everywhere the lasting and even decisive influence of romantic ideas. What A. W. Schlegel did for the history of world literature and Jacob and Wilhelm Grimm for that of the German language and Savigny for the history of law, all bears clearly the impress of those ideas. Herein lies, perhaps, the most important and enduring achievement of romanticism. If it had possessed nothing but the feeling for the "miraculous," for the obscure and the mysterious, on which it prided itself and which is often considered, especially by its purely literary champions, its best and most essential character, it would never have long continued in the cultural world. Its persistence in both literature and general intellectual history was due to the circumstance that it was also a search for knowledge and had forged a new tool for it: the instrument of modern historical criticism. Here romanticism worked hand in hand with the much-despised Enlightenment. A direct and continuous road thus leads from the eighteenth to the nineteenth century, from Bayle and Voltaire to Niebuhr and Ranke. And here, too, we must see its lasting benefits. Even as the poetic gleam and splendor faded away and long after the "blue flower of romanticism" withered, its achievement remained fresh in the realm of the science of culture. The usual view of romanticism makes this seem strange and almost paradoxical. For what sort of renaissance and new blossoming could *science* expect from a Weltanschauung that searched out the dark places rather than the light and found its own peculiar satisfaction in so doing? And what could history expect from a mood that exalted and glorified myth and endeavored to hold fast to the legendary and religious view of things? Nevertheless the finest and really productive minds of the romantic period themselves drew a very decisive line between science and myth. Thus the reader of August Wilhelm Schlegel's review of Jacob and Wilhelm Grimm's *Old German Songs* would hardly suspect at first sight that it came from a pioneer of romanticism, since it rigorously discriminated between historical sources on the one hand and legendary, poetical, or mythical sources on the other. All reliable history, according to Schlegel, depended upon such a distinction. He reproached the brothers Grimm for having failed in many cases to separate legend adequately from authentic history and for investing the former with a dignity the recognition of which would imply a doubt as to our best established and soundest knowledge.

All historical truth involves the simple question of whether or not something actually happened; whether it happened in the way it is told or in some other way; . . . contradictory statements cannot both be true at the same time. . . . Poor service is done to legend itself by charging to its account all the spurious, incredible, or absurd things that some chronicler reports. Not all erroneous ideas have a pedigree. There are totally uninspired fancies and prosaic lies . . . Yet even in fiction and nursery tales the brothers Grimm speak of "the old kernel of the legend, of later tradition, or myth, of the mythical nature of the whole."

In connection with this criticism Schlegel demanded, above all, a secure philological foundation for the treatment of literary records. "It cannot be often enough repeated that research on the old texts in the vernacular can succeed only through criticism and interpretation; and how are these possible without an accurate knowledge of grammar?" And he showed that until then more had been done for the history of German grammar by foreign than by German scholars.[3] This was what seems to have inspired Jacob Grimm's *German Grammar:* he was first set on his own proper career in historical linguistics by that review of Schlegels.[4]

Still more remarkable was the influence exerted on Niebuhr by the main tendency of romanticism. It gave him a feeling for the distinctive quality of mythical thinking and for its significance, but it led him on to draw more sharply the line between mythical and genuine historical thought. Above all he realized that there is a fundamental difference in the various sources of historical knowledge and that a well-founded view of history cannot be attained unless that difference is held constantly in mind. Just because Niebuhr understood the mythical so well he was able to separate it clearly and definitely from historical reality. Thus his lively sense of poetry and religion, due to romanticism, became the point of departure from

3. *Anzeige der altdeutschen Wälder der Brüder Grimm* (Cassel, 1813), Bd. I; see A. W. v. Schlegel, *Altdeutsche Wälder,* "Sämmtliche Werke" ed. E. Böcking (Leipzig, Weidmannsche Buchhandlung, 1847), XII, 383 ff.

4. G. P. Gooch, *History and Historians in the Nineteenth Century* (New York and London, Longmans, Green & Co., 1913), p. 57.

which he went on to discover a new form of historical interpretation. He believed in an epic of earliest Rome which in splendor of imagination and profundity far surpassed anything that later Rome brought forth.[5] But he saw the actual history of Rome in another aspect. He was not content with discarding old legendary tradition en bloc, but wanted to set in its place a new and positive reconstruction. Instead of the doubtful and precariously attested events of earliest Roman history he aimed to bring to light the history of Roman institutions. He conceived of the history of Rome as consisting essentially in the great constitutional struggles between patricians and plebeians, which had their roots in the opposition between conquerors and conquered. It was to social and political problems that he first looked, the connection of the Roman system with the distribution of landed real property.[6] In this way he distinguished appearance from reality, and the essence of historical events was freed from the covering of mystical and poetical symbols that had surrounded and obscured it in its transmission down the ages. It had not been in vain that even as a student he was inclined to yield to his "love for critical philosophy." [7] This love inspired his work, even after he had abandoned abstract philosophy and the metaphysics of history to devote himself entirely to historical research.

There is a characteristic and remarkable passage in Niebuhr which is graphically expressive of this newly established ideal of knowledge. He likened the historian to a man in a dark room, whose eyes have gradually become so accustomed to the absence of light as to perceive objects that one who had just entered could not see and would even assert to be invisible.[8] I have no doubt that when Niebuhr wrote these lines he was thinking of Plato's allegory of the cave, though he gave it an exactly opposite turn. Plato was convinced that one who had left his cave and seen the light of day, who was no longer restricted to the sight of mere shadows but could attain to real knowledge, geometry, the knowledge of the eternal, would return only unwillingly and think it not worth while to discuss with his fellows the differences and meanings of the shadows. But Niebuhr wanted to give full rein to this interest in interpreting such things; he wanted to develop and refine it to the utmost, and he once referred to the work of the historian as "work under ground." Upon

---

5. B. G. Niebuhr, *Römische Geschichte* (4. Aufl. Berlin, G. Reimer, 1833), I, 179; see Fueter, *op. cit.*, S. 467.

6. See Gooch, *op. cit.*, p. 18.

7. *Briefe aus dem Jahre 1794;* see E. Rothacker, *Einleitung in die Geisteswissenschaften* (2. Aufl. Tübingen, J. C. B. Mohr [P. Siebeck], 1930), S. 42, n. 3.

8. See Gooch, *op. cit.*, p. 19.

what does this difference in the manner of thinking depend? Obviously the object of knowledge was for Niebuhr something different from what it had been for Plato. Whereas the latter restricted knowledge to "pure Being," and declared that all knowledge not directed to this "eternal Being" was erroneous, Niebuhr was certain that "becoming" as such was not only accessible to knowledge but that it was the only form of human knowledge which is adequate to a living and developing existence. Man should, therefore, cultivate those faculties that would make the reality of *development* manifest to him; he must be able to descry and distinguish definite forms in that twilight and dusk. He who could not do this certainly had no call to be a historian.

Unlike the dialectician, the historian could not leave the world of phenomena behind him. In this world he was continually beset by appearances. His very task was to rise above them by developing precise methods of separating the actual phenomena from deception and illusion as he picked his way through the world of legend and legendary tradition. What Niebuhr demanded was that out of the ruins of tradition the form of past existence shall rise up anew and that we shall distinguish the good in the new or the old—what is useful tradition and what is mere "rhetorical glitter." [9] That this was a work of historical reason he never doubted. Thus irrationalism, so often taught by romanticism, was in principle overcome. It had been only a battle cry and a catchword after all, turned against the pride of reason in the Enlightenment; but no new positive, scientific result could come of it. There would be no advance until new powers of reason were set free and the mere love for the past and intuitive absorption in it had given way to a conscious and trustworthy historical criticism.

Here is the great achievement of Ranke, who was Niebuhr's pupil, for it was Niebuhr who introduced him to history. Through his master's example Ranke first realized clearly, as he later explained, that great historical writing was still possible in the modern world. The stage in his development at which he overcame his romantic sensibility and set up a new ideal of positive knowledge can be exactly fixed. He first learned of Louis XI and Charles the Bold in Scott's *Quentin Durward*, and later read extensively of the conflict between them in Philippe de Commines' history. Ranke wrote to his brother that he found the true account more interesting and finer than the romance. At once he resolved to eliminate from his own works all invention and fiction and keep entirely to fact. He explained what Niebuhr had felt

9. Niebuhr, *op. cit.*, S. 208; see Fueter, *op. cit.*, S. 470.

so strongly, that when the historian lays down his pen he must be able to declare before God that he has written nothing but what was true, to the best of his knowledge and after most sincere search.[10]

That this was something new to many representatives of romantic history writing is obvious from the reception accorded Ranke's earliest writings by an historian like Heinrich Leo. When Ranke published his first fundamental work, *Zur Kritik neuerer Geschichtsschreiber*, in which he sharply criticized Guicciardini, Leo declared such criticism futile: "Guicciardini's book will retain its interest," he wrote, "long after Ranke's has sunk into well-deserved oblivion." Evidently he did not like to have his aesthetic pleasure in Guicciardini's presentation spoiled by criticism of its sources, and was ready to sacrifice historical truth to this gratification. But such notions and standards had lost all value for Ranke. He recognized only the stern command of objectivity and insisted, like Niebuhr, that the historian must not add to his material anything that would merely increase its aesthetic charm or have the effect of "rhetorical glitter." Whereas Leo declared that Guicciardini had succeeded in portraying the spiritual stir of life, and that in comparison with this it was of little import whether every line of his presentation were literally true, such a distinction between "life" and "truth" was incomprehensible to Ranke. He found genuine historical life only where he had succeeded in penetrating to historical truth, and devoted everything to the service of this one task. Only so could romantic aesthetics and metaphysics be overthrown and the writing of history established on a new and secure methodological foundation.

The question as to the possibility and conditions of historical knowledge now appeared in a new light. For the first time it could be posed with perfect clarity and precision. Of course the answer could not be given in a word even by Ranke. One must be content with a few of his personal statements in which he tried to formulate his views on the nature of history and the task of the historical. It is obvious that a certain indefiniteness attaches itself to such expressions, and that they merely hint at the problem rather than come profoundly to grips with it. Even his famous remark, that he would like to eliminate self altogether in order to let the object alone reveal itself, suffers from this deficiency. He assumes there a relation between subject and object which from a general epistemological standpoint is doubtful in the extreme, and appears still more problematical when this object is not nature but history. In natural science itself, as we become clear about its real structure, we are inevitably led to see that knowledge

10. See Gooch, *op. cit.*, pp. 19, 78.

is never to be understood in the sense simply of a representation, and
that no object is known that way. We must recognize the participation of the "subject," and learn to see therein not only an essential
limitation but a positive condition for all our knowledge of nature.
Even in the field of mathematics and the mathematical sciences the
proposition that Kant put in these words holds good: "that only is
known a priori in things which we ourselves put into them." Thus
even physics owes the revolution in its mode of thought, which has
been of such benefit, solely to this conception: seek in nature (without imputing it to nature) that which reason itself has prescribed,
even though reason must still learn all that from nature, and purely
by itself would not know anything about the matter. If this be true
for physics, it is so to a far greater degree for history. Here "subjectivity" enters, in the general sense of theoretical reason and its
presuppositions, but in addition the individuality, the personality,
of the author continually asserts itself. Without that there would
be no active historical research or writing. Hence the problem of
"historical truth," posed in a wholly new and acute form by Ranke
and responsible for his "revolution" in historiography, really amounts
to determining and delimiting the part played by the "personal"
factor. Here Ranke deprecated every sort of *parti pris*, any advo-
cacy of definitely political, national, or religious programs. Authors
who succumbed to such projects were not historians to him but
pamphleteers. For this reason he ventured later to deny Treitschke
all right to the title of historian, and with full justification called the
parts of Treitschke's *German History* that he saw then a mere historical pamphlet in the grand style.[11]

It was said of Treitschke that he used history simply as a pulpit
from which to make known his political demands. Had he not con-
sulted only the documents of the Prussian archives, lest otherwise his
favorable opinion of Prussian politics might be troubled? [12] Anything of this sort would naturally seem to Ranke not only a deadly
sin against the spirit of historical truth but the expression of a personal weakness, for it represented to him some defect in the "will to
knowledge." With Ranke himself, everything personal—be it what he
himself could not possibly suppress or else what he had actually suppressed—was exclusively in the service of the "will to knowledge."
That was what permeated, vitalized, inspired his research; but he
would not allow it to prescribe in advance the conclusions which his
research should reach.

11. See K. Lamprecht, *Einführung in das historische Denken* (Leipzig, R. Voigt-
länder, 1913), S. 41.
12. See Fueter, *op. cit.*, I, 543.

It was on such a separation of the personal and the factual that Ranke's idea of historical "objectivity" was founded. His own concern with the events he described is everywhere unmistakable, though never expressed in the form of the merely subjective or personal. In his view history should be neither edifying nor directly instructive; it achieves its purpose of edification and instruction better the less directly it strives after them, for it can lay claim to instruct by virtue of its mere being, through the force of the facts and ideas, without help from the historian, constantly putting in his own personal comments. Ranke was without a peer in this art, though methods were subsequently developed that were not available to him. In my judgment he must be placed in this respect beside the greatest not only in the field of historiography but in that of general scholarship as well. Goethe said that "first and last what is required of genius is love of truth," [13] and we have to say in the present case that Ranke possessed this indispensable requirement as few gifted writers of history have had it. From this standpoint his achievements in history rank equally with those laid claim to by Goethe in the realm of the study of nature. "The whole of my inner life of thought," said Goethe of himself, "proved to be a vital instrument of discovery (*eine lebendige Heuristik*)—first having the intimation of an unknown law, then striving to find it in the outer world and establish it there." [14] Ranke's research was likewise imbued with and guided by the apprehension of such "unknown law." What gives his work its character and intellectual value is less the objective material itself which he amassed, enormous though it be, than that same "vital heuristic," the way of seeking and finding, which Ranke incorporated in it and made the very model for historical research.

Only on the basis of such an ideal of knowledge could a really universal historiography develop. To be sure it was still inspired by national and religious ideas, but not cramped by them in either its choice of subject or its judgments. By virtue of this ideal Ranke could become a historian of the Reformation as well as author of a book on the Popes, though Benedetto Croce said of the latter that the Jesuit was right who objected: "The Papacy is either all that it claims to be, the institution of God incarnate, or it is a lie. Respectful reservations have no place here. There is no third alternative. *Tertium non datur.*" [15] Such a verdict, however, quite misunderstands the character of Ranke's work. He was by no means merely

13. J. W. v. Goethe, *Maximen und Reflexionen*, "Schriften der Goethe-Gesellschaft," XXI, No. 382, 73.

14. *Ibid.*, No. 328, S. 6.

15. B. Croce, *Theory and History of Historiography*, Eng. trans. by Douglas Ainslie (London, Harrap, 1921), p. 300.

the unmoved observer, the agnostic or skeptic, as so often depicted. Every page of his *German History in the Age of the Reformation* bears evidence of having been written with the deepest feeling for events and of an unequivocal attitude concerning them. Nor did he deny himself even moral judgments. "What must have been the general political situation," he wrote, for example, in describing the period of Louis XIV,

when the King, prompted by one of his judges at Metz, was suffered to institute the "Chambers of Reunion," before which he haled great princes so that their rights to lands and peoples, rights guaranteed by treaty, might be determined by his courts as if they were matters of private right! What must have been the condition of the German Empire when it allowed Strasbourg to be torn away so forcibly and in violation of the very nature of things! . . . What more was there that Louis XIV would not have permitted himself? [16]

But Ranke wanted to see before he judged, and he could see only when he had found a point of vantage from which to survey all that had come to pass in history. For him it was no simple chain of isolated occurrences, but an interlocking and constant struggle of spiritual forces—forces each of which had a definite meaning to him and which he liked to call "thoughts of God." From this dynamic point of view it is manifest that a historian who does not succeed in reproducing clearly the totality of all operations cannot identify and describe a single one of them, for a force as such is nothing in the absence of the opposing force against which it must assert itself and with which it must operate. "Though it may easily appear so at first sight, history does not present a scene of mere accidents, of states and peoples invading, attacking, succeeding to each other . . . There are forces, and in truth spiritual, life-bringing, creative forces, and life itself . . . there are moral energies that we see developing in history. They are not to be defined or brought under abstractions, though they can be seen and perceived and one can train oneself to divine their existence. They flourish and take possession of the world and manifest themselves in the most diverse forms; they challenge, limit, and overcome one another. In their interactions and their passage, in their life and in their passing away and coming to life again, which always means that there is more complete fulfillment, higher significance, and wider scope for these forces, lies the whole secret of world history." [17]

16. L. Ranke, *Die grossen Mächte,* "Meisterwerke" (München und Leipzig, Duncker & Humblot, 1915), X, 432 f.

17. *Ibid.,* S. 482.

Whoever saw "the secret of history" in this light not only could become but simply had to become the historian of the Papacy as well as of the Reformation. It was impossible for him to take up the one phenomenon and present it clearly to view except in the mirror of the other. He could not have described the Reformation and what he believed to be its spiritual meaning had he not first tried to understand the power the Reformation was opposing, the power in its full significance and its plastic sort of definiteness as an entity. He had to make the antagonist visible to grasp the innermost purpose of the Reformation itself.

Von Below has urged us to abandon the customary characterization of Ranke as a "contemplative" historian and call him, instead, an "objective" or "universal" historian.[18] But in truth the two coincide in him, for he could become contemplative only by being universal.

There is no doubt that in history, too, the sight of the individual event as it truly is has inestimable value, as well as every particular development—the particular contains a universal within it. But we must never reject the demand that we should survey the whole from some independent point of vantage, and actually everyone tries in one way or other to do so—what happens is that out of the multiplicity of perceptions there comes, without our willing it, some view of their unity.[19]

This is what Ranke meant when he said, during the composition of his history of the Papacy, that all true history must be universal and also that he felt himself carried away by the inner consequences of the events, by the "logic of the works of God." [20]

It has often been asserted by the political historians who came after him, von Sybel for instance, that such a way of looking at history must discourage action and the setting up of any goals as well as paralyze the judgment. But nothing of the sort happened in the case of Ranke, even if he did require that the judgments of history shall follow research and not precede or anticipate it. Because his opponents misunderstood him on this score they themselves relapsed into the ways of journalistic, tendencious historiography.[21] In contrast with such bias, Ranke represented the truly *philosophical* spirit, even though he strongly deprecated all speculative philosophy

---

18. Below, *Die deutsche Geschichtsschreibung von den Befreiungskriegen bis zu unsern Tagen.*

19. Ranke, *op. cit.,* S. 426.

20. Gooch, *op. cit.,* p. 87.

21. Despite their different interpretations both Fueter (*op. cit.,* S. 536) and Below (*op. cit.,* S. 50 ff.) emphasized this.

of history. Historical thinking, he insisted, is valuable only for its universality, for the light that it throws on the course of *world* events.[22] In a letter written in 1830 he said that philosophically he had no fixed "system," but that "philosophical and religious interests are precisely what drove me to history." [23]

It is remarkable that a thinker of the caliber of Croce should so thoroughly misunderstand this philosophical element in Ranke, and portray him as a "polished intellect" who knew how "to pick his way among the rocks (*inter scopulos*), without ever letting his own philosophical or religious persuasions come to light, or feeling compelled to make up his mind about things." [24] Ranke not only let these convictions be seen on occasions, but held consistently to them throughout his rich and comprehensive career of achievement. For him the motto, "Work, artist, do not talk," applied not only to art but to the writing of history as well. He wanted to portray and not educate or admonish. The goal was reached more surely the more one abstained from all oratorical ornamentation and every sort of direct persuasion. In times of passion and excitement such a disinterested attitude is apt to be censored or to meet with strong opposition. On occasions like these it is certainly fitting to point out what a place of honor Ranke deserves in the history of the problem of knowledge. He was imbued with a new idea of the task of history, an idea which once established could never thereafter be forgotten, no matter how often it was attacked. Ranke owes his supreme authority to the very fact that he set up no program but instead set an example in himself and in his work. He forged an instrument for the knowledge of history with his critical art of analyzing sources, which every historian thereafter has had to use, no matter what line he took or what cause he advocated. The way he himself examined ambassadorial reports and diplomatic papers, checking them, sifting them, and then using them for the understanding of political affairs represented an entirely new procedure. He explained that he saw here a method in which modern history would no longer be based on official records, not even on those of contemporary historians, except in so far as they possessed original information, but could be built up from accounts of eyewitnesses and the most authentic and direct

22. See O. Diether, *Leopold von Ranke als Politiker* (Leipzig, Duncker & Humblot, 1911), S. 572; also E. Rothacker, *op. cit.*, S. 161 f.

23. Ranke, "Briefe an Heinrich Ritter—Venedig, 6. August 1830," *Aufsätze zur eigenen Lebensgeschichte,* "Sämmtliche Werke" (2. und 3. Gesammtausgabe Leipzig, Duncker & Humblot, 1890), XLIII–XLIV, 238.

24. Croce, *op. cit.,* p. 292.

evidence.[25] Yet the documents, the reports of the Venetian Ambassador, for example, which Ranke employed most extensively, were never for him the alpha and omega of historiography, since he was continually driven from the description of events and deeds to the true sources, which he found in great individual personalities. For this he had to develop the art of literary portraiture, which played such an important role in all his writings.[26] Even his "objectivity" would not have become truly "historical" if it had not been nourished from this source of the intuitive perception of living figures. In respect to this objectivity he, too, though he was the exact opposite of Herder in temperament and disposition as well as in the scientific formulation of his problem, had that same great virtue of Herder's, thanks to which he had won his new historical conception of things, for Ranke's own objectivity, as has been justly emphasized, was derived, in the last analysis, from such a "universality of sympathy." [27]

What Ranke did for historical knowledge through his gift of sympathetic understanding and through the clarity and certainty of his method is plain and incontestable. It is more difficult to do justice to another element in his thinking that relates not so much to the form of history as to its content or object. According to him the object could be designated neither in a positivistic sense as the sum of bare facts, nor in the speculative sense in terms of general concepts. He took a peculiar middle ground between these two poles which is hard to define. In order to indicate this "mean" position Ranke seized upon the term *idea*, which thereby underwent a complete change from its original Platonic meaning. The point of contact with Plato was the fact that the problem underlying Ranke's concept of idea was the very one that Plato wished to master when he proposed his theory of ideas. It was the problem of the relation between particular and universal. To solve this problem, to explain the participation of the particular in the universal, Plato resorted to mathematics. This would show how it is possible for the human mind to perceive and clearly understand such ideas as "equal" or "straight," while the world of phenomena always offers us only imperfect examples: the equal pieces of wood or stone strive after "equality itself" without ever attaining it. In this case there was no other solution but to make the idea transcendent to the world of phe-

---

25. See M. Ritter, *Die Entwicklung der Geschichtswissenschaft an den führenden Werken betrachtet* (München und Berlin, R. Oldenbourg, 1919), S. 376.

26. On Ranke as a historical psychologist see, for example, Fueter, *op. cit.,* S. 477.

27. See A. Dove, *Ausgewählte Schriftchen* (1898), S. 112 ff.

nomena and set it as the One and Eternal over against the change and "becoming" of the appearances. But this road is closed to the historian, according to Ranke, for in taking it he would lose sight of his special object. Like Niebuhr he demanded that the historian should not shy away from the obscurity of the changing world but must learn to become accustomed to the darkness and to see through it to the reality in the events.[28] Though he looked to the "ideas" and regarded the ideal vision as an essential factor in all knowledge, still he could not allow of any such separation as Plato assumed between appearances and ideas, between the particular and the universal. It was rather a new relationship that appeared, destined to overcome the Platonic dualism not through the concept of nature, as in Aristotle, but through that of history, and Ranke was not the only one to struggle with this problem during the first half of the nineteenth century. His theory of historical ideas was closely allied to certain fundamental concepts of Wilhelm von Humboldt, most clearly expressed in his treatise, *On the Problem of the Historian*. To be sure, there is no complete correspondence between their two theories of "idea"—individual differences of conception are clearly apparent. But for the general development of the problem of knowledge in history these divergencies are of no importance. Here Ranke and Humboldt represent a distinct type of thinking common to them both which they continually sought to define more accurately. What they practiced at first with intuitive certainty should be brought to a philosophic self-consciousness and justified. This was as far as they were willing to be philosophical thinkers. Both rejected a philosophy of history in Hegel's sense,[29] for notwithstanding Hegel's intention to reconcile "reason" with "the actual" and regard them as substantially identical, they saw therein nothing but an artificial separation of "idea" and "appearance." As Humboldt explained, agreeing with Ranke,

The problem of the historian is to tell what actually happened. The more clearly and completely he succeeds, the more perfectly he has solved that problem. Straightforward description is the very first and essential requirement of his calling and the highest thing that he can achieve.

28. See p. 229, above.

29. For further details see Richard Fester, "Humboldts und Rankes Ideenlehre," *Deutsche Zeitschrift für Geschichtswissenschaft* VI (Freiburg, J. C. B. Mohr, 1891), 235 ff.

Ranke expressed his disapproval of Hegel most clearly in his *Über die neueren Geschichte*, Vortrag I (Leipzig, Duncker & Humblot, 1888).

For Humboldt's relation to Hegel see especially R. Haym, *Wilhelm von Humboldt; Lebensbild und Charakteristik* (Berlin, R. Gaertner, 1856).

Looked at in this way the historian seems only to be absorbing and repeating, not acting independently and creatively.[30]

It follows from this view that the "idea," in the sense in which the historical investigator uses the term, cannot be known through any separate faculty of knowledge but only through events themselves. Little as Humboldt wanted to see history taken up into philosophy he was just as little desirous of seeing it reduced to art, though from the standpoint of the aesthetic idealism which he shared with Schiller art was to him something ultimate and supreme. But if esteem for art be the sign of an age of advancement, then, as he put it "regard for reality" is the mark of an age that has mounted even higher. [31] Of course the task of the historian was not to be mastered by intellect alone; it required, rather, a constant cooperation of the creative imagination, which alone was able to tie together into a genuine unity the isolated and widely dispersed facts. But the imagination of the historian is not striving to get beyond the actual events; it subordinates itself to experience and the investigation of what is real.

The writer of history encompasses every bit of terrestrial activity and all forms of preternatural ideas; the totality of existence, the nearer and the more remote, all constitute the object of what he is working at and so he must take account, too, of all the ways of the spirit. Speculation, experience, and poetry are not, however detached, activities of the mind that are set over against and limit one another, but different facets of it.

Even the historian, like the draughtsman, produces only caricatures if he sketches detailed circumstances and events merely as they seem to present themselves and as they follow upon each other. The apprehension of events must be guided continually by ideas; yet on the other hand these ideas must not be merely added on to history as an unrelated appendage—an error into which philosophical history so-called easily fell. The "idea" can appear only *in* the natural connection of things and can never be separated from them as something independent and existing for itself alone.[32]

Although this recognition of the imagination as an important

---

30. W. v. Humboldt, "Über die Aufgabe des Geschichtsschreibers," *Gesammelte Schriften,* "Werke," ed. A. Leitzmann, Erste Abteil. (Berlin, B. Behr, 1905), IV, 35.

31. Humboldt, "Geschichte des Verfalls und Untergang der griechischen Freistaaten," *ibid.,* III, 193.

32. Humboldt, "Über die Aufgabe . . . ," *op. cit.,* IV, 37 ff.

factor in all historical understanding is reminiscent of romanticism,[33] still the center of gravity is located elsewhere by both Humboldt and Ranke. They never succumbed to the danger of obliterating the boundary line between history and art or between history and myth. While Humboldt was deeply influenced by Schelling's "philosophy of identity," he formed his own theory of ideas independently. The idea is (as has been rightly said) nothing other than the completion of the metaphysical-aesthetic directives indicated in the *Critique of Judgment:* every phenomenon of individual existence, be it a human character or organism or a work of art, is the representation of a supersensible substrate; every sensory form is the effect of an intelligible principle.[34] "Sensory" and "supersensory," "nature" and "freedom" could never merge into one another, therefore, and must stand in a relation of tension with each other; and precisely in this opposition is the root of all historical life. Ranke saw in this polarity a fundamental phenomenon which the historian has to recognize without being able to explain it by reference to anything else. "The truly spiritual," he wrote, "which suddenly appears before you in its unexpected originality, cannot be deduced from any higher principle." Thus what we speak of as "ideas," or "tendencies," we can only describe and in the description come nearer to direct perception of them, but we cannot define them or sum them up in a concept. That there is a certain hiatus between the particular and the universal, the appearance and the idea, was no more denied by Ranke than by Humboldt, but both opposed the Platonic concept of "separation" χωρισμός without a leap; as Ranke expressly said, one cannot get from the universal to the particular. The historian may safely try it, however, for he knows he is in no danger of missing the firm ground of reality and landing in a transcendent world of metaphysic. All that he can apprehend is "universal-and-individual existence"; and thus it is the "truly spiritual." The formal is the universal, the real is the particular, and together they are the living individual reality.[35]

Humboldt, too, emphasized that the historian seeks throughout only the individual, but added that no matter how empirical the material of history may be, the particular phenomena always show a certain constancy, order, and lawfulness, and that these aspects

33. For the relationship between romanticism and the theory of historical ideas see Fueter, *op. cit.,* S. 425 ff.

34. See E. Spranger, *Wilhelm von Humboldt und die Humanitätsidee* (Berlin, Reuther & Reichard, 1909), S. 193.

35. Ranke, *Politisches Gespräch.* For the concept of the "truly spiritual" see Meinecke's *Historismus,* II: "Ranke Rede," 640 f.

loom ever more prominently with the broadening of our knowledge no less than with the ennobling of human nature itself and the progress of time.[36]

Here there is posed for the theory of "historical ideas" a question that is indeed difficult. In what sense the "lawfulness" of events is to be understood cannot be gathered directly from either Humboldt or Ranke. It is clear that they were not thinking of a mere conformity to rule and coercive order, as in the case of natural events and "mechanical" causality. Nor should laws be sought for here in the sense of either economic materialism or Lamprecht's psychological laws. What they were interested in was, as Plato put it, "another kind of cause." But now come the questions as to how such an interrelationship of two independent causal series is to be made intelligible from the point of view of a theory of knowledge.

Does not causal order mean precisely that between all phenomena in space and time there shall be a necessary objective connection; and is not such unity and objectivity endangered when, in addition to physical causality, we recognize another, and superior, "supernatural" causality? Neither Humboldt nor Ranke seemed able to escape this predicament. All that happens in time and space, declared Humboldt, stands in an inseparable connection and in this aspect history, no matter how many-sided and living it may appear as it passes before us, is like a mechanism that obeys "dead" unalterable laws and is driven by mechanical forces. But now it had come to be realized, after many years, that any such exclusively mechanical explanation would lead one directly away from an understanding of the actual creative forces of history. There was no doubt that "ideas" did manifest themselves here, and that certain phenomena which are inexplicable simply as the work of natural laws owed their existence to the inspiration of these ideas—and there was just as little doubt that at some point the historian, if he is to grasp the true significance of events, must transfer himself to a realm that lies outside the events themselves.[37]

For his part Ranke, too, had no hesitation in maintaining that the "ideas" are of "divine origin," and he then had to assume such an ideal origin not only for religions but also for nations and states as well. In his view all these phenomena stemmed "from the divine and the eternal," though never wholly so. For a period the ideas are constructive and life giving, and new creations issue forth under

36. Humboldt, "Plan einer vergleichenden Anthropologie," *Gesammelte Schriften*, IV, 396.
37. Humboldt, *Gesammelte Schriften*, IV, 48 ff.

their inspiration. "But complete and unalloyed existence is never attained in this world; hence nothing is immortal. When the time is ripe there arise out of that which has fallen new efforts of far-reaching spiritual meaning that shatter it completely. These are God's communications to the world." [38]

Here the conviction so painfully attained, the conviction to which the historian as such is committed—that he shall operate within his own field of fact alone—seems in danger of being weakened and of yielding to a religious or philosophical metaphysics. But Humboldt as well as Ranke rejected a teleology like that sought in the eighteenth century, for they saw no longer in history the fulfillment of any definite purpose, human or divine. Humboldt will not search for divine final causes in history; he explains that in the main the driving forces of world history are the productive forces, culture, and inertia. There are no purposes in these things. "The destinies of the human race roll onward as rivers flow from the mountains to the sea, as grasses and herbs sprout, as larvae spin themselves into cocoons and emerge butterflies, as peoples press forward and are pushed back in turn, destroy and are ground to pieces. The force of the universe is . . . a ceaseless rolling forward; hence there must be recognized in history not some sort of unknown and falsely ascribed purpose, excogitated after a few thousand years' effort, imperfectly felt and still less perfectly understood, but only the forces of nature and of mankind." [39]

Thus we see how the theory of ideas in both Ranke and Humboldt always poses the central question of the relationship between the universal and particular, the eternal and temporal, the divine and human, but in no way pretends to answer the question in a purely scientific way and in the dispassionate language of science. Ranke did not scruple to declare that the factors determining the course of world history are a "divine mystery," [40] and he wanted that mystery to be felt throughout his writings, though he laid no claim to be able to reveal it. This was the point of attack for the later positivistic criticism that attempted to tear the entire theory of historical ideas to pieces. [41]

38. Ranke, *Deutsche Geschichte im Zeitalter der Reformation*, "Meisterwerke," I, 81.

39. Humboldt, "Betrachtungen über die Weltgeschichte," *op. cit.*, III, 357 ff.

40. Ranke, *Befestigung des deutschen Protestantismus, op. cit.*, IV, Kap. 2, 67 ff.

41. See especially the criticism leveled by Lamprecht at Ranke's theory of ideas, "Rankes Ideenlehre und die Jungrankianer," *Alte und neue Richtungen in der Geschichtswissenschaft* (Berlin, R. Gaertner, 1896), S. 26 ff.

XIV

Positivism and Its Ideal of Historical Knowledge: Taine

THE THEORY of historical "ideas" in the form in which it was developed by von Humboldt and Ranke did not mean that these historians were averse to historical reality. The task set was quite the reverse: these writers clung tenaciously to the actual world. Both agreed that the universal could be apprehended only in the particular, the "idea" only in the "appearance." Respect for reality was the supreme commandment. But the conception of reality itself threatened to break into a dualism, for they saw everything that happened in a double light, as it were. They recognized the operation of physical causes inherent in reality, but that was not all. The physical or material always had simultaneously its "spiritual" side, and the "sensible" pointed to an "intelligible" meaning. Though the idea appears only in the natural connections and could be understood only so, still it could not be subject to natural causality. Certain phenomena, and, indeed, the most significant, could not be grasped in their full meaning unless we resolved to look beyond the world of phenomena.[1] In Ranke's *Politisches Gespräch*, states are called "spiritual existences," and not only as original creations of the human mind but actually as "the thoughts of God." Thus the idea of causality itself seemed to split into two parts, a cleavage which left its characteristic stamp on every historical judgment.

This was the point of attack for positivism as it was precisely formulated in Comte's *Cours de philosophie positive*. Comte seems to have had but little touch with German philosophy and scholarship, and it is doubtful whether he was acquainted in any intimate way with the aspirations of the romanticists. Furthermore, he came to his position not by way of history but through mathematics and natural science. Yet when we study the development of his system we see why he went on to history. In the hierarchic structure of science that he was searching for—in the belief that it was requisite for the first principles of all "positive" philosophy—mathematics, and then the sciences of inanimate nature (astronomy, physics, and chem-

1. See page 239, above.

istry), constituted the secure and necessary foundation, but still they did not provide the real goal of knowledge. This lay in that science which Comte called by the new name of *sociology*. Accordingly this science came to be for him the alpha and omega of all true philosophy. The less philosophy lost itself in the world beyond, the "transcendent," the more perfect it would become. Philosophy can only search for and teach a "human" truth, and it attains its goal the more surely when it restricts itself to the world of mankind. But this cosmos of humanity in turn can be understood only when we resolve to go beyond physics, in the ordinary meaning of the word. What we need is not a physics of the inanimate world merely but a "social physics." The development of this is the supreme goal of positivistic philosophy. Until that is accomplished philosophy will not have fulfilled its chief task, which is to exorcise the spirit of theology and of metaphysics not only from this or that special science but from science in general, and thus assure science of a firm, "positive" foundation. Only the creation of a sociology, wrote Comte in conclusion, can restore the fundamental unity in the whole system of modern knowledge.

The first indispensable condition for this was the realization that sociology and history no longer constituted a "state within a state," but that there was the same inviolable conformity to law here as in all natural events. As long as this fact remained unrecognized, as long as some sort of human "freedom" was sought—a freedom regarded as a breaking through of natural laws—sociology would be unable to make any progress. It would remain infantile, in the stage of theological or metaphysical thinking; it would be in reality not science but fetishism. We must break once for all with this superstition and proclaim the undivided sway of rigorous laws in this sphere also. "I shall bring factual proof," wrote Comte, "that there are just as definite laws for the development of the human race as there are for the fall of a stone." [2] He believed that he had discovered *one* of these laws, and the one absolutely fundamental, in his "law of three stages," [3] and he was already convinced that in a sense he had become "the Galileo of sociology."

But we must not be deceived by this analogy between physics and sociology. Many of Comte's followers who were most active in disseminating his ideas interpreted it as a denial of all methodological distinctions between the two sciences, as though sociology and history

---

2. A. Comte, Letter to Valat, September 8, 1824; see L. Lévy-Bruhl, *La Philosophie d'Auguste Comte* (2e éd. Paris, F. Alcan, 1905), p. 270.

3. For details on Comte's "law of three stages" see above, Introduction, pp. 8–9.

could be merged simply into natural science, physics or chemistry. But this was not Comte's meaning, for in his "hierarchy of the sciences" he taught that a later and more highly developed member of the order could never be reduced to any earlier one. Every subsequent member added to its predecessor a characteristic feature and had its own specific individuality. Even in mounting from mathematics to astronomy, and from this to physics and then to chemistry and biology, it always appeared that each new member brought an additional distinctive factor that was not present in the preceding one and could not be inferred from it by deduction. This distinctive character became more and more apparent the higher we ascended in the scale of the sciences and the more closely we approached the most complicated phenomenon of all, which was that of human existence. For this comprehension of humanity, Comte had no doubt whatsoever, certain new concepts were requisite, which were not available in the existing sciences, and these had to be newly created and independently developed. In so far as he recognized universal principles that determined all knowledge, Comte was a monist; on the other hand he was emphatically a pluralist in his doctrine of method.

And now these questions were outstanding: What is that characteristic and distinguishing feature that separates the theory of mankind—social statics and dynamics—from all other branches of knowledge? And again, what is its special contribution in regard to content and method? According to Comte there was no doubt as to the answer. When we reach the final stage of scientific knowledge, when we ascend from physics and chemistry to biology, we encounter two new features. We must make use of the comparative method and we are then led to the idea of development as the basic principle that obtains for all knowledge of organic life. Whether we deal with an anatomical structure or a psychological phenomenon, methodical comparison of the regular series of growing differences would always be the surest guide to a solution of the question down to its last details. Such clues ought never to be lost sight of in passing on to the study of mankind, anthropology and sociology, for man is a living creature like all others and thus he is not outside the laws governing animate nature. All that is said about man's "spiritual" nature, as something not subject to an animal existence and its conditions, is sheer illusion. Though metaphysics may be continually deceived by this illusion of a "pure" spirituality, the positive method must renounce it once and for all. But of course this does not mean that in the advance from animal forms to the human nothing new appears in the series. Even though there be no sudden jump, no complete transformation, still the very idea of evolution means that new factors are in operation, which manifest themselves in the development of speech, religion, art, and the intellect. There was only one method by which these factors could be recognized for what they were and understood in their significance and effect: the historical method. In the transition from biology to sociology the idea of development assumes the form of *historical thinking,* and according to Comte the whole of scientific knowledge culminates in it. It is the topmost point in the edifice of positive knowledge which, without it, would remain incomplete and consequently inadequately understood in all its other stages.

It is thoroughly understandable that such a fundamental point of view would offer strongest and most enduring incentives. In that connection it is especially significant that much as Comte depended throughout on scientific assumptions and facts, he never fell into a dogmatic "naturalism." The distinctive right and value of historical thinking, what might be called "the autonomy of the historical world," were recognized by him all along. He drew the lines much more sharply than many later advocates of positivism and many disciples and pupils of Comte who invoked his authority. As biology could not be reduced to physics, so sociology could not be reduced to biology. For the characteristic method of sociology, the method of history, could not be logically derived from the methods of natural science. "History is not a thing that can be deduced." [4]

In the development of the positivistic method and historiography in France and England this basic idea was not only relegated to the background but was at times either obliterated or else turned into the exact opposite. It was believed that Comte's intentions could not be better fulfilled than by tearing down completely the wall separating sociology and physics. In England it was Buckle above all who endeavored to carry out Comte's program. He, too, opposed the belief that in the world of man there is anything left to chance, anything exempt from the natural order and its rigid determinism. But he derived his evidence for this uniformity and necessity in human affairs not so much from history as from statistics, which showed that the alleged freedom of the human will is a delusion. Thus he did away at one stroke with all distinctions between the social world and the world of nature, between ethics and physics. The number of crimes

4. Comte, "Appendice général," *Système de politique positive* (Paris, Chez Carilian-Goeury et Vor Dalmont, 1854), Tome IV.
For further details on the relation of sociology to biology and psychology in Comte's system see Lévy-Bruhl, *op. cit.,* chap. ii, p. 266 ff.

committed each year was as subject to rigorous mathematical laws
as any natural phenomenon. Here the historian had to mediate between the moralist, theologian, and metaphysician on the one hand,
and the natural scientist on the other. "To settle the terms of this
coalition," declared Buckle, "will be to fix the basis of all history." [5]
But for him the result was simply the merging of history with natural
science, which differed from each other chiefly in the complexity of
their phenomena, not in the procedures employed.

The same conclusion was trenchantly drawn by Taine in France.
He cannot be called a pupil of Comte in the strictest sense, for other
influences connected with German romanticism were of much more
effect in his education, influences diametrically opposite in trend to
those of Comte. But it may have been his very endeavors to overcome these influences that drove him in the end to go beyond Comte
in important particulars and throw himself unreservedly into the
arms of "naturalism." Only there could he hope to find salvation
from Hegel's metaphysics of history, which, unlike Comte, he understood thoroughly, and which had wholly captivated him in his youth.
He had learned German for the express purpose of reading Hegel's
works in the original, and he never gave up until he had entirely
mastered the "monster" of Hegelian logic.[6] Then, however, on a sudden resolve, he discarded everything in Hegel's theory, which, like
every other system of metaphysics, now appeared merely hypothetical
to him.[7] He wanted facts, nothing but facts. Yet he realized, of
course, that the facts could be only the beginning, not the end. A
collection of facts alone could not provide a science. "After the facts
have been gathered, then search for the cause," runs the maxim. But
there must no longer be two different ways of investigating causes.
The historian should not leave the sensory world to seek the true
and final reasons for events in an ideal world. He must let phenomena
speak for themselves and explain themselves. Hence for him there
could never be a priori standards of any sort, and just as little personal sympathy or antipathy. The history of art included all forms
and all schools indifferently; it was like botany, which investigated

5. H. T. Buckle, *History of Civilization in England* (London, Longmans, Green,
1871), I, chap. i, 35.

6. H. Taine, *Vie et correspondance, 1853–1870* (3e éd. Paris, Hachette et Cie., 1908),
II, 70.

G. Monod, *Les Mâitres de l'histoire: Renan, Taine, Michelet* (Paris, C. Lévy, 1894),
p. 60.

7. "I have just read Hegel's *Philosophy of History*," he wrote in a letter of June 24,
1852. "It is a fine thing, though hypothetical and not sufficiently accurate." See Monod,
ibid., p. 85.

by one and the same method and with the same impartiality both the orange tree and the laurel.[8]

The program of the new positivistic historiography was thus inaugurated. It admits of none but natural causes and will have to show that the chain of causes does not reach into infinity but can be traced back to a few general principles that govern and determine all events. The general causes, whose operation could always be demonstrated and which sufficed to explain every particular existence and development, were called by Taine the triad of race, milieu, time. The historian had done enough and completed his scientific task when he had succeeded in demonstrating the participation of these three basic factors in all phenomena investigated. Thereupon an astonishing simplification appeared to have been reached: historical existence, so manifold at first glance, so heterogeneous, so incalculably rich, revealed itself to the eye of the analyst as so simple and uniform that three concepts were enough to make it completely understandable.

Of course the question immediately arises in this connection whether this is the right way to break the spell Taine wanted to escape in turning away from the Hegelian construction of history. In point of fact, Taine, the "naturalist," who thought everything depended on a simple description of the given reality, sinned far more often against the "respect for reality" than Humboldt or Ranke ever did. Never were they satisfied with such simple formulas as he constantly employed. On occasion he himself admitted that the urge to find an uncomplicated expression for the great complexity of events was the underlying motive in all his research. He felt a sort of admiration for purely syllogistic reasoning such as few other great historians have known. A true and strictly logical inference seemed to him not only the soul of truth but of beauty as well, and on one occasion this enthusiastic amateur of music cried out, after having played a Beethoven sonata, "That is as beautiful as a syllogism!"[9] Taine made the most extensive use of his talent for abstracting historical material and presenting it in a simple way; many of his formulas, indeed, are of such terse precision and inviting simplicity that they

---

8. Taine, *Philosophie de l'Art*. In the following account I rely on my paper, *Naturalistische und humanistische Begründung der Kulturphilosophie* "Göteborgs Kungl. Vetenskaps och Vitterhets-Samhälles Handlingar" 5e följden, Ser. A., Bd. VII (1938), No. 3.

For the historico-philosophical theses of Taine, especially his determinism, I refer to that paper. Here we are concerned only with describing the purely epistemological factors in his view of history.

9. See Monod, *op. cit.*, p. 64.

are immediately and almost irresistibly stamped on the memory.

But the important methodological question here is whether the concepts with which he operated were actually what he represented them to be; in other words, whether they originated in purely scientific thinking and were acquired and verified by strict induction. That this is not the case appears more and more clearly the further his presentation goes into details and the more lively and colorful it becomes. Nowhere is to be found in it the attempt to get on with those "general" causes that he valued so highly and proclaimed the true scientific basis of explanation. As soon as he came to present concrete individual problems he virtually forgot all about those general causes. Not only was he absorbed in the details; he actually reveled in them. Hence the curious double character of his historical writing, where deduction from simple formulas and joy in the mere painting of manifold and variegated events go hand in hand. Nor did he succeed in preserving toward his subject the cool, unruffled calm of the natural scientist.

He coined the celebrated phrase that the historian must regard virtue and vice just as the chemist regards sugar and sulphuric acid, satisfied to decompose each into its elements without attaching any sort of moral judgment to his analysis. In the investigation of causality there was no place for such judgments.

There are causes for ambition, courage, and truth just as there are causes for digestion, for muscular movement, for animal heat . . . Let us then seek the simple phenomena for moral qualities, as we seek them for physical properties. There is a chain of great general causes, and the general structure of things, and the great courses of events are their work. Religions, philosophy, poetry, industry, the arts, the framework of society and of families are in fact only the imprints stamped by their seal.

Considered from this standpoint history becomes not only anthropology but anatomy. We might be sure of finding in it, beneath all the diversity and variation of events, always the same more or less unalterable bony framework. Facts change but their skeleton remains. "History today, like zoology, has discovered its anatomy, and whatever be the special branch toward which we turn, whether we deal with a philological, a linguistic, or a mythological question, we must always proceed in this way to achieve new and fruitful results." [10]

10. Taine, *Histoire de la littérature anglaise* (Paris, L. Hachette et Cie., 1863), I, ix ff.

Only so, Taine believed, can the objectivity expected of the historian be wholly satisfied. Like Spinoza, he will henceforth treat human passions as though he were dealing with geometrical figures, surfaces, or solids. The emotions, such as love, hate, anger, ambition, sympathy should not be regarded as weaknesses but as manifestations of human nature that are as much a part of it as heat and cold, storms and thunder, and other phenomena of the sort are a part of the atmosphere. The demand for objectivity, as Ranke understood and sought to meet it, seemed thus to be accentuated and far surpassed. Not for an instant may the historian allow himself to be carried away by his interest in what has happened. It is not for him to judge but only to analyze and understand.

But here again Taine's own concrete presentation of history shows a picture different from what one might expect of his abstract ideals and postulates. The further he progressed on his way the further he departed from these ideals. In his earlier works, the *Philosophy of Art* and the *History of English Literature,* he appeared to be still faithful to his fundamental principle. He would not appraise aesthetically but simply describe the various schools of art and their development: Greek sculpture, Gothic architecture, Italian painting of the Renaissance, Dutch painting. The moment he entered the sphere of public life, however, in his *Origins of Contemporary France*—his great work on political history—this attitude changed completely. Here a sympathetic interest in events can be detected in every line, since the very plan for this work originated in his own concern and the shock caused by the outcome of the war of 1870–71, and this interest was now so strong that it not infrequently clouded his eye for sheer factual consistency, as his critics have often emphasized.[11]

Taine appears here among those political historians like Heinrich von Sybel who voiced the demand that the historian renounce his "noble neutrality" and act as a political mentor.[12] Everyone knows what a storm was aroused in all political camps by Taine's work when it first appeared. But the historians, too, reproached him for his "political dogmatism," which sprang directly from the romantic theories that he thought he had left far behind him.[13] Even where he appeared not to judge but simply to analyze, it was only in appearance that he moved in the characteristically scientific circle of

11. A. Aulard, *Taine: Historien de la révolution française* (Paris, A. Colin, 1907).
12. H. v. Sybel, "Über den Stand der neueren deutschen Geschichtsschreibung," *Kleine historische Schriften* (München, J. G. Cotta, 1863), S. 343 ff.
13. See E. Fueter, *Geschichte der neueren Historiographie,* S. 587 ff.

thought. He believed one of the important causes of the French Revolution to have been the intellectual development that preceded it. The classical spirit was for him the real moving force behind political affairs that contained the hidden reason for them. It formed a manner of looking at the world which blinded men to the facts of political reality, to all historical change and growth, and to the value of tradition, which finally had to lead to the fateful destruction of everything then established. All this Taine pictured in a brilliant performance of really dazzling style. But his description made use throughout of the methods and intellectual devices and modes of presentation that are valid in purely "intellectual history" or "the history of ideas." There was no intention of leaving the naturalistic scheme out of account, but the narrative moved so freely within it that one almost forgets about it. Furthermore, the causal concept used by Taine had but little in common with that of empirical or exact science. Its origin is elsewhere. Nowhere can one more clearly detect how mightily Taine had wrestled in youth with the Hegelian philosophy of history and how lasting its influence had been on him. In masterful fashion he traced the downfall of the *ancien régime* to causes within itself, and he saw there, as elsewhere, how the seeds of decay were contained in all that made that order great and famous. The Jacobins were, in his opinion, the real heirs of the ancien régime. When one considers how it produced them, nourished and cared for them, set them on the throne and brought them into power, the history of the regime can hardly be viewed as anything other than a slow suicide. Such a chain of causes does not correspond with what Taine called "the autonomy of history," but is more an offspring of the spirit of Hegelian dialectic and its principle of the "overturn of antitheses." In general the "universal causes" of events upon which Taine placed the greatest weight, in theory, actually retreated further and further into the background in his purely historical presentation until at last they function only as mere shadowy phantoms. Instead of being the real forces that rule in historical life they often seem but mythical creations.

This feature of positivistic and naturalistic historiography was strikingly described in the criticism that Croce leveled against it. Whenever, in his search for causes, Taine reached a cause which he called now "race" or again "century," he was wont to declare himself quite satisfied, as if further analysis were neither possible nor requisite. "There the investigation ended. One had come upon some primordial factor, some trait common to all the feelings and the ideas of a century or people and some feature inseparable from all the activities of its mind and spirit. These were the great causes, universal and permanent." But from the standpoint of natural science what were these universal causes that would overcome and supplant those of modern science, if not simply the "occult qualities" of the Schoolmen? What were they, after all, but names, offered us in lieu of causes? "Taine's power of imagination saw something supposed to be original and supreme in them, but the critical mind knew nothing thereof," remarked Croce, "for critical thought requires that one should give reasons for the genesis of the facts or groups of facts that are called 'century' and 'race'; and in so doing at once make it clear that they cannot be either 'universal' or 'permanent,' for so far as I know there are no universal and permanent 'facts.' Neither 'the German' nor 'the Nordic' are such facts, nor, I would say, are mummies, that last for several thousand years but not forever, which change but slowly, to be sure, yet change nevertheless." [14]

The dilemma in which Taine found himself increasingly entangled here is apparent also in his treatment of the really fundamental question in all historical knowledge: the relation between the universal and the particular. Because he started with a set of concepts along scientific lines he might have been expected to seek a complete subordination of the particular to the universal, and to declare all isolated occurrences historically significant only in so far as one could discover a universal law of which they served as an example. But this is in no way the case.

In the face of the supremacy of the universal as it appeared in Hegel's philosophy of history, Ranke and Humboldt had insisted that the historian should treat the universal not as something subsisting by itself but always as something made visible mediately in the particular. Both elements must permeate one another and come to an internal equilibrium. With Taine, however, this equilibrium was often in danger of being upset from one or the other of two opposing sides. Not only was he absorbed in the particular but he sometimes indulged so freely in the depicting of details that their description seemed almost an end in itself. He himself once said that it was precisely out of such "little significant facts" (*de tout petits faits significatifs*) that the authentic historical portrayal must be made. He was tireless in tracking them down, and with his incomparable literary skill he knew how to set them in their proper light. In this respect he followed not Comte but Sainte-Beuve, who was his real literary master.

14. Cf. B. Croce, *Theory and History of Historiography*, pp. 66–67.

In his *Portraits littéraires* and his *Causeries de Lundi* Sainte-Beuve created a wholly unique art of literary portraiture and anecdote, and he liked to describe even great intellectual movements by collecting a mass of apparently insignificant details through which to make them clear and vivid. Taine strove more than Sainte-Beuve did for general formulas, but his delight in what was individual and in pushing matters to the finest detail also gave life to his portrayal. As he explained in his Introduction to the *History of English Literature* there are at bottom neither mythologies nor languages; there are only people who use words and create images and ideas. Hence he was far from drawing the inferences for historiography from his naturalistic interpretation that other champions of naturalism or economic materialism have drawn. He would have nothing to do with a collectivistic view of history but, on the contrary, recommended an extreme individualism. In the end the individual remained the alpha and omega of history and was the source of all real knowledge. "Nothing exists save through the individual; it is the individual himself who must be understood." "Leave, then, the theory of constitutions and their mechanisms, the theory of religion and its system, and instead of these things try to see the people in their workshops, offices, fields, as they live under the sun, on their soil, and in their homes; see what they eat and how they are clothed. This is the first step in history." [15]

The question that must now be asked, and it is the one which is decisive as to the truth or falsity of Taine's theory in purely methodological respects, is whether he would have succeeded in taking this "first step" and have had access to the world of history had he depended exclusively on the form of scientific description and explanation which, as a philosopher, he had set up as the standard and ideal of historical understanding. Obviously this is not the case. He naïvely yielded himself to a sort of shrewd wisdom about man and a kind of "physiognomics" that had grown out of quite other ground than that of scientific analysis. He pursued a kind of "face reading" that had little or nothing to do with that "autonomy of history" he prized so highly.

But the central epistemological problem posed by Taine's history writing, as it is by positivism in general, lies elsewhere, in the concept of historical fact that underlay his writing and was ingenuously employed throughout. Here he could tie up with the oldest traditions of empiricism and positivism. One can say of him in a certain sense

15. Taine, Introduction, *Histoire* . . . , p. v ff.

that he transplanted the Baconian ideal of induction from physics to history. Bacon was convinced that the scientist must begin by collecting his material from the observations of sense alone and without any theoretical preparation or admixture of abstract ideas. Only when the task of assembling the data has been completed does the work of examining them begin. Individual cases must be compared, and positive and negative instances weighed against one another, until finally a single rule covering a definite set of phenomena has been found. Here two entirely separate intellectual operations come into play. The facts themselves constitute a self-contained whole, which only later is subjected to theoretical treatment and interpretation. But even with Bacon himself this separation led to the most difficult questions of principle. Much, if not most, of what served for him as simple "fact" was revealed by new critical methods of scientific research to be a mere "idol." [16]

Taine, too, did not escape this dilemma of positivism. When he is compared with "critical" historians like Ranke, it becomes evident immediately how little ground he had for extolling the superiority of his scientific method. He transgressed it from the very first with extraordinary naïveté in gathering his "facts," for he made no distinctions of any sort. An anecdote, memoirs of doubtful value, a sentence in a political brochure or a sermon—all were accepted with equal readiness, if only they provided those "little significant features" upon which he liked to base his presentation and with which he enlivened it. For in his belief the real intellectual and fundamental labors of the historian began not at this point but later: "After the facts have been gathered, then search for the causes." Thus it could be objected to his "facts," as to Bacon's, that they were not only uncritically gathered but for the most part did not even deserve the name, because Taine never suspected that the historian of culture would be unable to dispense with the methods of critical philology. [17]

Of course such an objection does not detract from the value of his historical writings and must not blind us to their peculiar excellence, for they depended far less than he would have us believe, or than he himself believed, upon the general principles that he set up as a theoretical historian. These were only the frame of the picture; its drawing and coloring were of quite another provenance. Here he gave free rein to his artistic nature, his imagination, and his gift of clear, telling illustration. He painted individual portraits that were very

16. For further details see *Das Erkenntnisproblem*, II, 16 ff.
17. See Fueter, *op. cit.*, S. 584 f.

true to life. He could capture the whole "face" of an age in a few strokes. It is this sort of mastery that makes his work so impressive and will ensure its survival, even though the theoretical foundation upon which he attempted to build, and which seemed to him the most important part of his work, be very doubtfully regarded.

XV

Political and Constitutional Theory as Foundations
for Historiography: Mommsen

THROUGH the efforts of Buckle and Taine the basic principles of positivistic philosophy gained a wide circulation
among both English and French historians and exerted an
increasingly strong influence. They made their way into Germany,
too, though they never found there such a favorable soil and ready
response. For toward the middle of the nineteenth century German
writers of history, also, had not only abandoned the ideals of romanticism but found themselves in steadily increasing opposition to
them. They set up other political objectives and stressed the fact
that romantic fantasy and quietism were irreconcilable with them.
The historian, instead of absorbing himself in the past and looking
back to it as a lost paradise, ought decisively to serve the political
future. In place of the ideology of romanticism and its theory of a
"national spirit" there was required a foundation for the science of
history free of all metaphysical assumptions.

In this respect even Ranke failed to satisfy the new generation
of historians. They held to a counterview, a new political realism: one
should no longer be content with mere study but ought to set up very
definite and concrete goals.[1] Between these ideals and the fundamental tenets of positivism there seemed to be no inevitable antag-
onism of any sort; on the contrary, they coincided in important respects. Nevertheless there could be no true alliance between them,
for the influence of romanticism was still far from dead in Germany
when historians were beginning to turn away from it and to declare
that the battle against it was "the order of the day." Even there
where the struggle was on for the new political aims the romantic
ideal of knowledge had not yet been renounced. "We observe," wrote
von Below, "that all political historians accept the facts attained by
the historical school of law and even rely in part on the leaders of
this school of thought. They are really the pupils of Ranke, and none
ignores his methods. They have profited by all the scholarly ac-
quisitions of the romantic period. In their academic judgments, so to

1. For details on the opposition of the political historians to Ranke and to romanticism see G. v. Below, *Die deutsche Geschichtsschreibung*, S. 38 ff.

speak, they have rejected romanticism, yet they cannot dispense with what it has achieved." [2]

So the fight against romanticism was often carried on with the very weapons that it had actually forged itself. Even its "organological metaphysics" had not yet been overcome by any means, but survived in its assumptions despite the fact that many of its conclusions were being denied. Besides these remaining metaphysical assumptions there were also the continued influence of the Hegelian dialectic and Humboldt's theory of individuality.[3] All this precluded any reconciliation with Comte's positivism or with historians like Buckle or Taine.

When Buckle's *History of Civilization in England* appeared in Arnold Rugge's German translation, J. G. Droysen, one of the most prominent representatives of "political realism" in Germany, published a thoroughgoing analysis and review, in which he sought to reveal particularly its methodological weaknesses. Buckle's assertion that positivism was the first philosophy to put history on a firm scientific foundation was contradicted in the most outright way. Unfortunately there was a tendency in Droysen's criticism to give the problem an ethical twist and to object to Buckle's work because of its unmoral "materialistic attitude." But apart from this it was apparent that Droysen was superior philosophically to his adversary both in the precision of his thought and in the range of his philosophical knowledge. This is obvious at a glance from his *Grundriss der Historik* (1864), which may be counted among the fundamental works on the modern methodology of history. The idea of "understanding," from which Dilthey started later to characterize the individuality of historical knowledge and the difference between it and scientific thought, was brought into focus here for the first time and described in its essentials.[4] With this as a starting point Droysen proceeded to ward off all attempts to measure history by the standards of science and eventually to reduce it entirely to science. He stood out resolutely for a "pluralism of methods," and on this score, as we have seen, he could have invoked the authority of Comte.[5]

If there is to be any "science" of history it is only possible because history has its own peculiar and specific subject matter. So we must demonstrate that a certain realm of appearances exists, for the understanding of which none of these other approaches to knowledge

2. *Ibid.,* p. 43.
3. E. Troeltsch, *Der Historismus* . . . , S. 303 ff.
4. J. G. Droysen, "Die historische Methode," *Grundriss der Historik* (3. Aufl. Leipzig, Veit & Co., 1882), § 8, S. 9 ff.
5. See pp. 244–245.

is suited—not the theological or the philosophical or mathematical
or physical approach. Here questions arise which theological or philosophical speculation cannot answer; and just as little empirical science, which conceives the world of phenomena entirely in terms of
their quantitative relationships. These are questions where both
"deduction" and what is called "induction" fail us; questions that
cannot be logically derived from general principles or "explained"
in terms of mathematical physics, or even shown in a simple empirical
way, but which must nonetheless be "understood," and for whose understanding the development of their own intellectual methods is
required. "Is there, then, always just *one* way, *one* method, of knowledge?" Droysen asks of Buckle. "Do not methods differ in accordance with their objects, as do the sense organs for the various kinds
of perception, or the other organs for their different functions?" [6]
There was no question, in these objections to Buckle as made by
Droysen, of a hostility on his part toward intellectual history which
many political historians later exhibited. Of course Droysen confined his own investigations to a definite field in political history,
and one may consider him as belonging not only to the "German
historical school" but also, in a narrower sense, to a "Prussian
school." [7] Still, a theory that placed the idea of "understanding"
at the center of historical knowledge could not stop at the study of
political events or orient itself one-sidedly in this particular. Droysen
actually struck out in the direction of what has been since called the
"history of ideas" or "intellectual history." He aimed to make history
appear lifelike as a world of intellectual and moral powers. In this
respect he connected directly with the classical tradition of Humboldt, to whose article on the task of the historian he referred as well
as to the great introduction to his work on the ancient Kawi language of Java, which was the concrete application of Humboldt's
basic idea. [8] This was the only way one could hope to reconcile political
history with the history of culture, instead of keeping them in constant tension.

A step further in the same direction was taken by Theodor
Mommsen. He also was an out-and-out political thinker and by no
means free of political passions. But his scientific genius lay in dis-
ciplining the passion rather than allowing it free rein. He would

6. Droysen, "Die Erhebung der Geschichte zum Rang einer Wissenschaft." A review
of the German translation of Buckle's *History of Civilization,* which appeared first in
von Sybel's *Zeitschrift;* reprinted as an appendix in *Grundriss der Historik,* S. 47–68.
7. For a discussion of this Prussian school see Troeltsch, *op. cit.,* S. 303 f.
8. See Droysen, Vorwort, *Grundriss der Historik,* § 17.

not advocate any particular ideal for the state but wanted to understand it as such and make its structure manifest. For this purpose he had to strike out in a new direction. In the outward expansion of the power of the state he saw merely one side of it; what fascinated him far more were the forces within civil life, and he went deeply into them. The organization of the state, especially its juridical organization, became the decisive question. Thus juridical knowledge and jurisprudence were accorded a wholly different role and a far deeper significance in the development of the historical world than ever before. Mommsen regarded both the separation of philology and history from each other, and of jurisprudence and political science from history, as quite arbitrary and unnatural. He wanted to remove such senseless barriers, which, he said, emanated principally from the departmentalization of university faculties and should not be binding upon scholarship.

Niebuhr had previously been able to lighten the darkness that enveloped the mythical history of early Rome because he had seen the problem in a new light—conceiving the rise of Rome as the rise of the Roman system of government and realizing that political struggles were the real moving forces. But in the opinion of Wilamowitz it was Mommsen's first work [9] that clearly revealed the antithesis between the jurist such as Mommsen and the historian Niebuhr, for Mommsen "drew a bill of exchange, as it were, on constitutional law." [10] This new perspective required the introduction of entirely new methods of investigation, which Mommsen had to create for himself. Jurisprudence not only called in philology but directed the latter toward goals, too, which until then it had not set for itself or had not recognized in their full significance. In his work on Athenian political economy (1817) Boeckh had already paved the way for this development and had aroused keen interest in Attic law and its importance.[11] He had called attention to the significance of inscriptions and in 1828 had begun his collection of Greek inscriptions. But all this remained only a preliminary study that had to be intellectually assimilated before it could be directed to some great use. Mommsen was the first to succeed with this synthesis. Compared with even the greatest of his forerunners he was the only genuine historian, as dis-

9. T. Mommsen, *Die römischen Tribus in administrativer Beziehung* (Altona, J. F. Hammerich, 1844).

10. See U. v. Wilamowitz-Moellendorff, "Geschichte der Philologie," *Einleitung in die Altertumswissenschaft* von Gercke und Norden (Leipzig und Berlin, 1921), I, Heft I, 70.

11. For further details see *ibid.*, S. 55.

tinct from a mere antiquary. He may be called the first to deliver the history of government from its antiquarian isolation.[12]

In fact Mommsen almost reversed the relationships in respect to what was the "ancillary science." Politics, which had been treated as a mere aid to historical knowledge, was made into its proper subject matter and became the problem for historical research. In this respect he went far beyond even Ranke.[13] Such matters grew so important for Mommsen that he drew from them the most remarkable and radical conclusions, even in a pedagogical respect. Indeed he almost demanded, in his rectorial address of 1874, that one who was to prepare himself for the study of history in the right way at the university should not study history. "He who leaves the university with a thorough knowledge of the Latin, Greek, and German languages and the political systems of these peoples," he said in addressing the students, "is prepared to be a historian; he who lacks it is not. If you work at these things, then it is certain that the search into sources and the portrayal of practical events will come of themselves, as surely as the fruitful clouds send down their rain. If you do not make this knowledge your own, you will pluck fruit that rots as you touch it." He had said earlier,

I confess, Gentlemen, if I find from your papers that you are students of history I shall be all anxiety. Of course you may be determined to acquire the necessary preliminaries of language and the knowledge of politics for a certain field of historical research, and I am sure that for not a few of you it does mean this. But it might also mean that you think these subjects are more or less unnecessary and that you will take refuge in history from all the difficulties of rigorous philology and rest content with a painstaking investigation of sources and a study of the method of writing history. Where this is the case, nemesis will not be long delayed . . . The lack of genuine preparation will bring vengeance upon you because the false account will be either dull or fantastic or both at the same time, and in any case barren of the historical spirit.[14]

Mommsen wanted to make "the historical spirit" count in every field. He demanded not only the guaranteeing of such fundamentals of historical scholarship but also an extension of the foundations. He was the first to organize scientifically the study of ancient inscriptions, numismatics, and the history of law, and the result was an entirely new picture of Roman culture and the Roman state. It was in

12. See E. Fueter, *Geschichte der neueren Historiographie,* S. 552.
13. See M. Ritter, *Leopold von Ranke; seine Geistesentwicklung und seine Geschichtsschreibung* (Stuttgart, J. G. Cotta, 1896), S. 20, and Below, *op. cit.,* S. 122 ff.
14. T. Mommsen, *Reden und Aufsätze* (3. Abdruck Berlin, Weidmannsche Buchhandlung, 1912), S. 13 ff.

his *Römisches Staatsrecht,* of the years 1871–75, that this picture first appeared in its authentic form, for here the style of narrative and presentation that Mommsen had employed in his *Römische Geschichte* and straightway developed in a masterly way was fully perfected and deepened by his analysis. It was only through this perfected analysis that he could reveal the permanent in the change of the times and in the vicissitudes of political systems. His analysis laid the ground for that synthesis which he had envisaged from the beginning. As long as jurisprudence ignored the state and the people, he now declared, and history and philology ignored law, both would be knocking in vain at the gates of the Roman world. Thus Ranke's work was completed. "Mommsen and Ranke," said Gooch, "stand together and alone in the first rank of nineteenth-century historians. Ranke's works were almost entirely of a narrative character, while Mommsen earned fame not only as master of narration but as an interpreter of institutions and an editor of inscriptions and texts. They resembled each other in their marvelous productiveness and their combination of critical technique with synthetic vision . . . Rome before Mommsen was like modern Europe before Ranke." [15]

But close as the two were in their aims they were entirely different in what may be called scholarly temperament. Historical research with Ranke was destined ultimately to take the form of an imposingly calm and pure contemplation of the whole scene. Yet he was by no means unmoved by events, and all the reproaches so often made here are groundless. For he too passed judgments, though he had to stand far back from his subject in order to do so, because he wanted to see things from a viewpoint higher than that taken by those who were in the midst of events and who were attempting to direct these events toward their own ends. Individual occurrences and even individual transactions were for him only the foreground; he sought for something behind them, something that he called "the story of world events, . . . that course of events and developments of our race which we must take to be the true substance, the very center and essence of its existence: all the acts and sufferings of this wild, disorderly, impetuous, this friendly, noble, calm, this corrupt and yet pure creature that we ourselves are." All this the historian aims to capture in its true nature and form, so as to attain at last his real goal and reduce the whole stormy course of history to the calm of pure contemplation. Ranke saw history as Goethe saw nature:

> "And all the turmoil, all our struggle,
> Is lasting rest in God the Lord."

15. G. P. Gooch, *History and Historians in the Nineteenth Century,* p. 465.

But for Mommsen there was no such quiet contemplation, no tower outside and above events. His contemplation of history was charged with the whole dynamic of his personality.[16] He believed that he could never understand the stream of events historically without plunging in and being carried away by it. He was no quiet observer but a participant in the great drama of world history, and so energetically did he play his part that in his hands the past almost ceased to be the past. The difference between eras was wiped out; we stand in the midst of Roman history, as though it were the history of our own day, and affected in one way or another we follow it with the same inner concern. Mommsen's *Roman History* has worked such magic on everyone at some time of his life. Like many another "political historian" he had no desire to instruct directly and he was far above all such tendencious prejudices as are in Treitschke. Yet he made no secret of his sympathies and his antipathies; indeed what may be called personal idiosyncrasies plainly appear in many places. When his account of the relations between Caesar and Pompey is compared with that of Eduard Meyer,[17] or his picture of Cicero with that by Ferrero in his *Greatness and Decline of Rome* there will be little doubt as to where the greater historical fidelity lies. And when Mommsen comes to speak of Euripides, in his review of Roman literature and art, it is hard to believe that one is listening to a philologist or a historian, for he treats Euripides throughout as if standing before him and speaks of him almost as the Attic comedy had spoken. Of the man whom Aristotle had called the most tragic of the Greek poets Mommsen says that he was able to destroy the old tragedy but not to create a new one.[18] Subjective though such an attitude must often appear, this very subjectivity was a conscious device for transporting us into the midst of affairs. Mommsen did not want the ancients to come before us in buskins and the grand style. He renounced all solemnity and all stylization and likewise abandoned any attempt to efface himself in order simply to let the facts speak for themselves. Meanwhile he gave the commandment of historical objectivity another meaning by locating it elsewhere. Personality could be understood only through personality, and this was impossible without close sympathy, without love and hate. Here the historian

16. See A. Dove's "Vorwort zu 'Über die Epochen der neueren Geschichte,'" L. v. Ranke's *Weltgeschichte* (4. Aufl. München und Leipzig, Duncker & Humblot, 1921), VIII, 161 ff.

17. E. Meyer, *Caesars Monarchie und das Principat des Pompejus* (2. Aufl. Stuttgart und Berlin, J. G. Cotta, 1919).

18. Mommsen, *Römische Geschichte* (9. Aufl. Berlin, Weidmannsche Buchhandlung, 1903), I, 911.

must give his feelings and imagination free scope, and he may even go so far that the dividing line between science and art seems to disappear. In this respect he did not enter any claim for history as a strict science. But " 'the shuttle that weaves a thousand threads together,' " he said in his rectorial address, "the genial insight into the individuality of men and peoples, can mock all teaching and learning. The writer of history may be said to belong more to the artists than to the race of scholars." [19]

This was, in fact, the sort of influence Mommsen as an author had on the general public and likewise in his role as a man of research in the advancement of knowledge. Often it was those very ones who disagreed with him in details and drew a different picture of occurrences and their leading figures that came most under his spell. "It is unforgettable," said Eduard Meyer in his memorial address, "how phrases in which he epitomized some deep truth of historical life or depicted events and characters with such glowing colors, have impressed themselves on the reader, who will delight in returning again and again as to the creations of a great dramatist, even though he should differ from the author on the Gracchi and Pompey, on Cato and Cicero." [20]

The balance between science and art—and the older he grew the more deeply he felt the need of it—was finally restored by Mommsen in another way. From first to last he still declared it impossible to describe characters without love or hate, but the purely personal delineation retreated further and further into the background in his writings, and he was most energetic in inquiring into the achievements of history rather than spending his time on the plans, desires, and activities of individuals. And this achievement had to be interpreted with complete objectivity and construed from documents. In his old age Mommsen regarded this as essential, and he was more taken up with the monetary systems, questions of government, and the *Corpus inscriptorum* than with the description of particular events and personalities. Here no one has imposed a more rigorous standard of objectivity. He knew, of course, that what he required could not be fulfilled by any single person. He called for cooperative work and placed this requirement more and more in the foreground. In his own case it was only because of the two elements of his make-up, the "factual" and "personal," the "objective" and the "subjective"

19. Mommsen, "Rektoratsrede" (1874), *Reden und Aufsätze*, S. 11.
20. Appeared first in *Gartenlaube* (1903) ; reprinted in Meyer's *Kleine Schriften zur Geschichtstheorie und zur Wirtschaftlichen und politischen Geschichte des Altertums* (Halle a. S., M. Niemeyer, 1910), S. 539 f.

interests, constantly complementing each other in a sort of ideal equilibrium, that he was able to bring to consummation his whole new picture of Roman history and the development of the Roman world. He now saw historical science in the light of its social function, which no one writer could discharge alone and for which strict organization of talents would be needed. Yet after all this had been done the historian proper came into his own again, with his individual temperament and genius, and this genius lay beyond what could be taught and learned. Whoever had the notion that history can be taught as a trade would find in the end, to his consternation, that it is an art.[21] On the other hand, however, this art is not given freely to anyone who has not passed through the hard school of knowledge.

21. Mommsen, *op. cit.,* S. 14 f.

XVI

Political History and the History of Civilization: Burckhardt

T HE LONG and furious quarrel that broke out in the last
decades of the nineteenth century between the defenders of
political history and the advocates of a general history of
civilization seems at first glance a remarkable anachronism, for questions were fought over again and again that might well have been
thought settled long before. The eighteenth century, so often maligned
as entirely devoid of "historical sense," had actually had a much more
open mind about these problems and from a purely methodological
point of view had made essential progress in them. It is among the incontestable merits of Voltaire that he had recognized the limitations
of exclusively political historiography and had broken its spell.
Here he did not stick to a negative polemic but established a new
and positive ideal and sought to realize it in his two chief historical
works. History should no longer be only an account of battles and
campaigns or of diplomatic and political intrigues. It should describe the whole intellectual complex; besides political events it should
portray the development of thought and the literary and artistic
trends of each epoch; and finally it should unfold to a synoptic view
of the whole moral life of a period. All this Voltaire attempted in his
Siècle de Louis XIV and, on still broader lines, in his *Essai sur les
moeurs*. In many respects the execution was of course incomplete
and one-sided, but the subject was presented with perfect clarity and
precision. That step forward could never again be reversed. The
form in which Voltaire cast the new enterprise also remained as a
guidepost for many years. Attention has been rightly drawn to the
fact that even Mommsen's *Römische Geschichte* was organized on general lines according to the scheme originated by Voltaire in his *Siècle
de Louis XIV*.[1]

In this light it affects one strangely to see how toward the end of
the nineteenth century the history of civilization still had to battle
continuously for "its place in the sun," and was expected to prove its
right to exist in competition with political history. It might be

1. See E. Fueter, *Geschichte der neueren Historiographie*, S. 355.

On Voltaire's historical works and his significance as a historian see E. Cassirer,
Philosophie der Aufklärung, S. 288 ff.

thought that this proof had long since been furnished when it is recalled that at about this time there were works in France like those
of Sainte-Beuve or Taine, and in Germany like those of Jacob Burckhardt. Nevertheless many of the leading political historians tried to
contest the point that these could serve as a standard of method or
be of decisive importance for the scholarly task of history. A description of civilization, they argued, might of course accompany an account of political happenings and wrap around it like a clinging vine,
but when such a mass becomes too thick it must be relentlessly cut
away. This view was defended with special causticity and bias by
Dietrich Schäfer, who was convinced that the writing of history
had always been vitalized by its contact with politics and that it could
never without detriment be separated from this, its true center.
"Whoever wants to understand the development of a state," he explained, "must investigate the origin, growth, and continuation of
its power. But the power factors are above all of a political and
military nature; hence the predominating importance of these in
historical research." [2]

But it was going back a century and a half to work in this fashion.
It meant staying, or trying to stay, where Voltaire had found history. Of course this turning backward was only apparent, for no
"political" historian, however radical, could ever forget the magnificent broadening of perspective that had taken place since those
days through the works of Ranke, Humboldt, Schleiermacher, and
Boeckh. If one still wanted to treat history as purely a history of
states he would, even if unwillingly, have to give the concept of the
state an entirely different meaning from that which appeared in
the external expansion of its power and in its political and military
struggles. Even Schäfer could not escape this requirement—and in
recognizing it he really dulled the edge of his own argument in principle. "When philosophical thinking assigns to historical research the
domain of free human activities," he wrote, "progress is to be sought
only in the increasing moralization of these activities. It is the moral
powers that rule in history. Thus the essence of historical progress
in general lies in ethical advance." Voltaire would not have disagreed
with this passage and could have used it as the motto for his *Essai
sur les moeurs*. He would have differed only in emphasizing much
more sharply that there could be no lasting moral progress in the
absence of intellectual progress; that without enlightenment of the

2. D. Schäfer, "Das eigentliche Arbeitsgebiet der Geschichte," *Aufsätze, Vorträge,
und Reden* (Jena, G. Fischer, 1913), I, 264 ff.

understanding there would be no vitality possible in the moral powers of man.

Schäfer's view was attacked by Eberhard Gothein, who, like Schäfer, had started as a historian of economics, and from this standpoint could show that one could never adequately understand the nature and growth of the state if he looked at it exclusively from the side of one single activity. One shuts out all insight into its essence and makes the state a monstrosity if he does not see it continually in its relations with other factors, and especially with law and economics. But the same thing holds for religion, science, art, and literature as well. All the branches of knowledge concerned with these problems presuppose a higher unity where all meet and so are members of an organism that possesses a concrete reality and is called "the history of civilization." "The genesis of this kind of history and its present significance are a necessary consequence of the whole development of the modern spirit." [3]

In the rivalry and conflict of these views the history of civilization was in one respect clearly at a disadvantage from the start, as compared with political history. The latter could point to a long and established tradition that had given it a fixed and definite character, as far as method was concerned. While there were some inner tensions even here and sharp contrasts of view as to content, still mutual understanding had gradually been reached as to the task itself and the scientific way of handling it. Ranke's monumental work in particular could be cited, which remained a decisive landmark even among those political historians who sought to go further and fight for ideals other than his. But the writing of the history of civilization had not attained such a status, nor had it any classically recognized achievement. Here a many-colored picture of the odd assortment that was included in the history of civilization presented itself. Gothein complained with justice that Schäfer had taken advantage of this state of affairs to attack the history of civilization as a whole. He insisted that it should be judged by reference to its best and greatest achievements only, and that no attention should be paid to the second-hand stuff so often seeking admission under the guise of the "history of civilization." But even if one follows this prescription he does not gain any unified impression from the leading works in this field as to what they were all aiming at. And when one looks from one country to another essential differences of view are found.

3. E. Gothein, *Die Aufgaben der Kulturgeschichte* (Leipzig, Duncker & Humblot, 1889), S. 6. Schäfer replied in his "Geschichte und Kulturgeschichte," *op. cit.*, I, 291 ff.

Voltaire's idea of the meaning and value of the history of civilization persisted most strongly in England in the nineteenth century. Buckle's *History of Civilization* and Lecky's *History of the Rise and Influence of the Spirit of Rationalism in Europe* (1865) were in agreement with Voltaire's view that progress in enlightenment and general understanding is the real, indeed the only, criterion of the development of a civilization. Next to that Buckle placed the technical and material advance which followed as a simple consequence of the advancement of science.

In France, under the influence of Sainte-Beuve and Taine, the emphasis came to be placed differently. The former's great work, *Port Royal,* employed for the first time all the methods of psychological analysis to explain a great religious movement, the origin and spread of Jansenism, and to enable us to see into its most secret spiritual motives. And Taine's *Philosophie de l'art* and his history of English literature sought to do the same thing for the great period of art and literature.

Scarcely anything of the sort was attempted in Germany at first. Men like W. H. Riehl and Gustav Freytag took other paths in writing on the history of civilization. They renounced great syntheses and devoted themselves with loving care to the delineation of details. They were wont to concede that the world of history had been "delivered over to the political historians," but they took refuge after a fashion in a realm which had not yet been taken over. They contrasted the description of great historical happenings with their own "devotion to the little things," as the relation of the drama to the idyl. A section in Riehl's *Kulturstudien aus drei Jahrhunderten* (1859) bears the heading: "Historical Still Life." He explained that he wanted most of all to paint little genre pictures which, when united into one, could constitute a great historical panorama. Freytag's *Bilder aus der deutschen Vergangenheit,* too, was replete with this interpretation and sentiment. He endeavored, as he said in his *Erinnerungen,* to paint the life of the people, which flows in a dark stream beside great political occurrences.[4]

Thus from the first the history of civilization raised no claim to be other than a simple accessory and ornament—an ornament that would be disdained by any one who was concerned with seeing events in the large and relating them to their underlying causes. A his-

4. For Riehl's and Freytag's works on the history of civilization see Friedrich Jodl, *Die Kulturgeschichtsschreibung, ihre Entwicklung und ihr Problem* (1878); also the more detailed statements of Fueter, *op. cit.,* S. 566 ff. and of Gooch, *History and Historians in the Nineteenth Century,* pp. 573 ff.

toriography like that of Riehl or Freytag might boast ever so freely of its "closeness to life"—nonetheless it would be brushed aside by those who declared war on a history written in the name of "life." "There were curious and talented writers," said Nietzsche,

who painted with a delicate brush the happiness, the comforts, the every-day life, the rustic health, and all the blessings vouchsafed to children, scholars, and peasants . . . The comfortable . . . took possession of history in order to guarantee their own peace and quiet and sought to transform into historical disciplines all the branches of knowledge from which any possible disturbance to comfort might be expected. . . . Through historical consciousness they saved themselves from enthusiasm, for no longer was this "enthusiasm" to create history, as Goethe had ventured to think. On the contrary, it is precisely such blunting of feeling that is now the goal of these unphilosophical admirers of *nil admirari* when they try to take everything historically.[5]

When Nietzsche wrote this passage he was already under the spell of a thinker who had given him a new and more profound view of history. In the second *Unzeitgemässe Betrachtung* (*Vom Nutzen und Nachteil der Historie für das Leben*) he seems to stand forth as an opponent of history. But what he opposed was not history itself, for this had always been a real and lasting source of enthusiasm to him, especially of his enthusiasm for Hellenism and Greek civilization. But now he saw Hellenism itself in a new light. He set in opposition to the classic humanistic view of the Greeks his own tragic view, as expressed in his *Geburt der Tragödie* (1872) and *Die Philosophie im tragischen Zeitalter der Griechen* (1873). For him the idyl that earlier German historiography aimed to delineate stood condemned once and for all. His objection was that it could not serve life but robbed it instead of its highest virtues. Nietzsche the philologist never could renounce history in any phase of his development. What he turned against was not history but a distorted picture drawn by modern historicism. "They are carrying on to such an extreme about history," he declared, "and they cherish it so, that life is stunted and degenerate. To bring this phenomenon to our experience, as one of the remarkable symptoms of our time, is just as necessary a duty now as it is a painful one."[6] To mere historicism, which simply delights in the past as such, Nietzsche opposed the "No" of "the man

5. F. Nietzsche, *Unzeitgemässe Betrachtungen,* "Nietzsches Werke," Erste Abteil. (3. Aufl. Leipzig, 1895), I, 190 f.
6. Nietzsche, *Vom Nutzen und Nachteil der Historie für das Leben,* "Werke," I, 279 f.

above history" and to antiquarian history the real, monumental interpretation of it.

Whether the meaning of their doctrine is happiness or resignation or virtue or repentance men of superhistory have never been in agreement with each other, but regarding all historical ways of seeing the past they come to be of one mind on this proposition: the past and the present are one and the same; that is, in all their manifold variety they are equally typical—an omnipresence of imperishable types, a fixed structure of unchanged values and of eternally the same meaning.[7]

This was the sort of historical view that Nietzsche found embodied in Jacob Burckhardt and saw applied to all the great epochs of intellectual life: Hellenism, the dawn of Christianity, the Italian Renaissance. It is strange that Burckhardt should have been classed with Riehl and Freytag simply because his interest lay in the history of civilization. As a matter of fact, all that relates him to them is the common name that they all used to describe the trend of their investigations. But this name denotes two very different basic views and tendencies. Even Gothein, in his work on the programs of the history of civilization, obliterated this essential difference instead of working it out clearly. He reproached Schäfer because, in his attack on the history of civilization, he had fallen into the serious tactical error of seeking the enemy where he was not. Instead of setting up a straw man as an opponent he should have tried his arguments on the writings of both Burckhardt and Freytag.[8] Yet this linking together of the two writers is of dubious value, for the trend of Burckhardt's inquiry is of such a peculiar personal character as to make it hardly possible to assign him to any definite school.

Burckhardt's way is distinguished from that of most historical writers of the nineteenth century by the fact that his personal and intellectual sympathies lay in an entirely different direction. He could have professed himself as little a follower of Hegel as of Ranke, for he saw political power, and power in general, with very different eyes. To Hegel the state had become an actual proof of his basic thesis: that everything real is rational and everything rational is real. The state meant to him not only the reconciliation but the very identity of the ideal and the real. "The state is a spirit that exists in the world and consciously realizes itself therein. It is the progress

7. *Ibid.*, S. 292.
8. Gothein, *op. cit.*, S. 5.

of God in this world; its foundation is the power of reason realizing itself as will." [9]

For Ranke the nature of the state could not have been summed up in any such simple formula. The state was, to be sure, an "idea," but there were also other equally warranted and fundamental ideas, other potencies and basic energies of historical life which the state could not displace or simply override. On his view the state must protect and improve civilization by means of its laws and government, but it could not create civilization by itself, and the production of the goods of civilized life must be left to other powers.[10]

Nevertheless, however little Ranke's view of history would try to explain individual occurrences by direct reference to any divine purposes, it was founded upon the idea of divine guidance of events as a whole; and thanks to that he, too, came to a sort of theodicy of power. He had no doubt that power in itself is the appearance of a "spiritual being." Whole generations of historians after him have repeated this notion, that the state is in highest measure a moral power and that it is the moral reason of the people. This is precisely why they refused to consider the history of civilization to be something separate from and of equal rank with political history.[11]

To all this Burckhardt returned an uncompromising "No!" at the beginning of his *Weltgeschichtliche Betrachtungen.* He was too much a pessimist to believe in any such reconciliation of the rational with the real, and to his realism the apotheosis of might seemed merely a fraud. He found deception, too, in the idyllic portrayals of the earlier writings on German cultural history. He declared it a foolish illusion to hold, as Freytag insisted in his *Bilder aus der deutschen Vergangenheit,* that the "sense of duty and honesty" or "solidity, proficiency, and sincerity" had improved, as contrasted with earlier and ruder ages. Our presumption in thinking we live in the age of moral progress seemed ridiculous to him. "We judge everything by that degree of external security without which we could no longer survive, and condemn the past because this breath of life did not exist then, whereas even now horrors of all sorts impend such as war, as soon as "security" is suspended.[12] When Burckhardt wrote

9. G. W. F. Hegel, *Rechtsphilosophie,* "Sämtliche Werke," ed. G. Lasson (Leipzig, F. Meiner, 1911), VI, § 258, 195 ff.

10. For evidence of this view see M. Ritter, *Die Entwicklung der Geschichtswissenschaft an den führenden Werken betrachtet,* S. 382, 388.

11. See G. von Below, *Die deutsche Geschichtsschreibung,* S. 120 ff.

12. J. Burckhardt, *Weltgeschichtliche Betrachtungen,* ed. A. Oeri und E. Dürr, "Jakob, Burckhardt-Gesamtausgabe" (Stuttgart, Berlin, und Leipzig, Deutsche Verlags-Anstalt, 1929), VII, 49.

these words in 1868, in a period when "security" appeared finally
won, no one would have suspected that the historian would turn out
to be a prophet. He believed power as such incapable of any development toward an ethical goal. It would always remain what it is, and
"in itself it is evil." "Power is never satisfied; it is greedy and therefore unrealizable; hence it is unhappy and cannot but make others
unhappy. Inevitably one comes under the power of dynasties ambitious to maintain themselves and of individual 'great men,' and the
like; that is to say, of forces that are least interested in promoting
civilization." [13]

The originality of this view of history is only apparent when we
grasp the motives that led Burckhardt to this condemnation of power
and continually strengthened his aversion to it. It is obvious that he
did not judge as a moralist, or shrink from the sight of evil. On the
contrary, evil seems to have held a special fascination for him and
he might even be labeled, though most unjustly, an advocate of the
"immoral." When he thought he recognized real personal greatness
in history he acknowledged it, even though disapproving of its aims.

> *Übermacht, Ihr könnt es spüren,*
> *Ist nicht aus der Welt zu bannen;*
> *Mir gefällt zu conversieren*
> *Mit Gescheiten, mit Tyrannen.*[14]

These words of Goethe could well serve as a motto for Burckhardt's
history of Renaissance civilization. He forgave the blind impulse to
power when he encountered it in great men. No one has more im-
pressively described "unfettered egotism in its most terrible aspects,"
the "extreme blood-thirst of unbridled malice," the "wretched and
sinister" in the tyrants of the Renaissance, the Italian nobles, or
Cesare Borgia. The features of the picture are indelibly impressed
on us all. On the other hand he did not withhold moral judgment—
though it was not the most important thing to him. For he recognized in all that display of power merely the expression of natural
forces which must be seen and felt as such before inquiry could be
made as to their value or their unworthiness. "There is no question
here of praise or blame," he once said, "but of understanding the
spirit of an age in its vigorous individuality." All this he not only

13. *Ibid.*, S. 25, 73.
14.   Superior force, as you will find,
                 Can from the world ne'er banished be;
                 To talk with men of active mind,
                 And tyrants, too, this pleases me.

acknowledged but turned toward with manifest pleasure, for in the picture of the Renaissance that he wanted to paint light and shadow belonged together. Above all the boundless depravity he saw rising the "noblest harmonies of personalities and a glorious art." Precisely in its deep contradiction, its irreconcilable contrasts, the Renaissance seemed to him the true picture of humanity. He praised it for having first discovered and brought to light the full capacity of man; for having possessed not only the concept of humanity but also the substance thereof, and for this he thought it deserved everlasting thanks.[15]

But what Burckhardt forgave individuals he did not countenance in collective power. Here his judgments were diametrically opposed to those of most other historians. The misuse of power seemed to him most threatening and dangerous when it was not individual but organized misuse, for organization brought about the disappearance of that factor which alone could reconcile us to what in power was bad by nature. The tyranny of individuals might be terrible, but it was not necessarily against the human spirit and therefore not immoral in every sense of the word. But when great collective powers appeared on the scene and gave rise to an organized concentration of despotism the last refuge of the human spirit and morality was threatened. Then there arose that caricature, "the police state," with complete suppression of the individual. Burckhardt could not even reconcile himself to Plato's sketch of the ideal state. He declared it at variance with the nature of man, and still more with that of the Greeks, since it suppressed everything that depended upon individual development. The free many-sided character, the enormous wealth of forms, the widest diversity of Greek culture, Greek art, and Greek religion, all that was what delighted him most. Not its simplicity, in the sense of Winckelmann, but its gay color and variety attracted him.[16]

In religion and the state he saw essentially stable powers, and believed that of necessity they should strive to maintain themselves as they do. To him civilized culture not only did not coincide with these two powers, but by reason of its true nature was actually opposed to them. "Civilization," he wrote, "we call the sum total of those developments of the mind that occur spontaneously and claim no universal or enforced acceptance. It works unceasingly to modify and

---

15. See especially Burckhardt's *Kultur der Renaissance in Italien* (8. Aufl. Leipzig, E. U. Seemann, 1901), II, Vierter Abschnitt, Kap. iv, 25 ff. For a complete discussion see Karl Joël, *Jakob Burckhardt als Geschichtsphilosoph* (Basel, Helbing & Lichtenhahn, 1918), S. 16.

16. Burckhardt, *Weltgeschichtliche Betrachtungen,* S. 42 f.

dissolve both of the stable powers, except in so far as they have succeeded in making it wholly useful to themselves. Otherwise it is their critic, the clock that tells the hour at which their form and substance will no longer coincide."

This drama of civilization, which in most fertile epochs appears again and again in the form of tragedy, the cultural historian watches, and it is this that he knows how to unfold to the eyes of the mind. Burckhardt did not believe in the possibility of a peaceful solution, a solution that would not be tragic. For where Hegel and Ranke saw an "inscrutable harmony," ἁρμοίη ἀφανής in the sense of Heraclitus, he saw only constantly renewed conflict. At occasional happy moments it appeared to have been stilled, but it threatened incessantly to break out again, for the internal differences among the three powers of world history could not be composed. The state would repeatedly try to bring knowledge and art under a system of authority by virtue of "divine right." What might it not have done even in Assyria, Babylonia, Persia, and elsewhere to check the rise of all that is individual, which at the time would have passed as synonymous with evil? In all likelihood individuality tried every possible way to assert itself but finally succumbed to civil and religious restrictions, caste distinctions, and so on, without leaving a trace behind.

Hegel regarded civilization as the "self-activity of the idea," which followed a definite dialectical law. The separate factors drive one another forward; at first they appear antithetical and hostile, but at the supreme stage all opposition is suspended and the idea, as Absolute Idea, absorbs and reconciles all differences within itself. Ranke, too, who refuted any such philosophical interpretation of history, advocated a religious rather than a metaphysical theory of harmony. "The ideal essence of the history of the human race can be seen," he wrote in describing the encounter between Rome and Teutonism, "in the fact that during the struggle between the opposing interests of the state and the people, powers of increasing potency arose that transformed the whole situation and gave it another character." [17] Ranke denied "progress" in the sense of a universal guiding will promoting the development of the human race from one stage to the next, or of a spiritual character inherent in man that would of necessity drive matters toward a definite goal. He explained that neither view was philosophically tenable or historically demonstrable.[18] But a belief in the "continuous progress of

17. Ranke, *Weltgeschichte,* III, 8.
18. *Ibid.,* VIII, 175.

the universal mind" and the conviction likewise that over the centuries the human race had acquired a heritage consisting of social and material gains, but especially religious ones, still remained true for him. And in his opinion the moral and intellectual value of world history lay in the fact that it increasingly confirmed us in this faith.[19]

At this point Burckhardt's radical break with the traditional view of history is clearly apparent. All previous historiography, no matter which of the various directions it took, was consciously or unconsciously determined by the question which had been placed in the foreground by the very first work to be really concerned with the philosophy of history. Is history a chaos of fortuitous events, or can a meaning and a design be perceived in it? Saint Augustine's *De civitate dei* was supposed to reveal this mysterious plan as a plan for salvation, and the belief has always found followers and imitators. Even after the first centuries of the Renaissance, when the force of this theological manner of writing history had been spent, its underlying idea survived in "secular" form. The difference between Bossuet's *Discours sur l'histoire universelle* and Condorcet's *Esquisse d'un tableau historique des progrès de l'esprit humain* is far less than appears at first sight. Voltaire still continued to admire the work of Bossuet, even though he voiced the reproach that it consistently mounted imitation gems in gold.[20] But Burckhardt went much further. He regarded faith in a higher world plan as in every case poor solace, which could not compensate for actual moral wrong or undo or justify any act of violence. "Every violent deed that prospers," he declared, "is, to say the least, an offense; that is to say, a bad example. The only thing to be learned from successful misdeeds of the mighty is not to value life in this world more highly than it deserves." [21]

Obviously this is Schopenhauer speaking.[22] But how could Schopenhauer's philosophy possibly develop a great historian? And how could it produce such a "gem of historical literature" as Burckhardt's *Kultur der Renaissance*, which was the opinion even of those who were far from sharing his fundamental views? [23] Here is a remarkable phenomenon indeed, and an anomaly in the history of the mind that calls for explanation. On the basis of his own metaphysical premises Schopenhauer was entirely logical in denying all possibility not only of a philosophy of history but also of a science of it. A philosophy of his-

19. *Ibid.*, S. 6.
20. For further details see Cassirer, *Philosophie der Erklärung*, S. 290 ff.
21. Burckhardt, *op. cit.*, S. 126.
22. For Burckhardt's relation to the philosophy of pessimism see Joël, *op. cit.*, S. 64 ff.
23. See von Below, *Die deutsche Geschichtsschreibung*, S. 70.

tory was to him a logical inconsistency, for philosophy is the investigation of the nature of things and this has no history. It cannot be captured in the forms of space and time, which pertain solely to our subjective mode of perception. Nor is it susceptible of any meaning in terms of sense, for all attempts to give it such meaning become merely optimistic misrepresentations. What appears to us as history in the form of becoming is in essence and being one and the same thing: a blind will that knows not what it wills. To seek order here, a cosmos, an inner meaningful relationship, is like trying to make out groups of men and animals in cloud formations. "What history tells is in fact only the long, hard, and confused dream of humanity." [24] Nor can science, any more than metaphysics, ever hope to find anything in this dream upon which it can depend or from which it can even develop any sort of empirical "truth." For science aims not at the particular but at the universal, not at the temporal but at the permanent and enduring. Seen from this point of view "history is full of deception, and this is so not only in the actual rendering of it but even in its very essence, for while telling simply of individuals and particular occurrences it invariably pretends to be telling of something else; and yet from first to last it is merely repeating the same thing under different names and in other guises." [25] In so far as manifold appearances and changes are capable of any definite shape, in so far as anything permanent or typical can be discerned in them, it is *art* and not history that is to lay hold thereof. For, according to Schopenhauer, art rather than science is the true ideal vision. Here mankind succeeds in what is apparently impossible; here he frees himself from the fetters of the will, and so doing stands outside the wheel of time. He becomes the pure subject of knowing, devoid of will and free from time. Instead of the world of events in the form of an unbroken chain of cause and effect, means and ends, existence as such envelops him here; an existence belonging no longer to "reality," however, but to pure imagination. The imagination of art is the first step by which man can free himself from reality, from the dominance of the will. History pursues the thread of events; science pursues the restless and transitory stream of causes and effects, where with every goal attained one is torn away to farther ends, but art alone repeats the everlasting ideas gained by pure contemplation, the essential and permanent amid all the phenomena of the world. Its sole source is

24. A. Schopenhauer, *Die Welt als Wille und Vorstellung,* "A. Schopenhauers Sämtliche Werke" (3. Aufl. München, R. Piper & Co., 1911), II, Kap. xxxviii, S. 504.
25. *Ibid.,* S. 506.

the knowledge of ideas; its only purpose is to communicate this knowledge.[26]

There is no doubt that this view is related in many respects to that of Burckhardt, and that it must have aroused many and strong sympathies in him. He, too, turned to the past not for its own sake and he, too, was not content merely to bathe in the stream of becoming. It was not the flow of events that charmed him; he wanted to know that which was ever repeating itself, constant and typical. And he, too, did not regard the collecting and sifting of material as the final goal of history. "General facts," he said in his *Griechische Kulturgeschichte,* "should be more important on the whole than particular facts, the recurring more important than the unique." The "eternal Greek," seen as a form, was to him the essence of Hellenism, something more significant than any single factor. He was convinced that purely empirical knowledge would never suffice to give such a view of history, and that scientific abstraction would finally have to be superseded by "contemplation" and "intuition." Hence Mommsen's phrases that the historian probably belongs more among the artists than the scholars and that therefore he is not made but born, that he is not trained but trains himself, apply to no historian of the nineteenth century more closely, perhaps, than to Burckhardt.[27] He prepared himself unstintingly for insight into the historical world, and the real and proper means of so doing was from the very first fine art. We cannot think of his figure of Cicero apart from his history of civilization and the whole corpus of his work—Cicero forms an integrating element in it all.

For Burckhardt, too, the highest value of art, as of all free intellectual activity, was that it gives release from strict subservience to the will, from entanglement in the world of particular aims and individual "purposes." Only here did he find something "universal," something above the existence of man in civil society, and something that can only be embodied in individuals of genius.

There is a great diversity in that sort of "universal" which culminates in great individuals or is transformed in them. First, the searchers, discoverers, artists, poets, in short, the representatives of the spirit, must be considered separately . . . Artists, poets, philosophers, investigators, and discoverers do not come into collision with the aims to which the majority relate their views of the world. Their activities do not

---

26. *Ibid.,* § 36, S. 217 ff.
27. Mommsen, "Rektoratsrede," *Reden und Aufsätze,* S. 11.

affect the life, that is, the weal or woe, of the many . . . Artists, poets, and philosophers have just two functions: to bring the inner significance of the period and the world to ideal vision and to transmit this as an imperishable record to posterity.[28]

Not content with merely knowing what is matter for the special sciences, nay, even of philosophy when it is conscious of its manifold and enigmatic nature, the mind suspects the existence of other powers that correspond with its own mysterious powers. It finds whole worlds surrounding it that speak only in metaphors to what is imagination in itself: the arts . . . The arts are a doing, a creative power . . . To make manifest what is within, to be able to portray it so that it is an inner thing fully revealed, is one of the rarest of gifts. Many can reproduce externals as externals, but the achievement just mentioned arouses in the beholder or the listener the conviction that only that One who has done it is capable of doing such things and that he therefore has become irreplaceable.[29]

This aesthetic individualism of Burckhardt still corresponds throughout with Schopenhauer's basic view. To Schopenhauer genius was nothing but the most perfect *objectivity;* in other words, an objective as opposed to a subjective direction of the mind aiming at the person himself, that is, at the will. Accordingly genius is the capacity to remain wholly perceptive, to lose oneself in seeing and to free knowledge, which originally exists only for service of the will, from such subjection; in short, to leave entirely out of sight one's interests, desires, and purposes . . . in order to be only the purely knowing subject, the clear eye that scans the world.[30]

"Where there is no inner image to transfer to paper, where I cannot proceed from pure perception itself, I can accomplish nothing," said Burckhardt. "What I construct historically is a result not of critical thought and speculation but of imagination, which tries to fill the gaps in what I have intuited." [31]

But now comes a great difference. The "intuition" of Schopenhauer is that of the metaphysician, which led him beyond time, which was for him merely the form of appearances, and as long as we do not free ourselves from time the nature of things remains concealed. The "intuition" of Burckhardt, on the contrary, was a *historical* intuition. The pure world of images in which he was absorbed stood out before him in full plastic clarity in an immediate and timeless present,

28. Burckhardt, *op. cit.,* S. 163 f.
29. *Ibid.,* S. 167.
30. Schopenhauer, *op. cit.,* § 36, S. 217 ff.
31. Burckhardt, *Basler Jahrbuch* (1910), S. 109 f.; cited by Joël, *op. cit.,* S. 73.

as it were, but he became aware of an inner movement, a metamorphosis within it. To grasp and pursue this "becoming in being," the
transformations in the imaginative world of art, poetry, language,
mythology, religion, seemed to Burckhardt the highest duty of a
cultural history. Philosophy, as he saw it, was unable to do this:
"for history, that is, the coordinating, is not philosophy; and philosophy, which is busy with subordinating things under principles,
is not history." [32] "Contemplation," of course, is also the characteristic of the historian: it is not only his right and duty but at the same
time a most pressing need for him. "It is our freedom amidst our consciousness of the enormous universal bonds among things and the
stream of necessities." [33] But, unlike the metaphysician, the historian cannot raise himself at one stroke to the world of pure forms,
nor would he want to do so. For him form has its own proper being
and meaning only after it has revealed itself to his inner vision. In
the face of the great drama of this revelation both our individual
needs and our individual wishes are finally lost to view; we desire a
standpoint beyond the realm of desire, beyond all that is ordinarily
known as happiness or unhappiness.[34]

The mind must make its own the recollection of having lived through all
the different times in the world. What was once joy or grief must now
become knowledge, as actually is the case in the lives of individuals. Thus
the proverb "history is the master of life" (*historia vitae magistra*)
gains a higher, and, at the same time, a more modest meaning. We want
to become through experience not so much prudent (merely for the next
time) as wise (for all time).[35]

In this fashion the aesthetic wisdom which Burckhardt attributed
to history finally became a high ethical wisdom about life. Where
world history is rightly seen, where it is not represented merely as a
sum of external events but recognized as a story of forms of life,
there it gives thinking man an openness of the spirit for all that is
great—and this is one of the few certain conditions of higher spiritual
happiness.[36]

This intensely personal mood colors all Burckhardt's works. It has
little to do with the traditional ideals of political historiography, and
from the standpoint of the latter we are often apt to reproach Burck-

32. Burckhardt, *Weltgeschichtliche Betrachtungen*, S. 1.
33. *Ibid.*, S. 7.
34. Burckhardt, "Über Glück und Unglück in der Weltgeschichte," *Weltgeschichtliche Betrachtungen*, S. 192 ff.
35. *Ibid.*, S. 6 f.
36. *Ibid.*, S. 191.

hardt for being impractical. But if we take its measure by the ideal standards that he established and observed, we should have to say that such historiography has been really too insensitive to art. In no case should one expect to answer the question involved here by calling him no "true" historian but "almost more of an antiquary." [37] An "antiquary" could never have given Nietzsche what Burckhardt gave him. He could never have stirred him to the conviction that "knowledge of the past is at all times needed only to serve the present and the future, not to enfeeble the present or to tear the roots out of the vigorous powers of life for the future.[38]

37. See von Below, *op. cit.,* S. 71.

38. F. Nietzsche, *Unzeitgemässe Betrachtungen,* "Nietzsches Werke," Erste Abteil., I, 310.

XVII

The Theory of Psychological Types in History: Lamprecht

IN THE struggle for a modernization of the science of history Karl Lamprecht long appeared to be foremost. He was considered the extreme advocate of a new concept of history that seemed embodied in his person and in his work. It was actually to his keenest adversaries that he owed this fame. They were wont to see in him the most dangerous revolutionary, against whom all must unite in defense of the existing order, and they charged him with disloyalty to the best and highest intellectual traditions of history and with having betrayed it to materialism.

He had enemies in all camps. Not only was he obstinately opposed by the entire school of political historiography; he was regarded for years as the exponent of a naturalistic theory which others thought they had rooted out and finally disposed of by purely epistemological measures, by distinguishing between the historical order of concepts and those of natural science. But reviewing today the literature on the vehement Lamprecht controversy [1] one finds that it yielded relatively little in the way of principle, and it is impossible to escape the impression that the battle was largely in terms of catchwords and over catchwords. Furthermore, "modernity," as claimed by Lamprecht for his theory and as his opponents accepted it, can hardly be conceded today. Thinkers like Mommsen or Burckhardt seem in many respects far more modern than does Lamprecht.

He did not give up the "organic" view of romanticism though he tried to transform such fundamental concepts as the idea of a national spirit, to bring them nearer to the requirements of modern natural science. Even the continued influence of Hegel's philosophy can be plainly detected in Lamprecht's writings. When he declares it a basic principle of all historical progress that, during the course of great human developments there is a heightening of intensity of the original life of the spirit, in the sense that more and more aspects are brought into consciousness, one might think himself reading *Phenomenology of Mind.* This "intensification," which was supposed

1. A review of this literature is contained in E. Bernheim's *Lehrbuch der historischen Methode und der Geschichtsphilosophie* (5. und 6. Aufl. Leipzig, Duncker & Humblot, 1908), S. 710.

to disclose the real purport of the historical process and its goal, expresses in the language of psychology the very same principle that Hegel, as logician and metaphysician, included in the phrase that everything depended upon understanding and expressing "the true not only as substance, but ever so much more, as subject."

Something similar was Lamprecht's great and constant ambition, though he resorted to other measures. He relied not only on Hegel but above all on Herder, whose enthusiasm he shared for "the fullness of soul" that expressed itself in historical existence.[2] If we look ahead rather than backward we find his closest affiliation not with any empiricist of historical science but with such a phenomenon as Spengler, whose notion of a "cultural spirit" comes directly from Lamprecht's circle of ideas.

In order to do justice to Lamprecht's conception of history one must keep in mind the principle for which it contended. It is obvious that there are many defects in its execution and that he was unable to carry out the ambitious program that he had in mind, but there is little of theoretical value in singling out these evident faults with a view to refuting his work as a whole. The very scope of the material that he included, which was enormous, makes it easy for a critic to expose his deficiencies or errors in detail. His canvas was so broad that history, in the Greek sense of learning by research ($\iota\epsilon\tau o\rho\iota\eta$), would have to include virtually all the information obtainable from mankind. What he disapproved of in the preceding historiography was that it had been guilty of a wholly inadmissible restriction of its theme, not only in the treatment but in the very statement of its problem. No wonder it never became more than a mere fragment, or that it never had been able to unite into one organic whole the welter of particular facts that presented themselves.

According to Lamprecht this unity emerges only after we have resolved to treat events no longer in a single plane but to pass continually from one dimension to another. Political happenings constitute only one sector; but besides that there are economic processes, science and religion, poetry, music, and the various forms of fine art. But even this is not enough; for our historical knowledge is mute

---

2. Herder's "enthusiastic appreciation of the sociophilosophical elements in history," which formed the basis of the whole romantic interpretation of history, was emphasized by Lamprecht in his lectures, *Moderne Geschichtswissenschaft* (Freiburg i/B, H. Heyfelder, 1905), S. 10 ff. He expressly noted that the forms of consciousness, whose national aspect is best designated by the term "national spirit," "quite evidently represent the living forces of the course of history," although following modern psychology he did not allow of any substantial reference in the concept of "spirit." See *Einführung in das historische Denken* (2. Abdruck, 1913), S. 66 f.

without inclusion of the facts of prehistory, of anthropology, and ethnology. To be convinced of the intrinsic law that prevails throughout the history of mankind the "whole remaining record of humanity" must always be worked through.[3] And just as little should there be any limitation in spatial bounds. Even geographical barriers must fall, and one's gaze must encompass the whole earth.

When it is recalled that upon Mommsen's death at the age of almost eighty-six even he had to leave unfinished his work on Roman history, and that eventually not only he himself, with his immense capacity for work, but nearly all the great academic institutions had been engaged on it, one is amazed again and again at the tremendous self-confidence with which Lamprecht went at his task. His *Deutsche Geschichte*, with its twelve volumes, was to be only the first essay. He was convinced that the "succession of eras" that he had tried to demonstrate in it represented a general law that could be established equally for Greek, Egyptian, Israelite, Assyrian, Chinese, and Japanese history. All that would be required was careful examination of the factual material and a consistent prosecution of the inductive method.

Lamprecht was in no way disconcerted when oversights or mistakes in detail were pointed out to him. Historical criticism that spends its time in demonstrating such flaws and believes it has fulfilled its office in so doing, he said in reference to Herder, can hardly be sure of its reward.

No man, and no product of all a man's labor either, is like a perfectly thought-out book, and merely to point out lacunae in some pages and deficiencies in others must seem much more an envious job of rival contemporaries than a historian's true duty where there are judgment and perspective. The historian is concerned rather with the total creative achievement of previous times, and he must base his particular judgment on any present case upon all this knowledge.[4]

Lamprecht complained repeatedly that his adversaries had shifted the real point at issue by representing the problem not as one of the distinctive nature of historical knowledge but of a general Weltanschauung. They had tried to brand him an adherent of some definite philosophical system, whether they called it materialism or positivism. But nothing of that sort was central to his theory, for the method by which he had discovered it had been "thoroughly inductive and practical." He insisted:

3. Lamprecht, "Der Normalverlauf geschichtlicher Entwicklung," *Moderne Geschichtswissenschaft*, S. 73 ff.
4. *Ibid.*, S. 22.

There can be no really scientific pursuit of history if it be regarded as depending on the assumptions of any philosophy whatsoever, be this idealism, positivism, or any other kind. The science of history is an inductive science, within the limits of those theoretical restrictions and supplementings that are admissible for induction, and that is why contrary principles and trends can be established, because of the interim character of the inductive conclusions and the varied approximations that are made.[5]

Any criticism that is to do justice to Lamprecht's intentions must keep this point prominently in mind and address itself not so much to his conclusions as to his point of departure, considering how far he has gone rather than the ultimate goal. Even the question of Lamprecht's originality can be answered only thus. Hence while the essential points of contact between his theory and Comte's philosophy are unmistakable, he quite rightly defended himself, it seems to me, against those who wanted to stamp him merely a pupil or an imitator.[6] For he had not found in Comte precisely that element which served as the whole foundation of his theory of history, nor could he ever have done so. If one surveys Comte's system of the sciences he will be struck by the fact that psychology had no place whatsoever in it. The advance of knowledge led from mathematics to astronomy, from there to physics and chemistry, then to biology, and thence straightway to social statics and dynamics. Thus sociology was affiliated directly with the science of organic life, without need of psychology as a connecting link. The reason was that Comte did not recognize any purely introspective psychology, because he regarded all self-observation as mere illusion. In his opinion a psychic fact could only be ascertained in its connection with bodily phenomena, and for this physiology was, and always would be, the only resort.[7]

Here a sharp distinction between Comte and Lamprecht is immediately apparent, for the latter regarded psychology not only as an ancillary science to history but as its only possible scientific basis. "History in itself," he wrote,

is nothing but applied psychology, and so it is clear that theoretical psychology must be the key to its thorough understanding. . . . But it is one thing to know of this relationship and quite another to corroborate it. For the latter it is necessary that historical appreciation should

5. Lamprecht, *Alte und neue Richtungen in der Geschichtswissenschaft,* S. 3; see also *Die kulturhistorische Methode* (Berlin, R. Gaertner, 1900), S. 26, 33.

6. Lamprecht, *Moderne Geschichtswissenschaft,* S. 89; *Die kulturhistorische Methode,* S. 33.

7. See above, pp. 243–244.

include the deepest elementary processes, or precisely those that psychology first of all elucidates, and necessary, too, that the development of individual psychology should at least . . . progress far enough toward intellectual comprehension of these elementary processes.[8]

When Comte rejected psychology and refused to see in it the basis for the Geisteswissenschaften he was thinking especially of the form of it that he saw incorporated in the French "ideologies" of Jouffroy and Cousin. Ideological psychology seemed to him only disguised metaphysics, and he denied it all title to strictly scientific value.[9] In Germany, on the other hand, the development of scientific psychology appeared for a long time previously to have entered upon another stage. Here one might well believe that it had gained a firm empirical foundation, and one rigorously exact. Herbart had developed a mechanics of ideas which he tried to fashion after the analogue of mathematics, and such disciples and pupils as Lazarus and Steinthal had gone on from there to found a social psychology. Then Fechner's *Elemente der Psychophysik* seemed to take the final step toward opening the way to the mathematicizing of the psychic, since the relation of stimulus to sensation had been ascertained to be a quantitative one.

All these preliminary investigations were brought to fulfillment by Wundt, according to Lamprecht, and he had no doubt that a "psychic mechanics" complete in its main lines was now ready. He believed it would shortly be possible to transfer this mechanics from individual processes to those processes of the collective mind. With that the last barriers would disappear, and history would be resolved into applied psychology. What had always been simply a desideratum in the system of historical materialism would at last find its scientific fulfillment.

Lamprecht thought that the earlier materialism could not fill in the missing element because it had either lacked the most important connecting link or had willfully overlooked it. Materialism had simply wanted to force an identity between the "mental" and the "material" instead of being satisfied with a continuous gradation from one realm to the other. Science as such needed no substantial identity of the two; it was enough if the circle of causality could be closed by showing how they interacted with each other in accordance with fixed and

8. Lamprecht, *Moderne Geschichtswissenschaft,* S. 16 f. See especially *Die kulturhistorische Methode,* S. 12 ff.

9. For details on Comte's struggle against contemporary French psychology see L. Lévy-Bruhl, "La Psychologie," *La Philosophie d'Auguste Comte,* Liv. II, chap. v, p. 219 ff.

general laws. This question was now settled in principle if not in all
its details, for proof could be confidently brought that the same
factors and laws which the modern psychology of the individual had
attained were valid for the mechanics of the great social-psychological movements of history.[10] "Today the demand for this application of psychology," wrote Lamprecht, "is beginning to determine
the way of studying the Geisteswissenschaften, and a new synthesis
is beckoning us on to that goal of its fulfillment, in contrast to the
mere disjointed patchwork of recent times." [11]

Lamprecht was certain that economic phenomena should not be
forgotten in any such synthesis; on the contrary, they had a central
significance. He himself had first arrived at his own statement of his
problem by this route, for his first work, which remained a guide for
him, had dealt with the development of German economic life in the
Middle Ages.[12] His method differed from Marxism, however, in that
he did not try to understand the spirit of an age through its economic
relationships, but sought conversely to understand the latter through
the former. He set up his own psychologism against economic materialism and explained that the motives of economic activities could
be understood with certainty only when one had succeeded in interpreting them psychologically, that is, by tracing them back to their
final psychic motives. Restriction to economic motives alone, in his
opinion, could result in nothing other than barren abstractions, for
the collective psychological character of human history would be
overlooked thereby.[13]

No less decisively, to be sure, did Lamprecht reject the "over-
idealistic view" that it is possible to isolate the intellectual powers.[14]
Economics was the supporting stratum of historical events and must
always be recognized as one of their essential foundations. But even
the history of particular nations could never be properly appreciated
in terms of economic, social, and political history alone; otherwise
the significance, past or present, of individual human societies for
universal history would never appear in its true light.

Correspondingly any theory of the character and progress of whole
cultural periods must never take its point of departure from economic
and social ferments alone in the conviction that they are throughout and
exclusively determined by such elements. The theory must take its prin-

10. Lamprecht, *Moderne Geschichtswissenschaft,* S. 15 ff.
11. *Ibid.,* S. 64.
12. Lamprecht, *Deutsches Wirtschaftsleben im Mittelalter* (Leipzig, A. Dürr, 1885).
13. Lamprecht, *Einführung* . . . , S. 44 ff., 143 ff.
14. Lamprecht, *Alte und neue Richtungen* . . . , S. 70.

ciples of classification from the highest life of the mind. Not by their roots but by their blossoms are cultural ages to be defined and classified.[15]

There can be no doubt that Lamprecht's theory fulfilled an important function in its time, that it was fitted to free political historiography in certain of its forms from the narrowness and bias into which it had gradually sunk, and that in this regard it worked as a significant ferment. The violent and often extravagant attacks to which he was exposed show what a shaking up his theory produced. But the criticism and polemic were one thing, and the positive establishment and working out of the thesis quite another. Lamprecht was in agreement with Taine and French positivism in his desire to raise history to the rank of a natural science and transform it from a purely descriptive to a scientifically explanatory discipline. Any critique of his system must begin at this point. It must ask whether his ideas corresponded with what he had set up as a standard and a guide. Here it becomes apparent immediately how far performance lagged behind intent, for none of the "type" concepts that he coined can logically lay claim to be anything more than simply descriptive. Even were the accuracy of the description conceded, the task of explanation on which his eyes were fixed as the true ideal would in no wise have been performed.

He arranged a "succession of eras," which by and large were supposed to recur in the same form. After an original period of "symbolism" there followed a stage of "typism" and then one of "conventionalism"; after these came "individualistic" and "subjective" periods, and eventually the age of increased sensitivity and reaction to stimuli (*Reizsamkeit*) in which we are living closed the series. It is strikingly obvious that none of these concepts can lay claim to being strictly defined in a *scientific* sense, much less to being unambiguous. We have the case here of a very wide-meshed net and a crude attempt at the provisional arrangement of highly heterogeneous phenomena. Yet in his hands this scheme, which Lamprecht employed as a means of survey and primary orientation, gradually began to take on life in a most remarkable way. Instead of a system of historical relationships beside which others equally meritorious could be placed, it became the expression of *objective forces* that determine and dominate historical events. He expressly stated that not only German history, for which he had first developed his sequence of periods, but the history of ancient civilizations as well was "constructed" essentially in accordance with the same pattern.[16] This

15. Lamprecht, *Moderne Geschichtswissenschaft*, S. 119.
16. Lamprecht, *Einführung* . . . , S. 131.

pattern gives the picture of the "normal course," which can never be changed in its typical fundamental order though on occasion, of course, it would be modified by the influence of local or temporal circumstances.[17]

Lamprecht realized clearly that the proof for such a thesis could be given only inductively. But what a mighty induction would be needed to do so! Audaciously he disregarded all such difficulties, being sure of his goal and expecting to reach it, even though a long road still remained to be traveled before its actual attainment. "The course and the character of the epochs that are demonstrable in German history," he insisted with unshaken and dogmatic assurance, "mark the history of other peoples as well, in so far as historical sources permit verification. Nay, more. No people have yet been found in which this course could not be authenticated." [18] When Lamprecht gave his lectures in America in 1904 and presented his thesis, he expressed the hope of bringing proof himself of its universal applicability to history during his own lifetime.[19] He thought he had reached a point at which one might confidently venture upon the step of transforming an inductive into a deductive theory. He could now grasp the remarkable and paradoxical notion of a "history" that was to sketch only the main features of events and establish their general order, and, moreover, even abstract them from space and time.[20] Thus space and time, the principles by which individual things are distinguished (*principia individuationis*) would be transcended. Out of a survey of the development of all the great human societies there had come the authentic and perfect types of cultural epochs, "by elimination of individual and singular elements and emphasis on the common ones." [21] The more energetically Lamprecht worked out the meaning of the formulation and put it into effect the plainer it showed the danger lurking in his theory. For the outcome of such disregard of the conditions of space and time can hardly claim to be a "theory" of history; it threatens to become a scientific "nowhere" (utopia) and "nowhen" (uchronia).

What an obstacle Lamprecht faced here can best be made clear by comparing him with other investigators to whom at first glance he seems very close in respect to his fundamental views. Not infrequently he has been placed directly with Burckhardt,[22] and he him-

17. *Ibid.*, S. 139 ff.

18. *Ibid.*, S. 131.

19. Lamprecht, *Moderne Geschichtswissenschaft*, S. 94.

20. *Ibid.*, S. 92; *Einführung* . . . , S. 149.

21. Lamprecht, *Moderne Geschichtswissenschaft*, S. 91.

22. See, for example, the concluding chapter in M. Ritter, "Die politische Geschichte und die Kulturgeschichte," *Die Entwicklung der Geschichtswissenschaften an den führenden Werken betrachtet*, Buch 5, Kap. v, S. 421.

self, in his struggle against political historiography, appealed again and again to Burckhardt's example and ideal.[23] Both agreed, in fact, in their intention to give not simply vertical sections but cross sections of the events of history. They would not have it devoted only to following a Heraclitean stream of things but sought something enduring and permanent in it. The subject matter of history does not simply merge with time; it possesses a dimension that more or less transcends time. Thus Burckhardt declared,

So it followed *after* history and provided vertical sections; it proceeded chronologically . . . Our starting point is the only permanent one and it is for us the only possible one: to begin with struggling, suffering, acting man as he is, ever was, and ever shall be . . . The philosophers of history always viewed the past as something in contrast to ourselves and antecedent to us, who are completely developed, but we see that which is *recurrent, constant, typical*, something echoing within ourselves and intelligible to us.

For in Burckhardt's opinion the spirit is changeable but not perishable; it creates new forms continually, but in each one of these it expresses its unitary and enduring nature.[24] In the same sense Lamprecht defined the "Kultur" of an age as an expression of the total psychic condition dominant at the time—a "diapason" sounding through all psychic phenomena of the period and hence throughout all its historical events: for all historical occurrence is psychic in nature. He therefore sought for concepts so inclusive that not only a definite single trend but all happenings of a given period could be classified under them. "They are concepts of a certain cultural age regarded as a certain psychic diapason of the age." [25]

But such psychological abstractions were wholly foreign to Burckhardt. By the recurrent and the typical, knowledge of which was the historian's task, he understood something fundamentally different from Lamprecht's notion. What he wanted to disclose in all his chief works—in his presentation of Constantine the Great as in his histories of Greek and Renaissance civilization—was the spiritual texture of certain periods. For him this was not just something transitory; it had a firm, definite, and concrete form. It was a pattern that had a distinct outline and whose characteristic features could be described. But this description, according to him, could never be anything but a product of "intuition." We can grasp in imagination what is "con-

23. See, for example, Lamprecht, *Die kulturhistorische Methode*, S. 31.
24. Burckhardt, *Weltgeschichtliche Betrachtungen*, S. 2 ff.
25. Lamprecht, *Die kulturhistorische Methode*, S. 26.

stant" but cannot express it in the purely conceptual form of general rules or laws.

This artistic intuition of Burckhardt was not enough for Lamprecht, who demanded that it have a scientific foundation. History became for him a sequence of definite psychic occurrences that were subject in their course to a general law of nature and had to follow one another in the way that they did. Always and everywhere an age of typism had to succeed one of symbolism, to be replaced in turn by an age of conventionalism, and all according to one and the same uniform rhythm. It was this iron ring of psychological necessities that embraced the life of humanity. What we call individuality was always only a local and temporal variation, never an infraction, of this universal rule. The further Lamprecht progressed on his way the more this rule threatened to harden into a stereotype that somehow as a generality applied to all that happened yet never showed us the concrete and individualized picture of history.

Burckhardt, on the contrary, not only remained at the level of what we can directly observe but thought that all abstractions should serve only to lead us deeper and deeper into the intuitive world. Filled with an insatiable desire for such insight, he said that his study of history, like his pursuit of art, was a result of this "enormous thirst." [26] In this respect he delimited his procedure quite as definitely from philosophy as from science. As a historian he had no desire to compete with either, and he did not strive for the same form of the "universal" that is determining for them both and sets their direction. If this sort of universal constitutes the scientific character of a discipline, then he was ready and willing to admit that "history is the most unscientific of all the sciences."

Lamprecht would never have been capable of such an expression, for it would have seemed a betrayal of all his ideals. But Burckhardt said, "philosophical and historical concepts are essentially of a different kind and different origin; the former must be as fixed and closed as possible, the latter as fluid and open." [27] This fluidity and openness are missing from the Lamprecht types and from the rigid connections, too, that were supposed to exist between them. It was precisely Burckhardt's restraint and moderation in regard to all speculation that made him capable of his highest accomplishments in the field of historical research. In a letter written when he was twenty-four years old to Karl Fresenius he renounced all tendency to abstract speculative thought. "My substitute for that," he added,

26. See above, pp. 278 f.
27. Burckhardt, *op. cit.*, S. 62.

is direct intuitive observation that is directed more and more every day toward what is essential, and every day becomes keener . . . You cannot possibly imagine how, through my perhaps one-sided striving for the facts of history, the works of art and monuments of all periods gain meaning as witnesses of past stages of development of the mind . . . The supreme end of the history of mankind is the development of the mind toward freedom. This is my leading conviction and so my studies can never play me false, never fail me, but must remain my good genius all my life long.[28]

In this frame of mind Burckhardt regarded as of little significance the quarrels over history as a science and the controversies about method in general that marked Lamprecht's whole life and scientific development. He saw no need of them, saying that to him history was and always would be "poetry in the highest measure." "It must be thoroughly understood," he added in explanation, "that I do not regard it as something romantically fanciful, which would lead to nothing, but as a wonderful process of transformation and a new, ever new, revelation of the spirit. On this edge of the world I stand and stretch out my arms toward the original source of all things; and so to me history is pure poetry that can be mastered through intuition." [29] Lamprecht had no inclination thus to stand still on the edge of things. He, too, was strongly drawn toward the fine arts and actually fell back on them again and again when he wanted help in proving the correctness of his theory, until finally this material seemed to him more important and more convincing than mere facts and written documents.[30] So he likewise emphasized that so far as historiography was concerned with the working out and presentation of what is intuited as individual, it could not be successful solely by means of general scientific concepts. Here art must enter, for art alone could succeed in giving life to that which was material for the imagination and not for logically elaborated concepts.[31] But for Lamprecht this was only the beginning of history, not its goal. Its end and scientific completion, after the absorption in details and collecting them inductively and comparing them, must always be to establish the final, all-inclusive, general concept. Such supreme concepts "for the exhaustive subsumption of all psychic phenomena pertaining to the development of human societies, that is, of all his-

---

28. See "An Karl Fresenius—Berlin, 19. Juni 1842," *Jakob Burckhardts Briefe,* ed. F. Kaphan (Leipzig, Dieterich'sen Verlagsbuchhandlung, 1938), S. 58.
29. *Ibid.,* S. 61.
30. Lamprecht, *Einführung* . . . , S. 71 ff.; *Moderne Geschichtswissenschaft,* S. 29 ff.
31. Lamprecht, *Die kulturhistorische Methode,* S. 6, 35.

torical events generally," Lamprecht believed he himself had discovered in his "epochs of civilization." This concept "satisfied for
the first time the demand for a truly scientific classification and
thoughtful penetration of the world of historical facts; the history
of civilization is the first really scientific historical method beyond
the mere critical working up of single facts and series of facts." [32]
This drive toward the classification of phenomena finally proved to
be far stronger in Lamprecht than that for the direct view of things,
and at times almost threatened to suppress the latter entirely. It led
to an intense concentration of material, which had to be reduced to
a few leading aspects because of this compression. It is characteristic
of his procedure that in his New York lectures Lamprecht could
venture to give an account of the history of the German people from
about 500 B.C. to the present in one single hour. He dared to do this
because for him this history had gradually become simply a "psychological history," and because he was convinced that it must always
take the same simple and uniform course exhibited in the psychology
of the individual in his progress from childhood to youth, to manhood, and thence to old age.[33] "The order of things that we have
become acquainted with," he said, "is similar to that of the psychic
mechanism of the individual, since the laws of social psychology are
now known to be only cases of the application of the laws found in
the psychology of the individual." [34]

Here, too, he certainly overestimated how much the scientific
fundamentals upon which he depended would sustain, for what biology or psychology has ever furnished empirical proof that the development of the individual passes through the series of stages that
Lamprecht regarded as necessary and decisive for mankind? Even
admitting a thoroughgoing parallelism between ontogeny and phylogeny, the former could not provide what was here demanded of it.
A canon of development that works itself out in an unbroken series
of a definite number of cultural epochs, as the individual mind completes its specific development in passing through the various age
periods,[35] might well be called a sort of inference by analogy, but
certainly not an inductive inference.

It is well known that analogies of the sort have appeared again
and again in discussions of the philosophy of history, but they are
far too indefinite, and leave room for so many different possibilities

32. *Ibid.,* S. 29 f.
33. Lamprecht, *Einführung* . . . , S. 66 ff.
34. Lamprecht, *Moderne Geschichtswissenschaft,* S. 82 f.
35. *Ibid.,* S. 98.

that they cannot be used to establish any such simple and unequivocal canon as that of Lamprecht. The assertion that "epochs of civilization" in their sequence and character can be traced back to the simple working of psychological laws that the science of psychology has succeeded in developing" [36] is the postulate of method upon which his whole treatment of history depended. But it is a long way from the setting up of such a postulate to its fulfillment, and the subsequent development of psychology has very definitely shown how little it was in a position, in the last decades of the nineteenth century, to establish such a simple law for all historical existence.

Even Wundt hardly ventured on anything of the kind in the transition from individual to folk psychology. If one meant to trust to psychology as a guide here it could be done only if the science were established on another methodological foundation. But attempts of the sort, like that of Dilthey in his *Ideen zu einer beschreibenden und zergliedernden Psychologie*, were rejected by Lamprecht, for he thought them refuted by the negative criticism of Ebbinghaus.[37] He believed himself on firm and unshaken ground when he relied upon the experimental psychology of his time, and roundly declared it to be the "normal foundation for the science of history." [38]

If one examines not his theory but his practice as a scientist, it will be found that he held very loosely to what science authorized, for the results of the psychology which he invoked were of a very vague sort and would never have sufficed to justify such concrete and detailed assertions as his theory contained. Sometimes he employed "laws" as general as the rules of empirical association by similarity from which to draw far-reaching conclusions on social-psychological processes.[39] In such instances the fulfillment of the psychological schemata was invariably left to historical "intuition." Psychology might have provided the frame, but Lamprecht was wrong in his belief that it could also draw the picture of historical development as such, or even sketch its main features.

36. Lamprecht, *Die kulturhistorische Methode,* S. 38.
37. Lamprecht, *Alte und neue Richtungen* . . . , S. 38.
38. *Ibid.,* S. 19.
39. Lamprecht, *Moderne Geschichtswissenschaft,* S. 114.

XVIII

Influence of the History of Religion on the Ideal of Historical Knowledge: Strauss, Renan, Fustel de Coulanges

LAMPRECHT once pointed out that in the struggle between the champions of purely political historiography and those of the history of civilization the real point at issue had been gradually lost to view. There could be no question of committing history to a more or less definite content and holding it exclusively to this: "A science is characterized only secondarily by the extent of the field to which it relates; only with the rarest exceptions, and never through the idea, however profound, of its own internal course of development, will it make progress through the conquest of new territory, for this happens only by an improvement of its methods." [1]

The boundary line thus drawn was justified, in epistemological respects, and might have served to bring the discussion back to its proper channel and keep it from going astray. But on the other hand the development of science showed at every step that although questions of content and method are logically distinct, conclusions as to the possibility or necessity of their complete *separation* cannot be based on this difference in the concrete work of scientific research itself. Here there is rather a constant reciprocal influence and mutual fertilization on the part of both factors. Every extension of the domain of a science reacts on the concept of its method; every step taken beyond its former territory drives it to deeper reflection on the character and individuality of the means by which it acquires knowledge. Hence the question of the content of history and that of its form are continually interrelated. We have already shown that fact in several typical examples. When Mommsen declared that the structure of a state could be understood only through its system of government and laws, the one-sided dominance of the purely philological method came to an end. The connection between philology and linguistics on the one hand and law and political science on the other was raised to a principle of historical knowledge.[2] For Burckhardt also it was of the highest importance to separate state, re-

1. K. Lamprecht, *Alte und neue Richtungen in der Geschichtswissenschaft*, S. 4.
2. See above, pp. 258 f.

ligion, and civilization as the three fundamental forces through whose evolution all historical activity took place.[3] He had to postulate and develop a special method for each, an independent way to historical knowledge. In so doing he was occasionally absorbed in the history of religion, although in his first work, on the period of Constantine the Great, he made use of Christianity, as the best and classical example, to show what changes a religious belief must pass through when it emerges from the stage of pure inner conviction to become a state and a world religion. But he did not go any further along this road subsequently, because art was more important and decisive than religion for his way of looking at civilization. In a letter of the year 1842 he expressly declared that history was for him a "series of the most beautiful graphic compositions." It has been truly said that Burckhardt "was always the aesthetic historian; he was also, as a historian, a seeker of pictures, and as a teacher he fell back ultimately on the history of art as his favorite domain. For him the picture always prevailed over the tragic emotion, the beautiful over the terrible, the humanist over the pessimist." [4]

But what form must the ideal of historical knowledge and the historical method necessarily take if both the history of religion and the history of art appeared on the scene with equal claims and strove after a fashion for mastery? It is obvious that in a purely *systematic* respect the germ of a profound problem lies here. By its very nature religion can never escape from the sphere of the "image," the sphere of intuition and fantasy. From them it derives its peculiar power; it would wither away and die were it not continuously nourished from this soil. On the other hand the image can never be treated as merely a picture, as an arbitrary play of the powers of imagination. The image has a meaning, in that it not only represents the truth but is the truth itself.

All philosophy of religion has constantly revolved about this conflict and sought to resolve it in one way or another. But the issue takes on a new form as soon as it is shifted from the philosophy of religion to the *history* of religion. This was first done in the nineteenth century, and with it came about, too, the "historicism" of that century in its peculiar and specific form. We have said above that it would be inaccurate and misleading to follow the custom of denying to the eighteenth century all feeling for the historical whatsoever. The period actually was possessed of such feeling but simply had not

3. J. Burckhardt, "Von den drei Potenzen," *Weltgeschichtliche Betrachtungen,* S. 20 ff.

4. K. Joël, *Jakob Burckhardt als Geschichtsphilosoph,* S. 105.

proved it in great and lasting works.[5] There could be very little
benefit for religion and the knowledge of religion from this quarter.
It is true that Semler's *Abhandlung von der freien Untersuchung
des Kanons* (1771) established the principles of historical biblical
criticism even in the eighteenth century, and Lessing understood the
development of the various systems of faith as a progressive and divine "education of the human race." Yet none of these suggestions
could be completely developed in that period. What stood in the way
was the fact that even where the historical character of religion began to be known itself, another of its essential features remained
as mysterious as ever. Its origin and nature could not be understood
without a grasp of the specific nature of the *mythical consciousness.*
But here the period of the Enlightenment stood at the limits of its
comprehension and found itself face to face with a riddle which it
could not even understand as such with the means at its disposal, to
say nothing of providing a solution.

Only one thinker of the eighteenth century escaped these limitations. Giambattista Vico may be called the real discoverer of the
myth. He immersed himself in its motley world of forms and learned
by his study that this world has its own peculiar structure and time
order and language. He made the first attempts to decipher this
language, gaining a method by which to interpret the "sacred pictures," the hieroglyphics, of myth. Herder followed Vico. Yet even
these two were not fully clear about the peculiar character of myth.
They recognized and clearly grasped the distinction between the
mythical and the rational but were not yet equipped to see the difference between the mythical in its distinctive and quite independent
nature and the world of poetry, the "poetic." In this quarter the
lines of division, of which they had just become aware, were liable
to obliteration. Myth was regarded and interpreted as something
purely aesthetic.

Herder's first writings show how far this interpretation could go
and how fruitful it proved. He had the feeling that here he was
standing on new ground, and was just as conscious of the significance
of his viewpoint as he was of its limitations. He boasted of having
read the Bible as no other before him had done, and believed that it
then became "a holy scripture revealed after centuries of mystery." [6]
But he had a suspicion, too, that this sort of interpretation contained problems within it for the future. "Then trouble will begin,"

5. See above, pp. 217–218.
6. See especially Herder, *Älteste Urkunde der Menschengeschichte,* I, "Werke," ed.
Suphan, VI, 195 ff.

he wrote to Hamann, "until the day arrives when, through *facta* and *acta*, all will be unsealed. I am happy to have prepared, proclaimed, and contributed to this from afar." [7] Herder's historical sense, which could penetrate the future as well as the past, did not betray him here. All the seeds that he had sown grew and flourished in romanticism, and it was believed that the harvest time had come.

Schelling followed upon Herder, and was persuaded that only on the basis of his own theory would a true philosophy of mythology be possible. His philosophy would not leave myth at the mercy of sheer intellect and its critical faculty, but defended the right of myth to that element of fantasy in which it lived and moved and had its being. Yet Schelling's philosophy did not make it merely the play of an aesthetic fancy but actually attributed to it a truth *sui generis*. Myth was thought to conceal within itself a special sort of "reason," reducible to or comparable with nothing else. Looked at from the side of content it seemed to be nothing but fiction and fable, and, so regarded, it is in the greatest contrast with philosophy, which should know only the truth. The form of the myth, however, is quite another thing. It is nothing fixed but is evolving and variable—and its variability too is no matter of mere chance, for it is the expression of an inner law of myth itself.

There are subjects that philosophy must regard as wholly without relation to it. Among them belongs everything that has no essential reality, that exists as something only in the arbitrary opinion of man. The mythological process, however, has arisen in man independently of his wishes and thoughts. . . . Mythology is a natural, a necessary growth . . . a true whole, something definitive and held within certain limits, a world in itself . . . In the end the dead, the motionless, is counter to philosophy. But mythology is essentially active and self-moving in accordance with an indwelling law. It is actually the highest human consciousness that is stirring in myth, and through the very contradiction in which it involves itself and which none the less it surmounts, it proves that it is something real, true, and necessary.[8]

With that a new fundamental principle for the understanding of mythology was established. For the first time within the frame of a philosophical system the proposition was consistently developed that the world of myth must be understood in its own terms and

7. Herder. See Hamann, "Brief Herders an Hamann vom Mai 1774," *Schriften,* ed. F. Roth (Berlin, G. Reimer, 1824), V, 71.

8. F. W. J. v. Schelling, *Einleitung in die Philosophie der Mythologie,* "Sämmtliche Werke," Zweite Abteil. (Stuttgart und Augsburg, J. G. Cotta, 1856), I, 202, 207, 221 f.

not in those of any other. Myth is not an utterly strange affair but
has its own real meaning. The light in which it is seen ought not to
be simply a reflected light but must originate within it. In place of
the allegorical explanation of myth given previously—so Schelling
expressed the idea—must come the "tautegorical" interpretation,
that it means exactly what it says. We must cease to see myth only
as the husk concealing another sort of truth, whether this be regarded
in the sense of an "explanation" of definite natural phenomena or as
a moral truth. But it would not do either to reduce it to art and try
to understand it merely as "aesthetic illusion." Myth is not a fiction,
for that is the work of individuals who abandon themselves to the
free activities of fancy. In myth there is no such freedom or, better
said, no such chance. On the contrary, everything in it is a necessity,
imposed on us not from without, by the existence of "things," but
from within, through the nature of consciousness. This consciousness is the real "active subject" (*subjectum agens*) of mythology.

"The things with which man is dealing in the mythological process
are not really things but forces arising in consciousness itself . . .
The mythological process has to do not with objects of nature but
with the purely creative powers whose original witness is consciousness itself." This idea of setting human consciousness itself in the
place of inventors, poets, or any other individuals and treating it
as something which is necessary and to that extent "objective" in its
unfolding is the essence of Schelling's "philosophy of mythology."
What was most important and fundamental in it was not the exposition given in Schelling's lectures but the fact that he set the task to
be performed.

We shall not go on to ask in what way this proposal proved fruitful for the systematic investigation of myth,[9] since we are now concerned only with the consequent reaction of this new interpretation
upon historical thinking. It was at once apparent that a barrier had
been removed, which in a certain sense must have seemed insurmountable throughout the whole eighteenth century. As long as myth appeared to be only fable or fiction, no more was to be seen in its dis-
semination, in mythical tradition, than a sort of thoroughgoing
delusion. One might try to justify this on moral or religious grounds,
to defend and uphold it as a "pious fraud," but nothing in its character was changed thereby. Mythical narrative continued to stand in
the relation to historical narrative that error does to truth. And the
Enlightenment had no hesitancy about drawing the conclusions from

9. E. Cassirer, *Philosophie der symbolischen Formen* (Berlin, B. Cassirer, 1925), II:
"Das mythische Denken," 6 ff.

this. As long as they could not succeed in purging religion of all mythical elements and reducing it to a religion of pure reason or of morality, it amounted to nothing more than a systematic fraud. It was the work of priests and theologians, who had an interest in perpetuating this fraud. Such a solution commended itself the more since in purely methodological respects it seemed to offer an extraordinary simplification of the problem. The ordinary "pragmatic" view and interpretation of all historical events could now be carried over immediately into the history of religion. It, too, became a texture of ends and means, of individual plans and the effects resulting from them. There was no need to leave at any point the familiar field of conscious purposes and individual will and intention.

Romanticism and Schelling's philosophy together put an end to this view. They reversed the relationship of cause and effect, teaching that man is not so much the conscious creator of myth as the being *created by it.* "Looking at the matter carefully," declared Schelling, "to regard the individual man as the sole author of mythology is such a monstrous supposition that one cannot but be utterly amazed at the thoughtlessness with which it is so commonly made, as if things could not possibly be otherwise." [10] Has the deep and mighty living stream of sacred lore and story that flooded the world of prehistory, as from an inexhaustible spring, such a casual and unproductive source as the association of ideas of one or a few individuals? "Could the story of a millennium of wandering of the ancient peoples ever have developed from mere reflective, abstract thinking about nature concepts and personifications concocted in the barren understanding —things which would be comparable at best to the play of a childish imagination and which could hardly merit a moment of serious attention? Could the darkly mysterious and tremendous power of the belief in divinities have possibly developed from a beginning at once so feeble and so artificial?" [11]

What gave the "art" of the few this power over the nature of the whole? No single individual and no group could have been able to gain this ascendancy over consciousness if they had not been in a vital primordial connection with its very roots. Before any reflective thought is possible consciousness itself is enmeshed in the life of the mythical process. It experiences this process as a fate, as a destiny, against which it can do nothing. "Mythology originates in a necessary process (in respect to consciousness) whose origin is buried and lost beyond history and which at odd moments consciousness may

10. Schelling, *op. cit.,* S. 56.
11. *Ibid.,* S. 59.

perhaps oppose but which on the whole it cannot arrest, still less prevent entirely." [12]

On this point those engaged in the critical study of history had to accept the decision of romanticism. Return to a purely pragmatic history of religion that explained its genesis through the conscious activity and purposes of individuals was out of the question. But they could not bring themselves to let the problem remain as Schelling had left it. The new power of historical thinking, discovered and raised to its eminence by romanticism, proved mightier than had been anticipated by those who prepared its way. The answer that the origin of myth and religion is "lost beyond history" was felt as an intolerable restraint on the historical method. This was useless if it could not be extended in principle to cover *all* human affairs—and which of these bore so clearly, so unmistakably, the specifically human stamp as the development of religious ideas? To slip away into "transcendence," into supernatural origin, to invoke an incomprehensible and impenetrable "fate"—all this can accordingly appear from this time forward to be sheer evasion.

For science, at least, there is no point in nor any possibility of such a subterfuge. It had to apply its characteristic principle of causality to the whole world of phenomena if this principle were to retain its force and validity; if it were not to collapse and become useless in the future. Historical knowledge, like a knowledge of nature, is possible only on the assumption of universal determinism, and as there are no forces in nature that do not fit into it so also there are no separate fields of historical activity outside its domain. So it must be taken for granted that consciousness is not free but bound in its forming of the world of religion and myth. The only question is how we can completely understand the nature and the laws of this necessary operation, and we certainly cannot do this as long as we give any precedence to speculation. This must be displaced by pure empiricism which contains a twofold factor and hence must always move in two directions. Only from a connection and constant interaction between historical and psychological analysis is a scientifically tenable result to be anticipated here. Romanticism, with its idea of the unconscious, had to some extent revealed new depths for psychology. But it had not yet ventured to plumb these depths with the line of historical thinking, for they were believed to be unfathomable. But modern scientific thinking should really deliver us from this awe and this prejudice. It should show us that even here there

12. *Ibid.,* S. 193.

is no *non plus ultra*, that we do not need to break off anywhere but must carry on with our science resolutely to the end.

It was from this conviction, and in this intellectual mood, that the first great achievements in the critical history of religion came about. No single person laid the foundation, but a whole generation of investigators working together. Numerous differences inevitably arose in respect to details, but on the whole the prevailing impression is one of agreement in principle, agreement as to what was desired and sought. Everywhere there is obvious the strong and almost inescapable influence still exerted by romanticism and by Hegel's philosophy of history even on the mode of stating the problem. Nowhere was there yet any important break with this view of the world. It was more the language that was changed than the essential content of the thought itself. The strong unifying power still exerted in every quarter by the Hegelian doctrine was especially apparent from the fact that when confronting it even national differences retreated more and more into the background; for at about this time not only did its sway in Germany continue unbroken but it was beginning to spread to France. We know from the story of Hegel's youth how intent he had been upon a plan for a life of Jesus, and in many respects this plan is the germ containing the whole of his later teaching.[13] Neither David Friedrich Strauss nor Renan was acquainted with this youthful work, for it was not published until much later, in Hegel's literary remains.[14] But it is as though both writers were drawn by some mysterious intellectual current back toward this central theme. Strauss began to work on his *Life of Jesus* in the 1830's, directly after Hegel's death, and not long thereafter, in the autumn of 1835, the two volumes of the book were completed.[15] Renan's book appeared much later but again the plan, which presumably he had conceived independently of Strauss,[16] goes back to early youth. He had already planned in his youth and the time of his first intellectual struggles an *Essai psychologique sur Jesus Christ*, which contained the germ of his future work. "From that time

13. W. Dilthey, *Die Jugendgeschichte Hegels,* "Gesammelte Schriften" (1921), IV, 5 ff.

14. *Hegels theologische Jugendschriften* (Hermann Nohl, Tübingen, 1907).

15. D. F. Strauss, *Das Leben Jesu, kritisch bearbeitet* (Tübingen, C. F. Osiander, 1835).

16. The name of Strauss is only once mentioned in Renan's diaries, and nothing in the entry suggests that his work had any decisive influence on Renan's intellectual development.

For further details see Walther Küchler, *Ernest Renan: Der Denker und der Künstler* (Gotha, 1921), S. 76 ff.

forward," he said later, "the life of Jesus was written within my mind." [17]

But when Strauss and Renan attacked this problem they found themselves in an entirely different position from that of Hegel. For their own idea as well as the contemporary idea of science was not at all like his. In the case of Renan, there is no doubt that it was philosophy and the history of the mind rather than natural science that delivered him from the dogmatic creed of the Church. The authors to whom he felt most deeply indebted in his youth, at the time of his first spiritual and mental crisis, were those of the classic era in German literature and the leaders of German idealistic philosophy. During his last years in the seminary of Saint Sulpice he had been deeply affected by Herder, Kant, and Fichte.[18] But after the decisive step had been taken he had to look around for other support if he were to maintain and defend his newly won standpoint. The influence of French positivism and its scientific ideal were then beginning to be felt and so it was Comte and not Hegel who became his guide. In his youthful work, *L'Avenir de la science*, this turning point in his development is clearly apparent. Science, he announced, will fulfill all that religion has continually promised in vain. But he no longer believed that salvation could come only from a science of mind, from philology, criticism, history. Through his friendship with Marcellin Berthelot he began to get his first glimpse into the working methods of empirical and exact natural science,[19] and its concept of law became thenceforth the strongest foundation of his work of criticism, for it alone sufficed to abolish, once and for all, any faith in the miraculous.

It was at this point, too, that Strauss began with his criticism. If faith can be preserved only by recourse to miracles, he concluded, it is irretrievably lost; there is no longer room for that in the modern world. But if this were true, and if we were honest enough not to evade the issue, how are we to understand the fact of faith itself, even if only as a historical fact? Was there any entrance for the investigator of history into the world of religion that natural science itself, now come of age, could not disallow him? Nay, through whose aid he might even be able to penetrate religion deeper than ever before?

17. E. Renan, *Souvenirs d'enfance et de jeunesse* (New York, Boston, Chicago, D. C. Heath & Co., 1902), Eng. trans., p. 214; see Küchler, *op. cit.*, S. 73 ff.

18. For details see Küchler, *op. cit.*, S. 13 ff., 30 ff.

19. For an account of this friendship see the correspondence between Renan and Berthelot, published by the latter, in Paris, 1898; *Letters from the Holy Land,* Eng. trans. by L. O'Rourke (New York, Doubleday, Page & Co., 1904).

Once again it was the analysis of myth that Strauss as well as Renan believed would provide an answer to this question. It is remarkable to see how exactly Strauss affiliates himself here with Schelling, only to enter afterward upon an entirely different path. Schelling had exerted a powerful influence on him even in his first student years, and had been largely instrumental in preventing his complete surrender to the dogmatic doctrine and sentimental theology of Schleiermacher.[20] Through Schelling he had become convinced that myth is no merely outward and incidental shell to be discarded at will but a basic form of religious representation. At this point, however, a new turn came about in Strauss. He renounced all purely speculative interpretation and vindication of myth; no longer would he construct the rise of its creations, one from another, according to a dialectical scheme as Schelling did. Instead, myth became for him a fundamental means of *criticism*. It showed how to purge religion of the miraculous, instead of founding it on the miraculous as before. "The miracle," Strauss explained, "is the strange, the historical, method of dealing with conflicting contents in the evangelical stories of Jesus; the concept of the myth is the means by which we remove these contradictions from our subject and make possible a truly historical view of the life of Jesus." [21] Note well it is "the concept" of the myth. In other words, the purely rational understanding of its significance and its historical achievement and influence. If we want to rely on this concept and make it into a universal instrument of religious historical knowledge, we must first of all rid ourselves of the notion that there is any form of religious faith or idea that can claim an exceptional position for itself over against this conception. Here we were concerned with the truth of myth as a whole, not with the truth of this or that single myth, and this larger question, the really philosophical question, must be answered uniformly for all religions. In this respect monotheism has no advantage over polytheism, Christianity over paganism. Even the purest idea of divinity and a "personal" God to which we might attain would still show the unceasing power of myth; the monotheistic idea itself is still a mythological one.[22]

Once this was made clear the key to an understanding of the biblical stories had been obtained. Now for the first time we could understand how these tales had originated, and more still, how they

---

20. H. Maier, *An der Grenze der Philosophie* (Tübingen, J. C. B. Mohr [P. Siebeck], 1909), S. 270.

21. Strauss, *op. cit.,* I, 185.

22. *Ibid.,* I, 87 ff.

must have done so. They were neither the simple expression of what
had been experienced and remembered, nor yet mere pretense and
fraud. They arose from the unconscious imaginings and ideas of
primitive peoples, and to this extent expressed in full truth and concrete clarity the faith that lived in them. In their tales of the character and destiny of Jesus the common people made their picture
of the Christ just as the Platonic demiurge, looking to the Ideas
and especially the Ideas of the Good, made the world.[23] This knowledge of the mythical origin of most of the biblical tales need by no
means imply any religious depreciation of them. Beyond any doubt
Strauss did not originally mean his criticism thus: it was to be only
a method by which he could define the limits of the religious and the
historical, and prevent a vague merging of the two through which
their specific content of truth must necessarily become dubious and
be lost. "Factual" truth and "religious" truth could never be one and
the same, of course, for they were measured by different standards.
But there was no contradiction in employing their two standards side
by side, if one only kept in mind the principle that Schelling had
defended so vigorously and made the central point of his philosophy
of mythology: Not the world, not objective existence and happenings
are the scene of myth and religion, nor do religious tales pretend to
be giving information on that score. What else is historical criticism
of these biblical stories doing if not following through to the end
Schelling's thought that the active subject of mythology is to be
sought in human consciousness itself and not somewhere outside
it? In some particular phase of its development this consciousness
might very well possess some truth, the claim to which was not wholly
lost at a later stage though it must be shared with other contents
and elements and in so far become relative to them. It was just this
relativity of the biblical tales that Strauss' criticism described. By
such criticism the stories would gain as much in genuine moral and
religious content as they lost when considered as purely historical
documents with demonstrative value. The modern idea of science
imposes on us the duty of separating in the original and primitive religious experience what could not actually be separated but worked
only as an undivided whole. Even in the Jewish idea of the Messiah
the moral requirements and the religious expectation could not be
separated from the mythical features with which, as redeemer of
the human race, the Messiah was endowed. "Through this interpretation," insisted Strauss,

23. *Ibid.*, II, 740 f.

the making of the primitive Christian myth was put on a par with that
found elsewhere in the history of religious origins. That is precisely the
advance that has been made in modern times by the science of mythology:
it has realized that myth, in its original form, is not the conscious and
intentional invention of an individual but a witness of the common consciousness of a people or a religious circle, first expressed by one individual, perhaps, but accepted because after all it only voiced the general
conviction; it is not a cloak from under which some wise man disclosed
an idea that has occurred to him which would be to the profit and advantage of the ignorant masses, for it is only with the story, indeed in
the *form* of the story he tells, that man himself is first made aware of the
idea which he is not yet in a position to grasp as such,

simply as an idea.[24]

So far as the general principle of explanation was concerned,
Renan took the same position as Strauss, though in many and important respects he differed in working out the details. For him,
too, it was certain that there was no great religious event, indeed
not even any great historical event, which had not engendered a
whole circle of myths. And he, too, placed at the center of the discussion not the question of objective truth but that of the psychological necessity of these myths. He had no intention of destroying
absolutely all faith in the miraculous thereby, but rather of freeing
it from the objectionable character it must retain when it is not
understood in its proper context. What we of today call a miracle,
what appears as such to the modern man, can be expressed only
through a definite contrast and difference. A miracle is something
that falls outside the field of "natural" occurrences which is governed
by fixed and universal laws, but for a consciousness that has not yet
achieved such a view of nature and its complete subjection to causal
order this contrast has no meaning; the idea of a miracle escapes it.
Hence our historical perspective is false when we transfer to primeval
times an antithesis that is valid and decisive for us. It is just this
naïveté from which historical criticism ought to deliver us. When
thus understood this criticism would not so much reveal the errors of
imaginative faith as make clear the truth to which it has a claim—
even if this truth proves to be historically conditioned and therefore relative rather than absolute. In this sense Renan explained that
the words "superhuman" and "supernatural," borrowed from our
traditional theology, were without meaning for the religious con-

24. *Ibid.*, I, 195.

sciousness of Jesus. For Him nature and the life of mankind were not realms external to and cut off from God, not paltry realities subject to hard laws that make men despair: "For Him there was nothing supernatural, because for Him there was no nature." [25] Hence Renan persisted in distinguishing times like ours, where everything occurs in the light of reflection, from those "naïve" times that gave birth to religious faith. "We should sin against the true historical method itself were we to follow our own aversions too far. The essential conditions of a true criticism are, first, the comprehension of the difference between eras, and then the ability to rise above our instinctive habits that are the fruit of a purely rational upbringing." [26]

Every religious form is incomplete, and yet without such particular form religion cannot exist. Only in its quintessence is religion true, and yet to make it too rarefied in that way would be to destroy it. The philosopher who, perplexed by the bias, the misuse, the error that lie in the form, believes that he can possess himself of the reality by taking refuge in abstractions only substitutes for this reality something that has never existed. The wise man is he who sees that everything in religion is at once picture, preconception, and symbol—and that the picture, the preconception, and the symbol are useful and genuine.

Just as one does not reproach a painter with having perpetrated a piece of childish nonsense in representing God as a material being of definite form, so one can admit and love a symbol in so far as it has its place in the consciousness of mankind and has fulfilled its role. This is the sense and the inner heart of all religious imagination: "Man, face to face with the beautiful, the good, and the true, rises above himself and, sustained by a celestial beauty, abolishes his own wretched personality, is exalted, absorbed. What is all this if not to adore them?" [27]

The influence of the works of both Strauss and Renan was tremendous, but it depended in large part upon the theological conflict that they started, which was carried on with the utmost violence and animosity. It was this side of the problem that was almost exclusively seen at first and all interest was turned this way. But for our purpose this need not occupy us, and from the standpoint of a history of the mind it was not the most important side. We can see the struggle today in a different light. The important thing is not

25. Renan, *Das Leben Jesu* (German ed., 4. Aufl. Leipzig, 1880), S. 250 f.
26. *Ibid.*, S. 256, 265.
27. E. Renan, *Questions contemporaines* (Paris, Michel Lévy frères, 1868).

what the criticism of Strauss and Renan overthrew but what it constructed. On an earlier page [28] we referred to an expression of Niebuhr, that every true historian develops an individual manner of seeing and that more and more he must achieve the ability "to see in the dark." In Renan we find a passage that corresponds exactly with this notion of the peculiarity of historical knowledge. "I have acquired a sort of habit of searching underground, and of detecting sounds that other ears do not hear." [29] This acute vision, sharp hearing, and delicacy of perception Renan had developed to the highest degree. Therein lies his superiority over Strauss, who always employed the whole armory of ideas and, as it were, the heavy artillery of theological criticism and polemic. Renan would invariably hint rather than exhaust; he was the master of nuance, of chiaroscuro, of the devious, and what has been called his dilettantism, skepticism, Epicureanism is bound up with this side of his talent.[30] He strove after strict science and demanded it of himself, but distrusted more and more the force of logical definition and distinction when penetration to the last details of the history of things of the mind was concerned. One might as well try to hit a winged insect with a club, he once said, as try to grasp the truth in a mental science with the thick claws of a syllogism. The nimble and volatile truth escapes, and one merely wastes his effort.[31]

This type of mentality allowed Renan to push further than ever before into the world of myth and make it inwardly intelligible. He saw it, of course, more with the eyes of a poet than with those of a historian or an anthropologist. The heavy solemnity of myth, its gloom and narrowness, the oppressive weight that it exerted on primitive man—all this he recognized, but did not care to have these features absorb him. He saw myth in a more mellow, poetically transfigured light and accordingly pardoned what it had of error and deception. For what great truth in the history of man has ever been free from some admixture of error? Even the idea of primitive Christianity was always with Renan far more an aesthetic than a purely historical idea. He hardly wished it otherwise. "Poetry and all," he once cried, "I would have it so." [32]

But with neither Renan nor Strauss should we place the main emphasis on their individual interpretations of the mythical and their

---

28. See above, p. 229.
29. See Küchler, *op. cit.*, S. 204 f.
30. G. Monod, *Les Maîtres de l'histoire: Renan, Taine, Michelet*, p. 38 ff.
31. Cited by Georg Brandes, *Ernest Renan, Mensch und Werke* (2. Aufl. Frankfort/Main, 1887), S. 77 f.
32. See Küchler, *op. cit.*, S. 49.

employment of these interpretations in treating the individual problems of religious history, for another factor is of greater significance in the general development of historical thinking in the nineteenth century. Both belonged to that group of investigators and thinkers who had the insight to realize that an understanding of myth is an indispensable *organon of historical knowledge.* Up until that time one saw in the creations of myth only an obstacle to such knowledge; they were like a veil concealing the real, the actual, truth of history. Even Niebuhr was of essentially this opinion in his reconstruction of the early history of Rome. His problem was to eliminate the mythical and the legendary in order to attain historical truth. On this view myth and history seemed, as it were, to be the opposite poles of the intellectual globe. Myth is a world of illusion that conceals intrinsic reality from us, the reality of things and events. But what if this view could be reversed? Is myth only concealment, or is it not also concealment *and* revelation that meet us here? Cannot insight into the nature of mythical thinking and imagination be made a real medium of knowledge? Can it not serve as a guide to historical knowledge? And would this guidance cover only the field of religious development, or could it not be extended to reach far beyond this?

As soon as all these questions had been posed in precise form, we find history again at an important turning point in respect to method. Even the problems of purely political history were now accessible to a wholly new mode of handling. The beginnings of political history seemed everywhere lost in the obscurity of myth. But here, too, it is the problem of the historian not to escape from darkness but to employ it in his task, for his particular scholarly purpose. We must learn not only to see in the dark places but, strange and contradictory as this must appear at first sight, to see with their help. Myth, which seemed to be a barrier to historical knowledge, must be transformed into an instrument of this knowledge.

The first historian of the nineteenth century to grasp this problem with a full consciousness of its importance, and to bring it to an issue in a great classical example, was Fustel de Coulanges. His work, *The Ancient State,* was not only significant in content by reason of its abundance of new information; it also introduced a fresh viewpoint whose importance went far beyond the field in which it was first employed. By his own spiritual make-up Fustel de Coulanges belongs in that class of historians who are not satisfied with devoting history simply to what comes to pass. He did not intend to immerse himself in the stream of events and be carried away in it, but sought there for certain lasting forms. In this respect his views are akin to those of Mommsen or Burckhardt.[33] He was nearer to the former, however, in so far as his scientific interest was concentrated chiefly on the life of man in the state. This is what he wanted to disclose in its full scope. He was not content to describe the outward history of the state and follow it throughout the development of its power or to its downfall. For him the essential thing was not its outward but its inner history. For that reason institutions became for him the real object of political history, and his most significant achievements are in this field.[34]

But Fustel de Coulanges did not consider institutions in the same way as Mommsen did. "He did not come to history by way of jurisprudence," said Fueter,

and was less inclined to consider legal functions as dramatis personae or to regard constitutions and systems of government as independently existing organisms. He preferred to attempt to construct the state and its government from the bottom upward, that is, to derive them out of the beliefs of the people or their social relationships. For him the organization of the state was not the saving power; it was merely the outcome of social conditions and views.[35]

In his work *The Ancient State* a consistent attempt was made for the first time to explain in terms of the fundamental form and tendency of the ancient faith not only this or that element in Greek or Roman life but also the totality of their political and social life. But this derivation was not understood in the sense of a historical materialism. In contrast to that, Fustel de Coulanges laid the foundation of a new and original form of "sociology of religion." The question which of the two factors, the social or the religious, is primary and which secondary, which is cause and which effect, was not a critical one for him. For the historian never encounters them separately; they are given him only in conjunction, in their living concretion. It is arbitrary to separate off one part of this complex, for everything depends on their correlation. But if one had to make such a separation, then Coulanges had to give the primacy to religion.

One can hardly say whether it was progress in religion that brought about the social advance, but it is certain that the two occurred con-

33. For Mommsen see above, pp. 260 ff.; for Burckhardt see pp. 289 ff.

34. Fustel de Coulanges, *Histoire des institutions politiques de l'ancienne France,* première partie: "L'Empire romain, les Germains, la Royauté Mérovingienne (Paris, Hachette et Cie., 1875).

35. E. Fueter, *Geschichte der neueren Historiographie,* S. 561.

comitantly and in remarkable accord. One must keep in mind the extraordinary difficulty with which the development of regular societies was confronted in primitive times. . . . To establish common rules of life, to introduce a governing authority and obtain obedience to it in order to give reason predominance over emotion and public reason dominion over individual reason: all this certainly demanded something stronger than physical force, more respected than self-interest, more certain than a philosophic theory, and more unchangeable than a mere agreement—something that dwelt equally at the bottom of all hearts and there had its seat and its authority. Just this is the role of faith. Nothing exerts such power over the mind as faith. It is a work of our mind, yet we are not free to alter it at will. It is our creation, but we know it not. It is human but we regard it as divine. It is our work, yet it is stronger than we are. It is in us; it never leaves us; it speaks to us at every moment. When it commands us to obey, we obey; when it prescribes certain duties, we submit ourselves to them. Man may rule nature, perhaps, but he is still subject to his own thought.[36]

This concept of the power of faith is different from that current in the eighteenth century, yet far removed from all romanticism. Fustel de Coulanges was almost the first among modern historians to approach the phenomenon of belief with entire impartiality, to see it wholly as a historical phenomenon, and to seek to know it and present it in its historical significance. He left far behind him the view of the Enlightenment and its pragmatic explanation of religion. The various forms of faith, he believed, are based as little on mere convention as are the varieties in human speech. Here other and more powerful forces are at work.

One seriously misjudges human nature if he thinks that a religion can be introduced by agreement and maintained by deception. Count the passages in Livy that show how often the Roman religion proved a hardship to the patricians themselves, how often it embarrassed the senate, involving it in difficulties and hampering its action, and then see if you can say that this religion was invented solely for the convenience of the politicians. Not until the time of the Scipios did the idea arise that religion was of use to the government; but by then it was already extinct in the hearts of the people.[37]

But now if one does see how the religious idea is the life-giving and formative breath of ancient society (*"le souffle inspirateur et*

36. F. de Coulanges, *La Cité antique. Etude sur le culte, le droit, les institutions de la Grèce et de Rome* (1864) (4e ed. Paris, 1872), III, chap. iii, 152 f.

37. *Ibid.,* III, chap. xvi, 254.

organisateur de la société") [38] how is one to explain the rise of the living from the dead, the emergence of the organism from a merely mechanical arrangement through a merely mechanical compulsion? The form of bond that is essential to all religion must come from within, not from without. And only when we get our insight into this essential bond and recognize it for what it is are we vouchsafed insight into the forms of life of the past.

It has been said of Fustel de Coulanges that his historic interest was in institutions, not in life.[39] But this characterization does not seem to the point, or at least it does not seem in the least to do justice to his real effort and his actual accomplishment. He was always making reference to institutions, it is true, but it was only in order to see and appreciate the life of the past. The true historical investigator, he insisted, does not describe the arrangements and constitutions or the legal standards and religious customs or the ideas and the morals of a society merely for their own sake. "History does not study material facts and institutions alone; the real object of its investigation is the human soul; it must strive to gain a knowledge of what this soul has believed, felt, and thought in the different epochs of the human race." [40] But this form of sympathetic understanding is no such simple process as romanticism had earlier assumed. It was not enough to transplant oneself into the past with all the powers of one's sympathy and try thereby to reanimate it. For here a limit is soon reached. There are primitive strata of belief that go back so far into the past and that have become so strange to us that we cannot by any process of sympathy awaken them again. When we try, notwithstanding, to do so we no longer see the past in its own light but only in the reflected light of the present. The longing with which we embrace it is a sentimental longing, but this is no guide to historical truth. Instead of identifying ourselves with the past we identify the past with ourselves; instead of seeing it in strictly objective form we read our own wishes and needs into it and in so doing fall into a sort of idealization—one of the most dangerous of all delusions for the historian.

For example, the notion we have come to form of freedom in ancient times, does not correspond with reality.[41] The ideal of Roman virtue and Roman freedom is not true to history; it is merely a wishful dream placed back in the past. There was no place in antiquity for

38. *Ibid.*, III, chap. iii, 154.
39. See Gooch, *History and Historians in the Nineteenth Century*, p. 213.
40. Coulanges, *op. cit.*, II, chap. ix, 106.
41. The copy of the German manuscript has a lacuna at this point which cannot be supplied. But it appeared to consist of only part of a line. Ed.

our modern idea of freedom. It is part of the main thesis in Coulanges' work that the ancients did not know personal freedom.

The ancients knew neither freedom in their private lives, nor freedom in education, nor religious freedom. The person of the individual was of little import compared with the inviolable and almost divine authority claimed by what one called the state, or the fatherland . . . It was believed that morality, justice, the right must all give way before the good of the fatherland. Thus it is the strangest of all errors to believe that in the communities of antiquity a man enjoyed freedom. He did not even possess the idea of it.[42]

Once we have become convinced of the fact that the ancient faith exerted an unconditional and boundless power over the whole of life, the next problem is to obtain an insight into the source and character of this faith. Here, too, Coulanges trod paths that had not yet been ventured upon at the time his work appeared. In respect to their ideas of Greek and Roman religion, both classical philology and the general science of religion had been for centuries under the spell of Greek poetry. Indeed it could be said with some justice that it was the Greek epic, that it was Homer and Hesiod, that had "created" the [faith] [43] of the Greeks. To get behind that creation seemed neither necessary nor, by purely historical means, even possible. Yet Coulanges did not stop there. He sketched a picture of "archaic" belief that is far removed from Homer's world of gods. What enabled him to do this and to see Greek and Roman beliefs in another light is the fact that he made use of a new means to knowledge whose significance he was one of the first to recognize. He did not trust himself simply to the guidance of myth, and no longer regarded it as the sole source of our knowledge of ancient faith. What the old mythology relates of the gods is in his opinion only a revelation and reflection of the essence of mythology but yielded no essential understanding. If we want to understand we must strike out in another direction. The ideas and opinions man forms of divinity and the pictures that he fashions of it are always but a varied and motley wrapping beneath which another and more substantial content is hidden. What man believes comes more clearly and sharply to light in the manner of his acts than in his ideas.

Here it is that the historian must begin, therefore, if he wants to uncover the real primordial stratum of religion. The rites, not the myths, must serve as his guide. Primitive religion was never a mere

42. Coulanges, *op. cit.*, III, chap. xvii, 266 f.
43. Word missing in text; "faith" is supplied. Ed.

collection of dogmas or doctrines. It was not theoretical at all but practical through and through. It required of men not certain "views" of the divine, but laid prescriptions upon them that permeated the whole of life and left not the slightest room for free choice. If we could succeed in surveying the whole scope of these rules, these commands and standards, and if we could grasp the immediately compelling power with which they ruled the existence and the activity of men, then only should we have acquired an adequate conception of primitive belief.

It was not by chance that Coulanges arrived at this conception, but rather as a direct consequence of his own individuality and the fundamental tendency of his historical interest. This, as we have already seen, concerned itself with the permanent and not the transitory. He sought the essence behind existence, and held himself to institutions, in which he saw the true substance of historical life. From this standpoint rites could not but appear more significant than myth, since they constituted the really constant, "conservative" element in all religions. Myths come and go, and move slowly from one scene to another. Each generation retells them in another form and each adds new elements to the store inherited from the past, but behind all these changes taking place from epoch to epoch there remains something permanent that defies the assault of time. It is in this we must recognize the real bearer of the religious tradition.

The intercourse of man with the gods, the cult that he dedicates to them, the names by which he invokes them, the gifts and sacrifices that he owes to them: all this is enjoined by inviolable rules. Over them the individual has no power, for any infraction of them and any innovation could only work harm. All the virtue inherent in prayer, in sacrifice, in sacred services depends upon carrying these out always in exactly the same way. The slightest alteration would be equivalent to nullifying them. Even the word "religion," as Coulanges emphasized, does not mean the same to antiquity as to us. The ancient religion had no intention of exalting man to the contemplation of an absolute and making knowledge of it accessible to him in any way.

This religion was a total fabric of detailed doctrines and very particular rites to be implicitly observed. There was no need to ask their meaning, nothing here to think out, nothing for which one had to give a justification. To us religion means a collection of dogmas, a doctrine of God, an imaginative version of belief in the mysteries that are within and around us. To the ancients it meant rites, ceremonies, outward acts of devotion.

Theory counted for little, all depended on customs. They were compelling, a ligature binding men (*ligare, religio*). Religion was a physical bond, a chain to which men were fettered as slaves. Man created it, yet he was ruled by it . . . Ancient law never gave reasons. Why should it? It was not obliged to furnish motives; it existed because the gods had ordained it . . . The old books of law, the νόμοι of the Greeks, the *carmina* of the Romans, were unalterable. To change even a single letter of them, to displace a word, to modify even the rhythm was to destroy the law itself by destroying the sacred form in which it had revealed itself to man. The law was like prayer, which was pleasing to the gods only when it was uttered exactly in accordance with the prescribed formula, and became sacrilege as soon as one deviated from this by so much as a word. There was no town that did not possess a collection of old hymns in praise of its gods. Speech, customs, religious ideas might change in the course of time, but the words and rhythms of these hymns remained inflexibly the same; the people went forth to sing them at their festivals without understanding them.[44]

With this key in hand Coulanges attempted to unlock the holy of holies in the faith of antiquity. We need only place ourselves imaginatively at the heart of the cult, and then we shall not miss the way to that knowledge. He believed himself able to prove that the inner bond uniting all the various and apparently divergent expressions of faith was worship of the dead. All systems of divine worship had their roots in the cult of the dead, for there is no stronger and firmer bond than that uniting the individual to his family, to his father and forefathers. In the earliest times the individual knew and felt himself to be not a detached and independent unit but a link merely in the unbroken chain connecting his own existence with that of his vanished forebears. Nor was this chain by any means of a purely "spiritual" sort; it was material, for the dead were only so in appearance. Their power had not been extinguished; it worked on and on and made itself known to the living as a constant presence, as an immediate existence. The host of ancestors lived on in the family circle. From it they received the prescribed sacrifices, in it they shared all the meals and occupied the place of honor beside the fire that was lighted for them and kept unchanged and unquenched from one generation to the next.

This was the basic stratum of ancient faith as Coulanges disclosed it, and by reference to it he wanted to modify and deepen the ideas of ancient "polytheism" that are well known and current among ourselves. Polytheism presented only one element of the religion

44. Coulanges, *op. cit.*, III, chap. viii, 197 ff., cf. chap. xi, 226 ff.

of antiquity, the recourse to nature. One can make the attempt to understand the pantheon of Olympus and of the Roman capital in this fashion by envisaging in every god the representation of some special force in nature. But we should never put these Olympian gods at the beginning of religion. The faith that took its form thus from external nature had been preceded by another, which had to do with the human mind and drew its force therefrom. It was concerned with the ancestors of the race, and its symbol was the hearth and home.

The fire kept burning on the hearth was not natural fire to the mind of man. He saw in it not merely the physical element that gleams and burns, that transforms substances, melts metals, and becomes a mighty tool of human industry. The hearth fire was of quite another sort. It was a pure fire, and could be brought forth only with the help of certain rites and maintained only with special kinds of wood. It was a chaste fire: sexual intercourse was forbidden in its presence . . . Later, when the hearth fire had changed to the form of the great Vesta, Vesta became a virgin goddess; she represented to the world neither fertility nor power; she was the order of things, but not the strict, abstract, mathematical order, the imperative and inevitable law of necessity ἀνάρκη with which man early became acquainted in natural phenomena. She was the moral order. She was thought of as a sort of universal soul that governed the various motions of the physical universe just as the human mind governed the activities of our organs.[45]

Despite all the diversity of the problems treated—and they extend over the entire field of political and social life—*La Cité antique* is a development of one single idea. Coulanges held fast to his thread, once he had seized it, with extraordinary energy and unerring certainty. He saw it as the thread of Ariadne, which alone could guide through the labyrinth of the ancient religious beliefs. Not only his adversaries, but his admirers and partisans as well, have emphasized that he followed his basic idea only too obstinately and developed it too one-sidedly, so that many features necessarily belonging in the picture of antique civilization were dealt with too summarily or else entirely suppressed.[46]

The objection to Mommsen's *Römische Geschichte* had been that he "modernized" the Romans too much, but the opposite objection was urged against Fustel de Coulanges. It was said of him that he described the life of Greece and of Rome in a style that was too

45. *Ibid.,* I, chap. ii, 28 f.
46. See P. Guiraud, *Fustel de Coulanges* (Paris, Hachette et Cie., 1896), III, chap. iii, 38 ff.

"archaic." The difference between the two historians shows with special force and clarity how much the answer obtained from history is determined by the viewpoint with which a writer starts out, and how entirely dissimilar pictures of the same subject can be obtained by changing the angle of vision. For what separated the two investigators was not only their temperaments and characteristic scientific tendencies; behind these individual differences there lay a general difference of principle as to the problem and "maxim" of historical research. Each gave clear and concise expression to the maxim that he followed. Thus Mommsen explained in a letter to Henzen that much could be said in criticism of the modern style in which his *Römische Geschichte* had been written, but that he had been mainly concerned with bringing down the ancients from the fantastic pedestal on which they had been placed; and that although he might have gone too far in the matter, his intention had been sound enough. But whereas Mommsen had to move his subject nearer both to himself and the reader in order to see it in sharp focus and with the fullness of life, Coulanges sought to retreat from it. "I shall endeavor," he explained in his introduction to *La Cité antique,*

to make clear once for all the radical and essential differences separating the ancient peoples from modern society. Our system of education, which from childhood on permits us to move in the company of the Greeks and the Romans, has accustomed us to compare them continually with ourselves, to judge their history in accordance with ours, and to explain our revolutions in terms of theirs. What remains from them in us and what they have bequeathed us prompts us to believe that they are like us; it is difficult for us to think of them as an alien people; almost invariably we see in them only ourselves. This has given rise to many errors, and errors in this field are not without danger. If one wants to learn the truth about ancient peoples it is well to study them without thinking of ourselves. We must consider them as if they were wholly strange, and we should do so with a mind as free and with as much objectivity as we would employ, say, in studying the ancient Indians or Arabians. Thus considered, Greece and Rome come before us in a wholly inimitable way. Nothing in modern times is like them; nothing in the future can ever be like them again.

Mommsen, in his *Römische Geschichte,* wanted to present the drama of Roman political life, and what captivated him above all in this drama was not the course of outward occurrences but the individual players in it; the way in which they intervened in events, how they fell into conflict with one another, and how in these quarrels they revealed themselves and their characters, the sharpest sides of their personalities. The intimate charm of his presentation consists in the mastery with which he carried out his task. But Fustel de Coulanges had neither the ability nor even the ambition to compete with Mommsen in this field, for his idea of scientific history forbade him to dwell on single characters and lose himself in their individuality. He believed that history should draw a picture of certain conditions and describe their development. In the works of his later years especially he lapsed almost entirely into what Comte called social statics and social dynamics. In such a presentation of social conditions and institutions individuals counted for little, since it is not from their isolated efforts that all this complex of life arises but from forces of an entirely different kind. It has been pointed out that Coulanges has described whole epochs with hardly a reference to the names of their most important personages, and that even when he did mention them seemed to ascribe to their bearers a very slight importance for events; they appeared to him as an almost unnecessary detail.[47]

It is obvious and incontestable that from the standpoint of pure historiography this is a deficiency, but it is remarkable how much this very lack is actually the defect of his virtues. For only by retreating from his subject, instead of examining it at close range and becoming immersed in its details, was Coulanges able to develop the sort of vision that distance requires. He penetrated far more deeply into past times than others before him had ever been able to do. He employed no methods other than those already at the command of the historian, and his faith in the reliability of historical texts and documents was implicit. By virtue of this material he was able to discover and present conditions for which there was and could be no direct documentary evidence, because it was lost in the mists of "primitive time." The characteristic and perhaps unique feature of his *Cité antique* was that with purely historical evidence it attacked a problem that really could no longer be approached by way of history alone, since it led back to the domain of prehistory. No wonder that this goal could not be attained at the first trial, or that it was easy for critics not only to point out mistakes in details but to raise general and serious doubts about the interpretation and presentation.[48] But the value of the work as a whole is hardly diminished thereby, for it lies in the *attack* on the problem much more than in the execution

47. See Guiraud, *op. cit.,* pp. 200 ff.

48. These misgivings were most sharply formulated by H. d'Arbois de Jubainville in his *Deux manières d'écrire l'histoire* (Paris, E. Bouillon, 1896).

itself. But this remained hidden from Coulanges himself in many respects, because he avoided giving a turn to his theme that applied it to universal history. Today an investigator would scarcely discuss the cult of the dead among the Greeks and the Romans without feeling obliged to compare it with the other great religions of civilization and with the anthropological and ethnographic material. How much Coulanges' presentation would have gained simply by a reference to China and the origins of Chinese ancestor worship! Yet all this he not only did not attempt but deliberately eschewed, because it was in conflict with his ideal of scientific rigor, according to which the historian himself must not be heard but must let the text alone speak. "History," he declared, "should not be made with logic, but only with documents." And he forbade himself the introduction of any documents that he had not read in the original and interpreted in the most careful manner, often going as far as the analysis of single words. This could not but deter him from employing comparative methods, in which he perceived the danger of dilettantism. Comparisons, he emphasized, must never begin until a minute investigation of the separate details has been completed to the very last dot. "I would like to have a first generation of investigators devoting themselves to these individual researches and leave it to the following generation to seek out the general law that might perhaps be derived from these special studies." [49] One may doubt whether Coulanges, in view of his type of mind and method of work, would think even today that the time for such a synthesis had arrived; but in respect to method he must be included among the earliest founders of that "sociology of religion" that attained fullest expression in the work of Max Weber.

If one wants to convince himself of this and to show what Coulanges' writings held in the way of new and fertile suggestions, one must not stop at what he taught in the theory of historical method, for it by no means completely exhausts the content of his peculiar achievement, which extends much further than his logical theory of historical knowledge would suggest. He belongs to those historiographers who have employed themselves intensively and unceasingly with problems of method, and in their writings have constantly referred to them. Here his great model was Descartes, and he said on one occasion that he had really done nothing more than apply to history the systematic doubt that he had learned from Descartes. But in addition to this, another influence was working on him; that of Bacon,

49. Coulanges, *Nouvelles recherches sur quelques problèmes d'histoire* (Paris, Hachette et Cie., 1891), p. 4 ff., cited from Guiraud, *op. cit.*, p. 222 f.

of whose logic of induction he spoke with enthusiastic praise.[50] Indeed, it is evident that Bacon's maxims left a lasting mark on him, and I know hardly a modern historian in whom the influence of Bacon's doctrine of instances can be so clearly traced. Coulanges was certain that once he had all the instances in hand and had carefully compared them with one another the truth must emerge more or less spontaneously. As the naturalist to his observations, so the historian was related to his texts. He needed neither to add to them nor change them but only to conclude the sum of their meaning. The whole secret of the historical method lay in collecting all available texts on a given question, forgetting none, studying them exhaustively, and where texts were lacking admitting no suppositions of any sort and no unfounded hypotheses. "The texts are not always trustworthy, but only from them can history be written, and one must not replace them with his own personal opinions. The best historian is he who sticks closest to the text and writes, indeed even thinks, only in conformity with it." [51] The demand for "fidelity to documents," has seldom been more sharply emphasized than here; it seems almost as though the phrase "What is not in public documents is not in the world" (*Quod non in actis, non est in mundo*) had been raised to the supreme principle of historical knowledge.

But this form of Baconian empiricism, this belief that the facts are immediately given in the texts, encounters, of course, a definite limitation as soon as it is put into effect. What assures us of the integrity, the completeness, the reliability of the historical material itself? The theory of Coulanges gives us no definite answer; indeed, he avoided this question with remarkable lightheartedness. His adversaries accused him, in return, of being as credulous of old texts as he was critical of modern views. But he was seldom disturbed in his work by such critical scruples and put evidence together from wholly different periods, of wholly different origin, and often of very questionable value. Every source of information was taken into consideration, and almost all were esteemed of equal worth. It has been maintained that a good third of the references in his *Cité antique* are to legendary tales or to later fictitious writings.[52]

50. For Coulanges' relationship to Descartes and to Bacon see Guiraud, *op. cit.,* p. 8 f., 162 f.

51. Coulanges, *Histoire des institutions politiques de l'ancienne France,* "La Monarchie franque," p. 33, 69. Cited from Guiraud, *op. cit.,* p. 186.

52. See C. Seignobos, "Fustel de Coulanges," *Histoire de la langue et de la littérature française,* éd. L. Petit de Julleville (Paris, A. Colin & Cie., 1899), VIII, 285.
The paradoxical thesis that even falsified documents are not entirely barren of

Though it is obvious that these criticisms, in so far as they are deserved, must seriously prejudice the purely historical value of the work, they do not rob of its significance and originality what he accomplished in presenting the problem. No matter how inadequate the evidence advanced by Coulanges, the validity of his thesis need not be impugned. Classical philology was relatively late in reacting to his stimulus but today it is common knowledge that we falsify the picture of Greek religion if we seek to draw it solely from the evidence of the Homeric religion. Erwin Rohde has expressly referred to the work of Coulanges in his own investigations into the Greek cult of souls and the belief in immortality, in which he, too, distinguished sharply between the Homeric religion and that of primitive times. To be sure, he added the following: "It does not diminish appreciation of the fertile ideas in the book to admit that its basic concept, in so far as the Greek world is concerned, has not risen above the dignity of an intuition, which may be right and true but still remains incapable of proof. If there ever were an era when Greek religion consisted only of ancestor worship, our vision does not reach back to those obscure primeval times, long before all tradition." [53]

From the standpoint of our own problem, however, we must pass another and more positive judgment, for we are not primarily concerned with what new historic insights the work had attained but with what it meant on the whole to the development of the *ideal of historical knowledge* during the nineteenth century. In this respect it was, and remains, not only an important but an epoch-making achievement. One may compare Coulanges' accomplishment in his *Cité antique* with that of a miner who drives a new shaft and strikes gold yet can hardly estimate at first the productivity of the vein and foresee its whole yield. It was not history alone, in fact it was chiefly the science of comparative religion, that was able to realize the benefits. In this field the ideas that Coulanges disseminated so generously in his youthful work were abundantly productive. To be sure, there is a peculiarly tragic irony in an after-influence of this sort when it is measured against the intent of the author himself. He was a convinced empiricist and positivist, who wanted neither to suggest ideas nor to set up hypotheses. He insisted that for the historian there must be only

historical value but not infrequently may provide important information was set up and defended by Coulanges in his book: *La Monarchie franque*, p. 23 f. Quite understandably it met with the sharpest opposition. For details see d'Arbois de Jubainville, "Fustel de Coulanges et les diplômes faux," *Deux manières d'écrire l'histoire*, p. 178 ff.

53. E. Rohde, *Psyche, Seelencult und Unsterblichkeitsglaube der Griechen* (3. Aufl. Leipzig und Tübingen, J. C. B. Mohr [P. Siebeck], 1903), I, 166 n.

facts, nothing but facts, and that the intimate study of documents and attention to detail should be his sole guiding star. Again and again he warned against "vague generalities" and premature syntheses. History, he said, is not a rationalistic science, but a science of facts; it is a science of observation that may be compared to chemistry.[54]

But here Coulanges experienced a bitter disillusionment. In his most important work, *Histoire des institutions politiques de l'ancienne France,* he brought to light an abundance of previously unknown facts, yet hardly one of his results remained uncontested and none has enjoyed general recognition. His relation to contemporary historians was one of unbroken warfare, and the polemic became so overwhelming that it almost threatened to smother under its weight his scientific work and his proper labor of research.[55] On the other hand, the fertility of his ideas was amply proved in a set of problems of an entirely different sort. What he could only infer hypothetically for the Greeks and the Romans, the significance of which for the ancient religions he had perhaps overvalued, was fully confirmed when later investigators decided to widen the field of study. Moreover, certain basic insights into *method* that he had won were now seen in full clarity for the first time. That a consideration of ritual leads us back to the primitive strata of religious belief, that cult and customs are more reliable guides than what is given us in religious ideas and in mythology, all this was a principle which could have been proved in fullest measure by the history of the Oriental religions. Robertson-Smith rested his entire portrayal of the religion of the Semites on this principle.[56] Even the researches into the religion of primitive peoples have led to the same result. The thesis that rites precede dogma and that an understanding of the latter is to be won only from an understanding of the former now holds for many investigators as a cardinal truth in ethnology and social anthropology.

But the agreement with the results of modern research goes even further, appearing also in fields where it could be doubted whether there was any measure of direct stimulation by the work of Coulanges. The thought that if the history of religion is to discover the true sources of belief it cannot stop at that form of the "particular gods"

54. See Seignobos, *op. cit.,* p. 287.

55. See the chapter on "Les Polémiques de Fustel de Coulanges," by Guiraud, *op. cit.,* p. 145 ff.

56. W. Robertson-Smith, *Lectures on the Religion of the Semites* (Edinburgh, Adam and Charles Black, 1889) ; R. R. Marett, *The Threshold of Religion* (London, Methuen & Co., 1909). See also E. Cassirer, *Philosophie der symbolischen Formen,* II: "Das mythische Denken," 50 f., 270 ff.

presented to us by the pantheon of the various polytheistic religions was developed especially by Usener.[57] But when we study *La Cité antique* we find to our surprise that here, a generation before Usener, the same fundamental view is advocated, in fact that it constitutes one of the germ cells out of which the whole work developed. Even the very earliest research of Coulanges, his doctoral dissertation,[58] was occupied with the problem of the religious significance of the hearth fire. His *Cité antique* went on from there to show that a cult of the hearth fire was in existence long before there had developed from it the worship of personified gods with fixed and individual character-istics.

When the peoples of Greece and Italy became accustomed to imagining their gods as persons and giving each a name and a personal form, then the ancient cult of the hearth became subject to the uniform law imposed by human thought in that epoch on every religious belief . . . The altar of the fire was personified and called ἐστία, Vesta . . . In accordance with a thoroughly familiar procedure the common name (*nom commun*) was replaced by a proper name (*nom propre*) . . . But the remnant of the primitive belief, according to which this divinity was simply the fire on the hearth, never died out.[59]

In exactly the same manner Usener described how the older religious common names, the earlier appellatives, became proper names, and how it was this philological process that went hand in hand with a quite determinate religious development and furthered it in the highest possible degree.[60] One might be inclined to assume that this was merely a fortuitous and isolated case, to which no great weight need be attached. But this is by no means so. We find, rather, a genuine agree-ment in principle. For like Usener, and even before him, Coulanges set up the basic principle that there is no more reliable guide in the analysis of primitive religious ideas than linguistic analysis. In this fashion he sought to illuminate the relation between *patricii* and *patres*, and the meanings of *agnatio* and *cognatio*, and other problems of the kind.[61] In his later writings he retained this method and even tried to develop it further in its essentials. Often it is word analysis

57. H. Usener, *Götternamen: Versuch einer Lehre von der religiösen Begriffsbildung* (Bonn, F. Cohen, 1896).

58. *Quid Vestae cultus in institutis veterum privatis publicisque valuerit* (1858).

59. *La Cité antique*, I, chap. iii, 27.

60. For further details on this theory of Usener see Cassirer, *Sprache und Mythos: Ein Beitrag zur Theorie der Götternamen* (Leipzig und Berlin, B. G. Teubner, 1925); also *Philosophie der symbolischen Formen*, II: "Das mythische Denken," 246 ff.

61. *La Cité antique*, II, chap. v, 58 ff.; IV, chap. i, 269 ff.

that has to point the way for him to an understanding of social relations and institutions and it produces some surprising explanations.
Experts have unanimously declared the investigations carried out in
this way by Coulanges to be models of the art of philosophic and historical interpretation.[62] It is obvious from this that his actual work in
research was richer, more varied, and more flexible than one would be
led to expect from his rather narrow and rigid conception of historical knowledge, which would not only bind the historian to his documents but seemingly meant that he had to confine himself to their
domain. His standard was that the historiographer himself should
not be heard but that the texts alone should speak. Yet in themselves
the texts say nothing until they are made to speak through the labors
of the historian. They are not only incomplete but in many, if not in
most, cases obscure or contradictory. To lighten this darkness and
remove these contradictions a special art of interpretation is needed,
a historical "hermeneutics," which becomes more difficult the further
removed is the object with which it deals. And this art requires entirely new expedients as soon as we approach the frontier where
history and prehistory merge. One of the most important scientific
services performed by Coulanges was the development of this hermeneutics. His achievement in *La Cité antique* may be likened to that of a
paleontologist who goes back to the older geological strata in order to
acquire through their investigation a new insight into the world of
living organisms.

Of course Coulanges no longer allowed his peculiar method the
same free sway in his more important work as in that of his youth.
He was under the obligation and the pressure of proving his individual theses, and this burden often deprived him of freedom of action
and involved him in a mass of detailed inquiries. In this respect his
later writings show a distinct change in style; indeed, it has been said
that there is a deep crisis, a wholly inner one that divided his life
work into two clearly distinct parts.[63] But the inner unity of his work
was not endangered or destroyed by the sort of division of labor
which he had to make up his mind to accept. That unity rested upon
a concept that he followed consistently from first to last. Fustel de
Coulanges, said Guiraud,

had a fund of ideas concerning the development of humanity that were
perfectly coherent with each other. Usually he preferred to keep them

62. See the opinion of Fueter, *op. cit.*, S. 563, and of Seignobos, who in other respects
met the achievements of Fustel de Coulanges with sharp criticism, *op. cit.*, p. 286.
63. See Seignobos, *op. cit.*, p. 280.

to himself, but occasionally it happened that he let some of them slip out. Let him limit himself ever so strictly to the observation of particulars, he would often break out on a sudden impulse from the narrow circle in which he had confined himself and, directing the view of the reader to wide horizons, would open up far prospects of the future and of the past. He did not resist this inclination of his intellect, for although he explained that history does not consist in undertaking profound research but in establishing facts, analyzing them, bringing them into relation with one another and determining the connection between them, it so came about that there developed out of this "a certain philosophy almost against the wishes of the historian." [64]

He once said of himself that it intrigued him more to burrow in the depths than to lose himself in the open,[65] and, in truth, he was successful, thanks to his method, in pushing forward into the deeper strata which historical research before his time had scarcely touched.

If we pause at this point to survey once more as a whole the development of the ideal of historical knowledge during the nineteenth century the chief result of our examination is, as I see it, that we do an injustice to "historicism" when we stress only its negative and destructive side and regard it merely as the forerunner of skepticism and relativism. In philosophical respects another and a deeper task devolved upon it. After the power of historical thinking had once been discovered and had spread to all fields, it was, of course, evident that metaphysics in its old dogmatic form could never rise again. It was necessary to renounce a form of explanation of the world that sought to define Being and Becoming in a few general propositions. From all sides there poured into the human mind a wealth of new material that could no longer be mastered in this way. There seemed to be no escape and no salvation in the face of this situation save to take refuge in isolated facts and specialism. Here the separation of knowledge went so far that in the end every group of facts seemed to constitute an individual "science," while all these sciences were connected with one another by only the loosest of ties. In this moment of danger from extreme fragmentation "historicism" showed its consolidating and unifying power. To be sure, it sought unity elsewhere than in metaphysics and aimed to secure it by other means. Diversity, variety, change, evolution, all these seemed no longer the antithesis to Being but its correlative. Historicism found Being no longer in God or in

64. Guiraud, *op. cit.,* p. 198 f.
65. *Ibid.,* p. 135.

the Absolute Idea, and wanted only to hold fast to it in the human mind and the totality of humanity. This was the great question in which not only the philosophy of history but also the science of history had a prominent share. Historical science itself moved, of course, in many different, even apparently divergent, directions while it was about this business. But if one surveys these different tentatives and tries to hold them all in mind, then it is clear that though they could offer no unified and common *solution* of the problem they did work at a common *task*. And in this work the particular elements of the problem are more and more clearly apprehended and each is recognized and fully explored in its own true nature.

Index of Proper Names

Index of Topics